Nina Eliasoph's vivid portrait of American civic life reveals an intriguing culture of political avoidance. Open-ended political conversation among ordinary citizens is said to be the fount of democracy, but many Americans try hard to avoid appearing to care about politics. To discover how, where, and why Americans create this culture of avoidance, the author accompanied suburban volunteers, activists, and recreation club members for two and a half years, listening to them talk – and avoid talking – about the wider world, both within their groups and in their encounters with government, the media, and corporate authorities. Unlike interview-based studies of political participation, civic culture, and public opinion, *Avoiding politics* shows how citizens create and express ideas in everyday life, contrasting their compassionate, curious, and open-minded private conversations with their mysterious lack of publicly voiced political engagement. This is a unique book which challenges received ideas about culture, power, and democracy, while exposing the hard work of producing apathy. Its clear exposition of the qualitative methods used also makes it exceptionally useful for students of political and cultural sociology, communications, and politics.

NINA ELIASOPH teaches in the Department of Sociology at the University of Wisconsin-Madison. She was a Visiting Scholar at the Annenberg School for Communication, University of Pennsylvania, 1994–95, and has published in the areas of sociology, politics, and communications. She has also produced news and public affairs programs for radio. This is her first book.

Avoiding politics

Cambridge Cultural Social Studies

Series editors:

JEFFREY C. ALEXANDER, *Department of Sociology, University of California, Los Angeles, and* STEVEN SEIDMAN, *Department of Sociology, University at Albany, State University of New York*

Titles in the series

ILANA FRIEDRICH SILBER, *Virtuosity, charisma, and social order*
0 521 41397 4 HARDBACK

LINDA NICHOLSON AND STEVEN SEIDMAN (eds.), *Social postmodernism*
0 521 47516 3 HARDBACK 0 521 47571 6 PAPERBACK

WILLIAM BOGARD, *The simulation of surveillance*
0 521 55081 5 HARDBACK 0 521 55561 2 PAPERBACK

SUZANNE R. KIRSCHNER, *The religious and Romantic origins of psychoanalysis*
0 521 44401 2 HARDBACK 0 521 55560 4 PAPERBACK

PAUL LICHTERMAN, *The search for political community*
0 521 48286 0 HARDBACK 0 521 48343 PAPERBACK

ROGER FRIEDLAND and RICHARD HECHT, *To rule Jerusalem*
0521 44046 7 HARDBACK

KENNETH H. TUCKER, *French revolutionary syndicalism and the public sphere*
0 521 56359 3 HARDBACK

ERIK RINGMAR, *Identity, interest and action*
0 521 56314 3 HARDBACK

ALBERTO MELUCCI, *The playing self*
0 521 56401 8 HARDBACK 0 521 56482 4 PAPERBACK

ALBERTO MELUCCI, *Challenging codes*
0 521 57051 4 HARDBACK 0 521 57843 4 PAPERBACK

SARAH M. CORSE, *Nationalism and literature*
0 521 57002 6 HARDBACK 0 521 57912 0 PAPERBACK

DARNELL M. HUNT, *Screening the Los Angeles "riots"*
0 521 57087 5 HARDBACK 0 521 57814 0 PAPERBACK

LYNETTE P. SPILLMAN, *Nation and commemoration*
0 521 57404 8 HARDBACK 0 521 57432 3 PAPERBACK

MICHAEL MULKAY, *The embryo research debate*
0 521 57180 4 HARDBACK 0 521 576683 0 PAPERBACK

Series list continues at end of book

Avoiding politics

How Americans produce apathy in
everyday life

Nina Eliasoph

CAMBRIDGE
UNIVERSITY PRESS

PUBLISHED BY THE PRESS SYNDICATE OF THE UNIVERSITY OF CAMBRIDGE
The Pitt Building, Trumpington Street, Cambridge, United Kingdom

CAMBRIDGE UNIVERSITY PRESS
The Edinburgh Building, Cambridge CB2 2RU, UK
40 West 20th Street, New York, NY 10011–4211, USA
477 Williamstown Road, Port Melbourne, VIC 3207, Australia
Ruiz de Alarcón 13, 28014 Madrid, Spain
Dock House, The Waterfront, Cape Town 8001, South Africa

http://www.cambridge.org

First published 1998
Reprinted 2001, 2003

Printed in the United Kingdom at the University Press, Cambridge

Typeset in 10/12½ Monotype Times [w v]

A catalogue record for this book is available from the British Library

Library of Congress Cataloguing in Publication data
Eliasoph, Nina
    Avoiding politics: how Americans produce apathy in everyday life/
Nina Eliasoph.
        p.   cm. – (Cambridge cultural social studies)
        ISBN 0 521 58293 8 (hb). – ISBN 0 521 58759 X (pb)
        1. Political participation – United States.   2. Political alienation – United
States.   3. Political culture – United States.   4. United States – Politics and
government – 20th century – Public opinion.   5. Public opinion – United States.
I. Title.   II. Series.
JK1764.E45   1988
306.2′0973 – dc21   97–27918   CIP

ISBN 0 521 58293 8
ISBN 0 521 58759 X

Contents

Acknowledgments

While writing this book, I have felt like one of those cartoon characters who has an angel perched on one side of her nose, arguing with a devil perched on the other. Luckily, I have had an imaginative, politically and morally committed, and gentle population of angels engaged in a good-humored debate there, on the bridge of my nose.

First, all the members of my dissertation committee went far beyond the call of duty in their discussion of this project. Praise for dissertation advisors often comes as praise for their warm emotional support or praise for their brilliant intellectual contributions; in Arlie Hochschild, the two magically come together. Robert Bellah offered thoughtful insights grounded in deep social commitment and broad scholarly vision. Ann Swidler scoured drafts, broadened my scholarly scope, saved me from my worst excesses, helped me clarify my logic, and offered wise advice. John Gumperz very productively guided me through the world of sociolinguistics. The best way to "repay" them all will be to do my best to pass along such careful, caring, and analytically sharp attention to my students.

I learned fieldwork in a wonderful independent study with Michael Burawoy, and then found everything I learned in it challenged in a course with Aaron Cicourel. Two excellent discussion groups inspired me early on. Marcy Darnovsky, Rich Kaplan, Paul Lichterman, Arvind Rajagopal, Mark Saroyan, Louisa Schein, and Lyn Spillman were in the Culture Club. The Lorax group continues to develop ideas, and, via e-mail, to prickle my political imagination, thanks to long-time friend Blair Sandler.

Other friends, colleagues and family members helped, in casual conversations and written comments. Mabel Berezin, Bob Blauner, Ronald Cohen, Stephen Hart, Magali Sarfatti Larson, Jane Mansbridge, Richard Merelman, Mary Nicholas, Gerry Philipsen, Diane Stemper, Jeffrey Weintraub, and Rhys Williams. Jeffrey Alexander and my editor at Cambridge, Catherine Max, have been patient, insightful, and extremely helpful. Olivia Eliasoph Lichterman said "Beep," and "roar," and asked really tough questions like, "Why do regular trees lose their leaves in winter and pine trees don't?"

The people portrayed in this study generously gave time and effort to interviews, for which I thank them enthusiastically. I enjoyed going to Halloween festivals, rallies, dances, meetings, raffles, hearings, and parades, and I hope that the people at these gatherings enjoyed having me.

The Institute on Global Conflict and Cooperation at the University of California gave me financial support, and its conferences helped me formulate my research. I am also grateful to have received a Charlotte W. Newcombe award, sponsored by the Woodrow Wilson National Fellowship Foundation. The Scholars Program at the Annenberg School for Communications offered a thought-provoking place for talking ideas. I hope that Elihi Katz and the scholars he gathered there – T. Dunbar Moodie, Nicola Evans, Lena Jayussi, Paul Lichterman, and Silvio Waisbord – continue our political and intellectual questioning together. The University of Washington was a beautiful, friendly environment for writing.

The Department of Sociology at the University of Wisconsin-Madison has been a congenial and intellectually stimulating place for claryifing my ideas, reading more broadly, and writing. Mitchell Duneier, Aimee Dechter, Emily Kane, Pamela Oliver, Jane Piliavin, and Leann Tigges have been especially talented at keeping me laughing and thinking (and usually doing both simultaneously!). Toni Schulze and Barb Schwoerer have been generous with office support. Students here have inspired me to rethink key ideas.

Paul Lichterman talked about this project with me endlessly and enthusiastically, on many hikes, bike rides, and urban strolls with me, from the Bay Area to the Northwest to the Midwest to Philadelphia and back to the Midwest. He wrote pages upon pages upon pages of exciting, clear-minded, inspiring and supportive comments on many drafts; came country dancing with me; took care of me, body and soul; and reminded me innumerable times why I care about political talk when I forgot. May we keep exploring this infinitely intriguing world together, and trying to make it better!

1

The mysterious shrinking circle of concern

A puzzle: "close to home"

Lisa, a volunteer with an anti-drugs group, circled over and over again to the topic of the local nuclear battleships base[1] during an interview with me:

There's probably at least four battleships over there at all times. You can *see* them ... they're black, and there's scaffolding on them and stuff ... They're dangerous ... scary ... I mean, half those shipyard workers are on dope all the time. It makes me nervous. There's a park on the top of the hill. They come up and smoke dope at lunch and go back to work on the battleship. They have spills quite often. I mean, we don't know about it, but my husband was on a battleship working, so I know.

Another interviewee, Carolyn, lived closer to the base. A chemical plant just upstream from her had had a huge spill a few months earlier; oil lapped up onto her house, which jutted out on stilts over the bay. "The beach was *covered* with oil. You could see it on the rocks and in the water. It was sad," she told me as we sat at her kitchen table with her eighteen-year-old son, in front of a picture window with an eye-level view of the nuclear battleship base and the glimmering bay, under a big sky of rainclouds streaked with sunlight. Every twenty minutes or so a battleship slipped by.

When I asked Lisa and Carolyn whether they would get involved in doing something about the battleships or the oil spill problems, they both said, in separate interviews, that those issues were "not close to home," and did not really "touch" them personally. And they both said, in almost identical words, "and anyway, what would I do, bomb the place?" referring to the chemical plant and the battleship base. Carolyn said it twice (another interviewee said, "What am I gonna do – burn it down?").

Instead, they were both involved in an anti-drugs group, in which I had been participating along with them for several months. Why were they involved in this group? What would they think of some of the other groups

I studied – one that worked on nuclear issues and another that dealt with environmental issues? I asked the anti-drugs volunteers these questions, in a group interview. Six members sat in a shabby, linoleum-floored public room on the spindly fold-up kind of chairs that help make public meetings so uncomfortable. All agreed about their motives: "It's close to home," and "do-able." One said that compared to nuclear issues, "this [the drug] issue's a lot closer to home." There was a chorus of agreeable murmurs from the others. He described the time his house was robbed, which he assumed had "something to do with drugs. So, it's a lot more immediate than nuclear war. You know, that's an important issue, too, but – " and here, Lisa filled in, weaving together themes of "close to home" and power: "that just seems sort of distant. I can't quite get to those people, to deal with – or even nuclear power. Shoot, with where we live, we can't be too allergic to nuclear power. There's six or seven plants on battleships here."

Another member soon summed up: "It has to do with something that's close to you. See, the nuclear stuff is all around us but it's not in our back-yard, or across the street, whereas *this is*," referring to the drug problem.

Would they consider getting involved in doing something about a foreign policy issue? Carolyn said, "I would much rather look for something close to home, close to me." But, she chuckled, she *was* very concerned about three whales that had been in the news that week, trapped in Arctic ice with an international rescue force trying to dig them out. "Now, whales, they were far away, but they're *animals*," she laughed, noticing that the habitual phrase "close to home" did not exactly fit. Lisa added, "You know, there's only three of them, there are not thousands of them." So, it was "do-able": there were only three. Carolyn agreed, continuing, "But they're defenseless and, I don't know, I would rather help closer to home, I don't know, that's just – and then the other is just so large, political, and – " and she trailed off.

Was this group unusual, in implying that whales on the North Pole "impact our lives" more than nuclear subs in our front yards? that down the street or on our front deck is not "close to home"? No. One interviewee explicitly translated "close to home," showing how it worked to prevent discourage-ment, by making difficult structural problems invisible. George, a member of a country-western dance club I studied, lived in the same town as the volun-teers. One cold rainy weekday when he was out of work, I interviewed him with his housemate, at home – about two miles from the proposed site of a toxic incinerator, four miles from the nuclear sub base, and a few blocks from a toxic landfill.

George also said he would work on something if it was "personal, close by, in my neighborhood." On the proposed incinerator and the nuclear issue, he said he would get involved if it were "close to home." "I wouldn't want a nuclear base in Amargo,'' he said. His housemate Jolene laughed; George paused, and said there probably already was one. Jolene lit into him, saying "*Think* about it!'' and "Do something about it – it's *in* your backyard!'' but then she felt sorry for him, and explained, "the point is, OK, I know what you're saying.'' I asked, "So, what's he saying?''

"Well, it's like: what do you think about nuclear – *all* the junk going on. They're gonna, they're gonna push a button while we could all just go up in – you know, what are you gonna – ?'' She shrugged, completing the sentence.

Why did the volunteers say the nuclear battleships and environmental problems were not close to home? All were within a twenty-minute drive that could pass through a nuclear battleship base containing a thirty-acre toxic pit that the Environmental Protection Agency called "dangerous''; an Air Force site that shipped arms supplies all over the world, was rumored to contain nuclear waste materials and weapons, and was slated for a Superfund cleanup; two other toxic military cleanup sites; six chemical plants – there were four major fires or spills in the two and a half years of my fieldwork; a planned toxic waste incinerator; and two other big plants eight miles upstream that emitted carcinogenic and ozone-depleting chemicals. During my fieldwork stint, various environmental and disarmament groups held demonstrations at several of these plants. As one volunteer pointed out, nearly all the fish had died, and all the fishing clubs had died, too. The area was about eight miles downstream from two other factories that, along with several other plants, emitted cancer-causing or ozone-depleting chemicals. It would be hard to convince anyone that this area did not have some political, military, and environmental issues worth at least discussing, even if the conclusion of the discussion was that nothing should change. Certainly, these issues were not literally "distant,'' or "removed.'' Literally, these problems were in their backyards.

A second puzzle: "speak for yourself" in public

In every meeting of another local group, which had organized to oppose a toxic incinerator, someone raised the question of where toxic waste *should* go, saying explicitly that members were not just involved for their own families' safety. Every one of the six core members of the group raised the question this way, some quite often. Typical was Maryellen, a mother of two, speaking at the very first meeting I attended: "If it's not our kids, it'll be someone else's kids. People always ask, 'Well, yeah, but what are you gonna do with all that toxic waste?' That's something we should talk about, since it's not just a local issue. We shouldn't just fight off the thing to have some other community that's less organized get stuck with it!''

In these meetings, and in casual conversations, broad political questions were foremost – the activists talked about where waste should go, why so much waste is produced (especially by the US military), what governmental policies could prevent corporations from producing more waste, why not to believe corporation or government statements about the proposed plant's safety, why to be in principle against incineration-for-profit.

In front of the press, though, group members spoke completely differently. Suddenly, the activists presented themselves as panicked "moms," and self-interested property owners. The discourse would often shift the very moment the reporters turned on the cameras and microphones, and shift back again the moment the cameras and microphones went off. One activist said to every reporter she met, "She's a new mom and I'm an old mom. That's why we're in it. We're worried." She had been an activist since the civil rights movement, but she always presented herself as a "Mom" in more formal settings.

In fact, activists were not simply "defending themselves," as reporters and officials assumed; many believed that citizen participation was important, and found this issue to be a good one for illustrating a general principle to the rest of the community: that grassroots political participation is a better way of running the government than behind-the-scenes corporate control. Of course, they may *also* have been worried about their families or property values, but in casual conversations amongst themselves, these were not salient.

Introducing a petition drive to a bank of reporters, another member, Eleanor, repeated the pattern of privately voicing broad concern and publicly silencing her broad concerns. Publicly, she presented her motives like this:

I care about the people living here, and I especially care about the children that are growing up in this unique and wonderful place.

I'm also a concerned property owner. The only thing I own of any substantial economic value is the home I own in downtown Evergreen City. And what's gonna happen to this investment when I have to sell it to support myself for my older years, older than I am even now? Nobody's gonna come banging on my door to buy a lovely home, with a lovely view, with some lovely toxic pollutants in town.

But the very moment the cameras and mikes went off, she turned to me and a fellow activist to say, "This is getting to be more than a concern to *me*; it's getting to be a matter of the lives of the future generations here." Suddenly, instead of speaking only for herself, she could speak for "future generations"; instead of speaking only of self-interest, she could speak of her usual broad concerns.

Later, Eleanor told me, "My mind goes blank when I get in front of an audience like that. I just sit there and forget what to say." What exactly "blanked out" of her mind? In the context of speaking to the press, she "forgot" what she said about "the future generations." In front of the press, she could not say that she had been involved in successful grassroots campaigns for decades, but listen to the stories she told me while we were driving through town one day. She had an inspiring story about every spot on the landscape: "See that creek? We organized and saved that from being covered over in the '60s when the country thought that creeks were bad. We worked hard on that one." And, as we wheeled around the corner,

Over there, on the other side of the river, that's where there used to be some industry that left mercury in the land and water. And our kids [she herself did not have children, but talked of all children as if they were her own] go fishing off the pier there and you could sometimes see the mercury in the fish. And years after the industry left, horses started mysteriously dying over across the river. Then they sold off the horses and now they're building new tract houses there, on top of the stuff [George, from the Buffalo, lived in one of them]. Up river from that is the old ChemFill dump, of course. At least we finally got rid of them!

In the context of speaking to the press, she "forgot" what she said about "the future generations." She also forgot what she and others had been saying in meetings for over a year, that the government and corporations should invest in research to prevent the production of toxic waste. She forgot that the local group was part of a loose national network whose project was to change industrial policies. One day, an organizer from a national environmental group came to give a short presentation about his group's lobbying effort, to pass laws that would make corporations minimize production of toxic waste. Eleanor gratefully exclaimed,

I applaud your coming here. It really solves a lot of problems for me. When people ask where should it go, I'm hard pressed for an answer . . . It would make us fragmented, it would be community against community, one saying "Put it there," and the other saying "Put it there." This gives us an answer: "It shouldn't go anywhere."

And she enthusiastically nodded and agreed when another member said, "You [national lobbyists] are saying that it's not incumbent on us to come up with a national level solution. We just have to work locally, and know that you're working on the national level." After a discussion about the connection between local activism and national policy, the lobbying group representative summed up: "We're helping make your short-term goals have long-term consequences. While you're here, defending yourselves, we're over there, lobbying, saying, 'Look, no towns want these incinerators, they're dangerous, and we have to have a better solution.' " Eleanor enthusiastically nodded, and said afterwards that she would start being more involved, now that she had an answer to the problem she described.

Behind the scenes, Eleanor was eloquent about her broad political commitment, so the group often begged her to make public speeches, but since she worried about "blanking out" in public, she usually said no. All the activists who spoke at demonstrations and to the press made similar speeches, emphasizing their seemingly natural, "unpolitical" motives, and silencing their public-spirited motives and policy suggestions. They assumed that the public forum was a place for plaintive individuals to expose their side of the story, to "speak for themselves."

Political evaporation

The puzzle in both of these cases is that citizens' circles of concern shrank when they spoke in public contexts. In both cases, broad political concerns surfaced and then mysteriously vanished behind very personal-sounding concerns: "my house," "my children," "close to home." People implicitly know that some face-to-face contexts invite public-spirited debate and conversation, and others do not; in contemporary US society, most do not. Examining where and how citizens can comfortably talk about politics might help us understand how so many Americans manage to make the realm of politics seem irrelevant to so many everyday enterprises.

We often assume that political activism requires an explanation, while inactivity is the normal state of affairs. But it can be as difficult to ignore a problem as to try to solve it; to curtail feelings of empathy as to extend them; to feel powerless and out of control as to exert an influence; to stop thinking as to think. There is no exit from the political world, no possibility of disengagement; human, political decisions permeate human life, whether we like it or not. Few Americans vote, many tell survey interviewers that they have little faith in the government,[2] many are astonishingly ignorant about the most basic political issues:[3] yet all are touched by this untrusted, ignored government. If there is no exit from the political world, then political silence must be as active and colorful as a bright summer shadow.

Apathy takes work to produce. This book shows how some Americans produced it in the course of conversations that engage, or push away engagement, with the wider world; many of the people portrayed here spoke, in intimate whispers, of a vague concern for homeless people, the environment, and even faraway victims of distant wars. Many had their own private analyses of the problems; many said in interviews that they had never voiced these ideas before. Empathy for foreign victims of war; worries about the environment; horror over injustice: only by speaking do people give these meaning and form, providing socially recognizable tools for thinking and acting.

The people I met did sound as if they cared about politics, but only in some contexts and not others. They did not just think everything was fine as it was, but there were too few contexts in which they could openly discuss their discontent. Most of the time, intimate, late night, moonlit conversations were the only places other than interviews where that kind of discussion could happen. In group contexts, such discussion was almost always considered inappropriate and out of place; informal etiquette made some political intuitions speakable, and others beyond the pale of reasonable, polite discussion.

Following sociologist Erving Goffman, I call the main group interactions "frontstage," while peripheral interactions that participants do not count as part of "what is going on," that are deemed beside the point, whispered, out of the spotlight, or hidden are "backstage." Goffman says that we often carve out a "backstage" space for ourselves, in which we can relax and stop paying so much attention to the impression we are making on an audience. Waiters in the kitchen of a fancy restaurant, for example, can shed their smooth aristocratic demeanors and yell at the cook; salespeople off the floor can make fun of their product and customers; teachers in the lounge can cuss and smoke:

The backstage language consists of reciprocal first-naming, co-operative decision-making, profanity, open sexual remarks ... use of dialect or sub-standard speech, mumbling and shouting, playful aggressivity and "kidding," inconsiderateness for the other in minor but potentially symbolic acts, minor physical self-involvements such as humming, whistling, chewing, nibbling, belching, and flatulence ... [B]ackstage behavior has what psychologists might call a "regressive" character.

(1959: 128)

Surprisingly, I found the opposite pattern. People sounded *better* backstage than frontstage; at each step in the broadening of the audience, the ideas shrank. In a strange process of political evaporation, every group fell into this strictly patterned shift in discourse: what was announced aloud was less open to debate, less aimed at expressing connection to the wider world, less public-spirited, more insistently selfish, than what was whispered. Focusing on the remarkably consistent pattern will tell us what Americans consider "public" to be, and why "public" speech is so often less generously open-minded than private.

When good manners prevent publicly minded speech in the potential contexts of the public sphere, the public sphere has a problem. In families, workplaces, and schools, we assume that open, forthright, active communication matters, as a good in itself; why do we value everyday political conversation so much less? Theorists since Aristotle have argued that regular political conversation is a defining feature of a healthy democracy; that in a democracy, the substance of political life is public discussion; that the ways we can talk about our concerns go far in shaping them; that the ability to discuss politics allows citizens to generate power together. So, how did public-spirited, open political conversation come to seem ''out of place'' in so many places in Amargo? Paying attention to the dramatic shifts in discourse from frontstage to backstage made it clear that citizens were not just lacking in public spirit, but lacked it only in some contexts. Most people did not usually talk about their concerns to an audience larger than one, in a voice louder than a whisper – how did their publicly minded ideas evaporate out of public circulation? Listening to citizens conversing about politics in everyday life can reveal how some cultivate concern for the wider world, and how so many manage to convince themselves and each other not to care.

In search of the American public

To observe how political ideas circulate in everyday life, I participated in a wide range of civic groups – volunteer, recreational, and activist groups, spending about two and a half years with the groups.

Volunteer groups included two anti-drugs groups, a high school parents' group, a recycling center, and a few meetings of the League of Women Voters. I went to the anti-drugs groups' meetings, and parties, and helped with their petition drives. I helped work the high school Parent League's concession stand at track meets, sell raffle tickets (at events like a Halloween Festival, a Farmers' Market, and other spots around town on weekends), folded envelopes, and otherwise did what members did. I also attended city meetings and other meetings intended to publicize officials' and volunteers' efforts – several Just Say No rallies, an anti-drugs parade, some family events that the volunteers announced in their meetings. I also informally interviewed people who were trying to set up a homeless shelter in a suburban mall. Volunteers' meetings are portrayed in the first half of chapter 2.

Recreational groups included a country-western dance club that alternated between meeting at a bar that I will call the ''Silverado Club'' and a fraternal organization (like the Moose, Eagles, or Redmen) that I will call the ''Buffalo Club''; and another country-western dance class. I went to rodeos, fairs, horse competitions, barbecues, theme parks, and other events with groups of country-western class members. I describe two different subgroups at the country-western clubs: one group's conversations are portrayed in the first half of chapter 4 – I call this group ''the Buffaloes,'' or ''the private people''; the other subgroup, which I will call ''the cynics,'' is very briefly sketched in the short chapter 6.

Activist groups included a group that was trying to prevent a toxic incinerator from being built in town, and a permanent peace vigil intending to block
US arms shipments to other countries. The activist group on which I most
focus, the anti-toxics group, changed so much during the time I studied it, it
offered in itself a good range of activist approaches to public life. I went to
their rallies, hearings, press conferences, meetings, informal gatherings like
poster-making sessions and subcommittee meetings, and parties. These
groups are the topic of the first half of chapter 7.

To trace the connections between these groups and the wider world, I
listened to the anti-drugs groups', schools group's and anti-toxic group's
encounters with social service and regulatory agencies. I observed how
powerful institutions influenced members' understandings of the role of citizen involvement, and vice versa – how citizens sometimes challenged the
official definitions of citizen involvement: On what grounds did social service
agencies, the media, police, schools, elected office-holders, and other institutions and cultural authorities surrounding the groups ask for citizens' political discussion? Where did they invite expressions of public spirit, and where
did they shut it out? How did groups interpret these invitations?[4] The story
of each group's interactions with larger institutions is told in the second
halves of chapters 2, 4, and 7.

I also spent time with members of all three sorts of group outside of the
group contexts – on the phone, and at movies, watching TV with them, going
for walks, or doing whatever they did in their spare time. I taped semi-
structured interviews with at least ten members of each category, and gave
interviewees a questionnaire asking demographic questions and some political opinion questions taken from national surveys; and I taped their efforts
at deciphering the questions. I also conducted group interviews in each category. In interviews, activists' speech was similar to their speech in informal
group settings. But interviews with volunteers and Buffaloes often revealed
ideas and feelings that went unspoken in group contexts. Interviews with
volunteers is the topic of chapter 3; interviews with Buffaloes is the topic of
chapter 5.

To address the question of how groups are connected to the wider world,
I also followed reporters around, as they covered local citizens' involvement
and local issues in general; interviewed the local newspaper reporters; and
analyzed their stories to examine how they talked about grassroots citizen
involvement. This is the topic of chapter 8.

Most Americans live in suburbs, and the region I portray is no exception.
The region surrounding the cities I will call Amargo and Evergreen City was
typical of a new kind of "post-suburb" that is growing especially rapidly,
and is very different from the stereotypical small, homogeneous, white,

middle-class bedroom town facing a vibrant central city.[5] These new, ethnically and class-diverse dwelling places are criss-crossed by giant 6-, 8- or even 10-lane highways, going through malls and business parks, instead of having one downtown with a main street, as earlier suburbs did. Orange County, near Los Angeles, is the prototype of this kind of suburb. Amargo and Evergreen County fit the mold perfectly. They had tiny downtowns with no grocery stores, no clothes stores in which people normally shopped, no movie theaters, no home supply stores, no hardware stores, no variety stores for practical kitchen items; everyone drove to giant regional malls for food, clothes, entertainment, and the rest (while I was doing fieldwork, though, activists colonized the back room of a pizza place in Evergreen City, and made it into an informal meeting ground – the presence of the activists transformed the setting).[6] In all of the volunteer and activist groups combined, only three regular members had gone to high school where they now lived. Over half had lived in the county less than eight years. Recreation group participants drove from a two-hour radius to get to the clubs.

I listened to political conversation and silence in a wide range of contexts, to find out how people manage so often to keep politics at arm's length in so many situations, and whether there were any contexts in which political conversation was possible. I do not make a causal argument here, but do hope to help society reflect upon itself in new ways, to refresh the usual ways of thinking about political disconnection, to offer a new question – a mental peppermint clearing out stale thoughts, a "sensitizing concept . . . an idea that suggests directions along which to look" (Blumer 1986 [1954]). My question is: *how do citizens create contexts for political conversation in everyday life*?

The concept of the public sphere

To examine this question, we have to fine-tune our ears to the unsaid, the taken-for-granted, and listen carefully to citizens creating "the public sphere" in practice. Many scholars have called for studies of the public sphere[7] or have argued for its theoretical importance, in very abstract terms.[8] Some have studied interaction in the public sphere historically.[9] No studies systematically ask, "How do – or don't – people create everyday life contexts for political conversation? How do civic groups create and enforce manners for political conversation?"[10]

Discussion, debate, disagreement: public life is hard work, not something for which every society or individual naturally comes equipped. As John Dewey put it, in *The Public and Its Problems*, "Faculties of effectual observation, reflection, and desire are habits acquired under the influence of the culture and institutions of society, not ready-made inherent powers'' (1927: 158). Theorists of public life say that face-to-face organizations are the basic schools for learning democratic principles and social responsibility. Unspoken ideas about *where and how* citizens can talk politics are at the center of any society's notion of citizenship. In the 1830s, Alexis de Tocqueville visited the United States from France and marveled over the enthusiasm with which Americans involved themselves in groups. Unlike passive subjects ruled by a king and involuntarily bonded together by a sturdy hierarchy of kings, lords, and peasants, active citizens ruling themselves in a democracy need the voluntary bonds of such groups: ''Feeling and ideas are renewed, the heart enlarged, and the understanding developed only by the reciprocal action of men one upon another . . . in democratic societies . . . only associations can do that'' (1969 [1831]: 515–516).

These ''associations'' form ''the public sphere.''[11] The public sphere is, theoretically, defined as the realm of institutions in which private citizens can carry on free and egalitarian conversation, often about issues of common concern, possibly welding themselves into a cohesive body and a potent political force.[12] It is not just a closed, hierarchical workplace and not just family but is a third setting for conversation, with three main characteristics: participation is optional, potentially open to all, and potentially egalitarian.[13] The settings I studied could have represented America's public sphere, made of thousands of local citizen gatherings like the ones I studied.

For theorists of the public sphere, moral and political understanding are not inert objects that people can carry around inside their own heads and implant in the heads of others. Rather, these theorists assume that people must learn how to understand the larger world by interacting and talking about social issues, in groups. In contemporary society, political life is, more and more, administered by forms, numbers, technicians, or the invisible hand of the market, which silently gives and takes away with no explicit considerations of morality or cultural integrity. Only plain talk, between citizens, can knit the bonds necessary for a more humane society, and can reveal the often morally unsavory assumptions hidden in the market and the bureaucracies (Habermas 1985). Without a vibrant public sphere, democratic citizenship is impossible; there are no contexts to generate the kinds of selfhood, friendship, power, and relations to the wider world that democracy demands. The point is dual: participation in the public sphere helps cultivate a sense of community, so that people care more, and think more, about the wider world; and second, participation becomes a source of meaning-making power. Let us examine these one at a time.

First, participation generates a sense of attachment to a wider world. In theory, the public sphere includes not only formal groups like political parties, and social-improvement-minded associations like the volunteer groups and activist groups described here. It also includes the free-form, sociable, playful, esthetic public life that happens in cafés, informal gatherings, bars, coffeehouses, theaters, salons, dances, poetry readings, even soccer teams: the country-western clubs portrayed in this book could fit here.[14] In seventeenth-century Britain, coffeehouses were centers for informal public discussion (Eagleton 1985). In one nineteenth-century Massachusetts town, working-class ethnic men regularly argued politics in neighborhood bars (Rosenzweig 1983). In seventeenth-century Paris, part of the fun of public life was the costume: women fitted singing birds in cages, pears, and flowers into elaborate "poufs" of hair on their heads (Sennett 1977). Singing birds, beer, pears, coffee: these physically vigorous gatherings embroiled members in each other's lives not just as brains engaged in calm, rational debate, such as some theorists describe,[15] but also as laughing bodies with tastes, passions, manners.

Such sociable gatherings can be fertile ground for political life. While not exclusively or even primarily politically motivated, these gatherings offer the familiarity that is a necessary precondition for some kinds of public life. Sociable familiar gatherings can create an infinitely nuanced stock of common sense and feeling, common knowledge and myths, common style, rhythm, and manners; background knowledge for how to act and how to be. Every day, people go to work, get stuck in traffic jams, pay bills, become involuntarily entangled with anonymous strangers; in the sociable public sphere, in contrast, people affirm voluntary connections to particular people. Whether for reading poetry aloud, debating playfully, playing music, joking, putting on plays, dancing, bowling, playing soccer, these usually unpolitical grounds for common life and meaning-making often make political life possible.

For this reason, theorists (Mansbridge 1991; Held 1989, for example) emphasize the importance of friendship in nurturing good citizenship. Good friends are not just nice to each other; they also help make each other become good people. Aristotle says that the opposite of a friend is not an enemy, but a flatterer (see Bellah et al. 1985): someone who tells you that you are being good when in fact you are being selfish or vain or stupid. Friends like these mutually raise each other to be good members of society. Such informal groups might easily grow into more explicitly community-minded groups of the more formal public sphere, such as activist or volunteer groups.

Ideally, this sense of connection helps people learn to think about the wider world. But Lisa and Carolyn, like nearly all of the people I met, *wanted* to be good, caring members of a community, they wanted to cultivate a sense of belonging and companionship. They wanted to care about *people*, but did not want to care about *politics*. Trying to care about people but not politics meant trying to limit their concerns to issues about which they felt they could "realistically" make a difference in people's lives – issues that they defined as small, local, and unpolitical. Volunteers worked hard to keep that circle of concern small – in cultivating a sense of connection to each other, they curtailed their ability to learn about the wider world.

To help each other and themselves to be really caring people, volunteers would have had to think about the large political forces that keep producing the problems on which they worked: the homelessness, the problems with schools and drugs, and the wars. How can people develop what C. Wright Mills (1959) called "a sociological imagination," a "quality of mind" necessary to grasp the constant interplay between our personal lives and the political world? Mills says that humanity desperately needs to cultivate this ability, in order to keep from feeling powerless and lost in a complex, overwhelmingly large global polity. Why are so many Americans unable to answer the most elementary factual questions about politics?[16] Mills would say that this is not because they are too dumb to memorize some list of facts that good citizens need to know, but because they lack this kind of imagination that could help them understand why facts matter. A sociological imagination comes from talking, reading – interacting in various ways; but for many, this sociological imagination is stunted, partly because the contexts in which people could stretch their minds and expand their sense of selfhood have evaporated.

A second way that participation in voluntary associations is supposed to help citizens create democracy is by generating a kind of civic power. The public sphere is very different from the kind of citizenship advocated by some politicians, who treat voluntary associations as the panacea for all social ills – former President Bush's "thousand points of light" and its British equivalent (Speaker's Commission on Citizenship 1990) are two examples. These officials ask apolitical citizen-volunteers to fill in for underfunded charity and welfare agencies, saying that such "citizenship" is more necessary now, in times of cutbacks. But the politicians do not ask the citizens to discuss the political decisions that made the cutbacks. Such citizens are asked to act like Lisa and Carolyn, to convince themselves that regular citizens "really can make a difference," without addressing issues that they would consider "political."

In contrast, the public sphere in theory, and at times in history, has been a doorway to political power. Unlike solitary "points of light," participants in the public sphere *generate* political power for common citizens: "power springs up between men[17] when they act together, and vanishes the moment they disperse. Because of this peculiarity ... power is to an astonishing degree independent of material factors, either of number or means'' (Arendt 1958: 200).

The "thousand points of light"-style volunteer, in contrast, simply tries to fix predefined social problems, and coolly avoids seizing the power to define political issues. The potential power generated in the friction of the public sphere is absent from a "thousand points of light" volunteer-style involvement. This is a cultural kind of power, the power to open up public contexts for citizens to question, challenge, debate; the power to become a different kind of person, to create new meanings and ask new questions; to inspire.

What is public-spirited political conversation?

What kind of conversation is supposed to work this magic? Political conversation, of course. But what is that? It is not simply ''conversation that refers to some group of objects out there in the world, called 'political' objects.'' Why not? Any object is potentially political – or not.

For example, race and sex are potentially ''political topics,'' but Buffalo Club women believed that the men brought them up to get attention – a playful slap or squeal – not to spark debate or to affirm a sense of connection to the wider world. The men's implicit referent was always the speaker, not the polity. When a Buffalo Club woman complained that her ''ex'' is ''a slime'' and ''a jerk'' and she wished that she had more money for her kids, she talked about it as a personal problem, unconnected to broader questions of who should pay for children's upkeep. Similarly, when I gave people questionnaires asking whether they had engaged in political activity or conversation, the varieties of methods of defining ''political'' and ''activity'' were much more interesting than the yes/no answers I eventually recorded on the questionnaire. For example, an activist in the anti-toxics groups answered a question about whether she had ''been to any political meetings in the last few years'' by saying ''no,'' and then backtracking: ''Well, I don't know, I guess you could call Communities for Environmental Safety Everywhere 'political.' What do you think?'' I shrugged and made an ''I don't know'' face.

The problem, as feminist scholars point out, is that ''politics'' can be hidden in almost any topic (Fraser 1987; Young 1987, for example). Recreation group members took racist and sexist jokes as purely personal statements, but an observer could say, ''Oh, but they really are talking about politics and just don't know it.'' There must be a way to write about the public origins and consequences of problems that fall outside of members' definitions of ''political.'' Is saying ''they are talking about politics and just don't know it,'' just like saying ''they have a toothache and just don't know it'' as some philosophers (Winch 1958: 79) argue? If so, then observers should do what some early anthropologists (Evans-Pritchard, e.g. 1976: 245) tried to do: simply leave their own theoretical and cultural baggage at the door, in order to explain the ''natives' '' own cultural definitions only from the inside. But the people I met *changed* their ideas of what counts as ''political'' from one context to the next – this context-switching would be invisible if the researcher tried to take the ''natives''' perspective on everything! That approach cannot be right. The person writing the story has to come down on one side or another eventually.

Indeed, sometimes an anthropologist must diverge from the natives' account of what they are doing, in order not to deceive his readers, because of the commitment in his act of speaking or writing. Suppose the natives engage in certain procedures that they tell him are ''making rain.'' How will he truthfully report what they are doing? If he says simply ''They are making rain,'' he is implying that their magic really can causally produce precipitation; such is the nature of our language. If he says ''They are engaged in a magic ritual designed to make rain,'' he is at least strongly suggesting that their actions cannot produce rain; in that case, he is true to knowledge but in a significant way false to their world, their way of perceiving and acting . . . there may be nothing completely neutral for the anthropologist to say.   (Pitkin 1972: 258)

If I were either to accept *speakers'* explicit definition of ''political'' and ignore what didn't fit, or apply my *own* definition and ignore what didn't fit, I would *miss the whole point:* what is interesting is precisely how citizens come to define some issues, and some contexts, as ''political'' and some as ''not political,'' in interaction. In the gaps between their various definitions – or between their definitions and mine – is an interesting and important potential dialogue.

Like the anthropologist who presumes that waving a stick does not cause rain, I also come with certain presuppositions. I presume connections between the people I met and the wider world, even when the people themselves did not overtly acknowledge any attachment. My question is whether or not speakers *ever draw out* a topic's public implications, whether speakers ever assume that what they say matters for someone other than themselves, ever assume that they are speaking in front of a wider backdrop. I am interested in a process of giving voice to a wide circle of concern – a public-spirited *way of talking*, not a topic (''politics'').[18] Political theorist Hanna Pitkin says that public-spirited conversation happens when citizens speak in terms of ''justice,'' which, as she eloquently puts it,

forces us to transform ''I want'' into ''I am entitled to,'' a claim that becomes negotiable by public standards. In the process [of making such claims] we learn to think about the standards themselves, about our stake in the existence of standards, of

justice, of our community, even of our opponents and enemies in the community; so
that afterwards we are changed.   (1981: 347)

This does not mean that people will always come to the *right* decisions when
speaking in a public-spirited way, but that such discussion forces a discussion
of who "we" are and why "we" care, and what "we" can do about it.
Appealing to common ground would have forced speakers to *create* common
ground, "making the path by walking it." In other words, public-spirited talk
is first, open to debate, and second, devoted to questions about the common,
public good, without blindly excluding questions of oppression and differences of opinion. Without such a forum, people have no place for actively,
collectively forming a will, a community, or a vision of the wider world.

So, a group could have a topic that I might consider "political" but not
treat it with public-spirited conversation, and vice versa. During the Gulf
War, I heard a conversation in the recreation groups about how the war
might impinge on members' travel plans. That was not a publicly minded
conversation. On the other hand, a conversation in the same group about who
would cook the food for a potluck, with jokes about whether the men could
do anything other than bring Kentucky Fried, boiled water, and microwaved
burritos, came closer to being a publicly minded conversation, since it
referred to systematic gender differences, with a slight twinge of righteous
indignation. Usually, I heard public-spirited conversation only backstage, in
hushed tones.

In making these constant, implicit distinctions between public and private,
participants simultaneously create a context for interaction and a relationship
to the wider world. People create the realm of politics in practice, when they
create, and recreate, and recreate again, this kind of "grammar" for citizenship, constantly drawing and redrawing the map that separates "public" from
"private."[19] The public sphere is something that exists *only between* people,
and comes into being when people speak public-spiritedly. Speaking public-
spiritedly creates the public sphere.

Objective self-interest?

This search for "publicly minded" speech might seem ridiculous to someone
who assumes that self-interest is the essence of politics. But even self-interest
must be cultivated socially: is it in Amargo nuclear battleship workers' interest to have a healthy workplace? a healthy home? a future planet? a job?
good schools and day-care for their children? low taxes? a strong American
military? In the long run, poisoning the environment is not in anyone's interest, so even corporate pollutors have to engage in some twisted emotional

gymnastics to define their own "interests"; even for them, there is no single "bottom line" that trumps all other interests. Nuclear battleships, toxic incinerators, and oil spills come to be understood as being in some people's interest, against other people's interest, and not of concern to others.

More importantly, self-interest is not always the only thing that matters to people, anyway. Citizens forfeit their own power when *any* preconceived definition of public life systematically filters some valuable kinds of speech out of the public forum – in Amargo, the prevalent definition of public life called upon citizens to speak in terms of self-interest in public, to speak only for themselves. The assumption was that "politics" is for getting what you want. But as Hannah Arendt says, this infinitely pliable "in-between" of public life (1958: 183) is not just an instrumental means to some other kind of power. It is also an end in itself. Arendt grandly states that "to be deprived of it means to be deprived of reality" (1958: 199). Powerlessness comes from being inattentively caught in the " 'web' of human relationships" (Arendt 1958: 183); power works, in part, by robbing the powerless of the inclination or ability to develop their own interpretations of political issues. With active, mindful political participation, we weave reality and a place for ourselves within it. A crucial dimension of power is the power to create the contexts of public life itself. This is the power to create the public itself.

Theorists like Arendt consider this meaning-making, public-making power an end in itself – being able to participate in decision-making, to learn democracy, is one of the great joys of life. But this power can *also* be a means to more instrumental kinds of power,[20] since it opens up some aspects of life for public questioning and closes off others, allowing some aspects to seem humanly created and changeable, and others to seem natural and unmovable. If Amargo residents accepted the seemingly natural connection between environmental regulation and unemployment, and entered the public arena solely for the purpose of promoting their predefined "self-interest," they might advocate keeping local jobs at the expense of the environment. Their lack of political imagination could be fatal.

The only way to discover what the choices are, or whether "self-interest" is the most important motive in play, is through public discussion. Once we drop the idea that promotion of self-interest is the sole essence of politics, the question becomes: how do people create contexts for talking about politics in a variety of ways, including conversation about "interests" but also including other ways as well? While we might rightly cheer when "the little people" rise up to defend their own, very local interests,[21] my point is that without this power to create the etiquette for political participation, citizens are powerless. Without this power to determine what sorts of questions are worth discussing in public, citizens are deprived of an important power, the power to define what is worthy of public debate, what is important, what is good and right, what is changeable and what is just natural – even if they sucessfully promote projects that are in their "interest" (Laclau and Mouffe 1985). These kinds of power – to make meaning and to formulate and promote one's interests – are inextricable.[22]

The point is not that once we figure out our real interests, and act on them, then we can stop talking and go home. The point is that being able to talk can be a good in itself, and a source of power in itself; people are always creating selves and communities and interests and power, one way or another, actively or inadvertently, in interaction.

Subjective beliefs?

So, despite one brand of common sense, "objective bottom-line interests" do not exhaust all there is to know about citizenship. Another typical common-sense understanding of politics points to "subjective inner beliefs and values." Research on inner beliefs, ideologies, and values is usually based on surveys, which ask people questions about which they may never have thought, and most likely have never discussed. Questionnaires provide a political vocabulary, a set of cultural "tools" (Swidler 1986), assuming that the respondent shares the ways of thinking and speaking about politics necessary to formulate the survey questions (Bourdieu 1984: 460). The researcher analyzing survey responses must then read political motives and understandings back into the responses, trying to reconstruct the private mental processes the interviewee "must have" undergone to reach a response. That type of research would more aptly be called private opinion research, since it attempts to bypass the social nature of opinions, and tries to wrench the personally embodied, sociable display of opinions away from the opinions themselves.[23] But in everyday life, opinions always come in a form: flippant, ironic, anxious, determined, abstractly distant, earnest, engaged, effortful. And they always come in a context – a bar, a charity group, a family, a picket – that implicitly invites or discourages debate. The survey is itself a context, that helps create the kind of person who will cooperatively answer a stranger's questions and not demand dialogue. When I had a job in college as a door-to-door survey interviewer, I encountered some interviewees who valiantly tried to convince me of their opinions, hoping to convert me; others who offered beer and outrageous opinions, hoping to date me; others who offered amusing debate, hoping to embroil me in an evening's entertainment. Others were like the Russian émigrée who refused to state her opinions unless she knew what mine were. My job, however, was simply to repeat the questions exactly as written in the question booklet until the respondent succumbed to the interview format.

Democracy, for this approach, rests on beliefs and values; add up all the private opinions to get one big "public" opinion; if all individuals carry inside themselves democratic psychological dispositions, like little ships in a bottle, then (presuming citizens have rights like freedom of speech and assembly) we will have democracy.[24] In this view, what is needed to repair democratic life are supreme acts of individual will; each individual should find the desire to become a good citizen and the rest will take care of itself. That idea is harmonious with individualistic American common sense, which tells us that what is inside is what counts: "they care because they believe in helping people," or "they don't care because they don't have good values," or "if parents taught their kids better values, there would be less crime" (so does a country like the United States, with the highest imprisonment rate in the world, just have too many bad parents?).

This approach misses the fact that public life happens *between* people, in relationships. What do these separate individuals do when they get together? What if they spend most of their days trying to ignore the fact that they work at jobs whose missions they do not particularly revere – manufacturing nerve gas, the 137th shade of pink lipstick for Revlon, personalized cat food bowls? Can people possess values, just as they possess other objects that may lie in the closet gathering dust? If institutions do not live up to values, then "values" are not directly in operation most days of the week. What is in operation is a practical sense of *where* to talk about "values"; of which "values" are supposed to be relevant where; and of where "values" are basically irrelevant.

Another way of trying to unearth inner beliefs and values uses one-on-one interviews, away from the respondents' friends or usual associates, in situations modeled after the psychotherapeutic session. Political scientist Robert Lane, for example, invited interviewees for several long, intimate sessions in his comfortable office.[25] He even offered them cigars. The results of his respectful, sympathetic interviews offer striking insights into abstract political beliefs and reasoning, but such intimate, therapeutic relationships between interviewers and their subjects may encourage respondents to speak in uncharacteristically serious ways about issues that they usually treat flippantly, or ironically, or do not discuss at all, or discuss in some contexts only for the purpose of showing that they are smart, or discuss in other contexts only to reassure themselves that the world is all right after all.

A variant on this type of research says that apathetic citizens are often "in denial," experiencing "psychic numbing" (Lifton 1968), trying not to care because they feel overwhelmed and want to protect themselves and their loved ones from despair. Psychological resistance could account for part of the political silence I found; but the next question should be, what interactions made such "psychic numbing" seem so necessary? In a fascinating study, *No Reason to Talk about It: Families Confront the Nuclear Taboo*, two psychologists (Greenwald and Zeitlin 1987) found a paradox: parents and children in focus groups tried to hide their fears from each other, to protect each other, but family members all felt more secure and empowered if they actually talked about their fears.

I add that one of the most important beliefs is an unspoken belief about talk itself – about where talk matters and about what kind of talk is appropriate where. This "culture of talk" tells us when we need to hide our fears, and when talking will help us work through our fears. When I asked the standard survey question "How much of the time do you think you can trust the government in Washington to do what is right?" many volunteers said something like what Carolyn said, "Most of the time. Well, at least I'd like to *think* it's most of the time. Of course, I'm not so sure it really *is*. But I hope it is. So, I'd say 'most of the time.' Yes, put 'Most of the time.' " Notice – neither yes nor no nor undecided was the most "real" belief here. Volunteers' beliefs *included* an effort at convincing themselves that they lived in a democracy, and an orientation toward talk itself. Being a good citizen meant being upbeat and encouraging; and volunteers assumed that that meant not talking too much about problems that one could not immediately fix. Compare that response to the typical activists' response to the survey question "Can a person like you make a difference?" Many said, "No," and then laughed on the side, exclaiming that it was amazing how active they were considering how little effect they thought they had. Typical volunteers said, "Yes," with an "at least I hope so" tagged on.

Ironic, detached, theatrical, hesitant, tight-lipped, resigned, clichéd, effortfully pious: the relations people have toward their own opinions, and the ways they explain those opinions, are part of what "holding an opinion" means. In other words, volunteers and activists shared skepticism about the government, but habitually expressed it and displayed it differently. It was not their "inner" beliefs that differed so much as their style, their willingness to voice some ideas and feelings and not others, in some contexts and not others.

In other words, the problem with psychological approaches is that what matters for democracy is not only what individuals privately hold inside their brains. What also matter are the ways that citizens mingle and interact. The "democratic norms" that really matter are unspoken norms for conversation, manners, civility, tact, that make citizens comfortable engaging in freewheeling political conversation in everyday life contexts. For democracy to survive, there must be a range of contexts that citizens recognize as appropriate places for broad political debate. Valuing this neither exclusively subjective nor exclusively objective, but "intersubjective," nature of politics means taking interaction seriously, as a social fact that is patterned, real, and important.

Making the path by walking it: civility, feelings, and social structure

I will call the process of creating contexts for political conversation "civic practices," or, interchangeably, "political manners" or "etiquette."[26] This etiquette implicitly takes into account a relationship to the wider world; politeness, beliefs, and power intertwine, in practice, through this sense of civility. The concept, then, refers to citizens' companionable ways of creating and maintaining a comfortable context for talk in the public sphere.

Goffman called this constant, unspoken process of assessing the grounds for interaction "footing" (1979, 1981).[27] Are there stairs here? loose gravel? ice? To walk we have to assess the footing. Talking is the same: are we talking to make conversation? to accomplish a task? to show off? The footing draws on that "inexhaustible reservoir" of "common knowledge" on which participants rely for interpreting each other's conversations, which members intuitively understand to be giving meaning to the interaction.

Investigating the footing means asking what members assume "being a member" requires; what kinds of talk and silence members consider appropriate for that context; whether talk is considered important at all or whether there is another, more non-verbal way of establishing a sense of companionship. That is, what does the very act of speaking itself mean to them? Until I assessed the "footing" in the volunteer high school parents' groups, I could not figure out why they ignored the political problems that they inevitably encountered in the course of their work – the race riots, caved-in classroom ceilings and flooded classroom floors at the high school, for example. By tuning into their political manners, I realized that volunteers assumed that volunteer groups exist to show that regular citizens really can make a difference, and that talking about these problems would sink the buoyant feeling of empowerment.

In the tenuous American public sphere, how people make sense of each other's conversation is an open question. Many of the people I met reported initial trepidation at joining a group, saying that they had feared that they did not know what to do in a meeting, how to talk, how to act. Even more blatantly than in other settings, members' unspoken answers to the questions "What are we doing here, anyway? What is this group for? What is talk itself for in this setting? What is the appropriate way of talking here?'' were not ready-made, but were improvised, in practice.[28]

This etiquette varies from one context to another, so one way of observing this process of creating contexts is to notice the dramatic changes in discourse from frontstage to backstage. This civic etiquette is always an active, culturally creative response to a particular context. Civic practices are the fundamentally sociable processes by which citizens create contexts for political conversation in civil society, by jointly creating a relationship to speech itself. In creating these contexts, citizens develop meaning-making powers together. These ''practices'' defy the logic of systematic thinking, but embody instead practical knowledge that participants share, that allows them to make sense of situations together. ''Practice has a logic which is not that of the logician'' but is a ''practical coherence,'' on the order of ''tact, skill, dexterity, delicacy, or *savoir-faire*: all names for the practical sense'' (Bourdieu 1990: 80–86).[29]

When I discovered that citizens' conversations in the public sphere were less wide-ranging than their conversations in intimate contexts were, my initial question – ''How do Americans talk about politics in these contexts?'' – quickly became ''How do Americans avoid public-spirited political conversation in these contexts, and what are they doing instead, that makes such conversation so rare?'' I realized that we need a new conceptual tool to help us ferret out the etiquette that undermines this freewheeling conversational ideal: we need *a way of listening* that makes us notice how people create contexts for public-spirited conversation – and how they neglect to seize that opportunity for free speech.

How did groups, and the institutions surrounding them, discourage or cultivate the expression and circulation of political ideas and concerns? And how did some groups manage to break out of this cycle of political evaporation? So many citizens wanted to be more than passive monads shuffling between work and sleep, so many were worried about the wider world, and yet so few were able to express their broader desires and concerns in public. A precious political, emotional, social good evaporated before reaching broad public circulation.

2

Volunteers trying to make sense of the world

The way to get a volunteer is to ask, "Who has a drill bit and can drill eight holes in this board next Saturday?" Someone will come who maybe never volunteered before, and then maybe they'll come again.

Geoffrey, volunteer, telling me how a volunteer group can grow

Part 1: *Trying to hide the public spirit*

Volunteers were poised to combat the specter of futility and to convince all newcomers that "You really can make a difference!" and that "Everyone has something to offer," as they often put it. They hoped to communicate that message through the very act of volunteering; and tried not to pay attention to problems that might undermine that message of hope. So, they tried hard not to care about issues that would require too much talking to solve, and tried to shrink their concerns into tasks that they could define as unpolitical, unconnected to the wider world. These citizens thought they could inspire feelings of empowerment within that small circle of concern; and they implicitly believed that helping people *feel* empowered was, in itself, doing something good for the community.

Advocates of democracy have long looked to groups that work on small, local issues as potential schools for wider political concern. Volunteers shared faith in this ideal of civic participation, but in practice, paradoxically, maintaining this hope and faith meant curtailing political discussion: members sounded less publicly minded and less politically creative in groups than they sounded individually. In the ideal image of the public sphere, citizens casually talk politics in voluntary associations, widening their horizons just by becoming members. In the ideal, such groups encourage "unrestricted communication" (Habermas 1974); usually, Americans imagine that any "restrictions" on public debate must come from outside of the groups themselves –

from laws preventing freedom of assembly (Scott 1990; Havel 1989), or, more subtly, from propaganda that prevents people from learning about politics (Chomsky 1988; Stauber and Rampton 1996; Parenti 1993, for example) – or, even more subtly, from long-standing oppression that makes people unable to stand up for themselves (Gaventa 1980). But here, participants did *some* of the work of restricting communication themselves: they assumed that talking about politics would only sap vigor from the healthy tasks which volunteer groups realistically could set for themselves, and it would intimidate new members.

Thus, in group meetings, volunteers never drew connections between their everyday acts of charity and public issues. For example, when requesting volunteers to watch over children at the pre-dawn playground, Julie never wondered aloud whether there were any larger issues involved – perhaps long work hours and short vacations; perhaps the commuting patterns that left parents with an exhausting, sooty, two-, three- or four-hour round-trip each day, with no public transportation alternatives;[1] maybe the absence of paid positions for caregivers to watch the children on the pre-dawn playground and at other times throughout the day – larger issues that made Amargo parents into "overworked Americans" (Schor 1991) who hardly had time to see their children.

In almost any meeting, the discussion *could* have widened out to broader questions like this, possibly encouraging citizens to begin permitting themselves to imagine broader solutions. But volunteers assumed that there was no sense sacrificing precious, scarce time complaining and feeling bad about something that could not be fixed; and here was a small, upbeat, hands-on solution that could work right away if enough people would help. Every volunteer meeting presented an example of this method of inspiring good feelings and avoiding discouragement. The first part of this chapter shows how volunteers created "frontstage" group contexts that made publicly minded conversation seem out of place and discouraging; yet, in their backstage conversations, volunteers recognized that there is a problem with this approach – that it is impossible to divorce caring about people from caring about politics; that there are few purely personal or local solutions to social problems.

The second part of the chapter on the volunteers will show how social workers, school authorities, and city officials aided this process of political evaporation. A refrain among the social workers and volunteers said, "If a child is home alone with a problem, that child could go to any of the neighbors in the community, because they'd all be part of the Caring Adult Network (CAN)." In that way, adults could all share in raising the community's children, "so that the community is like an extended family for the children," in the words of one social worker; any mom on the block would poke her head out the kitchen window if she heard a child in trouble. The beautiful image of the Caring Adult community contrasted sharply with the reality of the suburban city, with its empty streets, seven-lane strips, mobile nuclear families, and commuter parents. Portraits of this supportive, loving community always referred to the past, never to the present reasons that this type of community was absent. This "culture of nostalgia" (Skolnick 1991) encouraged people to change their feelings about the community, as if the feelings themselves were the only problem. Officials tried to inspire citizens to recreate that dreamed-of tight-knit community; the image helped vaporize volunteers' expressions of public-spiritedness.

Chapter 3 will show how volunteers spoke in interviews, when explicitly asked to discuss politics. They overly freely "admitted" that they "selfishly" cared only about issues that were "close to home," even when it required a tremendous stretch of the imagination to find any connection at all between their involvement and their self-interest. Those extravagant assertions of self-interest helped volunteers feel empowered within a small circle of concern: they could tell themselves that they did not care about problems they felt powerless to fix. These assertions aided the cycle of political evaporation, by preventing volunteers from voicing clear concerns, even to themselves.

Though volunteers inevitably encountered issues like race, child care, poverty, gender inequality, and school funding and policies in the course of their volunteer work – issues that in another context might fuel hot debate and political fire – these groups emphatically defined their work as "not political." When I interviewed the schools group and asked what they thought motivated members of a local grassroots group that was working on a foreign policy issue, Danielle succinctly summarized my question as, "She's asking, 'Why do they choose politics instead of schools?'"

In American community life, volunteer groups are to good citizenship as apples are to fruit; they are the very model – what linguist George Lakoff (1987) calls the "Idealized Cognitive Model" – of good, productive citizen involvement. Volunteering is the hegemonic image of good citizenship (Gramsci 1957, 1971). A great deal is at stake in the definition of the volunteer, and in the definitions of compassion, altruism, optimism, and everything else that goes along with volunteering.

The volunteers I met were unusually compassionate and optimistic, freely giving attention and care to their community, valiantly trying to create a community spirit. Even when someone got shot in the convenience store next-door to the high school, no new parents came to the high school parents' meeting – it was just the same old dedicated bunch that showed up. This small group filled an important spot in the civic life of Amargo, but still, something was missing. In trying so hard to maintain their "can-do" spirit, their optimism and hope, volunteers assumed that they had to hush any discussion of political problems.

Plugging into volunteer work

In my search for community involvement, I participated in two anti-drugs groups: "Vote B for Substance-Free" and the "Just Say No Team." Just Say No was a group made of volunteers and social service workers from hospitals, Youth and Family Services, the Recreation Department, Child Protective Services, the city police and the military police from the local nuclear base. Vote B had about eight regularly attending members; Just Say No had about twenty. I attended meetings, events like Just Say No rallies, anti-drugs parades, family events, and public meetings that these volunteers and officials held; and generally did what other members did. Incidentally, de Tocqueville's example of Americans' zest for forming funny little groups is a Temperance Union – perhaps not much has changed since then!

I also participated in the Parent League, a group of about twelve parents – both mothers and fathers – of high schoolers, whose general purpose was to help the school out. The group met in the musty old library of the high school, a room with big oak chairs and tables, crumbling paperbacks and twenty-year-old magazines on the shelves, fragrant with the cozy smell of library paste. Among their many projects were: selling candy and burgers at school games, holding a yearly dance, building the throne for the Homecoming queen, holding a "Career Night" – an evening at school to which representatives from various occupations were invited to describe their work (and give out brochures, pens, pencils, and pins with their corporate or military branch logo on them). I went to their meetings, helped run the concession stand, sell raffle tickets at events like the Saturday Farmers' Market and the Kids' Magicland Halloween Fair, and generally did what other members did. In my quest for volunteer opportunities, I also went to some events put on by the recycling center (including an exuberant celebration with a school marching band playing Sousa marches, and Girl Scouts in uniform!)[2] and the League of Women Voters.[3]

In the two core volunteer groups – Vote B and the Parent League – were three schoolteachers, one corporate scientist, one local realtor, two full-time homemakers (both with two years of college education), and some pink-collar workers. These groups were typical of American volunteers (Verba and Nie 1972: 99),[4] coming somewhat disproportionately from higher income and education groups, but including a wide range, and the plurality (but not always the majority) of members was white. I took part in the few, rare meetings which drew these volunteers together with groups around town that were less racially or ethnically mixed – all African-American or all Filipino, for example.

I place all the volunteer groups in which I participated in one category because the groups all shared a style of talking; they were a "speech community" (Hymes 1972), and volunteering was a "speech genre" (Bakhtin 1981). And members themselves referred to these groups as of a piece. When I told Sherry, a high school parent, that I was studying "what gets people involved in volunteer groups and how to get more people involved," she told me about a meeting sponsored by anti-drug social services, and mentioned Kiddie Magicland, a Parks Department-sponsored city playground. A group of volunteers made a booklet listing volunteer and social service agency-sponsored projects, calling it a "resources guide." Volunteers themselves assumed these projects formed a single category.

Vote B for Substance Free did try a political route, trying to increase taxes for more prisons, police, and some social services, so it might seem strange that I call it a "volunteer group." But the group never discussed the issue as a group, so when I asked members, in the group interview, why they were involved in this issue, members chuckled and said, "We've never really talked about that," and thanked me afterward, saying that they were glad someone gave them the chance to sit down and finally talk about it. The League of Women Voters similarly avoided publicly minded debate; for example, even in their pre-election meetings, they discussed politicians' strategies, but never discussed the merits of the politicians' political programs.

As a volunteer myself, I had difficulty finding a niche that was not simply working alone on a predesigned project. I asked often what I could do to help: I could drive around town alone delivering hot meals to the elderly, go door-to-door alone gathering petition signatures or make phone calls at home, meet an "at risk" child once a week to give support, supervise the playground before school, become a Block Parent, providing a "safe house" for children who were in trouble, sell raffle tickets for the Parent League at the Farmers' Market or at the evening Halloween Fair, and maybe another volunteer would show up, too, but if not, I could do it by myself. These were projects involving only one volunteer, when I was looking for a group. If I were a citizen searching for a public forum in which to learn how to participate in and clarify my thoughts about the wider world, volunteer groups would not usually have been good places to search.

When I asked how I could get involved, all volunteers enthusiastically told me to contact someone (always a woman) whom they considered a "real super volunteer" like Julie, an extremely active volunteer, or Claudia, the head of the local Meals-on-Wheels program, or a really dedicated social service worker like Virginia or Fiona, saying that if I really want to know about volunteers, I should talk to this person, because "she does so much." No volunteer referred me to a "real super group." In all the groups were many members who never came to meetings, but sent messages offering to help out with tasks. Volunteers did not think of themselves as doing good as groups, but as individuals.

Over tea one day, I asked Julie how people decided what projects to work on, where they got ideas, when they discussed the overall big picture. People did not spin out those kinds of ideas "any more," she said, though she "personally thought it was fun." Maybe people got them from "the sixties," she speculated. Others said something similar, except for two who were on the School Board, who told me they might meet now and then over coffee, on a *one-to-one* basis, for their "bigger picture" discussions – in private sessions, not in open meetings.

Volunteers said that meetings were a waste of time compared with the groups' real work. Compared to the activist groups, the striking feature of volunteers was just how little time they spent in group contexts. Though volunteers attended many meetings every week, each was very to-the-point, short, and task-oriented. When I said that I was studying "community life – what gets people involved in groups and how to get more people involved," many proudly recounted a long, long list of their volunteer activities, amazing me with how many evenings a week they devoted to volunteering. None mentioned why they were involved. Their point was that activity itself was a matter-of-fact way of demonstrating commitment.

"We accomplish a lot": what "the frontstage" is for in volunteer groups

What was missing was respect for discussion itself, willingness to debate about troubling issues that might not be resolved immediately; willingness to risk discouragement. This fear of talk itself became apparent to me in one of the first meetings of the Parent League I attended. Charles, the local NAACP representative, parent of a high schooler himself, had come to the meeting of mostly plump, pastel-clad parents wearing a black leather jacket and skinny black jeans. When the meeting was almost over, he had his turn to speak.

He said that some parents had called him about a teacher who said "racially disparaging things" to a student. The students in the class tried complaining to the "appropriate authorities" but the authorities all said they were "too busy" to deal with it. Charles said that the school had hired this teacher even though he had a written record in his file of having made similar remarks at another school. Charles also said there were often Nazi skinheads standing outside the schoolyard recruiting at lunchtime.

Charles' deadpan enumeration of the problems took my breath away. Since a race riot had erupted in the school a few months earlier, and another riot had occurred down the block at a movie theater, volunteers might have considered the teacher's remarks especially worrisome. But no volunteers asked what the teacher had said, to judge for themselves whether it was racist. They just sat, blandly listening.

First Sherry minimized the problem, treating the problem as a personal, generational one, saying, "It is often hard for parents to go talk to teachers – my mother used to be intimidated by them, too," as if to say that it was not really a race problem. "I guess some parents are still in that generation."

Mild-mannered Geoffrey cut in with a slightly cross edge to his voice: "And what do you want of this group. Do you want us to do something," not as a question, but with a dropping tone at the end.

Charles continued, "I just thought more people would be at the meeting and it would just be something parents should know." He said parents should be more involved in general, and not just to accomplish things, but to talk. Of course, members thought involvement was important, too – Charles' urging the parents to get more people involved seemed to be simply an insult, since they assumed that they were doing all they could to invite involvement. So, in defense of his group's efficacy, Ron exclaimed, "Don't underestimate us – we make efficient use of small numbers of people! We get a lot done!"

Charles slowly started restating the problem but now Ron was getting impatient. He interrupted, "It's not up to us to do anything about the incident. That should go through the proper channels." Turning to Charles, as if it were purely Charles' problem, he conceded, "It *is* unfortunate that the incident occurred – happened," using that officious bureaucratese that marked their discourse on "touchy" issues. "But it should go through the proper authorities," he repeated, even though Charles had already reported that the "proper authorities" were not doing their jobs.

I was shaken by the interchange, and eagerly awaited a discussion, but the only comment at the time was from Ron, a big, hefty businessman. He turned eagerly in his seat the instant the meeting adjourned, to correct an impression he thought a newcomer like myself could have got:

Were you surprised at how much money we made at our raffle? You were surprised that we got that much, weren't you? But it was just small amounts over the course of the six weeks [spent raffling an old Cadillac at the Farmers' Market and the Kiddie Magicland Halloween fair]. That's what I meant when I said to Charles [a new member], "Don't underestimate us." We may be small, but we're energetic! We can accomplish a lot more than you'd think!

Later, Danielle told me that the parents gave Charles a cold shoulder because they thought he "had an ax to grind."

Geoffrey's minutes for that meeting reported:

Charles Jones relayed an incident *for information* [my emphasis]. He is investigating on behalf of some parents who requested help from the NAACP. He is in charge of such investigations by the NAACP. The event involved a substitute teacher [notice his emphasis that the teacher was not really a real one] who made a racially derogatory statement in class.

Other minutes from that meeting included details of a discussion of what kind of fundraiser to hold:

Someone said that Bill McDowell [the principal] said we should have bingo games. An extensive discussion on bingo operations ensued. Pam had idea that we have one big fundraiser each year so that we would not have to work year round . . . Victoria suggested we have an auction as a fundraiser. Trudy suggested a crabfeed. Bob suggested a spaghetti feed. Joan suggested simply ask parents for $5 donations towards a specific project.

This continued for half of a single-spaced page, clearly indicating which topic of discussion was central to the group's purpose.

Was this lack of attention to Charles' presentation simply an example of racism? At first I thought so, but soon changed my mind – though I did have other reasons for suspecting that racism was the simple cause of silence: nearly every meeting of the Parent League included passing reference to yet another "incident," as parents and educators called racial name-calling and fighting. At one meeting, Ron pointedly erased race from a story. Two teenagers at Amargo High had fought and hurled racial epithets at each other. Ron asked rhetorically why the fight got "billed" in the paper as a *race* problem, when it was just a quarrel between jealous boyfriends. The other parents agreed. In another meeting, parents repeated a neighboring high school's rude chant, shouted at a basketball game: "You got no skill, go back to The Hill!" I asked a usually articulate white parent, Clara, what "The Hill" was, and she couldn't even bring herself to call it a "black" neighborhood, saying, "Well, The Hill. The Bowling Green Hill, is what it's officially called. It's a a a er, a – a *poor* neighborhood, yes, a *poor* neighborhood."[5]

Two black members of volunteer groups fitted in very well because they shared the other volunteers' practical style. At a track meet one day, one black high school parent told me about a group in which she worked, that was going to have its statewide meeting, managing to avoid even once mentioning that it was an all-black organization. I asked, "Is it a sports group?" "No." "Oh, so it's like the Girl Scouts, or a camp?" "No . . ." and only later did I read in a newspaper that it was a group organized on the basis of race. I wrote in field notes, ''How embarrassing! Trudy probably thought I was asking leading questions, when really, I was just confused! But if you have to worry so much about avoiding in this slalom course of dangerous topics, how can you even carry on a clear conversation?'' Trudy was acting appropriately here, group members would surely have said.

Sociolinguist Teun van Dijk (1987) would say that this hesitation and circumlocution is clear evidence of ''racism,'' but I do not think that would be a good explanation. Avoidance was the way the volunteers publicly treated *all* troubling social issues. The problem was not racism *per se*, but volunteers' relation to political discussion in general, including discussion of racism. Volunteers thought that Charles should not have brought up the subject of Nazi skinheads and racist teachers because there was nothing they could do about it – at least not without risking the discouragement that might accompany political debate. To talk about racism would have meant changing their political etiquette, to stop trying so hard to keep up that can-do spirit and let some frightening uncertainty in. Actively ignoring such tensions was considered a positive good, a moral act. Better would be to work on projects that illustrate how easy, effective, and enjoyable involvement is; then, they believed, everyone will get involved and race problems will dissolve in the busy harmony.

Their efforts at ignoring race were also part of their general effort to avoid snobbery; to be welcoming and encouraging meant treating everyone as an equal, not as a member of a category.[6] When I asked on the questionnaire what race they were, many responded as Sherry did: ''It doesn't matter what race you are. Anyway, it shouldn't.'' Having to talk about something, in fact, would be a sign that there is a problem; if things are going smoothly, regular people should not have to sit down and talk.

Avoiding discouragement and snobbishness, though, had costs, among which probably was the community's ability to deal with race problems. Many parents of color came to one or two meetings and then never returned. I spoke to one who had come only once; she had concluded that the Parent League was ''a bunch of white people who weren't interested in race.''

The Royal Dog Steamer

Instead of discussing potentially upsetting issues, most meetings featured in-depth discussions of practical fundraising projects. For example,

I looked all over for a machine that can roast hot dogs continuously so we don't get a backlog when all the kids come up to the stand at once. So, I found one at this restaurant supplier – they're offering us a discount, so we should write them a big thank you note. It's called a Royal Dog Steamer, and it can steam foot longs, Polish dogs, hot links, regular dogs, sausages, you name it, about twenty at a time!

Debbie, a sporty mom who wore sweatshirts and sneakers to Parent League meetings, chuckled while announcing this, as if to say that it was humorous, but understandable, that a group of ten adults should be so concerned with all the different types of dogs. When a topic was within the group's scope as members defined it, discussion was lavishly detailed.

What is remarkable about this emphasis on fundraising is that, for most volunteers, it would have been much easier to pitch in money from their own pockets than to spend that enormous amount of time and effort on fundraisers. It might possibly have actually been cheaper for volunteers to donate their own money than to spend it on building elaborate concessions stands and other fundraising equipment. But just chipping in money would have missed their point. The implicit moral of a fundraiser was to show the community that common people care (Wuthnow 1991), not to show that only rich people can effectively care, or politically sophisticated people care. Fundraising really seemed to be "doing something."

Another way to keep discouraging issues at bay was to hone in on a very concrete solution to an overwhelmingly large problem. In one meeting, Just Say No members talked about starting a collection drive for foster children who were turning eighteen. A member said 18-year-olds were not supported by the state, so many were simply turned out of foster care to fend for themselves. One volunteer said, "Those kids wouldn't have *anything* of their own." The first volunteer had a solution: "*One* thing that 18-year-olds would surely need would be *blankets*," so they began planning a drive to gather blankets. Emphasizing the word "one," the volunteers left tacit their doubts about the other things homeless teenagers might need – toothbrushes, clothes, beds, homes, jobs, education, love: thinking about all that would be overwhelming. The volunteers wanted to believe that regular citizens can solve local problems, but the perceived, implied political structures make it difficult to do.

Volunteers were certainly not oblivious to social problems; they could talk about them if there was something upbeat to say, if the problem already had been solved. In one meeting of an anti-drugs group subcommittee, a city official told a story that everyone present found outrageously funny: "a skinny Jewish guy with a shock of bright red hair" came to give a speech at a Just Say No rally and all officials, black and white, had been worried. The city official, Liz, said,

The people in the neighborhood were going, "Who dis guy? What he got to say to us? Who de heck is he?" Then the rally came and he was pawing at his shirt like maybe he was itchy or something, and he looked kind of sweaty and nervous. But he gave a rousing speech, everyone was thrilled, and at the end, he whipped off his shirt and had a Superman costume on underneath.

They could release the tension with gales of laughter and a story, but only because everything had already worked out fine. An interracial meeting that did not turn sour was a relief; that was what made the story so funny. The assumption was that racial tension *was* present; the problem could be acknowledged, but only after it had already been overcome.

The officials who worked with volunteers echoed this assumption – that talking about problems without immediately offering a solution is just complaining. I heard the pattern broken only once, in a Just Say No meeting, when a probation officer said:

One concern of mine is I see a lot of kids in my program abusing drugs and they need a place to go. They're over eighteen so funds earmarked for under eighteen and family intervention don't apply. They are adults, but they're still living at home. They don't have jobs, and they're not in school. That's a concern of mine.

The format was supposed to be to tell a story like that and then right away say how someone was solving the problem. So there was silence, while everyone waited for her to tell us about the solution.

After a long moment, she apologized with a giggle, ''I just have a problem, not a solution.''

The chair of the meeting said, ''I'm sure someone'll be coming to talk to you to figure out a solution.'' Perhaps volunteers and social service workers did indeed engineer a creative behind-the-scenes, quiet solution, but the general problem went undiscussed and unanalyzed in public.

The longest reflective conversation I heard in a volunteer group was one that a teacher practically forced on the Parent League. Wearing a cotton blend plaid shirt and sporting a crew cut, this teacher did not appear to be a hippie with wild ideas. Handing out a sheet entitled ''Prom Madness,'' he argued for putting a limit on spending on the prom, so that students would not be forced to work too many hours to pay for prom expenses. The problem was, there was nothing but fast-food restaurants there; the students wanted a more stylish prom than could be held at Pizza Hut or Taco Bell, and spent vast sums to travel by limousine to get it. Danielle passed me a doodled note halfway through the discussion, with an apostrophe-eyed smiley face on it, quizzically asking, ''Are we having fun yet?'' with the obvious answer being, ''No.'' Everyone looked bored – some wandered in and out for pop that loudly clunked out of the machine down the hall.[7]

What was most taboo was speaking about problems in terms of justice – publicly minded speech that was considered wrong, but addressing the same problem in a piecemeal way was considered all right. Charles committed a *faux pas* when he raised a principle for a group fundraising activity at a Parent League meeting, in a discussion about raising funds to buy computers for the high school:

> First, has anybody tried going over to Microchip Lane [the general name for an area nearby, known internationally as a center for computer production] and *asked* for computers? The big corporations take our money but they don't give it back. *Unless you ask.* They'll even send people to train the kids to use the computers.
>
> It's training them to work in industry, and the corporations need that as much as the kids. They should pay for the services the schools give them. Back in another fundraiser I worked on, we hit up Ford for four brand new cars. We raffled them off and made $2–3,000 per car. We also got "used trucks" from Seven-Up. The corporations will give if you ask.
>
> RON: What "we" is this?
>
> CHARLES: Excuse me?
>
> RON: What "we" got these things? What organization?
>
> CHARLES [very slowly]: At that point in time, it was 1969, I was in Texas. I was working with the [was I the only one who expected him to say Black Panthers?] YMCA. The second point is that you should put the money into an account to have it collect interest and just draw on that.
>
> BOB: I really like your idea of putting some money away and just taking the interest.

They ignored the idea of "hitting up" the big companies. But later on that evening, they talked about "requesting donations" from small companies, for an auction of "a night for two in the mountains," or "dinner for two at a nice restaurant." And still later, Bob said that a local black politician had mentioned "getting someone from Alpha" to donate some computer equipment, since he knew an Alpha executive who lived in town.

Talking about a special favor from one specific politician who might be able to get one particular individual to have his company donate a few items erased the principle of political justice that Charles had tried to raise, about corporations' obligation to the community. "Requesting" was okay, but holding companies accountable was not. Asking politely was okay, quietly negotiating behind-the-scenes was acceptable; but raising a matter of principle and trying to discuss it publicly was considered unseemly.

The point is that allowing political conversation in their meetings would have given a different meaning to volunteers' work, even if volunteers had kept on doing *exactly* the same tasks. But volunteers assumed that talking would not itself produce knowledge or power.

Backstage complaints and recognition of problems

Backstage, volunteers sounded quite different. In the tiny, closet-sized office where she worked, one volunteer told me and another volunteer a story she had heard at a get-together the night before. The story was about how Debbie hosted a family that was visiting Amargo from a rural county, to take part in a big, statewide high school football game:

When they got here, the [rural] parents said, "Oh, thank God." So Debbie said, "Thank God what?" They said, "Thank God you're not black. We were worried they'd house us with blacks." So Debbie said that she told her son to invite all his black friends over for a slumber party! Some of the kids from Auburn had never seen a black person before and they were asking them, "What clothes do you wear?" "What music do you listen to?" Debbie said it was quite a cultural experience.

This kind of direct action was something volunteers cheered, but quietly, never in the group context. Volunteers tried to be welcoming to all parents, and assumed, as Geoffrey told me, that it was better "not to make an issue of including minorities but just treat them like everyone else." In other words, working together on concrete projects would do more good than talking about race. Thus, I saw volunteers' children play with a mix of friends worthy of a United Nations utopian fantasy poster. Danielle's children were of mixed race. For most volunteers, racist *beliefs* or even subtly racist feelings were not the explanation for their silence.

Volunteers were not unconcerned or unaware or lacking in the "inner values and beliefs" that feed political concern. They were lacking public contexts in which to voice those concerns. Most volunteers were privately obsessed with political worries, but simply assumed that they could not do anything about them, and that volunteer groups were the wrong contexts for discussing them. Combating futility meant, above all, combating the *feeling* of futility, and especially, combating the expression of such feelings aloud in volunteer group meetings, where such feelings could be most destructive.

But backstage, conversation was quite different. Just before polls closed after an especially disillusioning state election, Cora, Julie, and I were shivering outside the junior high school cafeteria, potato salads in hand, giant coffee-maker at our feet. We were waiting in the foggy November evening for a janitor to unlock the doors of an old school cafeteria, in which the League of Women Voters was going to host a post-election potluck dinner for all volunteers. Cora, a friendly older woman, was embarrassed at how disgusted the election made her. She was a Republican but voted for the Democrat because he had done her a personal favor.

"Oh, I've gotten so cynical about this election!" she exclaimed. "I mean

it. Isn't it awful it's come to that – voting for him because he did us a favor?''
She apologized for sounding so cynical. With sympathy, Julie asked why she
was so cynical. Interspersing her criticisms with many more apologies, Cora
fumed at the politicians for putting so many measures on the ballot on the
same issues, saying that she was so mad she voted "no" on almost all
twenty-eight ballot measures;[8] she was cynical because, while she was calling
people to get out the vote, she could not stop herself from thinking that people
should not vote on issues that they know nothing about; cynical because there
are people who make their entire livings as paid political consultants.

Julie consoled her by saying that it really was not that hard to read the
ballot (it was over a hundred pages long). Chuckling, she offered her personal
solution: simply not to watch TV or listen to the radio. Cora spent the rest
of the evening whispering apologies to us, and Julie spent the rest of the
evening consoling Cora, whispering several times over dinner, "Oh, I'm sure
you'll get over it." When we were eating, I also whispered to Cora, saying
that I thought it was all right to feel cynical sometimes. Cora confessed, "I
really *am* feeling cynical today – partly because I've been volunteering all
day." Toward the end of the dinner, she declared that her mood had blown
over already.

In the high school, a classroom ceiling fell in and never got repaired for
lack of funds; there was a longstanding flood in another classroom, and the
school library was full of popular magazines from the 1950s. Considering
the generally dire condition of the school's resources, it could have made
sense for a school group to try to influence funding policy – or at least
complain about it. "There's really nothing you can do about it . . . I don't
have any control over it. I just have my one vote, but – " as Danielle said
with a shrug at a Boosters' dance. The "depressing subject" of school funding came up only when I was alone with Danielle and my husband at the
dance. Aside from the times Charles and other outsiders brought it up, it
never came up in the group meetings or in gatherings with more than one
volunteer. Danielle, who was not wealthy, told me twice that her son either
had to sell five expensive tickets to a band concert or pay for the tickets
himself. That fundraiser was better than an earlier one, selling chocolate
bars – Manuel owed "only" a hundred dollars for the tickets and had not
been stuck with junk food. The chapter on interviews offers many more
examples of volunteers' political worries: the point is, these "depressing"
problems – and imaginative possible solutions to them – never arose in group
meetings, but outside of meetings, in whispered conversations, or in interviews. Many volunteers were so eager to discuss them I could not stop them
once they started.

Backstage and frontstage among volunteers and officials together

Volunteers' political avoidance was absolutely consonant with officials' approach to politics. When the Nazi-skinhead concert came to town, the volunteers and officials alike hated the publicity the white supremacists were getting. Yet, they did not speak out about it. I interviewed the mayor, on the phone, as a reporter for a Stockport radio station (I had never met him in person; he did not pay attention to my name and assumed I was just one of the dozen regional reporters writing about the concert that day). I asked, "Is there anything local citizens or city government can or should do to prevent these kinds of racial attitudes from continuing?"

First he informed me that the press was operating on a factual error, that the concert was not actually happening in Amargo (it was a few feet outside city limits in a barren unincorporated area, on an prominent Amargo doctor's ranch), and that I should therefore call someone else; it was not under his jurisdiction, so there was nothing he could do.

I asked in several different ways if there was anything citizens should do to make it clear that they did not support Nazi skinheads. Again, he said the concert really had nothing to do with Amargo, that Amargo did not have problems like that. Clearly, he considered the event bad public relations for his town. His job as mayor, like the volunteers' job as volunteers, was to highlight the good, not analyze the bad. Then he said there was something people could do. "They should ignore it! Don't go. Ignore it. That's the worst thing you can do to people in that group, I think, is deny them your attention. Make it clear you don't support their views, you don't support that philosophy, and then: ignore it." After this, he said that he did not understand the question, saying that simply staying home would send a clear enough message. Finally, he said that they could "state it with their children,[9] and in their homes." Like the volunteers, the mayor treated attention to such difficult problems as a breach of etiquette. Political silence was not at all a principle of laziness or cowardice; it was considered a positive good. Avoiding the image that the town was racist was the same as avoiding racism, they thought. Was the mayor a racist? I heard a rumor that he would not let his daughter date anyone but whites. This style of treating politics could hide all sorts of viewpoints from public scrutiny; the volunteers' civic etiquette could serve as a cover for racists, though it usually did not. From the outside, their silence made them all sound like potential racists to the outside world.

This emphasis on happy public discourse systematically screened certain types of talk out of public circulation. One volunteer, Barney, often tried to start public debate, but social service workers repeatedly moved the debate "backstage." Barney was retired; he had developed a second career as a full-time volunteer and public gadfly, who constantly tested the limits of the official culture of political avoidance. At an evening meeting, oddly called a "public forum," a panel of social service workers and police gave speeches about crime and punishment to an audience of about ten people. After the presentations there was some time for questions.

Barney was the first to raise his hand. One officer joked, "You can always count on Barney to say something!" treating him, as usual, as an eccentric old fellow who could always chip in something odd.

Julie, who always stuck up for Barney, said, "I hope so!"

Barney said,

It costs $20,000 per year to put someone in prison, but that's not gonna help. What they need is jobs, and good jobs – a job at $6/hour only gets you $12,000/year. Why not just pay them the extra money, give them a well-paying job, instead of waiting till they have to go to jail and then having to spend almost twice as much for them to not do anything, in jail?

Another volunteer added another question, which the black lieutentant answered first. Then he got back to Barney's point: "It's not $20,000 a year, it's $33,000 a year. It's cheaper to send them to Harvard. Now, they don't all go through the whole system or every building would be a jail. But, it's a necessary evil, something society has to have, something society wants." The lieutenant treated Barney's question as a request for information (and probably the officer felt proud for having "successfully" deflected debate in public).

But backstage, the officer could acknowledge that he *did* understand that Barney was trying to start a political debate. Interestingly, after the panel ended and people were milling around, the lieutenant and Barney were standing by the perennial coffee-maker, and the lieutenant said, as if in confidence, that some huge percentage of the juveniles in jail were black. Under his breath, he said, "You know, you gotta wonder, when so many of the kids in jail are black and minorities." And the local head of Child Protective Services also scurried over to Barney, and also engaged his contentious question under her breath: "I appreciate your question. I read letters in the paper, saying 'put more kids in jail,' but I don't agree, either. Working with the family is key. That's the answer. Impact the child."[10] Backstage, expressing opinions was acceptable. The two officials made it clear that they had indeed understood that Barney had intended to ignite a debate, but that the public forum was no place for that. In public, arguing over opinions would just be complaining.

An expansive horizon glimmered for a moment and then quickly vanished in several meetings of the Just Say No team, when anyone would mention tobacco and alcohol companies' campaigns to recruit teenage consumers. Speakers always sounded astonished that a corporation would do something so terrible. At one morning meeting, a representative from a project which promoted a nationwide "smoke-free day" came from Stockport with a slide show, asking the group to participate. The show said that $3,800 goes for tobacco promotion every minute, and that the tobacco industry needs 3,000 new teenage smokers each day to keep up its business. By coattailing alcohol and tobacco onto the drug problem, the volunteers and officials potentially confronted big corporations. However, right after mentioning the advertising and the teenage smokers, the Just Say No team continued the meeting, focusing again on changing one teenager at a time, from the inside out, and no mention was made again of corporate culpability. Still, the fact that it came out once was exceptional.

In the Just Say No committee's short Mission Statement were some suggestions aimed at developing "a unified, positive vision of Amargo," including:

2. Call for adoption of a community slogan, such as "Amargo – a Place Where You Can Make Friends." . . .

5. Teach realtors to think in terms of selling a "home" instead of a "house". . .

7. Encourage media campaign advertisers such as First Hospital and General Gas and Power to run ads on "friendship."

This was the frontstage face that volunteers aspired to present to the world.

A small part of the officials' and volunteers' avoidance of debate was an eagerness to avoid offending potential official allies. For example, Liz took Shirley, me, and a third volunteer into her barren city office one weekday morning, to instruct us on gathering signatures for the Alcohol Tax petition. Liz told Shirley to contact the president of the Police Officers' Association, loudly laughing, "Just don't mention that lots of police officers have severe drinking problems!" Then Liz and Shirley together told a story of two officers who shot each other at 2 a.m. in a bar parking lot, drunk after hours, while wrestling and playing with their guns. Liz said, "The frightening thing is that these guys are legally allowed to carry loaded weapons with them twenty-four hours a day." Laughing, they told another tale of two officers leaving a bar and "slamming a guy against a car, grabbing the guy and really manhandling him, firing two shots into the air, and then finding out that they had nabbed the wrong guy!" Shirley said that they should have had their blood alcohol levels tested and publicized. Liz, the official, focused on technical and legal issues, saying that they were just officers, so they were not required to submit to such tests. After a while, they summed up:

SHIRLEY: There are a lot of = [11]
LIZ: = drunk cops =
SHIRLEY: = in Amargo!

Shirley joked that people will laugh at them if they see that the police endorsed the petition; but of course, she was only joking. There was no question but that they would seek the police's support. Alliances came piece-meal, one precisely defined issue at a time, not as a whole movement working on a range of interconnected issues.[12] Powerful institutions like the police were crucial allies. No matter how many drunken brawls local police officers had, their seal of approval was important – more important than the volunteers'. Publicly minded critique evaporated in the process of making alliances like this one.

Efforts at making compromises and avoiding conflict between institutions still account for only a small part of officials' aversion to discussion. More often, and more crucially, officials avoided public debate because they were like volunteers in assuming that public discussion itself was tiresome and depressing.

Backstage, volunteers and officials recognized the overwhelming nature of the problems they faced, and the limits of their culture of political avoidance. One tale told at an anti-drugs meeting illustrates the tensions that volunteers experienced with their entrenched political style. Julie had, a few days earlier, told someone a story that was then relayed to us at an anti-drugs meeting. "Julia Trenton Brooks was taking the bus one day," the story went.

She takes the bus every day [said with admiration, as if to say that it is good, but remarkable to take the bus] but this particular bus she takes every day. On this bus is a little boy who gets on poorly dressed, sometimes not dressed warmly enough, sometimes he doesn't come at all.

Well, over time, people on the bus have begun looking out for this youngster, and making sure that he not only gets off at the right stop, but waiting till he gets from the bus stop into the school. Every morning, they made sure he made it into that school.

Now, that's what we're after: a Caring Adult Network, so that the community is like an extended family for the children

The quaint story was full of archaic language: a sing-song storybook tone, with repetitive clauses like a nursery rhyme, old-fashioned words like "youngster," a child not dressed warmly enough – a stock image of a poor child from a fairy tale – and a character who rides the bus when normal people are insulated with their stereos in tinted-windowed, air-conditioned cars.

Backstage, a couple of days later, Julie and I were cleaning out the massive coffee-maker after another anti-drugs meeting. I told her I thought that that story was touching. She slowly turned toward me and said, "The poor little boy – he was so neglected, his hair uncombed, sometimes he looked hungry. He just stopped coming one day." I asked what happened to him. She said she didn't know. "That's the way it works. When the family does something, the kid will just disappear." I asked if there was any way to find him, to make sure he was all right. Looking at me with her big eyes, she sadly said no.

Volunteers knew that the care shown this child was unusual. Julie had been on the bus only because she could not drive – she had told me once, when I was saving her an hour and a half, by driving her a couple of miles across town, that she herself would love to be able to drive, so that she would not have to waste so many hours a day waiting for infrequent and slow city buses. But she had an eye impairment that made driving impossible. With empty sidewalks, few buses, few corner stores, there were very few public spaces where adults came into contact with each other or with children, in the normal course of a day. As in most car-centered cities, adults who would want to be part of a "Caring Adult Network" would have to schedule a specific time and place to encounter a child. So, an involuntarily present "extended family" on the bus lost track of the privately owned child. What if we were all alone in our cars – would we never notice the ragged, hungry child? Why were there not *more* public places like the bus, where adults could collectively care for the town's neglected children? Who was responsible for the community's children? Would contacting Child Protective Services have helped or harmed? Could anything be done on a more than one-at-a-time basis? What if the poor, small, young child had been a poor, violent-or-foul-mouthed, big, old child? Volunteers certainly noticed the problems with the "one child at a time" approach to social issues, yet they could not discuss them openly. In this and other moments, volunteers publicly wanted to tell the uplifting story but not the sad ending; that part could be told only backstage.

If troubling questions ever did arise frontstage, they quickly were swallowed up in silence. In a meeting of the Vote B for Substance-Free campaign, Julie brought up a question that she said "will surely be asked again." "Someone said to me, 'the drug addicts got themselves into this mess by becoming addicts; they can get themselves out of it.' That's what this guy said. They're saying the common citizen shouldn't have to pay for the rehabilitation programs that only the addicts use. How are we gonna respond?'' After a long silence, someone else brought up a logistical question.

To avoid unequal participation, avoid talk

Volunteers wanted to show that anyone, the common person, not just a saint or a genius, can make a difference. Their assumption, though, was that talking would be difficult for newcomers, even though it was not difficult for all of the volunteers, personally, when outside of the meetings. In second-guessing other people's capabilities and desires, volunteers perceived that some people are more eloquent than others, that eloquence is not randomly distributed throughout the population, that some people have more cultural wherewithal, more eloquence, more training in self-presentation, than others (Bourdieu 1984). Indeed, many activist groups – feminist, ecological, peace groups, especially – have faltered on mismanaged equality, a "tyranny of structurelessness" (Freeman 1973), in which talkative people can rule by default.

Talking about politics would especially threaten volunteers' egalitarian method of building a sense of togetherness. It would require taking stands on issues, distinguishing oneself, making a scene, while volunteers preferred equality to distinction. So, again, opposing abstract, political, or principled talk was, paradoxically, volunteers' way of looking out for the common good.

The parent group had to plan a date for Career Night that did not conflict with the school's other after-school events. Someone suggested April 20. Joan, a sporadic participant in the group, looked in her date book.

No, that's Passover.

SHERRY [laughing]: Joan [turning toward me and a new member] – she teaches our kids at Catholic Confirmation classes – Passover doesn't apply to you!

JOAN [in a mock hillbilly accent, so as not to sound too ponderous]: It's a matter of principle.

BOB [slams his hand down on the table in mock fury, then smiles]: OK.

JOAN [apologizing]: It's just that last year I learned my lesson. I scheduled something for Rosh Hashanah and got *murdered*. And it was only two families – or three.

What mattered here was not inner beliefs, so much as the form they took. Joan may have been *thinking* in terms of principles here, or in terms of avoiding conflict, or more likely, she was blending several forms of moral reasoning at once. She tried to offer the reason of principle first, but the pressure of the group forced her to say the more normal reason, of avoiding trouble. What is important here is that she could give voice to only one type of reason. Without talk of principles, publicly minded political talk is hard to imagine.

Volunteers did not like advertising their principles, and did not like it when other people advertised theirs. Being humble often meant claiming to be self-interested; the disclaimers were always instantly available. Joking with the mayor at a meeting, Ron was talking about an earlier meeting. The mayor said, "I was surprised to hear you ask, 'What's going on?' in a political meeting. 'Ya don't *ask* that about politics,' " he said, tongue-in-cheek. Ron laughed, "I wasn't asking about politics – I was asking about economic self-interest! That's different – it *really matters!*"

In this manner, even minor principles went unheard. When the school district was considering building a new school, Danielle brought in a magazine describing an "ecologically sound design for a school grounds," with native plants instead of a grass lawn. Danielle described the article, saying excitedly that it was about building environmentally sound schools as a method of educating children and saving money and saving the planet in a minor way. The group's only response was Debbie's, "Yeah, a lot of kids are allergic to grass!" Otherwise, they just said it looked like a nice idea, especially the redwood sundecks. Danielle's speech on the principle behind the design fell into a void of silence, as if she had not even said it. Similarly, the Parent League took it for granted that there were normal things a parent group sells at games, so members did not need to discuss it. We sold hot dogs, hamburgers, candy bars, pop – though many children asked for fruit and juice, which we did not have, and the Parent League members themselves joked about how unhealthy diet soda was, and how one child would be "bouncing off the walls for hours" after eating four candy bars, and how children would be getting a caffeine rush from the Coke.

The fact that volunteers disliked *talk* of principles certainly does not mean that they did not *have* principles. They wanted them recognized without having to announce them. Sherry and Debbie were offended when a woman at a track meet who bought a burger from their mobile outdoor stand treated them like servants. "The first time, she came back to have her hot dog split! Can you imagine? Then the second time she beckoned over to me and said, 'She knows how I like it.' As if we were making money on it! As if she was a regular." They wanted their voluntary efforts to be recognized as voluntary, their quiet egalitarian practice to be matched by the rest of the community, by the other parents they would have liked to see at meetings.

Many Americans avoided speaking in terms of principles when principled talk can be so dishonest, and eloquence so unfairly distributed. Deeds alone should show intent; talk is cheap. Distrust of rhetorical eloquence has a long history in American politics. In the 1800s, Americans loved plain, unadorned public speech because they believed that it was more egalitarian than the fussy, musty, fancy speech of European aristocrats. Plain speech was a mark of our difference, of our egalitarian spirit (Cmiel 1990; Rodgers 1987). A hundred and fifty years ago, Alexis de Tocqueville said that Americans' drab speaking style reflected actual social conditions: they were drab public speakers because they had experience only with equality, not distinction (1969). Now, haunted by a more vast, unjustified inequality among citizens,[13] Americans avoid principled political debate altogether; we suspect that if we open the door to discussion, inequality will inevitably slide in and take over. The quest for equality undermines the deliberation that makes democracy possible.[14]

Volunteers wanted to be sure not to make anyone feel dumb. Instead of feeling excited by the complexities of the political world, they felt threatened, and tried to carve out a set of concerns that would not reveal anyone's ignorance. The League of Women Voters showed a pre-election video, showing pro and con presentations of the twenty-eight measures on the state ballot. Trying to remember all fifty-six opinions made me dizzy, but afterwards, the volunteers all said it was very helpful, very useful, very informative, gave a lot of information. This continued for quite a while, until finally, a non-volunteer, a non-member, broke in with, "It *was* a lot, though, wasn't it?" Janice, a member, confessed that she "knew people who just voted 'no' on all of them because they don't understand them." But for the presence of the non-volunteer, the meeting would have ended with all the volunteers privately assuming that all the others were better informed than they themselves were (Merton 1968 [1949]).

Usually, though, volunteers did not stage public discussions of political issues, but framed concerns in a way that made them seem not to require knowledge. Why do we meet? It's obvious: we want to help the schools, or we are against drugs. Who could be against schools or for drugs? A person did not need knowledge to be against drugs or to convince others to be against drugs. At my very first meeting, I was asked to write a Letter to the Editor of the local paper in favor of Measure B, even before I had read the group's pamphlets. In contrast, activist groups like the anti-toxics group never assumed that a new member would know enough after one meeting to write a Letter to the Editor.

Participants in the Vote B for Substance-Free campaign could have considered their work to be deeply conflictive, but instead, they demonized drug dealers and users, imagining them as enemies beyond the pale of humanity, not human opponents in a political conflict. As the Vote B for Substance-Free committee's flyer stated, "Amargo is under siege. Our streets, school and homes are being overwhelmed by drug-related crime . . . to combat this plague . . . Measure B has been introduced to provide the funds needed to sustain an all-out war against drugs.'' The only conflict Measure B volunteers ever mentioned publicly was about raising taxes. When the measure lost, members were at a loss to explain why.

At another League of Women Voters meeting in which politicians spoke on video about how to become a politician, I said I would have liked to hear talk about how candidates decide what positions to take on issues. Janice got up to clean the coffee-and-cookie table at that point, and Jim said that he did not understand the question, adding, ''It's easy. They just have to have an inner conviction.'' A city council candidate who was there gave an example of a confusing policy decision: ''a proposed McDonald's – where no one already *has* a position. It's not like being for police, or for or against firemen, for or against growth. They don't already have a position on McDonald's in a residential area.'' But Janice, as a typical volunteer, still did not get the question, and reasserted, ''Get inside their heads,'' and ''They have to be pure as snow.'' If an opinion is there, inside, before anything else, discussion will not help clarify or change it, but, as Janice said later, ''would only make things worse'' and raise doubts and confusion.

Were volunteers just trying to avoid disagreement?

Many scholars have noticed Americans' aversion to political debate and love of unanimity (Hartz 1955; Varenne 1977). Were volunteers afraid of disagreement? ''You don't talk about politics with your friends. Not if you want to keep them,'' Geoffrey told me. Or perhaps volunteers all agreed already, and thus did not need to talk. If a group comes together for a specific reason, members do not need to discuss everything under the sun, they would say.

In interviews, several volunteers cited the maxim, ''Don't talk politics or religion with your friends,'' and explained the phrase by saying that people hold their opinions on these matters too passionately. However, as we will hear in the next chapter, most members barely held political opinions, and most held no political opinions passionately. Members were unsure what positions they *would* take if they had to take stands; in interviews, volunteers often reversed themselves several times in the course of a few minutes (and noticed the reversals, themselves). In the volunteers' case, what was silenced was not unpopular viewpoints, but debate itself.

Volunteers usually did not allow themselves the luxury of finding out whether or not they held opposing positions. They were against vocally holding political positions, period – of debating, talking, pretentiously holding forth. For the rare issues on which members did firmly hold opinions, some speculated incorrectly in interviews about the other members' opinions. Or, they just talked past each other. In one meeting Julie tried to convince members of the B for Substance-Free campaign that they should gather and recycle the wooden posts that had held their campaign signs. The other members said that it would be too difficult, and Julie gave a mock snarl, laughing, "Heh! I bet you're the kind of people that use Saran Wrap, too!" I laughed with her, but no one else got the joke (that using Saran Wrap instead of reusing old plastic bags could mark one as being unecological).

Elisabeth Noelle-Neumann (1984) coined the term "the spiral of silence" to describe the process in which people – who she says are by nature eager to get along with each other – refrain from expressing what they guess to be unpopular viewpoints to strangers. The spiral of silence sucks unpopular opinions out of circulation, by making them embarrassing to hold publicly. Noelle-Neumann bases her argument on experiments in which subjects are asked to imagine conversations between themselves and strangers on trains. But Americans rarely go on trains or talk to perfect strangers. More often, people talk to people they already know, in familiar contexts, some of which could invite debate and others which could discourage it – the texture of public life is more varied than the flat experiment supposes. Elihu Katz (1988) shows that when people establish ongoing everyday contexts with friends, relatives, neighbors, and colleagues that are very different from the context of meeting a stranger on a train, then they can create spaces in which disagreement is not perceived as a risk to solidarity. Context is all, here: over time, volunteers, unlike strangers on trains (or more precisely, unlike people talking in experiments about imagining strangers on trains), could have got to know each other's opinions, and could have developed a kind of trust that allowed for political disagreement. Instead, they worked together to establish contexts in which debate itself was unpopular.

Avoidance of disagreement is not universal; Israelis, talking among casual acquaintances, for example, "use political talk the way Americans use talk about sports: to create common ground, with political disagreements only adding to the entertainment value" (Wyatt and Leibes 1995: 21). So, the question should be: how do people create contexts in which disagreement is allowed or avoided?

Volunteers' political etiquette systematically silenced some *types* of ideas more than others: democratic ideas, participatory ideas, ideas with long time horizons, ambiguous or ambivalent ideas, ideas that would not lead to an immediate volunteer-style solution: in short, any idea that demanded talk was avoided. This is different from Noelle-Neumann's "unpopular opinions," a term that implies that we all already know what the possible range of opinion is and have staked out positions on that range. Here, it was not the opinion that was controversial but the style of discussing it.

The case of Charles was an especially obvious illustration of the importance of style. His was all wrong: it addressed conflict, and structural problems, like corporations that take from the community but do not give, and,
what must have seemed worst of all in the eyes of volunteers, he assumed
that talk could be a good in itself. All the volunteers agreed with him that
racism had no place in the school and most agreed that the school needed
more government funds; it was not the content of his ideas but the *style* that
made him appear rude. Julie's and others' ideas about community participation disappeared in the group context, in favor of more concrete topics like
the Royal Dog Steamer.

Disagreement itself was not taboo – what was out of place was public-
spirited conversation about discouraging issues and topics that volunteers
assumed to be beyond their scope. There were animated debates about fundraising options, how to transport soda to the annual senior class picnic, and
other concrete, hands-on projects. Ironically, when the group fell apart (after
I left), the problem was not political disagreement, but that volunteers decided
that Ron was too bossy. The care paid to avoiding political disagreement was
beside the point, considering that personality conflicts, not political disagreements, broke up the group.

Political avoidance was a culture, not a strategy aimed at avoiding disagreement or any other conscious goal. Part of what made it easy for volunteers all to avoid public-spirited political conversation was the institutional
context that supported volunteer work.

Part 2: *The institutional setting for volunteering: the "Caring Adult Network"*

> Virginia Woodward [a social services administrator] is looking for volun-
> teers to supervise the playground in the morning before school starts. A lot
> of parents have to leave for work at 6 or 6:30 a.m., and there are no before-
> school programs even in the elementary schools, so the parents have no
> choice but to just dump their kids – first graders, second graders, even – on
> the playground, sometimes before it's even light out, and just hope for the
> best.   Julie, volunteer, making an announcement to an anti-drugs group

Most officials seriously tried to encourage volunteer participation, partly to
save money and get desperately needed help in an era of cutbacks; and partly
because they considered volunteering an intrinsic good, knitting community
together with freely given care. Authorities encouraged volunteers to work
hard feeding the elderly and warming the poor, to act as compassionate individuals to compensate for the unspoken, unspeakable lack of institutionalized
compassion. Yet something was missing. Officials imagined drawing on a

deep well of citizens' goodness to compose that "Caring Adult Nework," but excluded political concern and conversation from that image of community. This institutional setting helped inspire political evaporation.

In the 1970s and 1980s, many leftist critics of "the welfare state" said that citizen participation was better than the cold hand of bureaucracy, and that the welfare state was good only at controlling people, "policing the family" (Donzelot 1979), "regulating the poor" (Piven and Cloward 1979), and extending tentacles of bureaucracy into the everyday lives of local communities.[15] The right agreed, adding that it was also too expensive, and cut the funds. The irony in Amargo was that social workers themselves had the same image of the social welfare bureaucracy that left critics, right critics, and volunteers had: that only the spirit of voluntarism can revive the community; that bureaucracies should not replace the webs of care that go unspoken in a real community; that bureaucratic rationality cannot replace loving community. These social service officials did not act as if they felt like cold arms of the state, bureaucratically controlling local communities.

Yet, the ways the social workers tried to steer away from the cold image of control actually worked to make the control even more omnipresent, drying up volunteers' abilities to think beyond the "It all starts with the family" philosophy. The ways the social workers invited participation not only did not address political issues, but colonized potentially free spaces – volunteer groups – in which citizens could have engaged in freewheeling, open, casual political conversation.

One of the most important things that freely organized citizens' groups can do that social service bureaucrats cannot do – no matter how thoughtful, warm, and sincere those service workers are – is engage in imaginative, improvisational, creative political conversation. If social service workers had consistently communicated to citizens that they valued citizens' talk in itself, and had not tried to encourage volunteers to be just like social service workers, then perhaps they all could have begun to break through the stalemate between the bustling, loving ideal of community care and the desolate reality of public neglect. But most officials shared volunteers' culture of political avoidance; I heard rare exceptions to that tendency – such as when the teacher tried to encourage the Parent League to talk about the expensive prom – but these exceptions were too rare to penetrate the volunteers' culture of avoidance.

The story of pupils waiting on the playground before sunrise was a common one. Another story told in the Just Say No team described the same problem: these children clustered at a bus stop in front of a church, so a minister sometimes took them into the church for hot cocoa, to warm up and wait for sunrise and the bus. The message was supposed to encourage us and help dispel the frightening image of children abandoned at dark playgrounds and bus stops. Volunteers were asked to supervise pre-dawn playgrounds and bus stops, but they were not asked to talk about whether scrounging for volunteers was the best way to solve the problem.

The beautiful ideal that officials presented was of a "Caring Adult Network." It comes at a moment in history when this ideal seems more and more unreachable every day. First, cuts in social services and a declining economy leave more children in danger. Second, the power that local communities once had over local concerns is eroding, as more important decisions are made for them in international summits and global corporate headquarters. Officials almost never explicitly addressed these trends in meetings, but did address a third: they often noted that fewer adults are home during the day to comprise this Caring Adult Network than there might have been in eras when workplaces were closer to home, or when wives stayed home, or when children lived in big, extended families, with many siblings, boarders, farmhands, and other adults.[16] Volunteers and social service workers alike assumed that the busy, old-fashioned, populated neighborhood was more safe and caring than the contemporary neighborhood.

Though most people in this booming new suburb had not lived there very long, and did not share a history there, social workers often repeated a tale told by an old, long-term Amargo resident, of a grandmotherly neighbor in Amargo who took children under her wing, protecting and disciplining them when the parents were not available. This is the volunteers' version of nostalgic yearning for a bygone "community." We could never say why so many parents were unavailable now; why anyone had ever left such idyllic communities; or if anything had changed since then except feelings; or if, even back then, such truly generous neighbors were typical; or if any neighbors in that cozy past had ever been narrow-minded, cruel, or overly inquisitive. Those thoughts might have invoked conflict or discouragement or required discussion.

Empty houses, declining welfare services, declining economy, declining local power, declining volunteerism:[17] the problems seemed overwhelming. In earlier eras, volunteers and social service workers like Jane Addams responded to the feeling of being overwhelmed by looking beyond the immediate problems, to their political, structural origins. They let themselves become activists, advocates, even crusaders.

But in Amargo, this activism, this expanded horizon that de Tocqueville said would come about from volunteering, was hemmed in by social workers' emphatic assertions that "it all begins with the family" and extends no further than a "Caring Adult Network." The social workers enthusiastically emphasized the idea that "community involvement" was central to any long-term improvements in the city, but did not treat political concern and publicly minded discussion as part of that "community."

The first mode of participation: lending a hand

Officials asked volunteers to "participate" in three ways. The first, most prevalent invitation was the one we have already seen among volunteers themselves: to "pitch in," "lend a hand" in work that understaffed social service agencies could not do alone, by plugging themselves into already existing programs, trying to hold back the overwhelming flow of problems by helping one person at a time. Many volunteers worked as substitutes for social service workers, doing the kinds of scheduled, routine work that does not necessarily open participants' political horizons. Officials – police, school officials, social service workers, the fire chief, the mayor and vice-mayor – usually encouraged this task-focused, non-verbal approach to citizen participation. Citizens' efforts were thought to be efficiently captured that way, because citizens themselves did not have to invent new organizations and solutions to problems.

Social service workers clearly communicated an implicit philosophy, despite their verbal emphasis on "community": individuals were important; groups were less important. Volunteers could lend a hand to pre-set projects. Thus, the ongoing groups that social service agencies, police and city officials set up were for children, drug addicts, and potential criminals: drug addicts and "at risk" people, who could go to a 24-hour-a-day drop-in center, a de-tox center, out-patient clinics, or courses in "building self-esteem." Groups of children and clients are not "publics" in the sense described in chapter 1. The implication was that healthy adults do not need public life.

But limiting volunteer participation to pre-set tasks has a cost. As the founder of a national research institute focusing on volunteering rightly argues, this approach is a scourge on voluntarism; volunteer groups in American democracy have not served and should not serve merely as substitutes for work that paid service providers should do (O'Connell 1989).

Collapsing the distinction between volunteers and officials encouraged volunteers to trail behind officials, unsuccessfully trying to be just like them instead of valuing the distinct contribution that unpaid, creative, passionate, opinionated citizens can make to public life. Each time the Just Say No committee met we all introduced ourselves by saying what organizations we represented. Volunteers usually sounded uneasy in these introductions: "Oh, me? [chuckling] I don't represent anyone. I'm just here as a regular old member of the community.''[18]

It is no surprise that public debate was considered unnecessary for obviously good acts like taking the children into the church to warm up in the morning; what surprised me was that this lack of debate carried over into issues that could easily have been treated as controversial. When Shirley came to a meeting saying she needed to collect signatures to help put the proposition on the state ballot that would raise the tax on alcohol, there was almost no discussion. Julie asked Shirley, ''Would you like to share with us names of some of the organizations which have endorsed it?'' Shirley could remember only some fire departments, and said that alcoholism is expensive to the state and the state's alcohol tax was low compared to other states. Quickly and flatly, she listed where the funds would go – I tried to jot it down, but it was so fast, Shirley clearly was not expecting anyone to pay attention, and I was not sure I got the proportions right.

Right away, Liz, a city official, started suggesting organizations that could help circulate the petition: ministers, hospitals, schools. She asked if Shirley was alone, or had help. Shirley was alone, so Liz said the first thing she needed was for the group to set up a committee to help her.

Since I had told Julie earlier that week that it was hard to find a group in which to volunteer, Julie jumped in: ''Here's your chance, Nina!''

I was put in the awkward position of having to offer to lend a hand on the project without hearing a discussion of its merits. I would have preferred a few seconds to think about it, and would have asked questions, but I was shy and felt the pressure of time. ''How did they all know so quickly that this was a good proposition? Had they talked about it before the group met? How did they expect me to work on something without knowing more about it? How do the other volunteers know what to do about an issue they have never heard of?'' I wondered to myself. In that meeting, I suspected that I lacked a brain. Liz volunteered herself.

Feeling cornered, I did, too. No one suggested that the group discuss whether or not this was a good proposition (later, luckily, I decided it was. It lost anyway). Knowledge was not seen as emerging from discussion. There was no talk of publicly showing the promotional video that the campaign headquarters in the state capitol had produced. Volunteers' strategy contrasted sharply with the activists', who worked on another ballot initiative in the same election. For activists, publicly showing an educational video and encouraging discussion afterwards was a keystone of their grassroots effort.

Members of the Just Say No team went far in their aversion to broad discussion. Volunteers were theoretically very welcome, but the regular meetings were at 8 a.m.; other meetings were often scheduled for work hours as well. About twenty people usually came, sitting at a U-shaped table on folding chairs in an overheated community center fragrant with Nescafé and CoffeeMate.

One meeting started with a city official announcing that between a new grant and older ones, the organization had raised a million dollars that year. "So, Just Say No has been a very successful organization this year," a city official, Liz, said. Julie, the dedicated full-time volunteer, chaired the meeting. She suggested: "Since the Just Say No team has been in existence for about a year, and is raising so much money, maybe it's a good time to talk about our mission and purpose before we raise our second million dollars."[19] She very briefly outlined an agenda for discussing the matter, but the group emphatically decided that it should not discuss its purpose. In fact, officials spent a fair amount of time discussing how good it was that they were not rehashing the group's purpose.

Barney was the only one who agreed with Julie: "At the beginning there was more publicity for Just Say No, but sometimes I go to some meetings where people don't even know what the Just Say No committee is. I think there should be more publicity. It's not in the newspaper enough." Julie got a very soft tone in her voice, as if she were talking to a child, and said, "So, Barney, you're saying . . . " and paraphrased his question. Nobody else's comments required a soft voice and a paraphrase; but Barney was treated like an eccentric uncle, especially when he brought up controversial ideas.

The head of the recreation department said, "Things are happening anyway. Maybe there's not a lot of publicity, but there's been a lot of new programs put in place."

Someone else added, "Some people aren't gonna pay attention no matter what you do. They'll just notice the Just Say No parade." A volunteer echoed the recreation department head's assertion, saying, "We've gotten a lot done and raised a lot of money, so we're doing just what we're supposed to be doing."

One city official was vehemently opposed to discussion. He argued,

I didn't think we really needed to get so exotic. It's simple. We're a catalyst, the center of a wheel. Our job is to say what's going on and could it be better. There's no use reinventing the wheel. Besides, if we really reorient our activities, we might overlap with other agencies, or with the Center Foundation Grant . . . Look, we started with seven amateurs and all the things have been taken over by professionals. That's our role. We're doing just what we should be doing. So I say, "If it ain't broke, don't fix it." We say, "You're professionals – we'll help in any way we can." You could say we're a support group for professionals.

The group was performing clearly necessary and useful tasks, such as organizing after-school sports programs, so, members assumed, there was no need to discuss it. These Just Say No meetings were the ones that volunteers told me to attend if I was looking for groups to join, but someone looking for people who casually engaged in broad discussion while volunteering would have been disappointed. Only Julie and Barney, the two unusually active volunteers, disagreed; for them, public involvement *was* the project, or at least a central part of it. Officials thought that it did not matter what anyone had to say about the various projects as long as the work got done.

Volunteers wanted to believe that authorities knew what to do, that the society was in good hands, that officials knew something that volunteers did not know, that they themselves were not as well-informed as the people who ran the city. So, though a few people worked full-time as volunteers, they nearly always deferred to the "real" work of the city. For example, Julie told me that "of course, most of the money the city receives [in a grant that was not earmarked for specific projects] goes to repairing roads and such – some of the roads are in really bad shape," taking for granted that those projects were more important than the ones she worked on – a homeless shelter and a children's after-school program, for example.

Meanwhile, officials sounded as if they felt as politically powerless as the volunteers. Social service workers and city officials operated what many have called "toy governments" (Gottdiener 1987); they themselves felt powerless and penniless, and thought that they could do their jobs only by relying on the kindness of strangers. Neither officials nor volunteers were eager to kindle debate when there was so much pressing work to do. At every meeting the vice-mayor passed the hat for a homeless women's shelter. No one mentioned housing policy.

Social service workers, police and other city officials, who were not supposed to be politically partisan themselves, wanted to make their projects seem non-political and non-controversial, and seem not to require discussion. But local problems are usually inseparable from the wider political world; avoiding discussion and controversy took a high toll on the quality of citizens' public conversations and on citizens' political imaginations.

The second mode of participation: "it all begins with the family"

A second, less usual approach to citizen participation was offered by social service agencies: inviting volunteers to heighten their own or somebody else's psychological sensitivity. The aim was to make families healthier. Citizens were not called on to lend a hand, in this approach, but to lend a heart.

Still missing was a tongue and a brain; still missing was a thinking, moral soul that is loyally connected to the wider world. This approach, like the first, funneled potential empathy and broad curiosity into small, private expressions of direct experience, enforced a relentlessly small circle of concern, and outlawed reflection about the common good in public.

Officials' informal theory about the roots of social problems told them that, no matter how big or small, social problems grew out of family problems. Social issues could best be addressed right here, in the privacy of one's own home, not by changing any structures or policies, not by getting adults more involved in the broader picture, but by ''building self-esteem.'' Over and over, I heard that the family was the root of youth's lack of self-esteem, and low self-esteem was at the root of drug abuse, and drug abuse was at the root of crime, poverty, even war and other problems. For example, a police lieutenant at a ''public forum'' in which a panel of social service workers and police spoke to a crowd of about ten citizens (of whom three were teachers or social service workers themselves) said, ''The crime is usually is a symptom of a bigger problem which usually goes back to the family structure. That's why the family has to come, too [to participate in a probation program in which teenagers clean streets and parks instead of being sent to juvenile jails].'' Or again, the police chief: ''There are ten thousand arrests in Amargo per year. We should focus on the source – the family is the first unit – next is the neighborhood, then the police, fire department, etc.'' This approach to volunteering saw the family as the unmoved mover, as ''where the buck stops,'' as the only real place that needs fixing.

If problems could be defined as psychological – as residing within the individual – then they seemed to fall into the realm of the ''do-able.'' A pair of counselors came to the musty old library to recruit Parent League members for a therapy program for youths who engage in ''out of norm behavior.'' The counselors were clear only about that one thing: they wanted to make the problems do-able. The way they did that was just like the volunteers' way – to break the social causes down into individual ones:

Because of the overwhelming nature of the four-day training [to learn to help run these therapy groups], you come out and go, ''Where do I start?'' There's so many things that have to be in place. Because of that, we decided to start very small, on things we could put our paws on. We decided to start on *one student at a time.*

Unlike the usual ''hands-on'' volunteer efforts, these projects did value discussion – but only discussion about feelings, only in special rooms, and only with special people. Publicly minded talk was still taboo, not surprisingly, since they never claimed that their goal was to create public space for exploration of public problems. Such programs can certainly help open up a psychological imagination in citizens, offering a wonderful way for people to think about intimate personal relationships. But the lopsided invitations to participate were never designed to open up a sociological imagination – a way of drawing the connections between personal relationships and impersonal forces; for thinking about social relationships that are not intimate, but that are important in children's lives as well. This is ironic, since when troubled teenagers got together to speak for themselves, as part of a school project, they twice organized panel discussions, both on social, not exclusively psychological, themes: nuclear war one year, child care another.

Social workers pressed the idea that once they created good, solid individuals, that community life would follow, rather than the other way around. That is, they clearly communicated the idea that healthy individuals create healthy community, but not that healthy community life also creates healthy individuals. For example, the Just Say No team eagerly talked about an Outward Bound-style program used in many cities, ROPES, in which groups of "at-risk" teenagers ran an obstacle course that could be completed only through group cooperation. Virginia enthusiastically supported her proposal, saying,

> There are some big "aha's" that happen when you discover the power within and the power to work with other people. What then, what do you do with it?

LIZ [the vice-mayor]: You build community with it.

VIRGINIA [with surprise, arguing against the implicit, prevalent idea that group life is only for teenagers and people who have problems]: And it's not just for troubled kids. Or youngsters. But for all kinds of people – me!

(Another social worker added that if even one child in 100 got turned for the better, it would save hundreds of thousands of dollars in treatment.)

Could teenagers tell the difference between ongoing community life and the kind of group life simulated by programs like ROPES? What if part of their problem was that they lived in a city where, as the probation officer said, "once you hit eighteen, there's nothing in town to do" – a town in which group life was so often disdained except as a diversion and cost-cutting measure for "at-risk" youth?

The project's aim was to create a different kind of individual (by simulating group life), not a different kind of community or wider world (by encouraging the creation of actual institutions of group life). Projects for "at-risk" teenagers worked on their feelings without asking them to think about the wider world – asking them, in fact, to *block the wider world out* momentarily.

The third mode of participation: rituals of care

A third type of invitation from social service workers asked for help in staging occasional festive events: activities like wrapping a giant Red Ribbon around the high school, to symbolize Just Say No, or arranging the children on a football field, in a formation, so that together their bodies spelled "I DON'T DO DRUGS" when photographed from a helicopter in the sky. A few adults attended a school-day ritual in which officials drove a fire truck onto a schoolyard, dipped elementary school pupils' hands in red paint, and then made handprints on a big white banner that they hoisted up in the air with the truck's ladders. The church that served hot chocolate before school also had "a guy who does Say No to Drugs skits on a bicycle for $100 a show," we learned at a Just Say No meeting. Local planners of the nationally sponsored Red Ribbon Week held another ritual in which volunteers extracted promises from some high schoolers to be "drug and alcohol free for two years," and had them write these promises down on paper.

Most volunteers thought these events were "kind of hokey," and stayed clear of them; but they got dubbed "community events" and the adults involved were called "volunteers," anyway. They were a very visible form of volunteer work, whose image circulated widely among non-volunteers. They were also the line of volunteering most enthusiastically supported by local corporations. Janice, of the League of Women Voters, said that donations like the free hot dogs, hamburgers, and sodas that businesses donated to a Just Say No event really helped get people to come. As *Newsweek* magazine said, in a laudatory issue devoted to volunteering a year before (July 10, 1989), "with corporate restructurings giving companies a black eye, and a growing low-wage labor shortage, many are finding volunteer programs an effective route to an improved public image." In the course of my volunteer work, I gathered a large collection of pens, pencils, rulers, pins, key rings and trinkets with corporate and military logos on them, some with uplifting messages such as "I don't do drugs." The vice-mayor, Liz, always used pens from the electric company or a computer company. The regional electric company and the Army regularly sent representatives to Just Say No meetings. Corporations used the groups for public relations, thus adding to a profusion of images of "care" and "community" without establishing costly institutions to care for local children.

These events filled a gap in Amargo, where there was little for families to do together, but organizers wanted to see the events as doing something much more important than entertaining children and parents. In contrast to ongoing, institutionalized voluntary caregiving, like Little League, Girl Scouts, and Headstart, this symbolic volunteering was aimed at "showing children that adults care" quickly, without requiring busy adults to spend too much time with children. The aim was to give them images, not just to interact with them. "The way to prevent drug abuse amongst teens," said the city manager, "is to give them models, so they can emulate caring adults like us."

These rituals were supposed to help create the emotional situation which they celebrated (alternately referred to as "community," and "the volunteer spirit"). Once again, participants were not asked to talk. These nationally directed rituals were re-presentations of an object ("the community") for which there was no original; demonstrations of something which was created only in the act of the demonstration, "simulacrum" rituals. These rituals gave no opportunity for volunteers to talk about the missing community which the image was supposed to represent, and indeed, they *prevented* volunteers from talking about the missing community.

The tone of these rituals mattered as much as their overt content. These social service agency-inspired events had that distinctive emotional tone of sporadic events produced *for* children *by* adults but not *for* adults: the adults who created these rituals were supposed to observe with bemused looks, if at all; children were supposed to show that they were duly appreciative of the extravagant image of care. Perhaps for the first time in history, adults have produced new rituals solely for the benefit of children. The religious parallel would be the "curbside religion" of parents who drop their children off at church but do not themselves go, as if to say that adults do not need rituals. What if the children noticed that their parents figuratively "drove off" after dropping them at the curb for the anti-drugs rituals? Parent League members and other steadfast volunteers were more interested in activities that took more work, and that would do more than "show" they cared.

Much social theory emphasizes the community-producing effects of ritual. Rituals represent a people to itself, hold up a mirror to the group, telling the group who it is, and giving members ways of thinking (Durkheim 1915). More critical theorizing emphasizes the ways such symbolic reflections selectively sift out controversial issues (Lukes 1975; Spillman 1996), reproducing inequality and political passivity through a distorted image of the society – a parade that includes all sorts of organizations but none that represent workers or labor unions, in Lukes' example. In one way, Lukes and the other critics are right: these rituals constantly replayed a nostalgic image of a happy, harmonious community devoid of real conflict. For example, if an anti-drugs volunteer were to make any demands on any institutions or request that citizens talk to each other, he or she would no longer be considered a member of this anti-drugs "community." While volunteers could show they cared by parading against drugs, parading against racism when the Nazi skinhead concert came to town was not considered a way of saying "we care." So, in that sense, the rituals worked the way Lukes and others say.

But the rituals also worked in a way that is even more subtle than this not-so-hidden message. The *practice* of ritual production was one of the most important messages of the rituals. This sporadic and indirect method of showing concern made "care for fellow humans" seem to be a special occasion, something that could happen just a few times a year, easily incorporated into a busy commuter's schedule without changing anything else. It collapsed "feelings of care" into care itself. The message of these social service rituals of care was that citizens could change feelings without engaging in wider social questioning; showing concern this way required passive citizens to follow national directives and not think or talk too much. National leaders rewarded volunteers, but only those who did not talk about politics too much. President Reagan, for example, set up a council on volunteering (the President's Task Force on Private Sector Initiatives, in 1982), and a new award for exceptional volunteers, while at the same time levying new taxes on volunteer groups and trying to force volunteer groups away from any focus on political advocacy, and toward charity (O'Connell 1989). The low value placed on citizens' independent thought and political engagement itself was part of the meaning of these rituals.

This kind of togetherness can be the yeast that leavens all other kinds of solidarity (Walzer 1992, for example). In a study of people who risked their lives to rescue Jews in Europe during World War II, for example, Samuel and Pearl Oliner (1988) found that one of the central features distinguishing rescuers from non-rescuers was the rescuers' supportive networks. These sorts of informal networks are an infinitely rich resource, that make life more livable in innumerable ways (Putnam 1993). But they do not necessarily inspire political debate. In fact, frontstage interactions between officials and volunteers preempted political debate, in assuming that larger institutions were too difficult to change. In all three modes, public debate remained devalued and limited.

Alternative institutional contexts: political condensation?

Not all institutions inspired political evaporation. Occasionally, volunteers from different ethnic groups and volunteers from the racially mixed groups interacted, as members of their respective groups. This pointed out the clear differences between different volunteer styles. In contrast to the volunteers in whose groups I participated, the black, Asian, and Latino volunteers who were working within ethnically or racially bounded groups were much more connected to institutional powers: churches, civil rights groups, nationalist ethnic organizations. The volunteers in the mainstream, racially mixed groups imagined themselves as representatives of "the common person," while the volunteers in the ethnically specific groups imagined themselves as representatives of the organizations, of a category of person. This difference was part of what made the ethnicity-based volunteers much more able to talk about politics. Their civic manners called for something the mainstream volunteers would call "complaining." But for them, as members of organized bodies, complaining was not as dangerous, since they imagined themselves to have a sympathetic ear in institutions like churches and ethnicity-based organizations that might pay attention to them.

Thus, the two types of volunteers talked past each other. For example, an older white woman of the League of Women Voters and black volunteers from an all-black church kept misunderstanding each other at a potluck dinner. The black volunteers invoked principles and talked much more than white volunteers tended to, and white volunteers, trying to be accommodating, kept missing the point. A big, bald black minister chatted in a bass voice about the corporate and government interests involved in the Gulf War. At the end of a long discourse on the impending war, he said, "Face it, Bushes, Kennedys, Rockefellers, Exxon, oil companies: they're the ones who want this war, because they benefit!" He added parenthetically that, by using plastics and styrofoam, we all were also personally responsible for America's outsized consumption of natural resources.

A black woman at the table said, "McDonald's is gonna stop using styrofoam." Frank said, "Good!" and a white member of the League of Women Voters agreed, saying, "That would help get rid of some of the litter on the highways." Throughout the conversation, this white volunteer kept adding *non sequiturs* like that, taking talk about corporate responsibility and reframing it as talk about individuals' bad habits, misunderstanding why the blacks at the table wanted to talk about oil companies and the President. She was trying to help them out of their "cynical" feelings.

Mainstream volunteers, from ethnically and racially mixed groups, avoided talking about principles or complaining, while the more institutionally based volunteers felt more empowered as members of particular organizations, and so were able to hear complaints without feeling threatened. The mainstream volunteers' burden was to have to represent "the common person," and to have to second-guess what could attract or repel such a person. Avoidance of discussion was often the result. The other kind of volunteer had more latitude, having access to organizations that encourage citizen debate, and not having to second-guess such an amorphous population.

Another explanation of this difference would say that the African-American rhetorical tradition calls for more dramatic, powerful language than the "anglo" tradition does, so any anglo public speech would sound bland and pallid compared to black public speech (Kochman 1981). An observer might think that black volunteers *had* to use the anglo style in the mixed groups, as if they were speaking a second language. But I heard as much variation among groups of the same ethnicity as between groups of different ethnicities – white activists sounded very different, for example, from white volunteers. And it was not just African-American groups that sounded more direct and "political" than the mixed-race groups. The institutional contexts in which groups exercised their styles mattered at least as much as the group's ethnic styles; institutions that marked out a distinct political territory for the group made debate and critique possible.

The pattern of miscommunication that I heard at the post-election potluck was repeated in many encounters in another gathering; this gathering brought together the mainstream volunteers, ethnicity-based volunteer groups, church members, and anyone else who cared to come. The question for this extra-ordinary meeting was how to spend a large grant that the Just Say No committee had won for the city. And a glimmer of broadened horizon again appeared momentarily.

After a predictable set of introductory remarks about how "it all starts with the family" and how "we need a community of caring adults," social service workers opened up the forum for actual conversation between citizens. They had us break into groups of eight, to "brainstorm" about how to spend the money. We were to pretend we had a magic wand and "think big." No idea was to be discarded.

Despite the standard refrains about the family and Caring Adult Community, I thought that the imaginative instructions, combined with the diverse audience, would finally open up a context for free discussion of social issues in the public sphere. And it was different. The groups reported on their meetings; many had used their "magic wands" to wish for more day-care, after-school programs, a community center, better library resources, more attention to ethnic diversity, better public transportation – public goods that the volunteers always avoided discussing, but whose absence I had suspected other people noticed. In my small group, the white volunteer notetaker had managed to miss most of those sorts of suggestions, maybe because a social worker in my small group kept arguing with participants' "big" wishes, saying they were not realistic; if my group was typical, others had had an even wider ranging discussion than was reported to the larger meeting.

The organizer, an honored Pacific City social services specialist with a doctorate, summarized the presentations in a way that reasserted the need to work on feelings above all else. She concluded: "I'm hearing a need for a place, for resources, but also a need for: *connections* between people. And *that certainly* can be done!" The implication, as usual, was that we can change the feelings more easily than we can change the resources. Still, this meeting showed me that this kind of boundary-crossing could open up American politics in surprising, unpredictable ways.

Conclusion: the culture of political avoidance

These stories portray an emergency. How did it happen that children were dropped off for the school bus before sunrise, that there was nowhere safe for them to go after school, that there was nothing for people over eighteen to do? In Amargo, nearly all of the group activity except the country-western clubs was devoted to repairing broken childhood. When everyone in a community who volunteers does so on behalf of children, is this public or private involvement?[20] Bringing out the public, political aspects of childhood, zigzagging between the common-sense boundaries separating public and private, could have caused an explosion of political debate in Amargo.

But in practice, volunteers and officials considered anything associated with children private, not public or up for debate. "For the children" seemed to imply a definite set of obvious answers, not a range of debates and questions (and yet, consider how few obvious answers there are even for the most simple, basic questions of childraising – how to get children to eat, sleep, dress, not pour molasses on the cat). Frontstage, no one asked, for example, how other wealthy countries manage to support families with free health care, good and cheap education, year-long paid parental leave, short work weeks and long vacations, safe and plentiful child care, prenatal care, and other political programs designed to support families. In practice, volunteers and officials took "a focus on children" to mean "a focus on private life," and "a focus on private life" to mean "a focus on feelings." That meant that the only real changes regular citizens could make were changes in feelings.

We were all already presumed to know the solution: that everyone should be more like Julie, the extremely dedicated, gentle, full-time volunteer. Could even that generous flow of care offer as much attention and love as even one child needs in a dangerous social and physical environment, in an impoverished school system, an unwholesome wider world? For every troubled child, the community would need at least one full-time Julie! Perhaps free, imaginative debate could have helped volunteers figure out why there were not more citizens like Julie, or whether anything else could be done to help children. But no one was inviting average citizens to change anything more than feelings.

Free, imaginative public debate might also have inspired children, in itself. An observer might argue that the parents were trying to help their children right now, not through dubious political struggles over the long haul that might not amount to anything, anyway. Perhaps volunteers were maximizing their effectiveness, by forgoing the broad picture, focusing on what they could do now, before their children were full-grown.

Yet, *could* publicly minded discussion have helped the children right away, in the short term? Many studies have found that children who express concern about political problems (nuclear war, in the case of these studies) are more likely to feel hopeful about the future and more likely to do well in school than those who claim not to care[21] (Goldberg et al. 1985; Berger Gould, Moon, and Van Hoorn 1986). Talking to their parents made children significantly more hopeful that they and others could prevent nuclear war than were children who did not talk to their parents; having activist parents helped even more. The evidence is clear: children who live in a politically open atmosphere will blossom more fully than those who do not. Children are not the apolitical beings volunteers assumed them to be; they are deeply aware of the wider world, and this awareness infuses all corners of their well-being.

No officials in Amargo ever said that creating a community of adults pursuing interesting, important adult activities could inspire the children, though teenagers often said out loud, in various ways, that adulthood looked boring in Amargo. Activists, in contrast, often let their children come to meetings and hearings, assuming that the process was educational and enjoyable for them, giving them a sense of power and control. Volunteers said, "It's up to the next generation to solve those problems." They saw themselves as bringing the children up to be good citizens.

There was a profusion of "prevention" programs designed to care for children whose parents were gone till seven or so every night: the Caring Adult Network, the ROPES course, the Neighborhood Network, the Fight Back program, Amargo Celebrates Youth Day, Red Ribbon Week, and more.[22] Volunteers and social workers recognized that there was "a spoiled moral environment" (as Vaclav Havel poetically puts it) and assumed that the way to fix it was to be "role models," but models of what? The goal was unspoken. The Caring Adult Network, the nostalgic ideal, provided a constant, unanalyzed goal.

Like most Americans, volunteers and social service providers assumed that the opposite of cold, bureaucratic control was warm, family-like care: a village. Americans often accuse bureaucracies of instrumentally enlisting workers busily to carry out orders without questioning the goals. The irony in Amargo was that social service workers' anti-bureaucratic nostalgia resulted in a flurry of activity toward an unquestioned, pre-set, given goal. I add here a third element that is neither cold bureaucracy nor warm, cloistered family: free, open-ended conversation, playful curiosity about the fresh, wide, open world. That was what was missing in Amargo.

Some people who work in homeless kitchens or schools or against drug abuse draw out the publicly minded side of their work. The volunteers did not. What could account for their eagerness to keep publicly minded discussion of their work out? It was not that they were unaware or unconcerned about broader issues; not that they all shared a political world so deeply they already knew whether or not they agreed without needing talk about it; and not that they simply avoided all controversy. Their "inner beliefs and values" were not preventing them from caring about each other and the wider world. They did not have enough faith in the government and corporations to rest at home while powerful institutions started wars and built nuclear weapons bases and destroyed the environment; they had not simply bought a "dominant ideology" that told them that the world was fine as it was (we will see this more clearly in the next chapter). And officials' efforts alone were not the cause of this strange political evaporation. Officials and volunteers shared an understanding of whether good citizenship includes political conversation.

Silencing public-spirited political conversation was, paradoxically, volunteers' way of looking out for the common good. Volunteer work embodied, above all, an effort aimed at convincing themselves and others that the world makes sense, and that regular people really can make a difference. To show each other and their neighbors that regular citizens really can be effective, really can make a difference, volunteers tried to avoid issues that they considered "political." In their effort to be open and inclusive, to appeal to regular, unpretentious fellow citizens without discouraging them, they silenced public-spirited deliberation, working hard to keep public-spirited conversation backstage – though open political conversation was just what someone like Charles thought the group needed to hold, in order to involve new members and address community problems.

Volunteers' creation of "the public" itself, their political etiquette, evaporated expressions of the public spirit from public settings. Community-spirited citizens judged that by avoiding "big" problems, they could better buoy their optimism. But by excluding politics from their group concerns, they kept their enormous, overflowing reservoir of concern and empathy, compassion and altruism, out of circulation, limiting its contribution to the common good.

3

"Close to home" and "for the children": trying really hard not to care

Sherry's speech came out in a jerky, halting rhythm when she told me, in an interview, that the issue of nuclear war was "not close to home":

If it's not something that.
Affects.
My.
Family. [each word said separately]
I don't see.
Me.
Doing it.
[speeds up] And-I-mean-of-course-nuclear-war-could-affect-my-heheh-family.
But I still don't – If it's not local, I mean,
I'm more.
Maybe it's small minded.

Sherry knew it was a problem, but did not want to know.[1]

Volunteers strenuously insisted that all of their efforts were motivated by self-interest. Over and over, they repeated that all people, themselves included, get involved in community affairs only out of "self-interest," "for their own children," on issues that are "close to home" and "affect them personally." In appearing self-interested, volunteers seemed at first glance to confirm the theory that people are "rational actors," that is, people who will bestir themselves to community action only when they think that time invested will be worth the personal payoff, and only when they cannot hitch a "free ride" to that personal payoff on someone else's back. But, as we heard in the last chapter, volunteers wanted to do more than live in a paradise engineered by someone else; they wanted to reassure themselves, through their own actions, that the world makes sense because good citizens really can make a difference on issues that matter. Volunteers were, above all, "moral" – in the sense of *meaning-making* – actors, rather than "rational" actors. The phrases "close to home" and "for the children" worked hard; they were pivotal in allowing volunteers to maintain that feeling that the world made sense.

Before listening to their speech, though, remember that everyone portrayed in this chapter lived within a mile and a half of the nuclear battleship station and just downstream from the Evergreen Island Air Force base, on the river which hosted six chemical plants that had regular blow-ups and toxic spills. Volunteers were aware of all that, and even when they tried to avoid it, their children brought it up.

Trying really hard not to care

Unlike members of the other types of the recreation and activist groups, nearly all volunteers offered "self-interest" as the explanation for their own and others' community involvement, saying over and over that they would care about an issue only if it affected them personally. There was something overly insistent about volunteers' revelations and admissions of self-interest:

CAROLYN: I don't think anyone does anything that is not going to benefit them in some form or another, or there'd be no point . . .

PETE: Whether we admit it or not . . . Someone like Gandhi, you know, he may be the pinnacle of altruism, but he was "doin' his stuff for his own people."

JULIE: [murmurs of agreement]

LISA: And he felt good about what he did [with the implication, obvious to all present, that feeling good is in itself a self-interested benefit].

In the individual interview, Danielle said, "We have a vested interest in whatever it is we're volunteering for. If our kid is playing baseball, it's in Little League; if our kids are going to a school, it's for that particular school." In fact, the two members of the Parent League involved in Little League had kids who were far past Little League age, and one did not even have kids in the school yet.

Fishing for ideas about how all involvement could be considered self-interested, Danielle said, in the individual interview, "Maybe we're just all doing this to achieve some kind of greatness in our own groups. We want to be admired and respected in the community [laughs]. I mean, I don't know – we're not doing it for *money*, that's for sure."

Pete described the relation between the "problems of the world" and self-interest:

I know there are things out there that affect me, you know, they, uh, bother me, but I guess I – my first priority is my home and my immediate surroundings and I'm not anxious to go out and solve the problems of the world. I guess it's just my personality,

I guess. I knew someone in college who just could not – who saw all these problems and took them on as "personal," as her personal responsibility to solve all these things [he describes her briefly, saying it made her miserable to be so overwhelmed]. Of course, everyone would love to, if they had the power themselves, to stop war or end drug abuse or whatever, they'd do it, but obviously there's a feeling of impotence when you're dealing with issues like that. Boils down to just, "Find the opportunity in your life to try to make a difference, even if it's a small one."

Later he summarizes this statement by saying, "That gets back to, If I'm gonna actually expend energy to alter my lifestyle to affect one of these things, I'm probably gonna expend it where it's closer to home." In the course of a few sentences, he has gracefully transmogrified "a feeling of impotence" to a feeling of empowerment on small issues "close to home."

Probably most people feel powerless sometimes. The question is how we present our powerlessness to ourselves; whether we protect our feelings of empowerment by saying we don't care, or admit to feeling powerless, or even proudly brag about how very powerless we feel (as the cynical country-western club members did). The closest a volunteer did come to saying flatly that "I don't work on it because I can't do anything about it" was Julie, the anti-drugs volunteer, alone with me in the individual taped interview. She said she used to be an anti-nuclear power activist, but stopped because "nuclear power wasn't necessarily a personal choice kind of issue. And at that time, you could write letters till you were blue in the face, and and we did that, you know, and did everything and and [pause] I'm trying to think about why we stopped [11-second pause]."

Then she started and stopped again a few more times, then said it was too hard to make people understand the issue. I repeated, "So, it sounds like it was too hard?"

She interrupted, saying,

Yeah, I think so. It's almost like, um, you know, the starving people in Africa and Bangladesh. I mean, what do you do? You send them a check for 20 bucks? [pause] I think, I think you get to a point where you really need to decide what can you really impact, and what can't you. And that's not to say you don't care about the other ones any more, but that I think sometimes one needs to step back and go, "OK really, what are my limitations? What do I want to get myself all stirred up about? What's worth killing yourself over?"

Then she started talking very fast about how getting too busy can affect one's marriage and how she quit smoking fifteen years ago. The difficulty of dealing with nuclear power caused the issue just to disappear out of the conversation, adding to the feeling that it was not really a real problem. She interrupted herself, hopping from one subject to another rapidly; like other volunteers, Julie noticed that she had digressed from the troubling political topic, and interrupted herself to chuckle at the fact.

Within two sentences of expressing concern about a political problem that seemed "un-do-able," out of their control, volunteers all would shift to the theme of "close to home" *without noticing the shift*. To grasp the texture of speech that so smoothly blended care and power, listen to a long interchange between Julie and Carolyn, that I taped in a group interview with the Vote B for Substance-Free campaign:

JULIE: I was trying to think when you said what else would you work on. I worked real hard against nuclear energy a long, long, long, long time ago, and I was trying to think if that came around now, um, if I would do that one again. Because that was a real hard one. It was one of those that no matter how many facts you presented, people couldn't relate because it wasn't close enough [the meaning of "close to home" again revealed].

[She continues, alluding to an earlier question about United States military involvement in Central America; she refers to torture as the main problem] I think as one human being to another, we do have a responsibility to um work however we can to say, you know, that's not the way we should be treating our fellow human beings ...

But when you're in the community, for me, since I started with Special Friends last year [a Big Brother-type program for elementary school-age kids] and some of these other things, I don't know what's going on in the outside world. And I also don't *care*! [Carolyn chuckles] Um, it's just too much.

CAROLYN: Yeah!

JULIE: [suddenly speaking in language that was so rhythmic, it was poetry]:
I can do *nothing*
about what going on out there, But I *can* here,
and so that here I don't watch TV ...
I don't turn on the radio any more either ... It just – it's got nothing to do with the kid I saw that was abused,
or the meal I took to somebody whose house is just I mean, they shouldn't have to live like that,
or I walk down and they're selling drugs – somebody just got shot over there, I mean:
it's just so much right outside your door.
The paper and the radio just mean *nothing*
[Carolyn makes more affirmative murmurs].
That is. to me. [Starts to chuckle] ... I mean, just,

that kind of stuff just
Makes No Sense.

CAROLYN: Plus, they're not down at the level we're working in is something
I've learned from the [something, inaudible] program.

JULIE: Absolutely no idea!

CAROLYN: And the councilpeople, who are so "caring" in this town, have
no-o-o idea!

JULIE [chiming in]: – have no-o-o idea! [laughs] Right, that's right, and it's
absolutely unreal. And so, you know, I can't waste my energy, of which I
have very little [everyone laughs] on stupid – no, it's true, I'm half asleep
right now . . . Um, umm it's just you know,
if they want to go play games
and call each other names
– it's really why I quit on television.

Were volunteers simply acting in rational self-interest, investing scarce
energy where it it will make a difference "close to home," on issues that
affect them personally? If that were the case, then it was a very strange kind
of calculation, that worked only when volunteers did not notice that they
were calculating. "Why are you involved in this issue?" I asked in the high
school parents' group interview. Danielle said, "Really, I'm involved
because my my kids are here." Elaine said it next: "All my efforts are
geared – I will get involved in anything that involves kids . . . So I'll join
committees like the Just Say No committee in Amargo, that you know, for
sure, is the issue of drugs, but, you know, my view, really is it's an issue
about kids."

I asked how they decide when something affects their kids, saying "the
people in the anti-nuclear group I'm studying are saying that they're involved
to make the world safe for their kids, too, and the environmental group says
it's for their kids – the anti-crime group I'm studying, they say that, too. So,
I'm wondering, uh –" Bob and Elaine murmured "mm," and "yeah," and
"that's a real good question. You could tie it all to kids." Danielle said the
same thing, and then the topic changed.

But the vocabulary of self-interest was so automatic that volunteers could
not abandon it even when they themselves had just said that it did not
adequately explain their motives. So, moments later in the interview, we were
back to "the kids." Bob offered, "Just about everything I've ever volunteered for in my adult life has to do with kids," and later, Sherry stated, "I
would do things that involve my children."

All of the high school parents said they felt concerned only about issues
that affect them and their children; but if we listen more closely, we can hear

how much effort went into dividing up the world into issues that were "for the children" and those "problems of the world" that were not for the children. When Danielle heard about a disarmament group in Amargo, she said with a sigh, "That would be something that would be nice to be involved in, when I didn't have to be involved in things related with the kids." Yet, she grimly joked in the Parent League group interview and several other times to me, "Manuel [her son] always tells me there's a bomb with Amargo written on it. 'Port Amargo.' [dry chuckle] We'll be the first to go." She had a Salvadoran refugee son-in-law, whose face was lovingly displayed in several wedding and family photos right by the front door of Danielle's house. But, regarding United States involvement in Central America, she said, "We are so removed from all that. And could we ever get the facts even if we wanted them," not as a question, but a statement, with a falling pitch at the end.

She did not have faith in the government to do what is right all the time, yet, she told me more than once, with alarm, that she had never talked to her son, who was just about to turn eighteen, about the draft, during a stretch of years in which the United States had sent troops overseas several times. This self-described "news junkie" said in the group interview, "You know what's funny? Manuel says to me about a month ago, he says to me, you know, I'm gonna have to register for the draft when I'm eighteen, and you know, we had never talked about it. Never! Never! Do you still have to register?? And I thought about that for days!"

The meaning of "for the children" becomes more and more mysterious; it is not obvious how not talking to one's children about the draft protects them from harm – though it might protect them or the adults from acknowledging fear. All of these avid expressions of self-interest become more mysterious; these phrases do not just communicate volunteers' straight calculations of self-interest. Volunteers did not just say, "I care but feel powerless about that issue, so I have chosen to focus on another issue instead." Instead, they strenuously tried to tell themselves that they simply did not care about issues they felt powerless to control. Paradoxically, they *wanted to believe* that people are self-interested, precisely *because* they were trying to convince themselves and their children that the world is good, moral, and makes sense.

Clarifying to each other whether or not powerlessness equals apathy

Intellectually, of course volunteers knew the difference between caring and power. Sherry said toxic waste was not something she worried about, and that she could not understand why anyone would, and Bob, her husband, "corrected" her.

BOB: Yeah, but maybe that's just because it's not an area of interest for you. But it's a pretty important area.

SHERRY: Oh, yeah, I agree.

BOB: And that fortunately someone is taking [action], is volunteering in that area.

SHERRY [faintly]: Yeah.

BOB: I think it's an issue of major importance . . .

DANIELLE: Well, look at back East, when they went to the beach, and all this waste, it's you know, rolling up on the beaches, I mean, you *can't deny* it [the implication being that one would want to deny it].

SHERRY [grudgingly]: Yeah.

DANIELLE: You know, you can't say it doesn't exist.

The same debate arose again, on US involvement abroad. Geoffrey said it would be impossible to find out the necessary facts, even though he thinks it is important to do so; and Sherry added, *as if in agreement*, "Yeah, I feel, to me, it would not even interest me to find out about that information." When Bob forced her to see the difference between the two approaches, she grudgingly agreed, but the fine distinction between considering an issue unimportant and considering it "un-do-able" was not one they normally made.

Pretty soon, Sherry was back to, "Most people do volunteer on something that affects their personal life," with Danielle chiming in on the last three words: again, the automatic response.

"You can have more of an impact uh . . . at least you feel like you can"

In interviews, volunteers managed both to see the problems and to turn away from them, describing them in lavish detail while simultaneously avoiding them. If they were unequivocally self-interested, they would have sounded more unequivocal in interviews, instead of circling around and around the issues about which they professed they "never thought" and "did not care."

Having only once heard in a meeting the story of the ceiling falling in on the shop class at Amargo High, I had begun to think that maybe I had imagined the story, or maybe it had not really happened, since no one had referred to it again. But then Sherry, in the individual interview, talked about the new school the district was planning to build:

I want to know, if we have all this money to build a new high school, where is the funds to fix up the existing high school! You know, I can't wait to go to my first meeting, Nina [about the new school plans]. It just really has got me bothered. You know, like we say, the roof falling down, while the kids are in the class! You know, the kids during wintertime, they're carrying blankets to school because they know there's no heater in their class because it doesn't work [this sentence ending loudly, on a high pitch]! And this is, you know, it's not just this school, it's the other one, too, and the elementaries.

Later, she said the teachers should be paid more. Volunteers were aware of the problems, but silenced that awareness in meetings.

Most volunteers brought up troubling issues – especially related to the environment and race – before I had a chance to, and then they circled back to these issues without my prompting. In fact, in several early interviews, I had tried unsuccessfully to *change* the subject, thinking that it was more important to cover my interview questions than to hear interviewees circling over and over again over those local but "undo-able" concerns. After eight interviewees all followed the same pattern, however, I realized that I should not try so hard to keep them "on track" – this pattern was itself a track.

Lisa, whom we heard in the preface saying that Port Amargo has "lots of unreported nuclear accidents," introduced the topic in the group interview by saying that there are six or seven nuclear battleships just over at Port Amargo, down the street. I was startled: "Really??"

MEL: Well, seventeen of 'em [which gave everyone a hearty laugh].
LISA: They're concerned about the battleship being up there; here these submarines they run right past Pacific City all the time.
CAROLYN: Sometimes you wonder if people have a clue as to what's going on here. [more laughter]. But I guess, you know, if we all decided that we didn't want the submarines at Amargo Flats, uh, it'd be pretty tough to change that.
MEL: Yup.
CAROLYN: ... You know I think you can have more impact uh, I don't know, at least you feel like you can [on the drug problem].

This phrase, "you can have more impact ... at least you feel like you can" slides over a crucial distinction, between changing situations and changing feelings.

As Sherry said in the individual interview, in the cinder-block walled office next to the car-repair garage she and her husband Bob owned, "Well, I don't worry about nuclear war too much because I don't think there's a lot to do. I mean, if they bomb us, we've had it. So, why worry about it ... I'm not that concerned with it." She was not saying explicitly that nuclear war was not a problem, just that she was not going to let it bother her. In their earnest efforts at shouldering responsibility for a small corner of the world, most volunteers felt they had to push the rest of the world away.

In the one-on-one interview, Lisa dwelled even more on the issue of nuclear weapons and power, only to say toward the end of the interview that it was not a problem after all. She brought it up, when talking about Augie Bradley, a local protester who had been run over by a military truck during a vigil against arms shipments to Central America. She could not remember what issue he protested, and inaccurately guessed that it was one that clearly weighed heavily on her mind: "probably bringing nuclear weapons into or – 'cause there's nuclear weapons over at Evergreen Island, I mean, there's, you know, all the nuclear power plants over at Port Amargo. On the battleships." She gave more details about the battleships, then tried to remember what their route through the Sound was:

there's at least two or three or four there's at least there's probably at least four battleships over there at all times, and they all have a nuclear power plant on them, because they're all nuclear power battleships. So, I have no idea about weapons. I'm sure there's no weapons over at Evergreen Island because they keep them all over at Port Amargo. But they do load up, I'm sure they go out and load up. And then they go out. Um, I don't know if they load up at Port Amargo, though. I don't think they go through the Sound with the weapons on them. I think they might load up at Sunshine Point [nearer to the ocean] . . . they toot in and out of the Sound all the time.

Using the same obsessively fine-grained detail, she describes the military workers' unsafe practices. I, meanwhile, was growing more and more agitated, worrying that such microscopic details of the battleships' activities was not part of my interview plan. I had not known about that weapons station until she brought it up in the group interview.[2] Her description continued for another two full pages' worth of transcript: "it is dangerous . . . there is a large factor for human error because there's a lot of idiots working and there's I mean, half those weapons station workers are on dope all the time. I mean it does, it makes me nervous . . . they have spills quite often . . . they had incidents once in a while . . ." So, she can "see why people in Pacific City do not want the one battleship there [stationed in the city's harbor itself]." I asked whether she thought she could do anything about it.

I can't do much about the Navy having these battleships at Port Amargo. I uh, and I can't do much about that the weapons station workers come up and smoke dope. I mean, you know, it bothers me, but no, I don't feel, I feel powerless actually, in a sense, I mean, I don't think about it because I don't – I know I have no influence over the fact that the battleships are there. Plus I mean I think they generally try to do a good job.

She then said that the Navy will do a better job than a civilian company would. Then a couple of minutes later she was back to *"But I do feel powerless, so, I mean, in a sense. That's why, uh, I'm not worried about it, uh, nuclear power."* I asked if something could happen that would get her to do something about it. She said,

Oh, well, I suppose if there was a meltdown or something over there ... I don't know, I hadn't thought about that. I mean, I guess I don't really feel that nuclear power plants are all that horribly dangerous. I know there's a potential for danger, but I'm not [then she starts talking extremely fast, to get it over with] I guess they don't affect me directly and they don't melt down on a daily basis and and the, I mean, they do emit radioactivity and all that stuff, but there's other ways to get radioactivity ... So, I guess it doesn't really bother me ... If there was a meltdown ... then, if nothing else, I just would not live here anymore. I wouldn't want to try to solve the problem for other people.

By the end of the interview, she had retracted her expressions of powerlessness and added an expression of self-interest, saying that the danger, if there was any, was a matter of personal choice, and she had control over her choices. She could feel less trapped than if she thought she were powerless and had no choice.

Like Lisa, who dwelled on the nuclear leaks, radioactivity, and stoned nuclear workers, only to end up saying that she was not bothered, Sherry dwelled on a "big," political problem, only to say that she was, after all, in control of her own world. I asked whether she would ever get involved in a group that was against building a toxic incinerator if one were planned for her town. She spent a few words on the topic of toxic waste, then quickly jumped to food. First she brought up apples, which had just been the focus of a national controversy because of a carcinogenic pesticide, Alar. Then she brought up bananas and potatoes, which she said, curling the very ends of her lips up into a flat, ironic little smile, have "something put in them when they are grown, And you can't wash it off. It's something in the soil. So, you know: Do you stop eating? Good question [said as a final statement, not an invitation to further speculation]." She said the grocery store had a sign saying their apples had not been sprayed with Alar, "And I – you know – but what do you do? You quit buying the stuff?" Then she brought up Halloween candy, saying that everything has some risk attached. Then she discussed chicken and beef, saying that there was something wrong with them, too. A while later, I asked again about toxic waste, saying that I wasn't sure I understood her answer, and she began talking about food again.

I have some control over that. I don't have to buy that fruit. You know, it's a personal choice, like, do I buy cigarettes and take the chance that I will or will not get cancer?

That's a personal choice. Same with the fruit. You know: do I still go buy the apples and bananas that my husband goes eats every day [laughing]? He still eats 'em; I still buy 'em [laughing]!

Then she discussed chicken again:

They say that Northern Poultry injects steroids or something like steroids [laughing] to make the chickens fatter. I have done this [she says this implying that it was a funny thing to do]: I have had the Acme Farms chicken that you can buy at Foodway's and I have had Northern Poultry that you can buy at Hick's, and if you pull the skin back there's this much fat under the Northern Poultry, and hardly any under the Acme. I mean it's just this loose stuff hanging from the inside of the skin of one and not the other!

First, she implied that she had no choice but to buy the chickens, apples, bananas, potatoes, candy, and beef, but then later repaired that idea to say she had a personal choice. Later, she began to say that writing letters would not have an effect, but then halted that thought mid-sentence to say "it really does count."

Aaron Wildavsky and Mary Douglas (1982) say that Americans tolerate much higher risks if we feel that we have independently chosen to inflict them on ourselves (cigarettes, diet soda, bungee jumping, car accidents) than if the risks are inflicted on us by entities beyond our control (water pollution, plane crashes). But I discovered that people can define almost anything as a "personal choice"! Sherry emptied out the whole contents of a refrigerator, saying that everything in it was the result of "a personal choice." Volunteers wanted the world to make sense – wanted to believe that individuals did indeed have control over their own lives – even if that meant saying that eating was a personal choice.

We should not take their discourse of self-interest at face value; neither should we just take them at their word when they tried to convince themselves that the world could be mended by bringing ceramic mugs to work and string bags to Safeway:

[from group interview]

PETE: You know, if you can, if a person can change one child's life by spending a couple of hours with them each day.
MARYANNE: It's self-esteem,[3] and if everybody has a good self-esteem [Pete: Exactly], then we wouldn't have all these problems, we wouldn't have – wars –
PETE [chiming in halfway through the last sentence]: All those other things are gonna just Disappear!

MARYANNE: Yeah, really . . .

JULIE: But you know, pollution? You can do that right here . . . You can take care of almost every global issue right here.

PETE: Start at home.

GLADYS: Ooh, I'll carry my string bag again.

JULIE: I mean, I carry a coffee cup with me in my briefcase 'cause I won't use styrofoam cups anymore. I mean, it's something.

Similarly, the League of Women Voters set *Fifty Simple Things You Can Do to Save the Earth* out on their sign-up table, a booklet describing private, household changes individuals could make to help the environment (for example, turning the shower off when lathering up the shampoo, or reusing plastic bags) without requiring any political changes (for example, regulating industry, or zoning to make driving less necessary). Like the discourse of self-interest, this discourse of individual efficacy covered up volunteers' pained awareness; they worked hard to ignore the problems of the wider world.

Volunteers *could* have thought that they were powerless and been angry about that, but since they wanted to think that they live in a democracy where citizens like themselves have power to work on issues that are "close to home," they assumed that their powerlessness was their own fault. They could have tried to "save face" and blame someone else for their power-lessness, but they preferred to think it was their own fault than to think that there was something deeply wrong with the world (contrast this with Goffman's understanding of self-presentation: he emphasized the face-saving nature of interaction, saying that most people are loath to admit to incom-petence; but volunteers were more interested in putting a face on the *world* than on themselves).

Notice, no volunteers unequivocally said that the "problems of the world," as Pete put it, were not problems. They did not give ideological reasons for their lack of concern; they did not say, "really it's fine, oil spills are neces-sary elements in an industrial society, and the refineries are doing a fine job," or "we need nuclear battleships to defend ourselves." Ron came closest, but when he did, it was not clear whether it was a joke or not: he gathered himself up, puffed out his nostrils and chest, and made his eyes into slits, declaring, "As society evolves, you use up resources. That's natural. You just find alternative methods to meet your needs." His son and wife laughed at Ron's joke on himself. Volunteers – perhaps aside from Ron – certainly did not think the world was fine as it was. Complacency was not their reason for silencing political debate.

Technical knowledge and passion: "no black and white issues"

Volunteers were very knowledgeable about frightening issues. Some volunteers were technicians, who used their technical expertise to try to avoid confronting such knowledge. Geoffrey, for example, was a nuclear energy specialist at a nuclear battleship station. I asked what he thought of anti-nuclear groups. With a friendly, bemused expression, he said, "Anti-nuclear seems broad. Are they anti-nuclear waste? Anti-nuclear weapons? Anti-multi-kiloton weapons because they're afraid they might blow up the world? Or they could be anti-tactical weapons. They could be anti-nuclear power plants because they block the view!"

Pete, a chemist, also tried to use his technical knowledge to argue, again and again, that "no issues are black and white," and that he would always need more information before he could arrive at an opinion on most issues. But doubts quietly and quickly sneaked up on him, despite his efforts to convince himself not to worry:

PETE: We talked about "passion" before, and I don't get very passionate about things like that [foreign politics] like some people do. This girl I knew in college, she got passionate about, about, uh, the environment. [chuckling, tongue-in-cheek] It's good that there are people that get passionate 'cuz they're willing to go out and sacrifice their lives for these causes and then I can sit home and watch it on the TV.

[Serious again] You know, that's a bit cynical, but, uh, that's basically where I'm coming from . . . I'm *very*, uh, I'm I work I work for a chemical company, a refinery, and so I'm very interested now in the perception of petroleum. Because it's like a dirty word. It *is* a dirty word. And you know, I'm very – I see the other side of it. And there is another side of it, but the media doesn't let you see the other side. And so, I'm real interested in that . . . Everywhere I go, someone asks me what I do and I tell them and then this wall goes up, "Oh, you work for a dirty refinery?" . . . All people know is what they read in the paper about problems, smells and uh, it's a real concern, because the industry has a black eye and you don't tend to hear the other side of the story . . .

NINA: Maybe it goes back to people not knowing who to believe.

PETE: People believe the papers! [more about the negative image refineries have] Unfortunately, the whole story doesn't always get told. I know there's no such thing as a black and white issue. That's one thing I've kind of, a conclusion that I've come to over time. You know no matter how passionate somebody gets about something, especially I feel that way about foreign politics, and other countries – you just can't say it's "getting rid of communism" and that's it – or uh, you know, whatever it is. It's never black and white, there's always somebody else's story to be told. Maybe the Sandinistas are doing good things for their people. Maybe – so what? Maybe they *do* have some communist influences. I don't know if that's all bad, but I – and that goes for environmental issues, too.

It's hard when you talk about environmental issues because I mean, there's – I know because I was trained in biology and ecology, that um, you do certain things to the environment and they don't recover, you know you can't stomp all over the earth and as if it's gonna keep coming back because it won't. So, there-there-there *is* almost a black and white issue to deal with. So, that's – that's a tough one.

As soon as Pete started talking, his dispassionate neutrality started to unravel; he talked himself into a corner, saying after all that some issues are not just all grey.

"I'd like to think that": beliefs and desire about what to believe are inseparable

When I asked volunteers in a questionnaire the survey question "How much of the time do you think you can trust the government in Washington to do what is right? just about always? most of the time? only some of the time? or almost never?" a good number of the volunteers said something like what Carolyn said: "Most of the time. Well, at least I'd like to think it's most of the time. Of course I'm not so sure it really is. But I hope it is, so, I'd say 'most of the time.' Yes, put 'most of the time.' "

Notice, neither "yes" nor "no" nor "undecided" was the most real belief here. The belief *included* an effort at convincing herself, and an orientation toward talk itself. As Goffman would say, people have a relation to their beliefs – "I'd like to think that," "I resent having to say that," "I must be dumb to think this third thing." "If I were a good person I'd think the other." Included in the belief is a relationship to the belief. Carolyn's 18-year-old son was listening in on this interview and pitched in his opinions. He said he trusted the government "only some of the time." In this and other moments, he sounded more cynical than his mother. Twice, Carolyn prompted him to fix his statement and say something more optimistic, and reminding him of incidents he had seen that contradicted his cynical analysis. She was teaching him how to feel better, too.

The volunteers did not simply assume they did not live in a democracy, as researchers (Almond and Verba 1963) found people in undemocratic countries doing thirty years ago: that is, easily saying without tension that "it's just up to the people in Washington,'' that ''politics is something that other people do,'' or that ''protesters have no business butting their noses into the government's affairs.'' The volunteers did not blame themselves for feeling powerless and confused, as the country-western dancers described in the next chapter did. And the volunteers also did not make jokes about pickled herring in acid rain-filled lakes, as cynical Buffaloes described in chapter 6 did – implying that the world out there was all just a big hopeless joke. Volunteers did not blame the government for their feelings of powerlessness. These would be other ways of distancing themselves. The volunteers also did not say ''I care about an issue but just can't do anything about it,'' as many of the anti-toxics activists said.

Don't talk politics: it is "just rhetoric"

Why did volunteers assume that they had to feel so upbeat? If they had not had that rule about how to feel, they could have discarded their ''close to home'' language. The final clue in this mysterious use of ''close to home'' lies in *volunteers' assumptions about what the very act of speaking itself meant*. The last chapter showed just how pervasive this tacit assumption was.

If drawing attention to political problems was an immoral distraction, protesters were immoral. Discussing the protester who was run over by the weapons truck during a sit-in on the highway at the Evergreen Island Air Force Base, volunteers did not imagine that the protesters' main purpose was to ignite public debate on the weapons issue. As Parent League member Clara said in an interview, people have to have power before they can talk.

NINA: How do you decide if an issue is distant or not?
CLARA: If it affects you personally and your family . . . You can hold your opinions about what a country can do, or can't do, about a situation, but that's rhetoric . . . I don't really think a person can really make a difference unless they have the power at hand.

They assumed that talking would not produce power. Someone had to have already given you power, if you wanted to make a difference. An issue that is ''rhetoric,'' that is not do-able, is not close to home, and talking about a problem like torture or war would only discourage people and distract them from the work they *can* do. Drawing attention to a problem without solving it was considered immoral.

Beliefs about talk itself were key here, in setting the boundaries of the do-able, setting the emotional tone – beliefs about who talks, about what talk accomplishes, about where talk belongs, about when talk is "just rhetoric" or dangerous, or depressing, and beliefs about how regular people talk.

The evaporation of voices

Not all volunteers used "close to home." Some did not share the volunteer culture of political avoidance. For them, the moment of political evaporation happened further along *en route* to public life, at the moment when they entered the public forum – or didn't enter the public forum.

For example, Charles and Luke, two black members of the Parent League who did not always share the volunteers' culture of avoidance, showed a side of themselves in individual interviews that no one who saw them only in the group contexts could have guessed. Luke, an articulate Jesse Jackson supporter, shop steward, workplace safety activist, minister of a home church, and backyard organic gardener, rarely spoke in meetings, and only once offered any ideas related to these interests – this was when he invited a representative from his union to come to "Career Night" along with dozens of other career representatives. But in the interview, he made it clear that he thought they were related. He had much to say in the individual interview that never traveled as far as the group discussions. In response to my question about toxic waste, for example, he said,

Toxics are a great concern. I've been looking at that as well, on TV – they show all these different toxic waste areas, how it's seeping into the ground, getting into our water and all this, and I don't know, for some reason, it seems like, [hesitantly] you know, it's almost like the politicians and whatever is selling America out.

That's just the way I feel about it, quite honestly [chuckles]. They're selling us out. There must gonna be this mass move to the moon, and they're gonna leave us all here to self-destruct. I don't know, that's the way I think about it sometimes. I say they're going overseas, for instance, all the industry, the major auto makers, uh, GE, Zenith, all these big uh, Hewlett Packard . . . What are they gonna do – just vacate this land period and everybody moving out of here? Because that's the way they seem to treat this country anymore! . . .

We don't seem to want to address issues that are life-threatening, and you have to look at it like, "Gee, whiz, if you don't deal with these things, we're gonna soon self-destruct! . . . I got a little grandson, and sometimes he'll be running around here, and especially if something flashed on TV, you know, let's just say, the toxic waste, then . . . I look at the little guy and think, "Man, what's it gonna be like for him!" Things are pretty drastic. And people don't seem to care.

Earlier, he talked about the "profit motive" as a cause of the problems. Unlike the other volunteers, he talked about his grandchild without using that "for the children" discourse, which relied on collapsing "close to home," power, and self-interest. He used the one child as an example of the future generations in general; and then he did not "correct" himself to numb his worry, but let his depressing thoughts stand. But in group contexts, as I said, he was silent, except to offer to work the concession stand and to make very concrete suggestions about where to sell raffle tickets.

And not all volunteers used the "close to home" discourse all the time. An illustrative case of the contextual nature of the "close to home" discourse involved Ron and his tired wife Clara. Ron and Clara were the only two volunteers who were reputed to argue about politics in any context. Other volunteers referred to them as a phenomenon because of it, and the disagreement was a stock joke among their four children. When Ron was talking to his wife about the nuclear battleships, he lorded over her his knowledge of their dangerousness. But when talking to me, he emphasized their safety, using the "close to home" discourse.

The exchange began when I asked Clara about the nuclear group – could she imagine ever getting involved in such a group? She said that a nuclear battleship was different from a nuclear plant, and safer. Ron interrupted, "A nuclear battleship *is* a nuclear plant."

She said she heard there were differences and again Ron interrupted, "If one of those babies melts down out there in the Sound there won't be any difference to you!" To her, he gave more detail about how a meltdown could happen, drawing on the large store of unspoken frightening knowledge many Amargans shared. Clara gloomily mused that they may already have been exposed to radioactivity and would not even know it, since the government would not tell Amargo. Their 12-year-old son, also in the room, silently listening to the interview, mumbled, "They wouldn't?"[4]

Ron said he knew some sharp people who work on the battleships and trusted them not to make mistakes.

So, I know accidents happen. That's why they're accidents. But you know, I could stay in my bed, and not cross the street and never get run over by a car, but never do anything . . . I don't worry about it. I don't worry about it . . . If the people out there were a bunch of Bozos and they worried me, maybe I'd be over there protesting . . . I think it's run pretty right, so it's not an issue. So I don't do anything about it.

But then a moment later Clara referred to her own ignorance on the matter, saying again that she had heard that they could not melt down, and again, Ron interrupted, "They told you Three Mile Island wouldn't melt down either, but it did." Addressing his wife, Ron wanted to display his knowledge. But when standing on ceremony, addressing me, a researcher, he wanted to avoid appearing worried about something he could not change.

Danielle also often stopped using the "close to home" discourse when she and I were alone outside of meetings. For example, when she and I were walking down the street one day in Newton, picking our way past the usual array of homeless people, she became indignant, saying that she remembered when America had no beggars, that she remembered visiting another country when she was a child and being shocked that there were beggars on the street and that people could just walk right by without doing anything about it. She blamed the change on the Republicans, for "not caring" about homelessness. Then, she went on to say that, as a single mother, she herself could easily become homeless. She did not easily screen the wider world out of her everyday thoughts.

Backstage, I heard righteous indignation over injustice, worry, and the whole range of ambivalence portrayed here. But volunteers thought that speaking this way would not fix any problems, so even people who privately spoke with great indignation, concern, or doubt avoided showing those emotions in public.

Conclusion: compassion and citizenship

Volunteers tried hard to convince me that they, and all human beings, were self-interested and calculating. They strenuously tried to fashion themselves after the kind of personage that has had a long history in Western social theory's cast of characters – "rational actors" who "calculate the costs and benefits to themselves of various action they are considering and then choose the alternative most consistent with their fixed preferences" (Levi 1990: 8).[5] In other words, volunteers wanted to assume that people know what they want, and then assess the options open to them to decide where their efforts will have the most effect, and invest their time and energy in those efforts. Volunteers' energetic effort at modeling themselves after this image of humanity poses some interesting questions about "self-interest" based on "calculation," "fixed preference," and "rational choice." These questions demand a cultural explanation.[6]

First, volunteers did not tally up the costs and benefits of caring about issues that fell into the category of "not close to home." As we saw, when I suggested in interviews that all the groups I studied said they were involved "for the children," volunteers would reconsider the phrase for just a moment, say that indeed anything could be considered to be "close to home" and "for the children," and then, moments later, all revert to the "close to home," "for the children" discourse. They could not force themselves into another vocabulary, even after they had intellectually decided that the "close to home" explanation did not really do the job. It would be a stretch to call this activity "calculation." The work they did to divide up the world into "close to home/do-able" and "not close to home/not do-able" was not conscious – if it had been conscious, it would not have had the desired effect. Theorist Jon Elster discusses how a person might calculate that a desire is unhealthy and try to avoid having the desire, like Ulysses in the *Odyssey*: Ulysses orders his subordinates to tie him to the ship's mast and not obey his commands to be untied when the ship passes the irresistible Sirens, because he knows that if he yields to the Sirens' call, he will never get home. But, as Bourdieu argues (1990: 46), this analogy works only if people are like Ulysses, who could calculate in advance that he would want to avoid the Sirens' once-in-a-lifetime temptation; in most of life, this calculation has to be automatic, cultural, embedded in everyday practices. Even if volunteers had calculated the cost of caring about the wider world, they would have had to forget that they ever did the calculating if they were to keep their belief in democracy afloat. Perhaps in deeply private moments, individual volunteers scanned a set of options before deciding to work on more "do-able" issues instead of less do-able ones; and then forgot ever having made this calculation. But even if that is true, that process of political evaporation is itself interesting: they *had to forget* that they had convinced themselves not to care, and, lest they risk discouraging anyone else, the more public the context, the harder they had to try to make themselves forget.

Thus, the second problem with this rationally self-interested image of humanity is that volunteers did not have "fixed preferences" at all; they made a huge effort to convince themselves that they preferred what they thought they could realistically get: to love their fate; not to "prefer" clean water and safe food if that preference was unlikely to be met.

The third, most interesting problem with that self-interested model of humanity is that volunteers would have experienced a feeling of powerlessness as a *moral* problem, not just a problem of wasted investment of time; and publicly voicing a feeling of powerlessness would have been even more immoral.[7] They did not simply think that worrying about a problem they could not solve was a waste of time. It was immoral; it was socially destructive and could undermine their sense of the rightness of the world. They made assessments of personal and group power in ways that ultimately were aimed not at preserving their interests, but at preserving the feeling that the world made sense.

So, if volunteers were not as obviously self-interested as they claimed to be, why did they talk as if they were? In *Acts of Compassion*, sociologist Robert Wuthnow rightly says that a floating, unspoken mix of motives often animates volunteers' involvement, but only a few of those motives gel into speech. Most of the volunteers he interviewed explained their own altruistic behavior in terms of self-interest – "I do it because it's fun," or "I get a lot out of it," or "It's a personal growth experience," or "I meet a lot of interesting people" – or in terms of effectiveness – "We accomplish a lot."

Wuthnow, along with Robert Bellah and others, traces this language to American political traditions, and says that Americans should begin to draw upon their other, less individualistic traditions. Wuthnow wants volunteers proudly to acknowledge to each other, out loud, that their charitable acts, no matter how small, have meaning in themselves for the larger society, apart from how efficiently they accomplish specific tasks. In a happy marriage, saying "I love you" now and then helps give a definite shape to a floating, unspoken mix of good feelings. In a good society, the presence of regular, unsaintly, plain citizens caring for their community is important in itself – it is society's way of saying "I love you" to itself.[8] Bringing the hot meal to the old person is a kind of a ritual, whose message is "someone cares." Wuthnow says that volunteers devalue their own work if they do not explicitly recognize the importance of that "display," that ritual of compassion: the act of compassion, no matter how small, has meaning for the larger society, in showing that people really do care about their fellow human beings.

In practice, volunteers implicitly *did* assume what Wuthnow says they should make explicit: that the main importance of their work was to show that being good and caring is possible. But I add something with which Wuthnow would probably agree: volunteers also wanted to show that good citizenship is possible. They wanted to show that their feelings of compassion mattered, and were not just wasted. And they wanted to show not only that *they* cared; they also wanted to show that *everyone* can care, not just exceptionally good people. Volunteers used the discourse of self-interest and "close to home," in practice, to protect precious, fragile feelings of hopefulness and empowerment. In practice, the way they tried to show that good, effective citizenship was possible was to limit their circle of concern, and try not to care about issues that were not "close to home." "Showing care" and "showing good, effective citizenship" often contradicted each other; affirming compassion meant curtailing democracy.

What if an ordinary person cannot make a difference without talking about politics, without letting political concerns have their due, without feeling alarm, without figuring out some way to trust the power of words – without, that is, becoming an extraordinary person? Then, showing that "someone cares" would inevitably entail a kind of political engagement that volunteers tried to avoid. Redefining "compassion" and "citizenship" so that they could harmonize instead of clash would be a serious risk, because volunteers implicitly knew that when it came to compassion, they were on their own, freelancers in a wider political world that was not out to support their efforts. They did not try to change that implicit institutional context.

"Self-interest" is not the only important topic for political discussion. People join groups for all sorts of reasons. But if they feel that they can speak only in terms of self-interest, then an important part of their public selves has been amputated. Their meaning-making powers are impaired. The "close to home" refrain represented a heroic effort at creating a small corner of the world in which everyone could feel important, welcome, and effective; a small corner that protects citizens from the overwhelming, dispiriting context of the wider world. The more public the context, the more urgently moral it seemed to be, to vaporize expressions of public spirit.

4

Humor, nostalgia, and commercial culture in the postmodern public sphere

Part 1: *Trying to create a community of private people*

refrain:
Down Home: where they know you by name and treat you like family.
Folks know: if they've fallen on hard times they can fall back home –
 those of us raised up Down Home.
verse:
In the corner of the hardware store,
gathered round a checkerboard
old men tellin' lies and crownin' kings.
Kids drivin' round the old town square
cops roll down in the cool night air
go and see what's shakin' at the Dairy Queen.

hit country-western song of 1990, by Alabama

I don't know anything about him – I guess I'm falling in love. I mean, how
do I know he's telling the truth about his house or his job or anything? And
I've never seen any of his friends, and – I know he's a good dancer, and I
know he's real cute, but how do I know to believe him about the rest that
I can't see?

a country-western dance club member, on a potential boyfriend
she met at the Silverado Club

Regulars at the Silverado Club and Buffalo Club's country-western dance
classes usually greeted each other with warm hugs and exclamations of
"Hey, there she is – at last!" and "Where've you been?" Many participants
in the clubs' country-western dance classes said they wanted the place to
have "a real community feel," and to be "not just a bar, but a community
center, a family place," as one member put it. An onlooker at these dance
halls would have guessed that participants were in a close-knit community.
Yet hardly anyone attended regularly for more than a year, and participants

came from all directions, most from as far away as my grueling hour's commute. On six-lane strips between Denny's, Carl's Jr., Arco, Shell, Kwik Stop, Pizza Hut, and Sizzler, these clubs were not neighborhood bars. Members did not automatically belong to the close-knit, longstanding "community" they craved, in which they could count on each other's presence year after year in their neighborhoods, their children's schools and the grocery store, the Dairy Queen and the town square, over intertwined generations.

If they wanted "community," they would have had to *invent* it, from scratch; but country-westerners did not want to invent community. They wanted to have it ready-made, but it was not. They wanted to be in a primordial, deep, longstanding community, but they were not. "Community" must be one of the most overused words in the United States – local news shows talk about the "heterosexual community" and the "cat-owning community," as if community means simply a set of strangers who share a taste. In contrast, "community" of the sort the country-westerners ambivalently wanted would have lasted longer; it would have allowed participants to rely on each other even outside of the group context; it would have made conversation itself less difficult by establishing a firmer sense of common ground; and it would have allowed for a broader range of interaction topics and styles than the few which the group context allowed.

Country-westerners wanted to leave references to the wider world behind and just appreciate each other as human beings, pure and simple, in a community of equals, with no one rewarded for having a better job, being richer or smarter or more charitable or more patriotic, nor for having any particular loyalties or attachments, exceptional eloquence, skill, or any exceptional qualities: just people. They wanted to avoid the kind of constraints, judgments, and obligations that theorists describe. They were *private people*; they believed that what really matters is what is "inside"; that the tender, flickering "real self" can almost never be expressed in words, and certainly does not brazenly display itself in group contexts. Their unjudgmental ideal of friendship rested on an anti-institutional and anti-conventional feeling that anything larger than that hidden sliver of real selfhood was less real, and probably tainted, so participants tried to create a sense of etiquette that kept the wider world and its stuffy, confining, annoying, contaminated conventions as far away as possible. Shared humor and a shared taste for country-western styles seemed to members to offer togetherness without constraint, very loosely binding a fragile and precious sense of voluntary community without having to intrude on anyone's very private sense of self.

To keep the wider world at arm's length, participants tried to break the rules that they imagined the outside world would impose on their face-to-face context. Trying so hard to appear to be breaking rules meant dwelling on a few topics: racist jokes, bathroom jokes, sex jokes; and teasing. Participants did not know what else they shared, but could count on those jokes to violate some very general rules which they presumed that somebody out there obeyed. This aversion to ''good manners'' was, however, a rule itself: do not talk seriously in the group context, and try to appear to be breaking rules. The private people wanted the taken-for-granted sense of community to *be there already*, so that they themselves could have something against which to rebel, but they did not want to have to create anything themselves.

This made them so free, so far from any landmarks on the social horizon, they were unsure what they could presume to have in common, beyond the stylized topics that they could be absolutely certain that they shared – country dancing and clothing and horses. So when describing a new acquaintance, members would mention whether the person was a ''horse person'' or, interchangeably, a ''country person.'' Meeting on such a stark social landscape, sure of sharing only one specific taste, they had little to talk about; making conversation was difficult, and political conversation nearly impossible. The way country-westerners used commercial culture undermined their ability to create a solid sense of togetherness, letting them act as if they already were ''down home,'' when they were not.

Yet, here were people ambivalently trying to create a community, driving far to seek out companionship, not drones shuttling between work, home, and mall, not sitting home watching TV, not just stalking quick dates in singles bars. The worst violation of manners, worse even than acting serious, was to treat the places like ''sleazy pick-up joints.'' When Charlene came in a slinky dress and left with a stranger, other members actively shunned her. Members did not have very active ties to other groups – religious, volunteer, or political groups – and they spent most of their free time at the dance halls. They relied on the dance clubs. Typical was George, a bachelor, who told us, after having come to the Buffalo four times in one week, ''I'll be sitting there at home, every night, eating my frozen microwave burrito, and then I say to myself, 'Oh, why not go see what's going on at the Buffalo Club?' '' But the clubs offered unsteady ground; members ambivalently wanted more than irreverence from them. Betsy would have liked to know more about the potential new boyfriend than what she could ''see'' at the club. Another member, Jody, would have liked some help or recognition when she painstakingly wrote her own vows for her wedding, celebrated in a ceremony at the Silverado. It was nerve-wracking to write the ceremony all alone, and she was disappointed that no one said anything to her about it afterward. Other members worried that they were not skilled at making conversation – anyone would have that worry in such a naked social landscape.

Can a group that comes together initially sharing only jokes and consumer tastes ever become an incubator of citizenship, of the sort that Aristotle and de Tocqueville described? There is good reason to think so: as free spaces for political conversation, bars and coffeehouses, rodeos and rock concerts could be crucial parts of the public sphere. We do not need to be nostalgic for "real," pre-commercial, traditional community; since the 1800s, leisure and commercial institutions have been completely intermarried (Rybczynski 1991; Rosenzweig 1983, for example). A person freely spouting ideas in a bar can argue both sides at once just for the sake of making a good argument, try out half-baked ideas on an audience that is not poised for immediate action, write the mental rough draft before the idea congeals into a platform. In theory, these sociable, joking, loud, musical, fragrant, colorful, stylish public spaces are not risky places for exposing unformed ideas. Unlike speech in more formal settings like union meetings, volunteer groups, activist groups, or parties, conversation in these free spaces can be non-instrumental and utopian, but spoken as if it mattered.[1] But, like many Americans, private people did not imagine fun and political debate in the same picture. As more Americans move to centerless suburbs like Amargo, creating common ground may often mean coming together initially unsure of sharing anything but a taste in commercial culture.

This chapter explores this desire for a kind of human companionship that tries to distance itself from all institutions except commercial ones. What are the political possibilities of such a setting? How did participants at the country-western dance clubs prevent publicly minded conversation from entering the fun atmosphere, "frontstage"? What did members assume group life was? Why did it always have to be so funny and irreverent? The chapter begins by outlining two possible interpretations of this group. After a sketch of the scene, the story analyzes non-verbal communication; then, hidden, whispered backstage conversation and one-on-one conversation; and then group conversation. At each step away from implicit to explicit, and from backstage to frontstage, the sense of public-spiritedness evaporated a bit more; backstage whispers and even eyebrow-wiggles communicated more generosity, less bigotry and racism, more public spirit, than frontstage, loud, group conversation. Finally, the chapter examines the country-westerners' group rituals, like weddings and public events.

Commercial culture, humor, irony, and community: monads or nomads?

What does this group's vehemently anti-conventional, anti-institutional humor and heavy reliance on commercial culture mean? On the one hand, many Americans repeat grim warnings about the evil power of mass culture and rootlessness, and we condemn the powerlessness of all the lost souls who lack community, who we say are brainwashed by media. With proud irony, we even confess out loud that we ourselves are "suckers," that the whole political field is dominated by "spin doctors," and that we ourselves are under the spell of tawdry, vapid, and materialistic mass culture's omnipotent power, that tells us what to buy and how to think. According to this perspective, Buffaloes would be considered passive dupes of the culture industry, whose junior high-schoolish joking was a pathetic substitute for "real" rebellion.

On the other hand, many Americans *also* like to assert with vehemence that we personally are free to mix and match fashions and tastes, irreverently and merrily fashioning lives out of scraps from the junkyard of commodity culture. This pop resistance repeats what fashion magazines say year after year, that this year "unlike last year, the only rule this year is that there is no rule" – that now we can "Just Do It," as Nike ads put it, that consumer culture offers freedom. Consider the following corporate slogans:

> Sometimes You Gotta Break the Rules (Burger King)
> The Rules Have Changed (Dodge)
> There's No One Way to Do It (Levis)
> This Is Different. Different Is Good (Arby's)
> Just Different from the Rest (Special Export beer)
> The Line Has Been Crossed: The Revolutionary New Supra (Toyota)
> Resist the Usual (the slogan of both Clash Clear Malt and Young and Rubicam)   (compiled in Frank 1995: 178)

The moral is that we should rummage through the cast-off platform shoes, go-go boots, Donna Read dresses, and love beads to make an "individual statement" about our personal uniqueness. American best-selling psychology books often offer a matching philosophy, that places custom, ritual, repetition, and etiquette in opposition to morality, honesty, and true selfhood.[2] According to this perspective, Buffaloes were fun rebels, overthrowing oppressive rules, just doing it – perhaps they were "The Dodge Rebellion!"

These two contadictory common-sense ways of thinking resonate with two strands of social theory: the first would sternly regard the country-westerners as dupes of mass culture, escapists who only ensnared themselves more tightly in their alienation by trying so hard to escape the limits of their conventionality. This line of thought, offered by critical theorists like T. W. Adorno and Max Horkheimer, would say that the relentless humor and irreverence at the clubs allowed country-westerners to feel undeservedly unconventional, to feel like rebels when really they were utterly conventional "monads." These writers would call the constant laughter an ugly anesthetic for country-westerners' painful alienation,

the echo of power as something inescapable . . . In the false society, laughter is a disease which has attacked happiness and is drawing it into its worthless totality. To laugh at something is always to deride it . . . Such a laughing audience is a parody of humanity. Its members are monads, dedicated to the pleasure of being ready for anything at the expense of everyone else. Their harmony is a caricature of solidarity.
(Horkheimer and Adorno 1972 [1944]: 140–141)[3]

This approach to humor and mass culture says that when culture is produced for corporate profit, the audience's job is to exploit itself, not to take itself or its pleasures seriously but to settle into a permanent smirk and ironically try to enjoy being swindled. "The culture industry's"[4] sole aim is to make money and the audience secretly knows it: "The triumph of advertising in the culture industry is that consumers feel compelled to buy and use its products even though they see through them" (167).

Mindlessly ironic pleasure taken in the culture industry's products helps consumers rearrange their inner lives, when what needs rearranging is the world, critical theorists say. This cultural passivity robs the individual of any true individuality and sells him or her a mass-produced "pseudo-individuality." This freedom to buy a fake personality is like the freedom one has in a mall: there seem to be thousands of choices, but really there is only one: the choice to buy something. And this commodification of everything, in which "everything is looked at from one aspect: that it can be used for something else" (158), penetrates every aspect of life until the whole of inner, emotional life is corroded by this commercial, distrustful, instrumental, ironic, smirking attitude.

The second tradition, that echoes the "just do it" side of our contradictory pop philosophy, would argue that the Buffaloes' merry distance from stuffy institutions is masked rebellion; their way of using commercial culture is liberating; their humor and resistance to systems of meaning is itself a subversive relief from the tight controls of "normal" reality. For a hundred years, theorists – from Friedrich Nietzsche to Erving Goffman, Michel Foucault, Michel de Certeau, Jean Baudrillard and John Fiske – have echoed this sentiment. Better to speak in jokes, aphorisms, and silence, they say: indirect speech that overturns dominant meanings without substituting another set of dominating meanings. Joking deflates, reverses, twists, shakes up, mocks, reframes the order of a given situation, reveals hidden, new interpretations, and resists standard, limited constraints, tips over taken-for-granted interpretations. "Resistance" theories celebrate the unexpectedly rebellious uses to which audiences put mass culture – absorbing it ironically, using commercial culture to their own idiosyncratic ends, using their humor as a small, everyday rebellion against the culture industry. Wandering through the desert of meanings that commodity culture offers, audiences like this are not the "monads" that critical theorists imagined, but "nomads" who improvise meanings piecemeal as they go. The country-western group would be an exemplar of a group that resists systematic meaning altogether, merrily taking pot-shots at any and all efforts to impose dominant order on the world. And Buffaloes themselves clearly shared this longstanding tradition in Western thought that abhors tradition and systematization, and celebrates humor, irony, irreverence.

In this chapter, I will suggest that the problem with both answers to the question of how people ingest or subvert commercially prefabricated meanings is that neither pays attention to how people *create contexts for political conversation together in everyday life.*

A description of the set and characters

My first two months of country dance classes were in Evergreen City, at a defunct junior high school next door to the chemical plant that had had a major spill or explosion eight years in a row and now was the site of protest staged by an activist group I studied. Children rode trikes on the street, the huge compound glowing behind them, filling the sky with a thousand points of light. The somehow homey odors of skunky, acrid gas and a slow, brackish bay wafted on a mild breeze. After the month-long class ended, members who wanted to continue dancing attended the Buffalo and the Silverado, which were about a mile apart on a five-lane highway.[5] Between 50 and 100 people came to the Silverado or Buffalo every night; 200 on holidays. I will refer to members as "Buffaloes," "country-westerners," and "private people," interchangeably.

These clubs, an Elks Club, and a bowling alley were the only public places in Amargo for adults to gather to socialize. Parents often brought children to the country-western clubs on holidays for whole-day barbecue celebrations. Dance class participants went on camping trips together, to each other's houses, to horse shows and rodeos and theme parks together. In the two years in which I was attending, members held several weddings and wedding receptions at local country-western clubs. Several times a year, country-western radio stations staged benefit barbecues at the Silverado, to raise money for a charity disease prevention effort. On fundraiser days, a dollar bought bread soaked in brown gravy, a meat and a vegetable, and a ticket to dance all night. At the Silverado, a glass of tap water cost $1.50; mineral water $2.00; beer, more, so an evening out was not cheap (I fall asleep after about four sips of beer, so I always just ordered soda water – luckily for me, people did not buy rounds for each other, but ordered separately). The Silverado Club owner threw parties with grab-bags or raffles for Valentine's Day, Halloween, July 4th, Christmas, St. Patrick's Day, and New Year's, and sometimes allowed merchants to host fashion shows. The USO hosted "Welcome Home the Troops" celebrations at several clubs throughout the region after the Gulf War. These places were not "just" bars, but served sometimes as churches, as charities, as community centers.

The Silverado huddled on a vast, rutted parking lot on what once was wetlands and now was a truck stop, a mile and a half from Amargo's nuclear battleship station. Occasional gulleys of saltwater cattails poked through the wide, flat miles of paved malls and gas stations. Giant four-wheel-drive recreational vehicles filled the parking lot, making my miniature Honda look like a toy (soon, I learned that nearly all the regulars worked indoors, lived in a paved, snowless suburbia, and used the towering recreational vehicles to carry their big dogs around, and to sleep in when car-camping in the mountains once or twice a year). Inside the windowless Silverado, initial blinding darkness gave way to a huge Confederate flag pinned up behind the bandstand, the standard collection of neon beer signs and beer mirrors, men in cowboy hats, cowboy shirts, and jeans; women in curly perms and tiered flounces of lace or denim skirts, or jeans, and belts with their names embroidered in glitter on the back.

In the entryway to the Buffalo Lodge, also windowless, were three pamphlets from the national Loyal Brotherhood of Buffaloes: one for a Buffalo Club retirement home, another for a home for orphaned children of Buffaloes, and a third advertising the national Buffaloes' campaign to fight drugs in schools. On one side of the entryway was a very smoky bar – one of the reasons some members said they joined[6] the Buffalo Club was for the cheap drinks. On the other side of the entrance were a large linoleum dance floor, dining tables, and the opening to the kitchen. Most nights, retired Buffaloes attended "feeds," big, meaty dinners.

The members I eventually got to know were between 34 and 50 years old, all suburban dwellers, all white. Some had children over nine; none had young children. Most were high school or two-year college graduates. Most men were blue-collar workers in Pacific City or its suburbs: a near-distance trucker, two union carpenters building malls and subdivisions; a mechanic, a supervisor of maintenance for state office buildings. Most women worked in "pink-collar jobs" (Howe 1977), in front of word processors or cash registers. But members of the country-western clubs definitely did not gather as members of a social class. On the contrary, most did not know what the others did for a living, or often purposely forgot. Asking would not be polite, since members wanted to appreciate each other as human beings plain and simple, not as members of categories or fillers of roles. As one member said, expressing a sentiment I had heard before, "Everyone comes here – doctors, lawyers, who knows what else?"

Solidarity without words

Why was there so little publicly minded conversation in this context? The short answer is that there was very little conversation of any kind there. Remarkably, considering how often, and how far, participants would drive to congregate there, conversation itself was extremely rare. Music and dancing, raffles and grab-bag drawings, contests and fashion shows and other spectacles made it possible to sit for long periods of time literally without speaking. None of these centralized objects of attention was loud enough or distracting enough to prevent conversation, if participants had wanted to talk, but country-westerners just usually preferred silence. And even when there was no music or show, I often found myself sitting in silence with other silent country-westerners, when several of us were riding in the back of a pick-up on the way to a theme park, or sitting in a car, or eating at a spaghetti feed.

Yet, the silence was not mute. A culture's rhythms, sounds, and motions can create a kind of physical togetherness, meanings that cannot be reduced to words or beliefs or ideas, but has to be experienced *in practice*. Part of what constitutes membership in a group is a way of existing in a body:

Cultural effects may or may not depend upon semiotic "content," meaning, or claims of representation. For example, the most powerful effects of video games may be determined less by ideological dimensions than by certain forms of embodiment, by the way in which the player controls/produces the sounds and lights that engulf, produce, and define a "rhythmic body."   (Grossberg 1988: 383)

At the country dance clubs, every man (except a visiting German and a wealthy retired high school principal who had no friends at the clubs and soon dropped out) wore very stiff, very expensive, wooden-heeled, pointy-toed cowboy boots. All the men walked in them with a strikingly exaggerated stiffness, a bow-legged, clunky strut, first the hard wooden back of the heel, then the front of the heel, then the toe. The stiffness allowed them to enjoy a certain kind of masculinity one normally sees only on TV. Each step offered a satisfyingly resonant CLONKclonk. Compare that to the slithery sexuality (Willis 1978) and "seaweed dancing" inspired by acid rock music! I heard two different men say they could not go dancing because their boots were wet or broken. Without the boots, learning to dance was embarrassingly girlish; without the boots, the manly strut was impossible; the manly, "strong, silent type" identity was impossible.

Since Buffaloes relied so heavily on non-verbal communication, they were serious about it. Each night, the dance teachers who organized all the group events called out several times, "C'mon, guys, smile! You're supposed to be havin' fun!" as dancers with pursed brows struggled to memorize intricate dances with dozens of steps. Everyone adeptly asked precise and urgent questions about the dance steps: in my first dance class, a bulky man with a smooth, pink, eyelash-less head asked the teacher, "Is it one, two, step, then turn, or do you start turning during the third step?" Compared to parties of university-educated urbanites in Newton, the nearby city where I lived, country-westerners were much more able to surmount the risk of displaying physical skill – dancing – and less willing to risk a verbal display – talking.[7]

Non-verbally, members very clearly communicated that these dance halls were more than singles bars, by dancing with friends who were "the wrong age" for them, who were already "taken," or who otherwise did not excite their romantic interest – like "the Mosquito," who was much shorter and skinnier than the husky, bulky men that most of the women found attractive. Further in keeping with the open atmosphere was the arrangement of the dance floor itself, arranged to accommodate both couple dances and "line dances," so that if everyone watched out, no one would bump into anyone else. Just from these ways of being in a body, and forming a group of bodies, members "said" a great deal.

Is silence enough?

Talking as an activity in itself was a special event. "Staying up till two talking" was one sure sign of love; it happened only at the moment lovers were falling in love, not after and not before. Since talk itself was such a potent sign, reports of these intimate moments focused on the fact that the new lovers talked, not on the content of the conversation. After this proud moment of intense talk, if it happened, there was little to say. Jody, for example, said, not quite as a complaint, that her new boyfriend Jim, a mechanic, was very quiet. I asked what they talked about that weekend:

We didn't have time to talk: Silverado Friday night; Saturday we made breakfast, then I had to feed the horses, then the Country Team practiced and then there was the Cattle Branders' dinner. Then Sunday morning we went out to eat, then went to the Silverado, then Monday we decided to make breakfast because he's a good cook.

He made pancakes from scratch. They were so good. Well, they were raw in the middle, so he said, "Here, Muffin," and gave them to him [her dog].

Then she described an interaction between him and her dog.

Doug, a driver for a suburban company, spoke so little his girlfriend had to read his non-verbal signs ("He brought two cans of dog food for Rusty so that means he's planning on staying at my house two nights"; "He left a T-shirt in the bedroom so that must have been like a sign that he's coming back – like a cat leaves its mark"). She liked him for his non-verbal qualities: he so lovingly cared for his house and vintage car, and was so sweet to his dog.

For a person like me who loves to dance, the absence of conversation at the Buffalo could be a welcome relief from the above-the-shoulders activities of talkative, intellectual city dwellers in Newton, the cosmopolitan university town where I lived. For those more cerebral types in Newton, the whole physical dimension of interaction was often just missing. At the country dance halls, in contrast, I learned to appreciate and like good dance partners, people who were fun to watch dance, people who had nice smiles or pleasant posture, who liked a song I liked. I scoured people for physical cues about themselves, and learned to value those cues. One member, for example, was endearing to me because he looked so very earnestly boyish and deliberate when learning a new dance; another, because she looked so happy in her new summer dress. Participants trusted physical communication, not words.

To me, the blanket of silence was calming after a day of demeaning work. Sue was a grounds-keeper for a suburban school, and lived in a little house on campus. Seven of us sitting in her living room one Friday night did not need to maintain a steady stream of talk. It was so comfortable just to sit and be assured that whatever we said or did not say was not important. What mattered was that we were comfortable together. We lazily talked a bit, about Sue's dogs, her bird, and her cat. We talked to her dog as much as to each other. Soothing night sounds of frogs and crickets from a nearby pond emerged during pleasant stretches of verbal silence. Later, we turned the cassette player on out on the porch and danced. One did not have to demonstrate any wit or verbal acuity to be popular. Other events at the Buffalo were also pleasant without much conversation. At one Christmas party, fronds of sparkling silver tinsel fluttered in streamers zigzagging across the ceiling; sequined Christmas sweaters and cowboy shirts glittered below; green, red, pink, and white potluck food gleamed brightly on long cafeteria tables. A humorous raffle occupied our attention for a long while. The situation was familiar and festive, and we did not need to talk much. Whatever community these dance halls embodied was communicated non-verbally. Talking was not members' reason for being there. Most activities were like that, so that when members reported on a day's activities, reporting what anybody said was not part of the story.

"Maybe," I thought, "this physical communication is enough to establish a sense of community." Yet, like the verbal city people, the country-westerner people wanted to get to know each other and feel like community quickly; they did not feel they had the luxury of waiting years to get to know one another. Non-romantic friendships developed quickly, and some private people got married after meeting at the Silverado only a few months earlier. Members did not keep coming year after year, yet the numerous wedding rituals celebrated there assumed that there was a community strong enough to bear witness to these promises of long-term, serious commitment.

The silence thus posed some problems. In a community where members have grown up together, perhaps a silent nod, a small gesture, a glance can be enough to evoke the shared past through which they interpret each other's talk and silence.[8] In a tight-knit community, members could rely on each other's knowledge: "No, don't go out with that guy – don't you know he ax murdered his wife?" or, "He's a known liar." But in a suburban bar like this, far from anyone's home, members could not rely on community knowledge or community sanctions if something went wrong. This silence might be dangerous. Should tall, blond, attractive Betsy go way out to the rural countryside to visit that potential new boyfriend, even though she knew only "what she could see" about him? This was one of the many instances in which participants worried about the lack of familiarity.

The silence posed other problems as well. Making conversation, not just political conversation, posed an often insurmountable challenge. One member especially admired a friend for "being able to make conversation up, out of thin air." Another complained, "My conversation just doesn't 'conversationalize'!" Nearly all of Jim's conversation in my two years there was about the bargain he got on the giant, black cowboy hat he always wore. His other topic was a popular one for all – the number of steps you had to memorize for the new dance ("Have you tried the 64-step yet?" Jim often asked with a proud grin). Members of the dance team often found that the teacher had given them a new partner without telling them. Members exerted a formidable effort in more intimate settings puzzling together over the various silences.[9]

The more verbal people with whom I usually kept company in Newton, the urban enclave, would not have considered these non-verbal forms of communication trustworthy. How could I know that the earnestly boyish-looking dancer is not a rifle-toter who is proud that his dog bites blacks? He was, in fact. The recreation group members, in contrast, distrusted verbal prowess:

"That's just talk," they often said, or "He can talk, but what's underneath?" As Betsy said, "How do I know what to believe?"

For private people, talk did not legitimately matter. Betsy sounded as if she felt unreasonable to want to know more about the potential boyfriend than "what she could see"; she *wanted* to be content with what she already knew about his most basic humanness. Backstage, in one-on-one or three-way conversations, women often noted that their boyfriends or husbands hardly ever talked, but could "go on a two-hour drive and not say a word except, 'You hungry?' and 'Let's stop.' " Women's tentative remarks about their silent husbands and boyfriends were not quite complaints, though, because the women were not sure whether they were justified in complaining about the silence, and men controlled the frontstage, group contexts. Women *wanted* to feel happy just to be in their husbands' or boyfriends' company, side by side in the truck. They did not want to want anything more, since the official belief about talk was that it is cheap. Expecting conversation was not considered legitimate. And so there was very little of it. What group conversation there was, was relentlessly unserious.

Backstage and frontstage in the postmodern community center

While Goffman describes "backstage" as the place for letting loose, belching, scratching oneself – just generally being gross and offensive – at the country-western clubs, there were back- and frontstages, but with a striking twist: the *group* context, "frontstage," demanded the "profanity, open sexual remarks, shouting, playful aggressivity and 'kidding' " that Goffman expected "backstage." At the country-western clubs, it was only *backstage* that members could squeeze in a moment of seriousness and stop straining so hard to appear so casual. Why?

Country-westerners made it clear that they wanted no connection with an organization that would restrain their behavior in their free time. They assumed that a group "self" is not really real, that group contexts are not places in which people are really "themselves" unless the group is totally unconstrained. An observer who wanted to cheer for resistance, who valued the "nomad," the irreverent, the topsy-turvy and unsystematic, who welcomed the breezy claim that "the only rule is that there is no rule" would applaud the banishment of seriousness.

Such cheer makes sense if people are only really "themselves" and free when they let go of all social anchors. But in fact, it took quite a disciplined effort to cultivate this impression of casualness. Seriousness bubbled out around the tightly casual impression-management, but only backstage.

Urgently whispering, stepping out into the dark parking lot, pretending to go to the Ladies Room: backstage, never in the group setting, was where members conveyed straightforward thoughts, information, worries and feelings about relationships, work, family, and health, and the wider world. So, frontstage was occupied by a big hole; often, the group conversation would displease almost everyone, but none would complain – or at least they would wait until they were backstage to complain.

Projecting an image of freedom required finding irreverent-sounding topics. For white Americans, talking about race lends itself especially well to the trumpeting of irreverence. As linguist Teun van Dijk shows, white Americans' speech about race in interviews or formal settings is like talk of sex and defecation; always full of pauses, delicate rephrasings, false starts, and repairs (1987: 102). White Americans feel nervous talking about race at all; they suspect they might have said the wrong thing, and usually consider any talk about it taboo. So, joking about it openly in a group is a way for whites to seem to be carefree violators of a sanctimonious taboo. The same goes for talk about gender differences and sex.

Thus, the group atmosphere was more racist and sexist than most of its individual members. More tolerant voices evaporated. For example, at a barbecue at George's house, almost every participant was chagrined at the group interaction, but none complained or criticized until they were in a one-on-one conversation, or at most, a threesome. First, Chuck and Charlene kept up a steady stream of rowdy jokes that made no one laugh: a long one about news reporter Barbara Walters visiting an Indian chief and his ''squaws''; lots of anti-gay jokes, ethnic slurs, race jokes, toilet jokes, sex jokes, animal jokes, and child abuse jokes. In the middle of this stream, Chuck took a picture of Charlene with her 9-year-old daughter Suzanne cuddling into her lap. That led to a round of jokes about Suzanne's underwear showing. After a while, Suzanne began to cry, saying George was making fun of her. George changed the subject by asking Chuck's wife whether her husband Chuck acted like this at home, too. No, Chuck does whatever his wife says. ''Oh, do you have a whip?'' George asked the wife.

''No, but I have handcuffs. Actually I have these itty-bitty handcuffs we put on the cat!''

Chuck chimed in, exclaiming how funny it was to see his cat flipping and wiggling in little paw-sized handcuffs. Everyone laughed. ''Where did you get such tiny handcuffs?'' someone asked.

''When I was a recruiter for the Navy.''

Everything else that was said was either about race or sex, except ''Want another beer?''

To be friendly, the ever-agreeable George laughed at all the jokes, but the nine others at the umbrella-table on the patio stretched their lips horizontally across their faces – were they slightly smiling? Or maybe they were squinting at the bright sunlight glinting off the white plastic table? They did not laugh but did not make a point of not laughing either. Were they just very low-key, unexpressive, shy or quiet, or did they not think the jokes were funny? I could not guess, while we were all sitting around the barbecue table.

The others could not guess, either; a little while later, after most of group had gone indoors, Chuck said to one of the women, "Well, Carla likes me," and the woman answered, "No, she's just being quiet. Who says she likes you?" Jody said Carla was just shy. Again, making sense of the enigmatic silence was difficult for everyone; such backstage conversation was often devoted to deciphering other members' minimal utterances.

Finally, Chuck said something so offensive that the others momentarily stopped the proceedings. Suzanne had sat on his lap again, asking him to do a split. He made a joke, saying "I'm not gonna spread my legs for you! I hardly even know you!" Charlene, the girl's mother, put on a serious face, saying "Chuck, it's innocent. She's taking aerobics at school and they're teaching them splits, I guess." Chuck persisted in his abusive jokes, till Carla said, "Chuck, that's not funny." Suzanne's mother agreed, and I added, "Then I guess we all agree." They laughed. He insisted, "After four beers, having a little girl sit on your lap, you never know what might happen!" Despite the reprimand, George and Chuck teased Suzanne this way until all but Chuck, George, and Jamie got bored and meandered indoors.

Then something remarkable happened. After staging that long session of joking, the trio of men found themselves alone, backstage. I had come back out momentarily to clear some dishes off the table, and overheard a quick change of topic – suddenly the nasty joking was no longer necessary, and they discovered that they were all construction workers. George asked, "What hall? Er – are you union, are you a union construction worker?" They discovered they were in the same hall. They complained about the slowness of the lottery for work and about the quality of workers, joking about how some guys could not even read a blueprint correctly. This conversation took place after they had known each other at the Silverado for almost a year, so it was striking that they did not know that they were in the same union and had the same line of work. Backstage, they could make it clear to each other that they did care about something – and even were proud of their own craftsmanship – while frontstage, they had to appear disconnected from the wider world.

In the kitchen was another backstage tête-à-tête. "All Chuck and Charlene can talk about is 'locker room,'" Jody and Betsy were whispering to each other. Jan said Chuck was "sexist." Later, Carla also commented to me on

Chuck's offensiveness, by making a face when she mentioned his name in a list of people who were planning on going out dancing together later.[10] Before this, Betsy and I had a whispered conversation about her dog, who had just gone to the vet for a problem.

Enigmatic silence and its complement, the loud, strutting jokes, were necessary in the group context, but backstage, on both sides of the kitchen wall, all members could talk more plainly, about everyday life concerns, and discover that they did have something in common. This is not to say that conversations suddenly were politically charged or highly verbal, just that they were less violently racist and less effortfully casual.

When we all got back together again, the abusive jokes started right up again. At first, George tried to protect Suzanne. When someone joked about doing a striptease, Suzanne asked,

What's a striptease, George?
GEORGE: It's a kind of dance.
SUZANNE: OH! Let's have George do a striptease.
GEORGE [flustered]: Hush. You don't even know what one is.
SUZANNE: Yes I do. It's a kind of a dance. You just told me.

But after a while, even gentle George got in on the abusive teasing – she sat on his lap, and he said, "Are you gonna steal all the men here?" and then added, "Only kidding, Suzanne."

Why were the people who objected to the offensive jokes silent – or even eventually drawn into them? Silence was the only possible frontstage response to offensive conversation.

Practice vs. belief: the example of racism

Mounting a public objection to racist talk was impossible. Objecting to it would have required reference to a more solid system of meaning than participants were willing to impose on the situation. Not all country-westerners held racist "beliefs" (though to state it thus shows just how difficult it is to point to a thing out there called "a belief," and how unnecessarily static is the prevalent social research idea of measuring "beliefs" as objects). In fact, most were trying not to be racists. Betsy tried hard not to be "prejudiced," even in her private conversations. Jody had a Filipino daughter-in-law and often brought her adored, part-Filipino 4-year-old granddaughter to the Buffalo. She also had a black son-in-law, who did not come to her wedding at the club. Kim said, "It's awful about the race thing – Jody brought her son-in-law one time and he was just sweatin' the whole time. He barely dared get up." I overheard Jody saying to Kim, in a backstage conversation, that "it's a shame he can't come," about the African-American son-in-law. She passively sighed, "It's too bad it's like that. It shouldn't be like that."

But it was like that. And it was not up to her to change it, she assumed. She would not know where to start or why it would generally be a good thing on principle, since the son-in-law was not exactly yearning to attend Silverado dances anyway. So, Jody just continued in the group context to add to the volume of enigmatic silence.

The only responses to the fierce joking that could keep the fragile group intact were either to go along with the joking or to "not say nothin'," as Betsy labelled this mysterious silence. When I told Betsy what happened when I first met Fred, she thought my silent response to him was the only sensible one. Fred and I, I told her, had been waiting in line for roast beef at one of the Silverado Club events. Fred said he hated going to Newton, where he worked every day,

> I hate those little cotton pickers . . . Those black kids that push you around on the street – I can't stand to see them jiving down the street like that, like you don't belong, like they own the place. I just want to bring my horse whip and use it a few times!
>
> NINA [staring dumbfounded into the roast beef with gravy pan from which we were serving ourselves]: Oh, my!
>
> FRED: My horse knows what it means! Hohohoh!
>
> NINA: [more stares into the pan of cooked peas; silence]

When I reported this conversation to Betsy, she outlined some of the motives behind the not sayin' nothin' principle. She said that if he said that to her, "I would just not laugh, and maybe he would get the idea. Or maybe I would say, 'That's not funny, Fred. That's not something I want to hear.' "

She tried to explain it, saying that "maybe he just wanted to feel like he belonged, or maybe it's an attention-getting thing." I asked how it could be a way of belonging, saying, "How would he think he knew how I felt, when so many other people there disagreed with him?" Then she said again that "maybe it's an attention-getting thing. Like when I was in high school and my friends would always tease me about blacks because they knew I was friends with Dan [a black classmate]. I would punch them, joking – so, getting mad would just give them the attention they wanted."

A moment after making the joke about the horsewhip, Fred tried to shock me with a violent joke about animal rights protesters – all this within the first two minutes of my meeting him, before I even had had a chance to tell him I was a student from Newton. He was making it clear that he was not trying to win me over, was not going to let the presence of a "lady" cramp his style, but was going to say "whatever he damn pleased." It was a form of flirting.

He was straining hard to appear at ease, by saying something that he knew was "wrong." The precious few scholarly studies of everyday racism note this generally hyperbolic, rebellious quality of racist talk in everyday contexts. White youth in Britain claiming "Wogs smell like six month old shit," for example (Billig 1989), do not claim fully to believe their own bigotry, which they present in the form of "ferocious joking" (Sartre 1948). Racist joking is a way of violating norms that "everyone knows" are there, in a way that does not pin the speaker down. It is a way of asserting an identity that pretends to debunk the pious dominant discourse on race, but yet without requiring the speaker to take a serious alternative position.

The only response to Fred would have been to make another racist joke or make fun of Fred himself; to do the latter would be to do just what Fred wanted: give him affectionate-seeming attention.

Betsy had more to say about Fred's discourse: "So, maybe I would just laugh at Fred, because that's what you do when you first meet someone. 'Course, if I said, 'That's not funny,' he wouldn't talk to me for weeks – which, now that I think of it, would be no great loss, anyway!" Then she laughed. If the group prides itself on being like a community, and is so fragile and utterly voluntary, excluding someone would be a "great loss." She added she did not "care for him" for other reasons, anyway. For one, she referred to the time he tried to "force" her friend. Again, while someone else might call it "rape," and treat it as a moral, political, and legal problem, she did not. For her, it was a form of really bad manners, Fred's personal problem.

I said, "I thought maybe there was something I could have said," though really I could no more imagine than could Betsy how to counteract his humor without ending the conversation, and in fact, had done exactly what she would have done when I was standing in the roast beef and peas line.

She said, "What can you do? Whenever you get races together there's gonna be things going on. That's why I don't live in a city. I would never live in a city!"

Finally, she has presented the type of data that most social scientists observe: a belief. But notice how long it took her to mention it! The "belief" was not a very salient reason for avoiding challenging Fred. Since Betsy had never talked about it, she was not sure of another solution to the problem of racism, though she vaguely wished there were one. Her interactional reasons for her "not saying nothin'" were as important as any beliefs she stated. If people cannot converse about a problem, then it might appear inevitable, and then, if political problems seem inevitable, "not sayin' nothin'" makes sense; the "belief" is as much a result of the conversation (or lack of conversation) as its cause.

Other participants who would probably not appear "racist" in a survey, interview or other context, also engaged in racist joking. Erin, for example, joked when one member forgot George's name, "What's your name? What's yo' name? His name's Leroy? Yo, Leroy, yo' lookin' fo' some watermelon, Leroy?" One January 15, one of the first times Martin Luther King's birthday was celebrated as a holiday, there were four birthdays at the Silverado. A woman was at our table who did not fit in with this circle of friends – she usually sat with the two people of color who frequented the bar; she wore no make-up; had no perm; was thin and small. She added an unusual note of attention to the larger society:

> Martin Luther King's too. See [turning a giant smile to one of the birthday celebrators], he gave you a holiday.
>
> BETSY [snorting]: All's he did was make it so the banks were closed so we couldn't get any money.
>
> GEORGE: The man was a womanizer. He was a real playboy. He had dozens of mistresses.
>
> THE NAMELESS WOMAN [who kept to herself, so much so that the other people there did not even know her name, exclaiming agreeably]: Oh, I'm sure of that!

Even this woman ended up agreeing just to keep the tone right. Racism, like other political stances, happens in contexts. Many Buffaloes wanted to have un-racist attitudes, but did not know how to create contexts in which these attitudes could find a social form.

Observers of white racism and extreme conservatism usually examine groups with serious political programs, like extreme right-wing activists campaigning for "racial purity" (Aho 1991) or anti-abortion activists (Ginsberg 1989) or New Right women (Klatch 1987). But most groups do not inspire such loyalty and commitment, and extreme opinions are usually expressed more casually, based less on dogma and more on implicit desires to make jokes, look casual, shock listeners, or otherwise get along in everyday life settings. Country-westerners were more typical than extremists, in the loose, distant way they treated membership itself. And most of them were typical in their desire not to be racists. The fact that most whites have for so long not wanted to think of themselves as racists should not be lightly dismissed.[11] For at least half a century, most Americans have not wanted to think of themselves as racists (Myrdal 1944); most Buffaloes were no exceptions.

Observers of public life might think that the bottom line is the answer to the question "What do they believe?" But belief is not the only motor behind ways of talking about the wider world. People use racist jokes and other references to the political world to do something in interaction. Thus, the wider world entered the conversation in a backhanded way, in members' efforts to create a certain kind of interaction and present a certain kind of self, in practice.

Jokes about sexuality also brought in reference to the wider world in a backhanded way, in order to make the speaker appear irreverent, breaking rules about references to sex in mixed company and simultaneously making oneself appear unsanctimonious about anti-gay speech:

SUE: Are you going to the George Strait concert next week?
DOUG: Yeah, I like George Strait. Oh, I forgot [rolling eyes humorously]. I'm near Pacific City. Guess he's not very popular here [a joke on Pacific City's large gay population].

Social researchers usually ascribe anti-gay joking to deep psychological fears (Halle 1984, for example; LeMasters 1975), but here, the popularity of the jokes was just as much caused by participants' need to appear outrageous as it was by any inner preoccupations and fears. Like expressions of racism, the proliferation of anti-gay jokes was a result of interactional needs and assumptions about the nature of "frontstage," and not just an inner belief.[12]

Opinion leaders by default: the aversion to equivocation

Since there was little time for talk of any kind, just a few words made a big difference. The group atmosphere was directed by the few, mainly male, members who were most eager to look comfortably unrestrained, most energetically trying to make themselves look like fools before someone else did. The result was a group context which was more complacently awash in racist, violent talk than most participants would have preferred. Even though most members sometimes privately objected to these opinions, they sometimes ended up quoting the vocal members' opinions, for lack of anyone else to quote. Opinion leaders had to wax certain. Their opinions had to be expressible in one line and could not require explanation, because the point of taking them was to present a quick rejoinder, a snappy line, a sound-bite, to appear knowledgeable, not to slog through a reasoned discourse. Their certainty on all topics was never totally serious though, but, like racist joking, worked through grand, semi-joking hyperbole.[13]

For example, Jody told me in confidence that she thought that Joe, a friend of Doug's, was obnoxious and "crazy," and that "all's he ever talks about is the Marines. He takes a hat and says to his kids, 'This is a "cover," not a hat.' " But she did not discredit his opinions. After one get-together (Jody reported, "He flew a Marines flag over it, even though he was never even *in* the Marines!") she told me that Joe had said that "the Japanese are buying up all of California and making golf courses because they know that it will be an investment they can use to build houses on some day. California will be owned by the Japanese soon.'' Yet, a few days later, I overheard her repeating almost verbatim the same thing, minus the attribution to Joe. Joe could lead by default, not because he was so respected but because he talked so much and the other people talked so little. In a 1950s study of a Midwestern city, Elihu Katz and Paul Lazarsfeld (1956) found that many people arrived at their political and consumer opinions by looking to the opinions of relatively well-informed ''opinion leaders'' whom they personally knew and respected. The followers thought that their ''opinion leaders'' *should* be leaders – followers respected the leaders. Here, participants like Joe led opinions by default – not by being respected, but simply by repeating ideas out loud often enough. Even though the other people at the barbecue thought that Joe was ''out of line,'' they still squirreled away the things he said, storing them up against the famine of political talk and information.

Teasing

The absence of straightforward conversation left the ''normal'' fuzzy, left it unclear what could happen in the group context aside from teasing. It left most members not knowing basic facts about each other – what one another did for a living, whether they had ever been married, how old they were, what their last names were, for example. Country-westerners assumed that serious group conversation was the uncomfortable thing that unfortunately happened when the new boyfriend met the family, when George's short-term girlfriend lectured about her born-again Christianity, or when stuffy speech-makers got on a high horse.

Unlike the classical ideal of friendship, in which friends mutually ''raise'' each other, private people's ideal was to have fun outdoing each other's ''lowering,'' instead. One typical Sunday, the conversation flowed from one tease to another, strung together with long stretches of silence:

[from fieldnotes] A raffle made it easy not to talk much for about two hours – though it wasn't loud enough to prevent talk if we had wanted to. We teased Betsy and Ray for eating a lot. There were the teases directed at everyone, but especially at George. Then we made fun of Betsy some more for eating too much . . . Betsy whispered some private news to me about Doug . . . George wants to know why Kim and Sue are not dancing, which leads to a joke about whether they should dance together. There's another meeting at the Cattlebranders' next week. Jody says the costumes for the dance team cost ninety dollars, which she says is a lot. But Betsy says they include a slip and absolutely everything from head to foot. Boots are extra, though, says Jody. They have to be black boots; you can't wear your brown boots. George still doesn't know if he's gonna join or not. Betsy wants him to, and that's why she isn't really saying how expensive the outfits are – they really cost more. We made lots of jokes about this guy Tom who everyone thinks is cute: "Tom showed me a dance," and "Tom and Cathy are gonna start teaching their own class – that'll be fun to watch," and "Tom winked when he passed us on the dance floor."

Though this may seem to be quite a bit of conversation, remember that most of the day passed in silence. Teasing was the only kind of talk in which more than three people at a time engaged for more than a line or two of speech.

On another typical day, Jim and Jody laughed about whether an earring he found was his. A round of jokes about men who wear earrings followed. Then followed some jokes about what members' dogs eat and rounds of jokes about George's birthday and about the condom he was given as a joke gift: "He's so dumb, he doesn't even know what one is!" and jokes about the balloon he was given as a gift, whether he would get to dance with everyone because it was his birthday; jokes about who was going to pay for drinks.

To tease each other, people need a shared idea of what is suitable for teasing, so teasing might *seem* to be a reflection of deeply shared culture. Jokes about being dumb were by far the most frequent (followed by teases about being gay). At the barbecue in which George and Chuck had discovered that they both were carpenters, we joked about how dumb carpenters are. Chuck said he tried to teach George to plaster and he got covered from head to foot in the stuff. Charlene continued:

> George, for one, is so dumb, he loaded up the dishwasher and put his hat in, too, to wash it. He's so dumb it frightens me!
> SUZANNE [Charlene's 9-year-old daughter]: What's a carpenter?
> CHUCK: Uh. We uh. Build. Uh – buildings.
> CHARLENE [through her hoarse laugh]: Case in point!

Another time, George made fun of himself for living in the poor part of town; Doug made fun of George for having "grown up and still not knowing how to barbecue chicken right"; we all made fun of him for having a ratty, smelly dog. Betsy made fun of George for having so many cans of Spam in his cupboard, but even this joke stretched the limits of what members shared: Doug did not get the joke about Spam (that Spam is a particularly tacky canned thing to eat) and assumed it was a joke about eating out of cans in general, so he picked up where he thought Betsy had left off and joked about eating out of cans. We teased George for getting lead poisoning from cans, and then made more jokes about the relation between his dumbness and lead poisoning.

Participants hoped that teasing would make everyone comfortable. As Betsy remarked (just before the group started to disintegrate, with regulars coming less often), "It's just nice because everyone kids everyone else. I'm beginning to feel part of an 'in crowd' – not cliquish or anything, but you know what I mean.'' Members worried that speaking would reveal their lack of some obvious bit of common sense or common knowledge, but then teasing transformed that worry into a harmlessly amusing point of commonality. The point was to make it clear that one did not take oneself or the situation too seriously.

In a way, teasing did create a thin common ground, based on a common lack of pretentiousness. It revolved around members' supposedly stupid consumption habits, rather than, say, bad voting decisions or dumb political positions or unfounded religious preferences. But whether George ate Spam or drank coffee or used the right barbecue sauce was not something that deeply concerned fellow Buffaloes. Relentless teasing helped bolster members' belief that they were not smart enough to be good citizens, but that that did not matter.

Teasing closed the door on other kinds of conversation. Perhaps the mark of delightful, free conversation is that conversationalists never hammer away at any particular message, but just take joy in the artful process. Sociologist Georg Simmel makes this argument; and like Simmel's playfully unserious conversationalists, country-westerners lightly played in the flow of banter without trying to pound away at any particular message. No one at the country-western clubs except for those who insisted on "getting on a high horse" ever allowed the topic of conversation at the clubs to become significant in its own right. However, Simmel adds, sociability is an art that "feeds on a deep and loyal relation" to concrete reality. If it "cuts its ties with life" it becomes "a lifeless schematism which is even proud of its lifelessness" (1971: 56); vapid, precious, or boring.

The private people did refer to topics that someone else might define as tied to life, tied to the wider world: race, sexuality, and gender relations, war, work, and housing prices. But their teasing transformed anything anyone said into a purely personal statement about the individual speaker, not a statement about the world. It relentlessly refused to express attachment to the wider world; teasing let members keep the wider world at arm's length, secure only about their shared *dis*regard for the world. Perhaps if Jody, Betsy, George or Sue had heard Jim, Chuck, and Charlene make jokes about race and sex *in another context*, they would have reacted differently. But they assumed that the very fact that the conversation was happening in the context of the Silverado Club made it *by definition* ''not political.''

Topics in the news

This is not to say that publicly minded conversation always should be serious and solemn, or that jokes are always apolitical. Three times, I heard jokes that drew out the political and moral implications of the treatment of animals. Animal rights was an unusual issue; that and Charlene's promiscuity were the only two issues about which members expressed strong and fixed opinions. The other issue on which participants had a clear opinion was homosexuality, but their homophobia was not seen as an *opinion*, since it did not seriously occur to them that anyone could disagree.

Throughout this book, I define "publicly minded talk" very broadly, trying to draw out the implicit politics in everyday topics, rather than focusing only on topics that are debated in Congress or on the front pages of the newspaper. But if we turn for a moment to "politics" defined narrowly as "what's in the news," perhaps we can see why participants so rarely engaged in broader publicly minded conversation. I kept going back to the clubs night after night, weekend after weekend, hoping, since I was studying "political talk" (which I had initially defined quite narrowly), that I would hear some explicitly political talk this time, or this time. It kept not happening. With such a small number of instances of explicitly political conversation, the overwhelmingly obvious point was that members did not talk about politics, and the most obvious question was why and how not. In this chapter and the next, I have recounted *all* the group's explicitly "political" conversations I heard.

Those few times when members joked about the news, nobody responded, and the jokes fell into a silent void. Ray, a chunky man with a salt-and-pepper beard, was an exceptional character because he kept track of political affairs. At a Buffalo Club feed in 1989, he made a quick crack about Jesse Helms, a vocal arch-conservative member of Congress, and Helms' efforts to censor art. The response was total silence. I wondered if maybe everyone disagreed with him – but then, I knew that several had had abortions themselves, at the time when Helms was most famous for his condemnation of abortion. I tentatively guessed that they were silent because none knew who Helms was, and each feared that the others did.[14]

But I was not entirely sure of this interpretation until Betsy explained how silence worked to hide ignorance. I had asked if she had to read the newspaper in whose ad department she worked. "No, only for layout, to make sure the graphics are straight." The week before, her boss told her to ask one of the paper's advertisers whether his organization wanted to continue a longstanding ad, concerning voluntary aid to help the leftist Nicaraguan government of 1979–90, a few weeks after the leftists had lost an election. The elections had been on the front pages for quite a while, "and the advertiser said, 'Well, no, not since the election in Nicaragua,' and I just said 'Yeah, sure, OK,' as if I knew what they were talking about, even though I didn't."

I had puzzled endlessly over this vague political silence emanating from Buffaloes. Betsy provided a key:

I didn't know anything about it [the Nicaraguan election]. I've heard people say what they said, but I've also heard people say the opposite, that it was a good thing, and I don't know how to tell the difference. I don't even know enough to know what to believe. It all goes back to my bad memory. I just don't have a memory. That's why I can't get a better job, too. Other girls at work can remember all the different word processing programs, and I can't even remember one.

Though millions of our tax dollars had been spent on weapons aimed at overthrowing the leftist government, *most* Americans could not remember anything about it, even during the height of national controversy about the issue (ABC/*Washington Post*, 1987).

Others gave similar explanations of other silences. I had commented to Ray and George, on the day after the US invaded Panama in 1990, that I had just been listening to the radio news in the car. News of the invasion had interrupted prime time TV three nights in a row before this conversation, so this was not an obscure incident at the time. Ray had a detailed analysis of it (which I will discuss later). George, the ruddy construction worker, constantly interrupted, with unrelated comments. Later, I reported to Betsy,

Ray had this whole long analysis of the thing – I was surprised he said so much, because he's usually so quiet, but when I brought up Panama he really got into it. It was interesting.

BETSY [laughing]: Uh-oh, that's time to get up and do the Chantilly Cha-cha!

When offered an explanation, make a quick exit. I countered, in his defense, "No, it was interesting – I was just surprised, since he's usually so quiet."

She replied that the conversations she had with him were "all about fat – Ray especially likes to kid people. He teases me about how I'm always getting a second helping," and then she told a story about what he said to her the last time she piled food high on her plate. It did not occur to her that I might have been interested in Ray's analysis. In some other group, Ray's monologue could have been taken by other members as an easy opportunity to learn something, or argue, or tease him for his opinions.

Another time I heard reference to an issue in the news was Doug's one-line joke about a wealthy female tax evader, Leona Helmsley. And once, Betsy and Doug shot pointed jokes at each other over the issue of fur, at a theme park, when Betsy teased me for buying a rabbit skin. I reflexively made the requisite joke on her, "But you *eat cows* at McDonald's every day!"[15] Doug topped off my joke, adding, "That's right – environmentalists want for themselves but don't want anyone else to have anything." This was a coherent political debate, conducted in joking shorthand – the only one I heard at the clubs, not accidentally, about animals, the one topic about which both Betsy and Sue felt justified in having opinions.

And finally, for my inventory of references to issues in the news: George was a union member – though not a very active one – so when the waitress at the Silverado offered, ''Coors or Bud?'' he said, ''Coors, that's scab beer. I'll take a Bud,'' though several other people there were drinking Coors. No one said anything for that split second during which someone was supposed to interrupt or chime in with a teasing rejoinder, so he continued, in a self-mocking tone,

Me, ah like Bud. Gimmee a Bud. Boood.
KIM [laughing at how funnily he pronounced ''Bud'']: Bud. Sounds like Boood. Boood!

George would never dominate a discussion, never ''get on a high horse'' or ''soapbox''; he laughed along with Kim. The next week, coincidentally, the topic of Coors arose again. A man learning a new dance next to George was showing us his new giant silver Coors belt buckle. George politely did not say anything about his boycott of Coors. Instead, he nodded and smiled, complimenting the ornate metal buckle.

Avoidance of disagreement is only part of the story. George's position would have been difficult to sustain here because it was difficult to take a ''position'' on a landscape that was so unmarked. Taking a political stand means knowing where you are, literally ''standing'' there; but in this precarious reality, that was not easy. George was often the butt of jokes at the Buffalo. They called him a ''clown.'' But I used to like to imagine him in another time and another place, where he might have been less of a ''clown.'' Imagine George – with his plain jeans and shirt, plain face and plain shape, trim from work, not from aerobics – as a member of the Knights of Labor, for example, a strong US workers' movement of the late 1800s. The Knights fostered solidarity through informal community-based picnics, dances, and festivals, open to all,[16] and not just tedious, members-only, top-down meetings of the sort that George's union held. If George had been at a working-class dance festival instead of the Buffalo, he could have got into a playful argument over the belt buckle. Playful disagreement could have served an educational purpose in a playful form. Here, positions were taken passively, given by forces beyond the group; members continued to buy Coors without having discussed George's objection one way or another.

The high horse

Anyone who appeared to be taking a stand was ripe for a pruning down to size, and the pruning had to be a quip of no more than one or two lines.

Obvious attention-getting was a mistake, especially for women. At the Silverado one night, for example, Jim was in a particularly talkative mood. Pointing to a plump woman in a flamboyant miniskirt, he said to Jody and me, "She looks like she's standing on two stuffed sausages." Jody agreed. He continued, cheerily, "I'd like to take this beer bottle here and ram it up her ass." Jody "didn't say nothin'."

Trying to speak seriously was called "getting on a high horse"; that is, pedantically reciting facts and opinions in a monologue. People – again, women especially – who did this violated the rule of enforced joking and were not very popular. For example, according to Betsy, whenever Sue disagreed with a person, she "got on her high horse" and lectured about it. Sue was a pedantic collector of interesting tidbits of information, about everything from dog pedigrees to the meningitis epidemic in a town two hundred miles away. "Most people are like that," Betsy said. "They can't just have an opinion, but have to lecture on it," adding that maybe this lecturing explained why Sue had no boyfriends. Another person who "got on her high horse" (also called "getting on a soapbox") was the born-again Christian girlfriend George had for a few weeks. No one wanted to listen to her talk about her new-found faith, but rather than disagreeing with her or changing the subject, the members simply "didn't say nothin'." Getting on a high horse and appearing uncasual would ruin the atmosphere and the self-presentation.

Part 2: *Rituals of consumption*

Aside from dancing, what made this group into a body and not just a string of separate friendships were activities like lotteries, grab-bags, and raffles in which the whole group participated. These celebrations were "rituals," in the broadest sense – group activities that reflect and produce a group's sense of collective life. Rituals can offer windows into groups' self-understanding and their understanding of their place in the world. Emile Durkheim (1965 [1915]) says that rituals offer members a representation of the group, showing the group to itself in a concrete form, giving the group a name and a body. Rituals indirectly honor society itself, as the source of all meaning. Without direct acknowledgment and celebration of the bonds between people, sentiments of glad solidarity dry up, and a healthy society falls apart.

At these clubs, rituals were usually sponsored by institutions that were, one way or another, poised to sell something: the country-western culture and entertainment industry, the bars and liquor companies that courted country-westerners' business. Or they were sponsored by the national government that used the private people to sell its policies, by staging patriotic celebrations, and casting country-westerners as the cheering audience. The private people tried hard to keep their distance from such institutional life, in which employers, politicians, showmen, bartenders, priests, country-western fashion peddlers, the music industry, and entertainers all seemed poised to take advantage of the solitary private person.

What held their rituals together was the dismissive, distant stance toward the rituals, not the rituals' explicit messages – that is, what members shared was an unspoken relation to rituals more than an ideology. Members shared this practice more than they shared a theory. Constant raffles and country music at the clubs helped create the image of a rich common culture without actually creating a rich common culture. They kept us busy and let us spend time together without feeling a need to talk. The private people celebrated every holiday in exactly the same way: Valentine's Day, St. Patrick's Day, Halloween, July 4th, New Year's, Christmas: all called for raffles, grab-bags and lotteries. Local radio stations, the bar owner, beer companies, and other sponsors donated the raffle prizes for publicity. These rituals lasted over an hour, sometimes two. Buffaloes paid attention to them because they wanted to hear when their number was called, and to take note of the prizes other people won, so they did not carry on focused conversations during raffles. Though not a focus of direct attention for the full hour, the rituals nevertheless made the absence of conversation comfortable. Similarly, the loud music at both places was not too loud for other people at the bars to talk over non-stop, but it made conversational silence more comfortable.

It would have been embarrassing if anyone took the raffle gifts too seriously. One was supposed to strike a slightly ironic, slightly acquisitive, tongue-in-cheek pose – noticing whether the gifts were worth anything or not, accepting that most of the donations from the local country music radio station and beer companies were in the form of ads for themselves (such as T-shirts with a radio station call letters emblazoned across the front), comparing the price of the gift one put into the Christmas grab-bag with the price of the gift one took out. In my time there, I won: a glitter and cardboard tiara with a shamrock on it, a giant heart-shaped red plastic pin and matching earrings, a tie-tack with a Moose head on it (all present agreed it looked like Bullwinkle), a finless, eyeless stuffed goldfish from one of those 50¢, mechanical try-your-luck games at the entrance to the bar, two feed hats and two extra-extra-large T-shirts with radio station logos on them, another with a beer ad on it, a plastic creamer, sugar bowl and salt and pepper shaker set with Rudolph the Rednose Reindeer on them, and more. The comment upon opening the typical present was usually, "Oh. Lovely," though everyone was very attentive to the calling out of raffle numbers and hoped for a nice gift, which sometimes came. Some people won really good or valuable gifts in the raffles. None of us made enough money to buy these things, so, along with everyone else, I eagerly eyed the raffles and bought my share of tickets.

An exception was the Christmas celebration: each participant had to contribute a wrapped gift, and had to trust that the other participants had contributed an equally valuable wrapped gift. Really bad gifts were rare, and they caused members to whisper and speculate about who contributed them. One Christmas, I won a dirty ceramic Santa figurine, posed exactly like Michelangelo's Moses – the people at my table sized it up, saying it smelled bad and was stained, and that someone maybe got it last year at some other Christmas party. But usually, the gifts people contributed were pretty good – liquor, country music cassettes and CDs, handy gadgets. As individuals, most private people were honest; when participants agreed on a set of rules, they were trustworthy. The Christmas grab-bags worked because the teachers' tight choreography of the event offered a context in which members could trust each other; the rituals in turn may have helped build a sense of trust.[17] But members did not usually like rules – just once a year, as part of the Christmas spirit. None of the rituals during the rest of the year called upon members themselves to exchange gifts; commercial institutions provided the gifts "free," thus preempting the need for participants themselves to create group events.

All the group events were tongue-in-cheek rituals that celebrated consumption itself, through the constant barrage of trinkets and gifts. These rituals affirmed distance from convention, rules, tradition – distance from ritual itself. Though nobody was very attached to these rituals, they took up a large portion of the air-time at the country-western clubs. They were a mildly amusing diversion, but not anything that anyone really would admit to caring about. The point is, a distanced attitude marked a competent performance of the rituals. The meaning of those rituals is contained in that semi-caring, distracted, slightly acquisitive, playful, sometimes bored, humorous tone. That is, the *practice* of the rituals tells us something beyond their specific verbal content.

American holidays like Thanksgiving and the Fourth of July can embody a "civil religion," bringing Americans together, to look at who they are and celebrate their peoplehood (Bellah 1967). But, in practice, the recreation group's way of celebrating these – and all other – holidays revealed a "civil religion" whose object of worship was consumerism itself. Compare Buffaloes' celebrations to earlier incarnations of the same holidays. In Orange County, California, in the late 1880s for example, prominent local men would get up at July 4th celebrations to read the Declaration of Independence (Hansen and Ryan 1991). The whole town would attend a parade – a homemade affair – and the celebrations were like one in 1885 Anaheim, which celebrated marchers as "citizens" and members of civic organizations. The big display was a float of modestly clad girls representing the different states of the Union.

By the mid-1900s, the celebrations were depoliticized, private and commercial. The public focus, presented mainly in ads, was on the food and entertainment equipment individuals could buy for private celebrations held with family and friends. "Public festivity now seems to promote passivity and privatization, turning citizen into audience – an impassive consumer of images and products" (Hansen and Ryan 1991: 182). Nobody took the collective meanings seriously. In a bemused study of a 1970s working-class New Jersey suburb, David Halle says American celebrations like July 4th, Thanksgiving, and Halloween were dominated by blow-up turkeys, helium Mickey Mouses, papier mâché Kermit the Frogs, Popeyes, Snoopies, goblin witches, giraffes: symbols that nobody he met claimed to take seriously (1984: part 5; see also Caplow et al. 1982: chapter 10).[18] Not surprisingly, Halle found the same inattention that I found, which he attributes to the lack of serious political content in the rituals, saying "[n]ational rituals that are apoliticized and trivialized skirt serious views about politics and society at the cost of making themselves less pertinent to people's real concerns and interests. As a result they often have difficulty arousing enough interest to sustain them" (p. 286).

Instead of focusing on the explicit meanings that people attribute to holidays like July 4th, I am highlighting the everyday etiquette these holidays required – the attitudes that members are supposed to strike in relation to the rituals. Inattention is itself important; it embodies an orientation toward group life. That is, the rituals at the Buffalo were not just "trivial," as Halle says, but seriously showed participants precisely how to enact that distracted, slightly acquisitive, bored, humorous orientation toward group life.

Rituals without institutions

This pervasive distant stance posed a problem when the ritual was a wedding, since participants seriously wanted to have faith in private relationships. Many couples consecrated and celebrated weddings at the dance halls. The weddings showed the private people at their most communal moments, but the lack of explicitly shared public life made the affirmation even of private commitment difficult.

At these weddings, spectators kept asking each other questions like, "What part of the ceremony are we in now?" and "So, are they married yet, or are we waiting for something?" and "Have they cut the cake yet?" and "Is that a minister, or a justice of the peace, or . . . ?" One ceremony included the groom's singing along to a boom-box cassette of country music. Another ceremony was mostly inaudible because the built-in radio behind the Buffalo hall's stage kept blaring the local "'forties" station, with Frank Sinatra tunes and repeating ads for Ultra Slim-Fast Weight Loss Program. No one could figure out how to turn it off, so finally the wedding participants just talked louder than the radio, battling the ads.

Afterwards, the women would queasily question the power of these rituals, compulsively replaying in great detail the sing-along-with-the-boom-box-groom, which was called ''kind of weird,'' or the Ultra Slim-Fast vows. But they did not contrast the bar weddings with church weddings or any other more institutional[19] or intentionally experimental alternatives when they voiced their doubts. Buffaloes were not actively connected to religious institutions; some defined themselves in opposition to people who were more ''churchy,'' who never danced or drank. As Ray, who was sharing a house with his more pious brother, said sourly, ''My brother's and my lifestyles are real different.'' People who hold their weddings in the bars are clearly not strongly attached to churches. (There were other reasons for members' nervousness about the rituals, since most had been married before – a fact that silently contradicted the absolute, unequivocal, totally insistent country image of eternal romantic love. Members did not want to take those doubts seriously; they wanted to take the weddings seriously.)

Jody and Jim's wedding was at a country-western club. Jody carefully set up an arched trellis on the Silverado dance floor in front of the mirrors advertising Miller Lite and Coors Silver Bullet; she had carefully woven flowers into the trellis, to make it look like vines growing outdoors. Jody handmade decorations and party-favors: lace fans, cloth flower pins and bracelets, a little lace outfit for her granddaughter. Jody wrote all of the vows herself – the minister/celebrant had told her she had to. She had even gone to the library to find books to help her write it. This was not a flippantly conceived ceremony.

Finally, the short ceremony began – it was two hours late, because the bridesmaid and several other key helpers got lost on the way, having never been in Amargo before. A woman wearing a denim skirt and a bolo tie presided: ''Is she a minister?'' we asked each other. For all of Jody's care in writing the vows, the celebration leader/minister was nearly inaudible because she misused the house band's microphone, speaking into it as if the wedding were a show. I strained to listen. There were two themes: first, that women and men are different but equal: ''Woman was taken from Adam's rib, not from his head or his foot, so man and woman should be side-by-side, she at his side. But woman is made from man, not the other way around. Man and woman are not the same.'' Second, the country-western celebration leader, reading the vows written by Jody, said that men and women will inevitably argue. ''The only people that do not argue ever are dead ones. Living people will argue, and that is all right. Just that their arguments should

not be brought out into public, but will be just something they two will learn
to discuss.'' Jody was gently making the case that wanting to talk *is* legitimate, but still very special – something that is supposed to happen only
between lovers.

At the end of the vows, the bride and groom lit two candles from one
flame, and then a friend strummed the dignified superhit anthem whose
solemn refrain declares, ''You are the wind beneath my wings'' on the guitar,
accompanying a cassette. Afterwards, I said to Kim that the vows were really
nice. She said that she had not paid attention. Later, Betsy said she hadn't,
either. It was hard to pay attention to the minister/celebration leader, because
she read the vows in a sing-songing lilt that violated a normal speaking
cadence, clearly not expecting anyone to listen or analyze.

After the vows were exchanged and the candles lit, no one knew what to
do next. I heard whispers at my table. ''Is it over?'' ''I don't know – wait
and see what other people do.'' Some of the people at the bar were strangers
who had not known that there was going to be a wedding there. For a long
moment, we all sat waiting for the next thing to happen.

Finally, Jody, Jim, and the denim minister left, because there was another
mix-up, involving the wedding certificate. While they were gone, the rest of
the party first did not know what to do, then after a while, we got in line for
food. As soon as the newlyweds came back, the dancing began and it was a
normal night at the Silverado.

Betsy informed me later that a wedding has to proceed in a certain order.
If it does not, everyone will be confused and unhappy and not know when
to leave: first is the toast, then the bride cuts the cake, then is the Parents'
Dance where bride dances with groom's father and groom with bride's
mother, then the parents dance with each other and bride and groom with
each other, then party favors are given out, then the bride throws the bouquet,
then the groom throws the garter, then the wedding party throws rice, then
the bride and groom leave before anyone else does, preferably with some
unusual means of transportation, etc. ''It all has to happen in the right order.
If you don't do things in the right order, people won't know when to leave.''
If the ceremony does not go according to predetermined rules, country-
westerners at a wedding did not want to ask what is happening; they wanted
to know already and not need to ask.

Weddings are not as easy as they used to be, before writing one's own
vows and holding weddings outside of religious institutions became common.
Some highly verbal, deracinated people, like the activists I studied or the
people I knew in Newton, savored the discussion that went into inventing a
ritual together. The country people, in contrast, wanted to have more of a
tradition than they in fact had. Jody was left entirely to her own devices in

designing her ceremony – an anxiety-provoking prospect for anyone. The bride's and groom's parents were not there for the Parents' Dance; there is no ready-made traditional role for the bride's children or grandchildren. Jody herself was willing to experiment, but the group was not, as a group, so willing. If a wedding is not going to be firmly embedded in a tradition and a longstanding community, then members have to invent a tradition. But the private people wanted one to be there already; and it was not.

Several months after Jody's wedding, I told her that I thought her wedding vows were beautiful. She said no one else had said anything to her about it, nobody had praised her for the effort or creativity she put into composing the vows, or even mentioned the ceremony. She had no way of knowing whether or not it made sense to her friends. Instead of creating the "collective effervescence" and feelings of glad solidarity that Durkheim discussed, weddings like that often made participants nervous, tenuously drawing them into a celebration that underscored the tenuous texture of their community.

The desire, primarily on the part of women, for community was overridden by the desire, primarily on the part of men, for mandatory casualness. The only rituals intended for serious participation were the weddings, but the lighthearted, slippery footing of all the other rituals and conversation made it difficult for the weddings to achieve a solemnity worthy of a lifelong vow.

Coming together as consumers

Since the private people came together as consumers, instead of as volunteers or activists or church-members or people who made something together, they were especially open to being made into somebody's market. They expended lavish amounts of energy trying to avoid being "suckers," but they wanted the freedom that only consumers have, to select exactly what they wanted and not be encumbered with anything else. For example, when a group of us went to a local theme park, the Medieval Feste, our only remarks at the mock jousting pageant were "Oh, that must hurt a little," "Look, he really did fall off his horse," and, "Oh, that fence he's jumping over is just PVC tubing [that is, it is not heavy enough to hurt the horse when he tripped over it]," and "They're not really clubbing each other with those clubs." Country-westerners wanted to walk the tantalizing, tense line between being fooled and being too smart to be fooled.

Demystifying the hype was exciting in the context of total immersion in it. As critical theorists like Adorno and Horkheimer would say, if the mass culture audience wants to participate in the fun, it has to enjoy being "swindled." Complaining about prices, we bought funny hats, played a rigged game of chance (complaining that it was rigged), watched the pretend clubbing match and the pretend jousting match (remarking on the painlessness of the pretend falls), bought overpriced food. Of course, most Americans have gone to theme parks and have had this experience – the question is whether or not this is a group's typical context.

Their big question was usually "who was selling what to whom." When I asked Mark, one of the dance teachers, if I could put up a flyer asking to interview some members, his only question was whether or not I would be making money from the interviews. Since the answer was no, he said yes to my request.[20] Later, his teaching partner warned me that she had made an announcement last year about someone who wanted to interview members, and "people were offended." Why? "People thought it was inappropriate." Later, she too asked "where the money to pay people was coming from" (I offered interviewees in this group $15 compensation from my own pocket. At the same time that Debbie worried about my possible pecuniary motives, she offered to be interviewed, and refused the compensation herself, saying that she was doing it "as a friend," not for the money. As in other groups, we see participants assume that other people are more suspicious and self-interested than they themselves are). Several weeks later, she again said she was concerned that "someone" might think I was making money from the interview.

Still, most entertainment at the Silverado involved outside agents coming to the clubs to try to sell members something. For example, country-western fashion boutiques came to the clubs to stage "fashion shows," in which members themselves modeled the clothes. Women swirled around the dance floor, floating inside flowing, wafting billows of lace and flowery cotton; and then commented nervously afterwards that modeling the dresses made them want to buy them even though they were extremely expensive. Members sometimes yielded to the temptation to buy the wonderfully graceful hand-made garments.

Members relied on taste to say a great deal about themselves. Twice, Ray told me about the music he listened to as a teenager: the Beach Boys, Creedence Clearwater Revival and Santana. Now he listens to country. This capsule description of what he consumed was his succinct way of telling me who he was: not as old as he looked; used to like to party; once was into drugs and the counterculture; recently gone straight. The fact that he told me the same story twice says that this form of self-presentation was no accident. Commercial culture provided a set of reference points to a wider world, but it would be hard to trust commercial institutions and take attachment to them seriously.

Being sold something was what brought them together. When they said they were "country" people, it did not mean that they shared implicit country values or a country way of life. Members did not know what "values" or "beliefs" other members held. [21] A pervasive distant stance toward each other and the larger world, not just a set of beliefs and values, was what identified a person as a member of the group.

The political ritual nobody noticed

The thinness of wedding rituals made members nervous because they so much wanted the weddings to be real and solid. In contrast, members treated political ritual as something to avoid. Politics was yet another thing that someone was trying to sell them, and they were not buying. Their everyday attitudes towards their own participation in rituals and conversation made it hard for them to get a firm grip on the meanings of any collective representations: weddings, elections, states. Political institutions made money from the recreation group; but they also misrepresented[22] the group, both to the group itself and to the rest of society. The most striking example of this was a "Welcome Home the Troops" celebration, after the Persian Gulf war of 1991.

The Navy, the USO, a Pacific City-area country radio station, and Budweiser sponsored the celebration, in the rutted Silverado parking lot. Picnic furniture on loan from Redwood Deluxe, an outdoor furniture store whose name was prominently advertised on every bench and every table, provided the seating. Like a church steeple presiding above a medieval European village, a two-story-high blow-up vinyl Budweiser can loomed above the gathering, puffing in the bay breeze.

The radio station and the USO broadcast a medley of songs and a long monologue about the war, live from the parking lot "party." The first half-hour was a military history of the war; the second about "what it means to be an American." Most of the medley was supposed to be funny. The songs interspersed with the speech were all take-offs on pop songs: "The Leader of Iraq" sung to the 1960s pop tune "The Leader of the Pack" with bomb sounds instead of the gunning motor sound that is part of the original song (which was itself an ironic commentary on 1950s songs about bad greaser boys); and a long pretend ad about how to "get rid of roaches: make sure you face the spray in the right direction to avoid deaths by 'friendly fire' " (the large number of Americans who had been killed by their own troops' weapons had been in the news).

The radio medley matter-of-factly called the war "the Nintendo war" that was "live on TV." But unlike the politically minded media critics who originally made up these phrases, these radio station announcers were not using those phrases as ironic commentary on the distant, unreal treatment US reporters gave the war. This radio station was using the phrases simply to make the war sound more exciting, fun, funny, and marketable. It gave the announcers something to say about the war without having to say anything about why it happened or how it affected anyone or what the result was.

In keeping with this uncritical and unironic acceptance of the commercialization of the war, some party-goers wore T-shirts showing a map of the Middle East, with a plane zooming away from a bomb it had dropped, spelling ''It's Miller Time!'' in smoke in the sky.

Like Jody and Jim's wedding vows, the radio station's medley was hard to hear. It took Pam, a new member, about five minutes of listening to figure out what it was about. Almost everyone, including the people I knew, ignored the spectacle. They were there to have a party; it was an excuse to get together.

The second half of the show was about ''what it means to be an American.'' It started with a USO announcer saying that what she liked most about the troops was the names, listing an Italian one and a Polish one. The announcer's voice grew more and more shrill as members paid less and less attention. At my table, we were talking about Shannon's new dance outfit and how she was going to change clothes in time to be in the dance show, and asking each other to pass ketchup and mustard.

The USO announcer screeched even higher. ''Do you know how many Americans exercised our precious freedom to vote in the last presidential election??'' And Shannon exclaimed quite loudly, ''Who cares? I don't care how many people voted in the last election! When's the music coming on?'' Everyone at my picnic table smiled, but no one said anything.

Betsy came late, in the middle of a small round of applause for some young men who had just returned from Kuwait. People were applauding, so she did, too, willing to offer the benefit of the doubt and clap even when she did not know what she was applauding about. When I told her that the dance music was just about to start, and she had just missed a patriotic medley that was broadcast live from the party, she said, ''Oh, good, so I didn't miss nothing!'' I laughed, and she backtracked, saying, ''I only have so much patience for that stuff. I've heard it already.''

The USO-sponsored ritual continued, with a boy singing ''America, the Beautiful.'' We were all supposed to sing along, but no one did (this made a remarkable contrast to an anti-war demonstration I had attended a few weeks before, where I stood with some of the anti-toxics activists I studied. There, scores of people sang ''America, the Beautiful,'' in an effort to reclaim patriotism for dissenters). Then there was another sing-along to which no one sang along. We clapped a little from time to time at most of the designated places, without having heard the messages we were applauding. After one act, no one applauded, not because they disapproved, but because they were not listening. At that point, the USO announcer practically gave up, saying, "Oh, well, I guess you guys are doing something else."

But the ritual continued. The announcer awarded tiny bottles of champagne to some young men who had been in the war, including one who was wearing a Bart Simpson T-shirt that said, "I was there and it sucked." Jody straightened her granddaughter's dress, Shannon talked about the dance that the dance team was going to do, Ray asked if anyone noticed where the ketchup was.

The ritual continued, even when a drunk teenage Marine grabbed the mike from the USO announcer, live on the air. That momentarily got some attention. Pam said "Oh, she's handling it very well." Shannon said later that this drunk young man was whooping too loudly for the dancers to hear the music. Ray said his howls were scaring some of the little kids on the dance team. In other words, members were not particularly sympathetic toward this Marine, but they did not try to quiet him down, either. They were not going to treat him differently from anybody else. Their distanced attitude gave his action wide berth, thus making it possible.

The ritual continued, and suddenly the audience was transfixed: twenty local Asian children gave a demonstration of their Karate school's activities. Serious, with a pure mindfulness, the Karate students focused everyone's attention. "Uh-oh, we're surrounded," I heard, and "I hope those kids don't go out on the dance floor or I'm dead meat!" The audience had about two hundred whites and one black in it. The Asian children's parents stood among the cars in the parking lot, in a ring around the area that was roped off for the party. Whether it was the restrained violence, or the wonder of such focused attention in a usually distracted environment, or the racial frisson, the people at my table concentrated.

Concentration evaporated the moment the next act began: a nervous, thin 10-year-old white boy wearing a string tie and high cowboy boots, singing "I'm Proud to be an Okie from Muskogee" (whose most famous verse begins, "We don't smoke marijuana in Muskogee"). His wispy voice was off-key, and he got many words wrong. It was sadder for being right after the Karate school's spectacle, which had shown clearly that this audience was not simply constitutionally incapable of concentrating on anything. Recreation group participants had it in themselves to pay attention, but just usually did not.

Toward evening, we filtered indoors. Before the dancing began, we had some more patriotism. A bald World War II veteran was introduced as "someone from the USO who is going to say just a few words." He spoke for about one minute when Ray joked, "They're never gonna invite him to say 'just a few words' again. That's way more than a few!"

Betsy laughed, saying "I just want to dance!"

"That's what we're here for," Ray agreed. Another member agreed, with a chuckle.

An announcer told us that the event raised more than two thousand dollars for the USO, from the lunch ($3.00 for an "all-you-can eat All American barbecue"), and the raffle.

This USO raffle was not exempt from the distant, issue-free approach members had to the raffles. When Betsy and Pam saw how useless some of the Navy's raffle prizes were – day-glo fluorescent pink windshield wiper blades, brown denim jackets that one said "look like UPS drivers' uniforms" – one said to the other, "If I had known what the prizes were I never would have bought a ticket!" They did not treat it as a fundraiser specifically, but as a chance to win something.

Was buying raffle tickets a non-verbal sign of members' patriotism? Shriners, the Salvation Army, a child abuse prevention program, disease prevention societies, and other causes used the Silverado for fundraising raffles – I wondered if my overly verbal approach to life made me overlook country-westerners' quiet, low-key support of such vital causes. Maybe members really knew what they supported and just did not need to discuss it. So, I asked at various raffles what the raffle was supporting. No one ever knew, though everyone automatically bought many raffle tickets at the Silverado (Ray was an exception: he never bought raffle tickets, no matter what the cause. He was the only one who ever said anything about any of the charities: that money given to some charities never makes it to the people who need it, "like if you give money to a starving child, they funnel the money into a water project instead of buying food for the kid" – an odd objection to voice at the Silverado, where the tap water was undrinkable, forcing members to buy water. As usual, no one responded).

Jody, who had been sitting right across the picnic table from me during the entire radio medley, did not remember that it happened. She told me this later that night, when I referred to the medley about the war. She said, "What medley?" I described it. "I don't remember it. When was it? I must have been inside."

Spontaneous-seeming patriotism like this had appeared to explode in all of the country-western bars in the area. Much of this spontaneity was fabricated by bar owners, who used the war as a marketing device. The owners festooned their bandstands with flags and yellow ribbons, next to the omnipresent Confederate flag, hoping to attact patriots. The USO party raised more for Budweiser and the Silverado than for the military. The Silverado owner took part in a national letter-writing campaign to service members, that also ended up being profitable for the owner himself.

Still, these festivities alarmed people like the anti-toxics activists I studied. There were the drunk teenage Marines, like the one who grabbed the on-air microphone, hunky and sweating, carried away with enthusiasm. There were the "Saddam-ize Hussein" T-shirts. The anti-toxics activists, who opposed the war, watched the proliferation of ribbons and flags from afar, with alarm, taking the festoons as displays of political engagement and patriotism. Events like this looked to them like frightening, cheering crowds of crazed nationalists.

Yet, nobody at the Buffalo talked about the war, except as it impinged on travel plans. And there was no reason not to take part in activities that supported the troops unless the raffle prizes were not good. But that participation did not mean that they all actively believed in the rightness of the policies.

The distant way members treated the USO event was typical. They treated initiation into the National Order of Buffaloes similarly, as silly, boring, and possibly a waste of money. A few country-westerners were members of the Buffalo Club, but none ever referred to "being a Buffalo." Eight-page pamphlets at the door to the cigarette-smoke-filled liquor bar advertised the national Buffaloes' Just Say No to Drugs campaign, aimed at teenagers who used illegal drugs. The campaign was never mentioned. An elaborate initiation ceremony into the Loyal Brotherhood of Buffaloes had tried to impress members with the idea that being a Buffalo meant "enclosing each other in a circle of concern," and offered a long sermon which began, "Behold: The Buffalo. He forages on the prairie, taking only what he needs." The national Buffalo Club sponsored Buffalohaven, a home in the Midwest for orphaned children of Buffaloes; at 8:30 every night, members were supposed to turn toward Buffalohaven, facing an oil painting of two rosy children, and say, "Suffer the little children to come unto me." Needless to say, no one ever enacted that ritual. Members themselves did not consider symbols important. Buffaloes' distracted relation to this ritual illustrates my more general point: what marked membership in this group – what marks membership in any group – is not just a body of beliefs or inner psychological traits, but a way of relating to membership itself.

White country folk down home: implicit politics in practice

Private people did embrace one institution: the country-western culture industry. A huge body of research analyzes media's effects on individuals' ideas. In contrast, I would like, here, to illustrate another way of understanding media effects, that emphasizes media's effects on social interaction. Here in suburban Amargo, country themes enabled private suburban people to feel as if they shared more than they actually did.

In its earlier, less suburban incarnations, country music lyrics were about everything from parenthood to unemployment to poverty to prison life, as well as the more standard love-and-romance fare (Gregory 1989). Here, in Amargo, all the songs were about love, dancing – and nostalgia. The sprightly house band and teachers' cassettes played a repertoire of about twelve songs, played four or five times each, each evening. The house band's repertoire included "Pink Cadillac," "Redneck Girl," "Cherokee Fiddle," "Queen of Hearts," "The Wanderer," "Margaritaville," "All My Ex'es Live in Texas," and "Livin' on Tulsa Time," and a few other songs that were played less often.

To demonstrate the presence of media effects, researchers usually analyze the media's *content*, and then try to find out how much of that message sinks into audiences' *brains*. But a "content analysis" of these songs would simply not reveal the racial tinge of country music (the one exception at the Silverado was a song written by a local band that played at the club once, one evening when I was absent: a "country-western rap tune," which featured a fake black accent singing about "working 9–5 to get my crack" to the tune of Dolly Parton's "9–5"). Country music is considered, by culture industry leaders, to be for white suburbanites; yet, as industry leaders attest, racism in country music simply does not come from lyrics (Feiler 1996). This absence is remarkable, considering that everyone knew that "country" included this unspoken toleration of racism. Thus, one member announced that when he drove by a car that was blasting rap music, he would "blast Alabama back at them" (Alabama is the band whose hit recording at the time was "Down Home" quoted at the beginning of the chapter). An analysis of lyrics and beliefs would not tell us how groups use these artifacts, in practice. In this context, of deracinated suburbanites who shared very little, the irreverent attitude toward racism was one of the few things they shared. In another setting the lyrics would have a different meaning – regulars at a lesbian-run organic foods grocery store I stopped at in New York City, where a loop of Patsy Cline played, or in the coffee shop in a small town in Idaho where country music played, would probably have different relations to the music.

Here, Buffaloes picked up on the theme of nostalgia in country music, and leaned heavily on it to provide a sense of community. Ray (who, as we have heard, was opinionated in one-on-one conversation) talked in the group at length only about his grandparents' long-gone farm in what was now a wealthy suburb; how much it would be worth now if his grandparents had not sold it; how different the area was now, full of malls and highways. At least twice, he told us about his Idaho farmer relatives, including precise details of farm living, such as what time his relatives eat breakfast and what animals they have and what the animals eat; and all about bringing his children to visit the farm, where life was healthier, his chubby daughter lost weight, and people were nicer. It was considered a problem that "out in the country is going further and further out these days," as Doug, who grew up in Los Angeles, put it. They spoke openly about the fact that even suburban homes were becoming too expensive for them, but never talked about any solutions except moving even farther out.

While members liked to dream of an era when people could rely on each other and mind each other's business, they did not try to make the dream a reality. In fact, they were so extremely unwilling to interfere in each other's affairs, they did not consider doing so even when someone was clearly in danger. When a group of them let George drive home roaring drunk one night, Sue – the one who tended to "get on a high horse" – lectured Betsy and Jody about it in a whispered backstage conversation. But Betsy and Jody insisted that it was none of anyone's business to tell George what to do, that he was an adult and could do what he wanted. An even more worrying instance of this hands-off approach came at the end of that barbecue in which Suzanne, the 9-year-old with big freckles, was the target of jokes about her underwear and striptease dancing. Everyone saw her clinging embarrassingly to me when I tried to leave, saying, "When are you coming back? Will you come to my birthday? Why are you leaving? We have a sleeping bag here, upstairs. Please stay, please stay, *please*!" She begged me for my phone number. She begged her mom not to leave her alone at home that night – to take her to the bar. I was worried about her. "Isn't there anything we could do about Suzanne? I feel sorry for her, having such a weird mom," I wondered. Kim shrugged, "But what are you gonna do?" A few months later, her mother disappeared with her, and no one knew where they went.

The nostalgic image of community offered a warm feeling of a cozy, shared past without forcing us to mind each other's business in the present. A special, archaic language for "talking nostalgia" marked it off from real life with a sprinkling of phrases like "these days," and "nowadays," and words that implied that we all share a past that had, once upon a time, been different. In practice, nostalgia made country-westerners able to feel "together" without having to talk. Nostalgia offered an atmosphere of shared community and a feeling of having a shared past without requiring members to create a shared present.

Thus, nostalgia was more than just an inner belief. It made a certain kind of interaction, a civic practice, possible, by helping to maintain Buffaloes' non-committal, non-verbal style of interaction. Country-western culture gave private suburbanites an attitude, a "genre" (Bakhtin 1981), not just a set of particular beliefs, not just an abstract "message" or "ideology"; this commercial culture helped members create a relationship toward group life and membership itself (and, as is the case with most dance music, it was impossible to understand most lyrics, anyway).

Certainly, some audiences actively filter mass culture through their own lively subcultures; for example, Israeli Arabs read "Dallas" as a moral lesson about how corrupt Americans are (Katz and Liebes 1990; see also Gans 1962). But Buffaloes' shared culture *was* commercial culture; it did not preexist commercial messages.[23]

Many audiences have managed to come together under the auspices of commercial culture, and to go on, to create a more active face-to-face culture. For example, punk rockers in the 1970s twisted the meanings of mass cultural objects into emblems of resistance to the boring dominant culture: safety pins, Vaseline, Clairol, even suits, ties, white shirts and short hair became "symbolically 'repossessed' in everyday life, and endowed with implicitly oppositional meanings" (Hebdige 1979: 16). Punks showed that they themselves, not the commodities, were in control of meaning-making. For this approach, commercial culture is no obstacle to creativity; audience members become themselves *through* the media, imaginatively using media fragments to fashion identities for themselves (Fiske 1987; Hebdige 1979; Schwichtenberg 1993; Radway 1984).

But the private people did not *want* to interpret mass-produced images or resist them or combine them in outlandish ways, as Hebdige's punks did. Country-westerners did not *want* to revel in disjointedness. They did not want to be postmodern, or even modern; they wanted a stable set of taken-for-granted relationships, a shared, taken-for-granted sense of how to make a joke or how to tell when someone is being honest. They did not want to "resist." They wanted coherent, ready-made tradition – a whole, not fragments. They wanted community. They wanted to go home. And then – only then – they wanted to resist. Instead of coming to terms with their commercial roots, country-westerners imagined that they were rebelling against a home that is no longer there and never was.

Many moral philosophers share the private people's nostalgia for wholeness and community.[24] These philosophers ask us to participate actively in traditional, longstanding communities and religions; but for many contemporary Americans, joining a church or a traditional community would feel just as artificial as joining a cat lovers' club or country-western dance team. Paging through the phone book, why pick one church rather than another? It all starts to feel like shopping.

Instead of mourning for an imagined "down home" tradition, we should focus on how people could start where they are now, to create the kind of community that could make conversation – publicly minded and other kinds – possible. That kind of community would come to terms with its modern, "imagined," "invented," maybe even commercial roots. Consumption, playful joking and commercial culture have long marked the sociable public sphere. Surely, this lighthearted drinking, dancing, eating, playing, flirting, loud public has some potential for public-spirited conversation; the question is what can block this potential.

Everyone's a rebel in the simulated community: or what's so great about "subversion"?

Were critical theorists like Horkheimer and Adorno right? Does snide, permanent defensive ironic disengagement from all institutions corrode all human bonds, leaving nothing but commerce holding people together, as those theorists say? Is humor[25] a numbing agent, an anesthetic, a method of cutting jokers down so that they can fit inside their cramped lives instead of changing them? Were the private people simply plugged-in individually as monads into dominant meanings? Were they powerless in the face of the culture industry – does commercially simulated community become a dangerous substitute for face-to-face interaction?[26] It might seem obvious that the answer is an unequivocal yes: in the country-western groups, the manufactured image of community seized the possibly political desire for community and transformed it into rituals of irony, disconnection, and hatred. The image of community made palatable their fierce disengagement from stable institutions, their scattered sense of togetherness, their buyer–seller relationship to the larger world. Buffaloes were unsure of whether or not they shared anything beyond a conceptual cupboard full of Jell-O™ and Kraft™ Mini-Marshmallows.

But it took a great deal of effort and interaction for members of this "laughing audience" to remain isolated and disconnected from each other and the wider world, after having driven so far to meet and worked so hard to establish a non-verbal sense of togetherness. There was some reason, beyond being passively plugged-in, that the private people avoided public-spirited conversation. A group culture comes to life between people, not just inside them.[27] Country-westerners joked to give each other space, to avoid imposing order or getting on a high horse, or because they felt they had no other options for interaction. And when the constraint to appear casual was gone and they were backstage, seriousness burst forth. Critical theorists missed the mark when they focused only on individual psychology – examining the deeply psychological bases of "the authoritarian personality," start-

ing even before potty training: the public sphere and its problems are missing
from this overly psychological analysis. At these clubs, obstructed communication was a matter of civic practices, etiquette, not just individual, psychological barriers. The group's definition of "frontstage" made publicly spirited conversation seem out of place. And the constant frontstage joking about
race and sex, the half-hearted rituals, and the simulated community required
and reinforced Buffaloes' distracted, distant, hands-off relationship toward
membership itself.

Their imperviousness to ritual, institution, and meaning resembles just
what scholars from Nietzche to Goffman applaud.[28] For these scholars,
humanity's best hope lies in laughing at the tedious efforts of the systematiz-
ers, rule-followers, and upholders of good manners. While the serious mode
of interaction enforces a single interpretation of the world, joking is liberatory
because it keeps more than one version of reality in play at a time, lets all the
alternative, repressed realities flower, turns the tables on dominant meaning
systems. For this approach, laughter offers subversive liberation from what
these theorists call the "univocal" appearance of naturalness of our social
world (see, e.g., Baudrillard 1981: chapter 9; Bakhtin 1981). Such theory
assumes that what is shared is oppressive. Buffaloes, like many Americans,
agreed with that sentiment, assuming that humans' natural state is unsocial,
that any coherent meaning system pinches individuals' naturally sprawling,
expansive, unformed experiences, and that humor breaks through the crust of
dominant meaning (Fry 1963; Douglas 1975; Scott 1985, 1990; Goffman
1959, for some examples).

The problem with lauding "resistance" is that at the country-western
clubs, it meant disorientation, racist jokes, dogs trained to bite blacks,
unsatisfying weddings, and face-to-face silence. Jokes invoked a common-
sense racism, sexism, and feeling of being someone's market; but resistance
to the dominant pieties surrounding race made the group more violent and
uninclusive than the sum of its individual members. When the group's focus
is only on reversing and resisting, common meanings must come from elsewhere, unquestioned. When trying so hard to appear unconstrained, participants needed common reference points, common rules, so that they could
know how to appear to break them. These had to come from outside of the
group context, when they came at all, and were not examined by the group.
The effort to avoid constraint relied on members second-guessing what meanings they shared with the others. Common meanings had to slide surrep-
titiously into the interaction, so that members could have something *against
which* to feel rebellious. Without the standard, common meanings ascribed
to racist and scatological jokes, for example, this "rebellion" would have
been unintelligible.

This big "No" easily becomes a big "Yes." This political etiquette, the practical stance, is exactly the relation to politics that politicians count on when they blame all of our problems on "politics." It is just what right-wing politicians rely on when they strengthen giant bureaucratic corporations, lengthen the work-week in the name of global competitiveness, and otherwise advocate policies that would make a real rebel shudder. In the officials' new anti-politics, politicians all want to position themselves as "political outsiders," and the private people's "resistance" resonates with politicians' adamant insistence that political debate is a waste of time. In fact, the big loud "No" that these groups shout *is* the dominant way of relating to politics. This anti-institutional sentiment has become mainstream. In the 1996 election, candidate Dole claimed not even to have read his party's platform! Everyone wants to appear anti-politics, be a rebel, to proclaim that politics and talk are wastes of time.[29]

The idea that aversion to coherent meaning is subversive boils down to a very unsocial, individualistic, and nasty image of humanity. Goffman's backstage "belching and humming" is a sign of freedom only if one imagines that people are most free when least interactive. Making racist jokes is a sign of freedom only if one imagines that people are most free when most mean. Here, appearing "free" entangled participants even more deeply in dominant meanings without offering a way to change them. The private people still relied on the traditional American ideal of a real, authentic, inner Lone Ranger who stands up against the group. This is not "smashing all codes," as Baudrillard would like – it is replaying the same, tired old story; these "radical" theorists end up agreeing with Buffaloes, that liberation must be an entirely private, internal affair, conducted in opposition to group life.

This type of theorizing developed as an antidote to critical theorists' humorless gloom, which left no real hope, left nothing to do for those wishing for social change but to wait for a new era to blow in, somehow, despite the masses of passive "monads." The image of the subversive "nomad" offers cheer for the irrepressible creativity of "the people" in the face of repetitive and mindless commercial culture. The problem is that this idea assumes that there is a constricting, dominant order of meaning in place, and that it is always in need of subversion. Joking can be subversive if it undermines a stifling organization. In a traditional society or an oppressively rule-bound bureaucracy, jarring the frames is perhaps a form of rebellion. But at the country-western clubs, the atmosphere was the opposite of stifling. In an eyeless suburb like Amargo, the problem is that there is not enough common ground, rather than too much. Perhaps passive political subjects were comfortable in traditional societies, where they could quietly go about their business without feeling lost because tradition was already built into the very fabric of everyday life, giving it unspoken meaning. But when the figure presiding over the gathering is a two-story-high vinyl Budweiser can instead of a medieval church steeple, membership feels less secure, and establishing solid common ground in a scattered suburbia requires more talk. Participants wanted to get together as a group, but the only way they could do it was under the auspices of the giant, looming Bud.

This group seems to represent the picture of apathy; but that image took interactional work to produce. Political resistance and disengagement is not any more natural than involvement – mandatory irreverence and disconnection can be stifling and painfully tight, too. Buffaloes could not accomplish what they ambivalently set as their own project; lighthearted, easy, recreational conversation was too difficult when there was no trustworthy larger world to resonate with the smaller, private one. Because there was so little that members shared, or wanted to share, except for their very personal, intimate lives, establishing common ground in the group context was difficult. This is a step in the cycle of political evaporation: Buffaloes could barely carry on conversations together, and when they did, the conversation silenced all but the most vehemently irreverent, the most eager to express political disconnection and hatred. Most Buffaloes' ambivalent craving for community – for contact with a world that might be wider than their separate, individual friends – was a precious emotional, political resource, lost to the common good.

5

Creating ignorance and memorizing facts: how Buffaloes understood politics

Since the "private people" at the country-western clubs so rarely talked politics at the clubs – where they spent nearly all of their free time – members had little or no companionship in developing methods for analyzing politics. How do people like the Buffaloes, who had so little opportunity to talk politics, ever learn to think about politics? Interviewing them showed me just how risky and strange it was for most members to talk politics. This chapter reports on ten interviews and backstage political conversations with country-westerners. What most overwhelmed me in the interviews with this group was that their political worries, though often strong, were far-flung, even eccentric, not overlapping with other members' concerns. For example, Charlene had been so worried about nuclear war in the early 1980s, she read a book about how to grow potatoes in underground caves and live in the Yukon, "because of wind patterns making it a place fallout wouldn't land"; another member devoted a large portion of our interview to his worry that we receive radioactive rays from light bulbs and toasters. Another "would fear for [her] health" if she were to become politically involved, giving as an example a popular docudrama about whistleblower Karen Silkwood, killed by the nuclear power company whose crimes she exposed. These varied worries almost never made it to everyday conversation. Country-westerners were worried – sometimes devoured by worries – but they did not talk about their concerns, and so experienced them as purely unusual, personal fears that demanded purely personal strategies to vanquish.

They experienced the world of politics, in contrast, as an inert, distant, impersonal realm, a boring and scary jumble of facts that did not really touch life. Buffaloes just could not get a handle on all the millions of facts they thought they needed to know if they were to be good citizens; they had no framework for sorting through the facts or finding patterns, no one upon whom they could rely in thinking through their own opinions, no place to figure out how all the facts fitted together.

Buffaloes were private, not public people; they *wanted* to believe that the separation between politics and life was fine – that people should leave institutions alone and should be left alone by them. But they were not entirely comfortable with this privatism. While many social scientists say that Americans are ignorant about politics because they simply do not care and simply prefer to leave the wider world in the hands of experts, this case of the Buffaloes shows, once again, that what looks like apathetic "ignorance" is actually much more complex than that. Buffaloes knew many, many technical facts, but just had no way of grasping them all, no analysis.

The very private and very technical, fact-oriented approach go hand in hand – both ignore the interactive nature of politics, making political discussion seem superfluous. Their approach echoes the common-sense idea that politics happens inside the person or outside in the world of facts, but that nothing important happens in *between* regular citizens, in dialogue.

In interviews, no Buffalo referred to political conversations she or he had had with other people – except one, who referred to a conversation she had had with her mother ten years before. Without political conversation, analysis was impossible, and the world of politics seemed to be a collection of spare parts that did not fit together and was probably best avoided altogether.

"It's a shame"

Country-westerners labeled political problems inevitable, "a shame," and considered it best not to focus on them; anyone who did was considered a fool. One black, rainy night as I was about to get out of my car in the frightening Buffalo parking lot, I saw a skinny teenager smash the window of a pick-up truck, take a big, heavy-looking toolbox, and try to climb over the parking lot fence with it. He struggled a while to heave it over the tall chain-link fence, then sat down on the broken glass and litter next to the fence and started to cry. I sat there in my car a long time, trying to decide what to do: go into the Buffalo and risk setting a lynch mob on the young man – who looked Asian or Latino from afar – or ruining his life by sending him to jail? Counsel the teenager to go home before he got in trouble? What if he had a gun? If he's so afraid, maybe he'd use it, and my effort would end with me dead and him in jail forever. Finally, I just drove off in the greasy rain, and went to the Silverado. When I got there, I was unsettled and told Jody the story, without all of the equivocations, asking what she thought I should have done.

Without any deliberation, she said that I did the best thing. "It's best not to get involved,'' she stated firmly. Then I tried to bring out some of my equivocations, but she just gave me a reassuring, slightly pitying smile again, "No, you did the right thing."

More problems seemed inevitable to them than to me. Most problems were called inevitable facts of life – ''a shame,'' ''too bad,'' but not things that regular people could change – that is, not political, or even moral, just natural. For example, they recognized that everyone cannot live out in the country, but their desire to do so seemed inevitable to them: *"Of course* you don't want to live in a place that shares walls with someone else's house if you can help it,'' Betsy said, referring to her apartment. She had actually once gone to a city council meeting to lobby to keep some open spaces and horse trails, but never matched up that desire with her desire to live on a big lot: both were natural. In this way, country-westerners inadvertently reassured each other that there was nothing they could do to change things.

If social problems are simply out of regular people's control, talking will not help solve them, and must just be ''complaining,'' like complaining about the weather, as in Mark Twain's quip ''everyone complains about the weather but no one does anything about it.'' ''I don't let it bother me,'' and ''It's a shame'': I heard these refrains used to describe demeaning, low-paid work, the Persian Gulf war, racism, and urban sprawl. And the refrain ended the conversation. The best approach to such inevitable problems was silence.

Betsy's housemate was not a club attendee. The fact that she talked about the Gulf War was one of the many manifestations of her being from another, more socially engaged milieu altogether, one of the many social differences that led her to move out in frustration, after having lived there only three months. She was around the house one day when the TV had an ad for the upcoming newscast. The housemate said, ''There's gonna be a war. I know it,'' and Betsy and Doug ''didn't say nothing.'' Later, on the phone, Betsy told me that she was getting sick of her housemate.

About once a week since about October she's been moping and complaining and saying, ''There's gonna be a war. There's gonna be a war [said in a voice of mock dread, as if Betsy was imagining her housemate as a cartoon image of a bearded man wearing sandals and a robe, holding a sign saying, 'The End is Near'].'' But I say, ''OK, so there's gonna be a war. There's no point worrying about it. It's gonna happen and you're not gonna *do* anything about it by worrying about it every week [not emphasizing 'you' here, which would have made this statement into an implicit criticism, but saying you as a substitute for 'a person']. I mean, if it's gonna happen, it's gonna happen, so I don't want to hear you complaining.''

I said, ''There's no point worrying – *unless* you can do something about it.'' I was thinking of this as a question, as another way of asking if we could do something about it.

But she took it exactly as a statement, and agreed, "Exactly!" She continued matter-of-factly, "I'm not gonna do anything." While on the topic of Middle East conflict, she asked, "Did you see that movie last night on TV? About the hostages in Lebanon?" She described the movie; her point was that she knew the person who did the hairstyling for the cast.

Country-westerners rarely mentioned problems that were "a shame" in their group conversations; there would be no reason to do so. When Jim, Jody's boyfriend, got a concussion and whiplash when something fell out of a motor he was fixing at work, he grinned, "You know, Workman's Comp don't pay nothin'." Fred nodded silently, and that was the end of that topic. The fact that Jim was pale evoked concern, but the cause of his paleness was totally irrelevant, since there was nothing private people could do about Workers' Comp or working conditions. He might just as well have been sick with flu. It was unusual that Jim even mentioned Workman's Comp. Saying it did not pay enough was a simple statement of fact, like saying that it is snowing outside. But the silence did not indicate a lack of sympathy. Later, Jody told us again that Jim had been hit in the head at work, and again no one said anything, except that various people noted sympathetically, then and throughout the night, that Jim could not walk straight and was pale. "Look at him. He doesn't look too good."

Most often, the joking problems were about "ex'es," and everyone's ex was bad in a different way, so problems with ex'es were taken as purely personal issues. No one once extended the personal problem of "ex'es" to any broader, shared concerns, like child support or women's low pay – issues that feminists and even some legislatures were discussing at the time. "I don't let it bother me" was the best approach for a range of social ills.

Erin, a waitress in a mall, watched new young men with degrees get promotions while she kept selling muffins and malts. In some cultures, looking on the bright side would mean joining an organization, like a union, to make it so that one job was enough, instead of the three that Erin's boyfriend had. But, here, since no such organizations were visible on their horizon, the only optimistic thing to do was to not let the problems bother them.

Who is "the public"? People who think they can make a difference are fools

Political silence was based on, and helped reproduce, Buffaloes' ideas of citizenship: if the only people qualified to hold opinions are those who "have all the facts," then politics is not our responsibility. Politics is something that other people do, but not us.

NINA [in an interview]: Do you think there would be something you could do about nuclear weapons?

MARK [a military engineer]: Nope. Can't do nothing about nuclear weapons. There's just. No. Not a, not a regular person. Because. The reason being it's all just government-ran. The government feeds the terrorist and the terrorist feeds back to some other terrorist and stuff. Ain't nothing you can do about stopping the weapons. It all depends on the government. Sure, people can do their anti-nuclear protests, but a lot of good it's been doing. It's never done any good at all, as far as I've seen.

Buffaloes who did more than profess complete ignorance about activism said something like, "Well, I'm not gonna go out there and carry a sign!" They equated citizen involvement in toxics, disarmament, and foreign policy with "protesting," which meant "carrying a sign," "standing out in a parking lot with a sign," "wearing sandals": making a fool of oneself, ineffectually standing out in the middle of nowhere. People who think they can have an effect on politics are fools, who are puffing themselves up – and that would seriously violate country-westerners' political etiquette.

In interviews, I asked what "the public could do" about a range of political problems. After conducting several interviews with Buffaloes, I realized that when I said "the public," they thought I was referring to *someone else*, not themselves! Country-westerners did not consider themselves to be members of "the public." The public lives elsewhere. Mark, a white-collar civilian military worker, for example, thought "the public" lived in Pacific City. A local refinery kept having spills and fires, even after a giant spill the year before had made headlines. I asked why he thought the public did not stop the company from polluting.

MARK: Well, apparently, there was not enough public outcry. Pacific City should've done something about it when that happened.

NINA: Yeah. Like what?

MARK: Those [inaudible] people are always doing things.

NINA: The which people?

MARK: Pacific City? They're always doing marches and stuff to stop this and that.

The public exists elsewhere, not in our town, where regular people live. Many other interviewees talked of "the public" as if it did not include themselves, speaking of the public in the third person – "they." Another private person misunderstood the standard survey question I asked – "Are you a member of any of the following types of groups [followed by a list of various types of citizens' groups]? Do you play an active role in the organizations and generally go to meetings?''[1] He thought I was asking whether he received literature from such groups, or gave money, but it did not cross his mind that I was asking whether he himself attended meetings.

Several said that if they really felt strongly about an issue, they would get involved by trying to get elected to a government position. The idea that regular citizens can have a say in their capacity as regular citizens did not come to mind when I asked what ''the public'' could do about an issue.

Technical knowledge and the authority to speak: how many protesters does it take to screw in a light bulb?

The purpose of ''the public's'' existence was not clear to most country-westerners. Political questions, they assumed, can and should be decided by lining up the right technical facts – citizens can challenge the *technical means* of reaching political goals, but it did not occur to most of them that citizens can question the goals themselves.

Ken, for example, described protesters who were against a plan to store nuclear weapons, saying that the government's plan, of driving the weapons around in railroad cars, was the only realistic one, because it was the only one that could keep the weapons hidden; protesters were simply not well informed, because they did not have a better plan for storing nuclear weapons. Did the protesters say anything about the *goal* of storing nuclear weapons, or did they just worry that the weapons might blow up in their backyards? From Ken's discussion, a listener would not know that the protesters criticized both the goal of storing nuclear weapons and the means of reaching the goal. Questioning the *techniques* requires becoming an expert in nuclear physics; questioning the *goals* requires being able to reason about broad social and moral issues. Country-westerners discounted this second form of political reasoning, so they assumed that citizens would always be at a disadvantage when trying to participate in political affairs.

Another example of this focus on technical issues comes from private people who ventured an opinion on a protester who had recently been run over by a truck at the local weapons depot, during a sit-in protesting arms shipments to the Third World. His arm was severed and his head seriously injured. Private people laughed at him for his ignorance – he should have known that an eighteen-wheel truck traveling at full speed in potentially slippery conditions simply cannot stop that easily. What could this protester, Augie Bradley, know about military policies? He did not even know the exact destination of that particular truckload of weapons!

BRIAN [in an interview] [very fast]: *All he saw* was arms being shipped to South America. I don't know if he – to me, he had no knowledge or background of where it was doing [*sic*], where it was going, what it was doing, who it was going to, what it was being used *for*, except that something was going on down there. But as for the *details*, for a man to lose his right arm over something he didn't know all the inside about really amazes me. I didn't think – he didn't seem to know everything that was going on. I mean, [laughs] I saw maybe two or three interviews in *Time* magazine and – later on he found more information about it. I'm not saying the man was wrong by protesting about it. It was going probably *to* maybe a bad source, but *he didn't have all the background on what all maybe was going on.* When they interviewed him in the news and a couple of guys said, ''Well, it's not going there, it's doing this, this and this.'' . . . You lose your arm and you don't even know what the hell is going on, well, ''Sorry.'' The guy's got a Baggie for a brain.

Brian faults Bradley for not knowing where that specific truckload of weapons was headed. Very, very rapidly and parenthetically, he added that ''probably,'' ''maybe'' Bradley was not in the wrong, but the main current of his analysis was about knowledge (''Did Bradley have all the facts at hand?''), not about power, as it was with the volunteers (''Could Bradley realistically do anything about the policy, and if not, why was he stirring up ineffectual concern?''), or about morality, as it was with the activists (''Was Bradley right to try to block arms shipments?''). *Not one country-westerner mentioned whether the protester's position was right or wrong.* And none mentioned whether Bradley knew anything about US arms shipment *policy* – just whether he knew about *that particular truck's* stopping capacity and its specific payload.

Brian here, along with many others, shows how much ''in the know'' he himself is. The naive dupes out there protesting sophomorically believe that they can know everything, but Brian knows more because *he* knows that *they* are ignorant (Reisman [1950] describes this kind of citizen as an ''inside dopester,'' someone who always thinks he has the inside scoop). Similarly, on the issue of toxics, country-westerners said that there is no way for regular citizens to know whether they are safe or not, and many added that protesters are silly for thinking there is. Along with nearly all others, Brian did not say whether or not he thought it was right that citizens are kept so ignorant. And like the others, he discussed activists' tactics as effective or ineffective, but did not discuss policies as ''right'' or ''wrong,'' ''good'' or ''bad.''

Some recreation group participants possessed a piece of technical knowledge that made them feel better informed than protesters. Near Fred's work site, for example, animal rights protesters had locked themselves into the compartment at the top of a high crane, claiming that the crane was building a laboratory that would be used for animal abuse. Fred said the protesters were fools:

FRED [at the Silverado Club]: *I* know what could have got them down real fast.

NINA: What?

FRED: Just loosening the bolts on the crane – hahahahah.

NINA [What a Pollyanna!]: Wouldn't that be dangerous?

FRED: Well, the crane would start swayin' like – they'd come down. They'd come down all right. One way – or another – they'd come down. Those protesters – they don't know *anything*! *Right next door, we experiment on animals all the time*! And they're so stupid, they'd go protesting a new thing, when the old building has had experiments going on in it for *years*! They're *ignorant fools* [his emphasis]!

From the protesters' point of view, the main point was a general political and moral one; but, if protesters were trying to make a general, political point, Fred proudly missed the point. Some country-western men spoke as if *they* were the powerful ones looking down at the ineffective crybaby protesters. And indeed, sometimes they did have some knowledge that only a person working on the inside would have.

Buffaloes treated all activists this way, not just the ones with whom they might have disagreed – they reserved equal animosity for anti-abortion and pro-choice protesters, for example. "Agreeing" and "disagreeing" implies more of a political stance than country-westerners had. The kinds of groups country-westerners liked were ones that they assumed were unpolitical and did not involve knowledge, such as Neighborhood Watch groups.[2] Unless proven otherwise, citizens who did not respect the boundary between private citizenship and public affairs were considered "ignorant fools," who were wrong to interfere in affairs that were none of their business.

In these examples, it is clear that Buffaloes assumed that moral reasoning does not lead to the truth. If only memorized facts can lead to the truth, then trying to find the truth *through discussion* is not a good reason to talk. Only the possession of very specific technical knowledge allows one to speak – but then there is little reason to speak, except to exchange facts. The Buffaloes' exacting technical standard made it difficult to hold opinions, since they were regular citizens, not technical experts on all topics.

Betsy laughed when I asked about groups involved in the issues of foreign policy and nuclear war, and said that she really could not answer any questions about those kinds of groups because she did not know anything about the issues at all. In our interview in December of 1989, when the Berlin Wall was coming down and dramatic changes in Eastern Europe and the Soviet Union were breathtaking daily headlines, I asked whether she would consider getting involved in a disarmament group and she answered,

[in an interview] I'm just so – *uninformed* on all that. I *am*! I don't read – I mean I read the papers but I kind of like, I read things that are of interest to me but not things that are really like life-threatening or – You know, like the wars, or or what's his name that the President's talking to? Gorbachev? It's like, "Who is he?"

Oh, good, Brian's here [her housemate]. OK Bry, you're on. There's a Coors in the fridge. [To me:] You sure you don't want one? Ask him, because he knows more!

Country-westerners assumed that to form legitimate opinions, one needed technical expertise that was beyond almost all citizens' reach. Charlotte, an older woman from the Buffalo, for example, explained that she would not join a hypothetical group that was trying to prevent a toxic incinerator from being built in its community because she would not have the right scientific knowledge:

[in an interview] I don't know anything about that. I wouldn't know how to get involved . . . I wouldn't know how to be involved in it because I don't know when they say it doesn't really hurt the environment I don't really know that they know that . . . Like the spraying – malathion – it's sad, because they're gonna let the bugs kill all the fruit, but if they spray, *people* get sick. So who's to say what to do? I don't know.

NINA: Well, how would you decide?

CHARLOTTE: I was watching them on TV the other night and I was thinking, "What could they do to kill the fly without spraying this stuff? There must be other ways. There's – what came to *my* mind when I'm watching it is that there's what they call, you know what "systemic" is?

NINA: Yeah.

CHARLOTTE: Well, there's this systemic, OK – an example is there's this systemic rose, it's a combination fertilizer and bug killer. OK, because roses have aphids, which are bugs, and when you have rose bushes and you have all these bugs and they eat your flowers, or it was a fruit they'd be eating your fruit. So, they came out with this stuff a few years ago that's called systemic. It's a fertilizer but it also kills the bugs. And what you do is you dig it in around your rosebush and it doesn't get in the atmosphere . . . Why can't they have something like that that they dig in the ground, a systemic, that's not gonna go around and it's not gonna hurt all the people? Then I thought, "I wonder why no one ever thought of it or maybe it wouldn't work." See, I don't know because I don't know that much about it . . . I'm not a scientist and haven't had chemistry and so what do I know? If I went and joined something like that, I'd have to sit there and listen, because I wouldn't know enough about it.

Their standards for technical knowledge required for citizenship were impossibly high. Similarly, Cathy, the dance teacher, said that when two groups have opposing facts in a controversy,

> [in an interview] there's no way to decide ... You can come to me and ask me a question and go to somebody else and get a whole different answer ... You have to do your own research and make up your own mind.

NINA: That's so hard!

CATHY: Yeah, but something I've learned is, I don't take what somebody tells me at face value until I know *all* the facts. Until I've done my research and I've done my homework and I know all the facts, and then I make my opinion. That's how gossip gets started – this person says this and this person says that. Find out your facts yourself, and then make up your own mind.

NINA: How do you do that when there's so many things to learn about?

CATHY [interrupting]: That's what a library's for.

Later, she repeated, telling me how she made voting decisions on complex ballot measures and dozens of referenda, "Like I said, that's what libraries are for." A full-time worker like her, who also worked most nights and most weekends, cannot possibly go to the library to research every political issue. Nobody can.

The constant focus on protesters' technical knowledge made some speakers fear even venturing opinions if they were not fully technically informed.[3] In the interview with Betsy and her housemate Brian, I asked if the issue of nuclear war was something they could do anything about if they joined a group. Betsy pointed to Brian, inviting him to speak, since she felt unqualified.

> [in an interview] With the right people, yes. It would depend on the group of people I'm with.

NINA: How would you find them?

BRIAN: I don't have any idea how I would go about meeting those ... some professional people with knowledge and background, not just people who want to come from Woodstock and start stompin' on the ground. Knowledgeable people who know what can and can't be done, you know, safety factors. Some people who would be experts in the field, of nuclear fission, maybe, and energy and conservation. I keep rappin' off. I better shut up here.

BETSY: No, no! That's why it's you [who is speaking, and not Betsy herself].
NINA [laughing]: No, no, it's your turn [to Betsy]!
BRIAN: I have to sip – that's *my* kind of nuclear fission! [laughing]
BETSY [laughing throughout]: I don't have anything to add because I basically agree with what he said. No, I don't have the knowledge even to say half the stuff that he just said . . .

The focus on facts also made conversation and debate intimidating and irrelevant: if all I can do is offer facts for someone else to memorize, why not just leave that effort to the news and the textbooks? Betsy told me that Soviet TV had been at a nearby theme park and Gorbachev was in Pacific City. I had not heard about it, since I had been out of town, so I idly asked, expecting speculation more than a factual answer, why they picked the theme park. She said she "could not remember any of the details." Expanding her case, she added that she cannot remember anything "like that."

So, if I can't remember what started World War II or even what happened in Vietnam, how can I understand or remember what's going on in Poland, in Eastern Europe? OK, the wall is down, so they're free. So, what does it mean? And Nelson Mandela? I didn't even know who he was till he was freed. Then I thought, "Wow, twenty-seven years in jail and you're still alive? That's pretty good!" But I didn't even know who he was till he got out. And Forbes' birthday party? I heard about that five days after it happened. "Oh, good, he had a birthday party. Who is he?" There's just too many things going on in the world to know about all of them. And you know me – I just go to work, come home, and go to sleep.

Charlotte similarly explained political silence, while we were standing at a Buffalo party, after asking me how my "paper" was shaping up. "All I said in my interview was 'I don't know, I don't know' – it was pretty worthless, wasn't it?" She said she had walked by someone who was passing out flyers about a demonstration, and said, "I don't have time to find out about it," which, she said to me, "sounds really awful but it's also that I don't know." She said, "I got nothing to contribute and besides, I'm not gonna risk getting my house bombed or nothing, about something when I don't even know what it's all about."

All private people circled around and around this theme of political ignorance. Some focused on activists' political ignorance, either for being dumb enough to think they can have an effect or for getting the facts wrong, or both. While some people (like the activists and cynics I met) focused on the government's and corporations' role in keeping citizens ignorant, I heard this approach only once from this circle of country-westerners – from George, the joking, ruddy union carpenter, discussing arms shipments to Central America in the interview with his housemate, Charlene. He said, "First, they

say the government asked us in and the people say the government didn't
ask us in or ask for our help – you don't know who to believe or how to
make a logical decision."

When people simply shrugged and said that there was no way to know the
truth, since the government lies, they were not always saying it as a criticism
of government secrecy. Sometimes, they were simply stating a fact, as Betsy
did when discussing her housemate's annoying fretting over the Persian Gulf
war. Some, like Fred and Brian, said this as a way of simultaneously displaying superior knowledge to protesters ("the protesters think they know
what's happening, but they're wrong"). But instead of blaming himself for
his ignorance or blaming protesters for their ignorance, George blamed the
government's active effort to *keep* us ignorant.

Given all members' focus on facts and ignorance, it is no surprise that the
only long political discourse I heard at the country-western clubs was a display of information. A few days after the US invaded Panama in December
of 1989, I was waiting in a line with Ray, the chunky, bearded Kenny Rogers
look-alike who worked as a word processor for the military. In the previous
chapter, I described George's response to Ray's discourse (he ignored it).
Here is what George was so actively not hearing: I had told Ray that I had
just been listening to the car radio, and they were talking about Panama. He
proclaimed, "It's all politics." I asked what he meant.

It's all about money. And when you've got money, you've got: war. That's just the
way it is. Noriega was on the CIA's payroll through the early '80s so they don't want
him there telling what he knows, so they keep making up all these phony excuses for
the invasion. He probably just got greedy. He was dealing drugs back then, and you
know he was giving the CIA a cut – maybe he decided he wanted to keep more and
then all of a sudden, he's "a big bad guy." It's just like Vietnam – money got us in
there, too – Shell, Exxon, and mining fields.

[I asked, joking, if he was "some kind of radical or something."]

I'm generally a conservative, but some things I'm a liberal on, and then there are
a lot of important issues in between. You can't be a single-issue person or you're
sunk. How can you just look at Panama? What about Honduras, Costa Rica, El Salvador, or Mexico? Mexico is more important than El Salvador. And the Middle East!
The Middle East is really what's gonna matter. Israel is really crazy – they could go
to war in a minute and we'd supply them! The Israel lobby is so strong.

He listed recipients of Israel's aid: "South Africa – they set up South
Africa's whole system; Honduras; the drug barons in Colombia." He said,
about Israel, "They're not these nice, sweet people everyone thinks!" For
Ray, one cannot legitimately have an opinion about one country without
knowing all about every country. Are there any patterns? Is there anything to
be done? Ray was imparting information about a problem that he considered

inevitable, not trying to convince me to do anything or to cheer for the good side. There was no good side. He did not ask what George or I thought and made it hard for us to squeeze a word in.

If debate does not accomplish anything, protest must be for the purpose of grabbing attention

If problems are purely technical, discussion is irrelevant: there is one answer; it takes only one expert to screw in a light bulb. Country-westerners assumed that since debate on technical issues, such as the best way to store nuclear weapons, is certainly beyond the expertise of most citizens, citizens who enter the public arena must not genuinely be interested in kindling debate, but must only be interested in standing on a soapbox, on display, grabbing attention for themselves, or getting on a high horse. We saw how avidly country-westerners tried to avoid being "in the limelight," so it would be hard to imagine them appreciating someone else for wanting attention. If the public is rarely in a position to arrive at better technical solutions to a bug infestation than scientists themselves offered, then the public involved in such issues is there only for the purpose of getting attention. Debate does not accomplish anything.

Cathy, the cigarillo-smoking country-westerner, also assumed that when activists got up on the public stage, it must be for the purpose of getting attention, not for instigating public discussion on an issue that activists thought needed discussion. She was outraged at protesters' grab for attention, talking about it as a form of self-promotion.

90 percent of the public that I've found thinks demonstrators are a pain . . . Demonstrating doesn't get the public's attention. If it does get their attention, it's in a negative way. But if you have someone who's done their background and is knowledgeable on what they're fighting for, people are gonna take notice, because they're gonna know what they're talking about . . .

A lot of people just like to be in the limelight. They don't – that's not to say they don't believe in their cause. But they're not willing to go that extra mile to make people realize what's going on.

All people are gonna see is what you present to them. If they see a bunch of people standing in front of a building or in front of a site, holding a picket sign, that doesn't say anything. It says, "This is my opinion." . . . You know, for me to get involved, I have to know the hardcore facts.

"All people are gonna see is what you present to them"; whether the activist groups really were ignorant or whether they only seemed ignorant because of shallow news coverage was not worth distinguishing, for country-westerners. Instead of being angry at the press for devoting attention to the protesters, interviewees *could* have been angry at the press for doing such a bad job of presenting protesters' reasons for involvement. But, interestingly enough, no country-westerners criticized the media on that score; they assumed, probably correctly, that most environmental activists are not expert biologists, most disarmament activists are not expert nuclear physicists, so in Buffaloes' estimation, they had no license to talk.

As we saw in the previous chapter, conversation in the country-western group context was seen as a reflection on the speaker's own personality, not as a contribution to a common project, not as a reflection of something larger than the self. Likewise, they assumed that protesters' talk was a simple reflection on the speaker and the speaker's private personality. Therefore, Buffaloes shone their lights on the protesters' personalities and not on their messages; and then they criticized the protesters for wanting to be on display, as individual personalities. It would be difficult for a protester to break through this cycle.

Since country-westerners considered political talk to be a reflection on the speaker's personality, it was much more personally risky to talk politics than to discuss seemingly personal troubles: at the very beginning of an interview, Cathy sharply warned me that some topics were off-limits, too private: all of the survey questions about political efficacy and alienation, such as, "How much of the time do you think you can a trust the government in Washington to do what is right?" and "How much influence do you think a person like you can have over government decisions?" and others, were too personal. "How often do you read a news magazine or newspapers?" was too personal. "Whom did you vote for in the last election, for president?" was too personal. "How often, if ever, do you go to religious services?" was too personal.

But she spoke eloquently and at great length about her ex-husband's drug problem and her effort to help him kick his habit; how she stayed up nights with him to help him through withdrawal; how she nursed him through his nausea, fever, and sickness; how she pleaded with him to stay off drugs; how he went back on drugs and finally, how she separated from him. She also disclosed the sorrow she felt over her father's early death, when she was a child. I felt a bit awkward hearing so much about her very intimate sorrows, but to her, this was a more reasonable, easier topic of conversation than her political preferences and opinions. In the first chapter on the recreation group, I described the "reversal of frontstage and backstage." Here, Cathy echoes that relation. Talking about politics is just as personal, just as much a reflection on one's self, as talking about intimate relationships, but it is riskier. Her eloquence on very intimate matters shows a depth of practiced comfort in speaking about personal issues.

Deep jokes: the extraordinary case of animal rights

Aside from Ray's discussion of Panama, the only moments I heard participants at the Silverado staking out positions on public issues involved only one topic – on this topic alone, members made their positions public and even argued for them, though never for more than one sentence at a time, and never for more than one back and forth exchange at a time. Why was this topic of animal rights exceptional?

In one conversation with me, Betsy described some of the nauseating ways factory-farm animals were treated, according to an ad she dealt with every week. I said that I had just read something about people being treated that way; that it's even worse when you think about that kind of thing happening to people – and children, even. She said, "Yeah, but then you don't know whether they couldn't help it, or whether they brought it on themselves. Animals can't help get themselves out of it."

She was more concerned about animals than people *not* because she was an inhumane person, but because, unlike concern for people, concern for animals seemed to her to require no expert knowledge. Her attitude perhaps goes far in explaining why many Americans appear to care so much more unequivocally about animals than children. Concern for animals appears to require less knowledge; there is no way to blame the animal for its own condition.[4] Thus, on the issue of protecting animals, Betsy could allow herself to connect her private actions to faraway problems. We were talking about wearing an Earth Day T-shirt, and whether it did any good:

BETSY [on the phone]: Well, there's not much more I can do – I *already* do my recycling! And I snip my rings.
NINA: Snip your rings? What's that?
BETSY: The rings? On six-packs? You know how six-packs – or six-containers of soda, any can thing – come with plastic rings, around the tops of the cans, and if they end up in the ocean, baby seals and stuff get their necks caught in them and choke when they grow up.

She felt confident in this case: the issue of animals was not as confusing as other issues. Thus, she could *let* herself care, and even talk about the issue in casual interactions.

Referring to the media

The political silence among friends and family left country-westerners very open to media messages. Thus, in interviews, almost all referred to a movie or TV show in which a "political" topic arose; country-westerners rarely had the confidence to refer to a news story, but instead referred to talk shows, sit-coms, and movie stars.

BETSY [in interview]: I wouldn't get involved in trying to prevent a toxic incinerator from being put in our town because of fears for my health . . . like that movie about the girl who gets killed when she reports on a nuclear power plant.

On the phone, she said,

I saw Paul McCartney on TV, giving a speech at a music awards ceremony, and he said, "No one would have thought two years ago that the Berlin Wall would come down and everyone just said it was impossible, it would never happen, and now here it is, it's happened." So why can't that happen here? Who knows? If people start taking recycling seriously, and driving less, then maybe things won't be so bad in twenty years. If we can figure out how to stop polluting so much.

Others also used a non-news source to ground their thoughts on politics:

CHARLOTTE [to me, at the Buffalo Club]: You know, your interview made me think that I should get involved in something – a homeless shelter, maybe. I was watching *Donahue*, and they had a Russian fellow on . . . Donahue asked him if he could think of any *criticism* of this country. He said homelessness – he thought it was shameful that the richest country in the world should have homeless. It isn't right. Of course [Charlotte offers her opinion here], there are homeless in every country – there are homeless in Russia, too – but you know, I thought, "He's right. It is a shame that in a country where we have so many *things*, that there should be homelessness. It *isn't* right."

When they allowed themselves to express opinions and not just repeat facts, the authorized opinions came from an entertainment TV show – the *Emmy's*, *Donahue*, or a docudrama – not TV news and not personal conversations.[5]

Politics as natural disaster; the individual as victim

Topics that a person from the university town, Newton, might have considered "political" were almost never taken that way by Buffaloes. I mentioned some of these in chapter 1 – war, divorce, child support, low wages were all talked about as purely personal problems. Yet, while no one ever seemed to remember the political issues in the news, everyone saw the news about my plane destined for Chicago, stuck in the Stockport Airport with a bomb scare for nine hours on the day the Gulf War started. They remembered that news item because they thought of me, a personal acquaintance, knowing that I was supposed to take the plane from Stockport to Chicago that day. And they knew about my trip because the only other discussion private people had as a group about the Gulf War was also about our travel plans and whether the war would disrupt them.

Besty and I were on the phone talking about our plans beforehand. She also had planned a trip to the East Coast that same month. "Here I am going on a trip to Washington at the end of the month and there's gonna be war breaking out," she worried. I said I was worried about my trip, too. She said that at least Chicago, my destination, was not a target, the way the coasts were. Again, she said she was worried; again, I said I was, too. She confirmed, "You'd have to be weird not to be worried."

BETSY: They're saying to watch for terrorist attacks on the coast and I'm wondering how far in that means. And they're being really careful at airports for terrorists. They're saying people are getting to the airport six hours early.

NINA: That means I'll have to get there at 4 a.m!

BETSY: It's just something I heard – just a rumor. I don't know if if it's true.

Even though I was afraid in some ways, I was also skeptical about taking the war so personally, thinking that the worst aspect of the war was not the immediate effects it would have on me personally. "Well, what could happen to us, anyway," she said, adding that she just hoped it would end soon.

The intellectuals and activists I knew appeared not to take it personally: we are not supposed to take political issues personally, not supposed to worry about our own particular cases. Strikingly, not one of the university-educated, politically engaged people I knew in Newton noticed the report on the local evening news about my particular plane, though they also knew I was taking a plane to Chicago that day. Compared to the other intellectuals and activists I knew in Newton, I felt primitive, emotional, unable to attain a sufficiently abstract perspective on politics. But compared to Betsy, I was treating the war very abstractly, as if my own personal condition were irrelevant. I had not been as worried about the bomb scare on my own plane as country-westerners had been.

These differences in ways of relating to war illustrate the concept of the "habitus," a habitual way of organizing perceptions, that Pierre Bourdieu discusses (1977). The habitus allows some types of people to formulate a *political* response to policy questions, and opens to others only a *personal* response. For Bourdieu, the habitus is class-based, but this example shows that it is also based on group membership, which is not always exclusively class-based.[6]

If regular people have no say in politics, then we can only stand by and hope politics do not come too near us. Betsy brought up, in a one-to-one conversation, the question of whether she would ever want to get married and have a baby with her boyfriend.

> With all the problems, I don't even know if I'd want to bring a kid into this world.

NINA: Which problems?

BETSY: You know – pollution, overpopulation.

Then she shifted back to the topic of her relationship. Later, I asked, disturbed (feeling myself like a "volunteer" from my study – that is, not wanting to hear someone say something so discouraging),

NINA: Would you *really* have doubts about having kids 'cuz of all the world's problems?

BETSY: I would, but I have lots of family and if I had a kid it would have lots of cousins and relatives since my brothers and sisters have kids.

NINA: But that wouldn't protect it from pollution and stuff.

BETSY [in a self-dismissive way, as if to say that private cravings are irrational and silly but irresistible]: True, but sometimes what you really crave takes over.

Then the subject changed again. What struck me was that she did *not* say that maybe our children can repair the world, as a volunteer would have said, or that we can be an inspiration to our children by working to fix the world, as an activist would say. She was taking political problems personally, and assuming that she could nullify the importance of political problems with individual ingenuity. Betsy's brother, for example, was in the military, she said. "He's over there in Europe. *That's what got me worrying in the first place.* But he's smart. He'll be all right – he's smart . . . Well, he got into the Navy in the first place." She could not express worry about the war in the abstract, but could say only that she was worried about it because her brother might be hurt – the way she spoke made it sound as if she would not care about the war if her particular brother were safer. Ken echoed this extreme personalization of politics:

KEN [from an interview]: You know, everybody's gotta die. What makes it any different if you die in a car accident or I die in a nuclear war? You're still dead.

NINA: Well, gaaawd. If you die in a nuclear war and everybody else dies too, then –

KEN [interrupting quickly]: Well, then there'll just be a longer line at the Pearly Gate! That's all! [laughing]

NINA [laughing]: Well, seriously, if just *you* die, there's still *humanity* there, carrying on a tradition, a civilization –

KEN [interrupting]: But see now you're thinking in television terms: saturation bombing, nobody survives. You know, *somebody's* gonna survive. It doesn't matter how bad it gets, but *somebody's* gonna survive. You may be the *last person on earth*-type syndrome, but somebody's gonna survive [tells a joke about cockroaches] [repeats the idea that somebody will survive four more times] . . . Yeah, there's that chance it's gonna be a total annihilation. But then who cares? There's nobody left to care.

What matters above all is if individuals, not civilizations, survive.

When I asked country-westerners if they would ever consider getting involved in a group that dealt with the homelessness issue, and if they thought there was anything regular people could do about that issue, they all had the same kind of answer. Betsy said she could invite a homeless woman to sleep in her apartment, since she had an extra bed, but then, she was not sure that it would be safe for her to have a homeless person living in her house. Cathy talked about giving homeless people quarters and making friends with a homeless person. That is, country-westerners all assumed that they could help only *as individuals*, not by working in a homeless shelter (as the volunteers assumed), and not by pressuring the government to build more low-income housing (as most activists assumed). And on the issue of drugs, again, private people all referred to people they knew who had drug problems or people they knew who knew people who had drug problems. They did not refer to problems in schools and on the streets but instead treated drugs as a purely personal problem. Personal issues were always more important: after saying that toxic waste can cause birth defects, Cathy said, "If the [anti-drugs] program helps just one person, then I think it's worthwhile . . . I think if you could save one person's life, I think it's more important than spending years on the environment."

There was no category for politics. Remember the puzzlingly neutral response to Fred's and others' violent jokes. If there were a movement or a community or a reason for members to think it would do any good to confront Fred about his violent "jokes" about blacks, or if it mattered what anyone thought about unions or the environment or workers' comp, or if Betsy could feel that it would have been right to stand up to her friends about the black boyfriend, then maybe they would take a stand. To take courage and swallow, to say, "What I'm doing is right," an act has to represent more than just a random risk to the actor. One would have to see that people like oneself make a difference. Otherwise, making an issue of anything would just be a purely personal risk, like chastising someone for having bad table manners.

What difference would it make to Jody, Kim, or Betsy to say something to Fred, or Chuck, or Jim about their race and gender jokes? For them, it would be saying something to Fred as an individual, not Fred as a representative of a way of speaking which is wrong. It would be like taking a stand against Fred for disliking blondes – people would assume that you had some personal reason for wanting him to like blondes.

This is what it means in practice to be "not a public person." It means that you think that what you say and do is not part of a larger scheme and will not matter for anything but the most personal reasons, as a reflection on yourself. What you say matters for how it makes you look, not how it makes the world look. That is what living in "personal" instead of "historical" time means (Flacks 1988). It means not feeling obliged to worry how you and your companions are affecting things in the long run, not feeling obliged to monitor everything you say and do, to make sure it is right. But this personalized approach to life does not just come naturally; it requires interaction to learn how to define everything as "purely personal."

Conclusion: the sociological imagination in reverse and the devaluation of talk

Some might say that Buffaloes were obviously just too ignorant and apathetic to be good citizens. Such ignorance is not unusual; surveys of Americans over the years reveal a gaping hole where most Americans' political knowledge should be. In many polls, the winner is "don't know," "no response," or opinions based on incorrect information.[7] This endless abyss of political ignorance has long plagued democratic theory: if people don't know anything, surely they cannot be responsible citizens. And if one really believes that the majority of people are too dumb and uncaring to participate in politics, the bottom falls out of the whole idea of democracy.

W. Russell Neuman is one of the many scholars who would say that democracy is just too difficult for some people; he says we should just give up people like the Buffaloes. "[P]rocessing political information has costs," he states. "If individuals opt not to . . . pay much attention to the flow of political information, that may well be a rational and quite reasonable decision to marshal scarce resources and energies for other more directly rewarding pursuits. The stratification of political attentiveness and involvement is a natural and inevitable factor of mass political life" (1988: 177).[8]

On the other hand, other scholars argue that if researchers would just listen and probe and listen more, they would find that most Americans really know more than it seems – that they can reason, after all, even if they do not know all the facts (Lane 1962; Reinarman 1987; Gamson 1992; Hart 1992;

J. Hochschild 1981). These scholars show that if a curious, open-minded researcher offers free, unjudgmental, unhurried contexts for interviewees to reason aloud, instead of getting quizzed about facts and numbers – that most people can *become* thoughtful, reasoning citizens. If given this rare opportunity, almost everyone turns out to have the potential to think about politics. So, surveys show that most Americans are ignorant; open-ended interviews show that they are not stupid. Who is right?

Both are right. The surveyors are right to be chagrined at the amazing depth of political ignorance, but the interviewers are *also* right to protest that the ignorance is not based on stupidity, and not inevitable. Buffaloes, for example, were not illogical, and were sometimes impressively able to memorize facts, and often eloquent when talking about private life. But they did not focus their intelligence on political reasoning and thus, when it came to formulating opinions for an interviewer, they had to start from scratch, without enough reference points or information on the horizon. Of course, memorizing lists of decontextual facts is boring and does take time away from more "directly rewarding pursuits," but citizenship is not just a matter of memorizing lists of facts. Engaging in playful debate *could* create "resources and energies," and could be "directly rewarding," and could make learning about politics interesting and fun. So, while Americans are able to reason about politics if given the kind of opportunity that the sympathetic, open-minded interview researchers give them, this opportunity almost never presents itself to most Americans

Given the atmosphere at the Buffalo, Buffaloes themselves seemed to agree with Newman's position, in assuming that democracy was not for them; they did not consider themselves to be "the public," and were not sure that "the public" was useful to society, anyway. But they did recognize that they were victims of politics; they were not just simply, rationally, cleanly disconnected from politics.

Buffaloes were not simply "more" or "less" distant from politics than the other groups. They were both closer and more distant than activists and volunteers and intellectuals – simultaneously more open to naming political problems than the volunteers – calling them "a shame" – and less open to feeling responsible to fix the problems. They took politics very personally, but not at all politically: where others might see a foreign war, they saw dangerous implications for personal travel; where others might see the end of civilization in nuclear war, they saw the end of billions of separate individuals; where others might see a systemic structural problem, they saw individuals coping; where others might see moral or political questions, they saw dead, inevitable facts and very personal, private woes. They collapsed all social issues into natural or purely personal troubles.

C. Wright Mills connected such absence of a "sociological imagination" to citizens' worship of facts, not to their lack of information. "It is not only information that [citizens] need – in this Age of Fact, information often dominates their attention and overwhelms their capacities to assimilate it" (1959: 5). They need, he says, a way of thinking that connects the everyday to the global, a sociological imagination, and "the first fruit of this imagination . . . is the idea that the individual can understand his own experience and gauge his own fate only by locating himself within his period."

In contrast, country-westerners assumed that they had to know "all the facts" in order to have an opinion on an issue, not an analysis, not a broad overview. There was no way to connect very personal fears to such neutral, unanalyzed information – they could not locate themselves in relation to these inert, indisputable facts. The *devaluation of talk itself* is a thread running through all of this, connecting the overly individualized, personal approach to the assumption that there is a world of neutral dead facts out there, unconnected to us.

Having a sociological imagination would mean not just memorizing all the facts, "going to the library, to get an opinion," as Cathy said. Solitary individuals cannot possibly do all the research necessary to take positions on all the important issues in the world, and nobody can memorize many facts without an implicit theory to hold them. When the activists I met heard a new bit of information, they would ask, "What organization said that? Why? Who benefits from asking the question that way instead of another way? What organizations say something different? Why should, or shouldn't, I believe this organization?" Their implicit theory – that too much corporate power was incompatible with grassroots democratic groups like theirs – helped them organize the facts (and if a fact contradicted their theory, then they could remember it because of the clash). In many countries, class-based political parties tell people how to take political positions (Mann 1970).[9] People need an organized map of the political world, not just a huge pile of unsorted facts.

It's certainly possible that talking more could propagate incorrect facts – Jews control all the banks, you can get AIDS by standing next to a gay person, etc. – and perhaps country-westerners preferred to maintain silence rather than risk being swayed by the propagation of inaccuracies. But if we are going to continue to have a political system in which everyone can vote, and which has no entrance exams screening out voters who do not know basic facts, and if we are going to continue to hold on to the ideal of democratic participation, then we have to have faith that the free exchange of ideas will generate better, better-informed citizens.

Hating politics has a long history in the twentieth century; it has been a characteristic of military dictatorships throughout the world. Fictional characters in Isabel Allende's novel, *Of Love and Shadows*, about a Latin American country ruled by a military dictatorship, illustrate this approach to politics. "It's better to have a little abuse than to push the armed forces back in their barracks and leave the country in the hands of the politicians," says one sergeant (1984: 238). Another military man muses about his entry into the armed forces, "I thought the nation needed a respite from the politicians, and that we needed order and discipline if we were to eradicate poverty" (255). Why should millions of people learn all the facts, when ten experts will come to the same conclusions? If we agree with the Buffaloes, that experts should rule the country and leave the rest of us out, then there is no reason for us to talk about the common good, or to talk about politics at all, and we are left very alone with our very personal worries. An alternative would be to make civic life more educational.

6

Strenuous disengagement and cynical chic solidarity

The private people were not the only group at the country-western clubs. Another group usually sat together, went on outings together, and generally formed a subgroup at the clubs. Considering how continuously this second group of friends made morbid, despairing political jokes, and how much detailed political knowledge they exchanged, and how strong and bitter their opinions were, I was puzzled that they managed not to get involved in doing something about the problems that they so attentively, lovingly catalogued. Clearly, these Buffalo members did engage in political debate, in a potential context of the informal public sphere, but the point of their conversation was always to convince each other that they were smart enough to know that they could not do anything about the problems.

The point of including this comparison case is to show a range of methods for creating politically disengaged public conversation. Making such a strong effort to convince oneself and one's friends of citizens' powerlessness *is* a way of taking a political position, but it is one that closes off avenues for involvement that go beyond expressions of vehement disengagement. Thus, in the "cycle of political evaporation," such bitter cynicism enters the potential contexts of the public sphere, but only in order to neuter feelings of political engagement, to keep politics at bay. Ironically, this group, that talked about politics more than any group I encountered, was also the most actively distant from politics.

Like the other country-westerners, these more cynical country-western club participants were strenuously unserious, but talking did not pose a danger to cynics, as it did for the other recreation group members. Shortly after the Exxon Valdez oil spill covered thousands of miles of Alaskan coastline with oil, Maureen, Hank, Tim, and I were speeding past some refineries and grassy hills to the Buffalo. Maureen, a private secretary to the head of public relations at a pesticide company, Tim, a waiter with a college education,

Hank, who was part owner of a lucrative business he had fallen into by luck when he was in college, and I had no trouble keeping conversation going. Each eagerly overlapped and interrupted to be able to get a word in. [1]

First, Tim mused over his taxes, which were due tomorrow. That led to a conversation about Exxon's rumored plans to let tax money fund the Alaskan clean-up efforts. Maureen just exploded, ''Oh, that's *ridiculous*! And I heard the reason it took them so long to start cleaning it up was that it was cheaper for them to sit it out and get fined, since the fines are so small.''

TIM: It's the profit motive.

HANK: That's what makes them all work – it's the bottom line.

MAUREEN: Yeah, they should be given really big fines – nothing else would make them be more careful.

HANK: But that's hard to do.

MAUREEN: And the way they're blaming the captain, saying he was drunk. There's always gonna be human error. They should have safeguards against that.

HANK: Like a breathalyzer they have on some cars – if he breathes into it and his breath breathalyzes, he can't start it.

TIM: Then he'd lay into it after he already started it.

HANK: Or get someone else to start it. I heard the bears are all gonna start dying too.

TIM: Yeayup – the bears eat the oily fish and birds.

NINA: And it's such a huge area – as big as New Jersey or something.

MAUREEN [speaking very fast]: The whole world's being destroyed. I really think that. I just feel so helpless. There's nothing I can do about it. That's why I don't have kids. I figure the world's too much of a mess. It'll be destroyed by the time they'd grow up.

HANK [ever reasonable]: There's still some places left. The world's pretty big.

TIM: Oh, great – you're gonna find some *corner* somewhere – Micronesia or something?

HANK [suddenly talking extremely rapidly]: And I don't have kids or anything but I figure if I did *they'd* have a chance to grow up and it would be *their* kids with the problem. They'd have to solve it or their kids wouldn't be able to grow up. Anyway, there's nothing *I* can do about it.

MAUREEN: Oh, great. Hank, you give it fifty years, I give it twenty-five. It's just like nuclear war. That's another thing I never think about. [This assertion that nuclear war was *another* thing that she ''never thought about'' was interesting considering how often she talked about those topics.] There's *really* nothing you can do about that – even more than the environment.

HANK: I just figure if there's a nuclear war, I'd do what the anti-nuke people say: bend over, put my head between my knees, and kiss my ass goodbye. It's like a fly getting smashed on your windshield: what's the last thing that goes through its mind?

[Tim and Maureen laugh ironically.]

NINA: I don't get it.

HANK: His asshole.

NINA: Huh? Oh – augh.

TIM: I always thought that if I could know ahead of time there was gonna be nuclear war, I'd find out where ground zero is, buy a bottle of champagne and sit there and drink it.

HANK: In a tuxedo.

TIM: Yeah! In a tux!

HANK: And charge it to your credit card.

NINA: Yeah, I know a guy who takes out these huge loans and figures he'll never have to pay them back because there'll be nuclear war or something.

HANK: But you always have to pay them back. Never assume you won't have to pay them back. You will. I did that, with the same idea, and just now finally got them all paid back.

At this, we turned into the Buffalo parking lot.

Already in my first few nights with the cynical chic Buffaloes, they joked about nuclear war, oil spills, extinction, drug abuse, acid rain, toxic waste, the educational system, hippies, sexism, blacks, gays, and themselves. Talking about politics was entertainment for them. While the mainstream Buffaloes tried to avoid talking about politics by simply "not sayin' nothin'" about issues that might test their knowledge, and so were much more isolated in their political anxieties; and while the volunteers used the group forum to reaffirm to each other that the world makes sense, and actively avoided talking in terms that might challenge that belief; these strenuously disengaged cynics talked about it all. But they invited the problems only to demonstrate that they were immune to their unforgettable allure: morbidly fascinating petroleum-soaked otters, perversely voluptuous green hills filled with toxic waste, acid-filled ponds in the pristine mountains. They wanted to demonstrate to themselves and to each other that they had not been fooled, and devoted their political conversations simultaneously to displaying and pushing away all their ideals and knowledge, their sorrow and curiosity. They tried very hard not to care, and the more they leaned on the door to keep the world out, the louder the problems knocked.

On the way to the Buffalo another day, I made what I thought was a totally innocuous comment, which they managed to turn into a springboard for jokes about pollution. By watching how they interpret each other here, we can see how quickly and subtly the conversation turns from joking to serious and back again, seamlessly. Try as they might to be completely disengaged, one or the other of them would always surrender to concern, and express distress directly.

It was a splendid, breezy spring day. We drove along on the stretch of highway with a refinery on one side and oil storage tanks and soft, pretty, light green hills on the other. "Those hills are so beautiful. They're so green and soft!" I said.

TIM: Guess what? They have toxic waste buried in them!

NINA [playing the gullible, wide-eyed female act, which conveniently coincides with the appropriate action of a curious, non-native fieldworker]: No! Really??

MAUREEN: Yeah, I used to want to go for a walk in them 'cause they looked so pretty but now I'm glad I didn't.

NINA: Well, but what kind of waste is it? Is it something that could –

HANK: It's probably just oil that's seeped in over the years.

TIM: And see those little hills? Each one is a big pile of toxic waste, covered with grass!

HANK: No, they're piles of dead Gasco workers.

TIM: Right! All the Gasco workers who've died cleaning up explosions over the years there [there had been an explosion at the refinery a few weeks before].

MAUREEN [who had worked at the Gasco pesticide plant, and knew]: That's ChemOil.

HANK [not expecting anything serious]: What?

MAUREEN: That plant is ChemOil.

HANK: OK, ChemOil.

TIM: And see those white things? That's to mark where all the workers died. [a short silence]

NINA: Oh, look! Toxic cows! How cute!

TIM: They probably are.

MAUREEN: Can you imagine? Toxic burgers! Toxic T-bone! Let's open a restaurant!

TIM: No, seriously, they probably absorb all kinds of residues.

HANK: Everything's toxic. Look at that deal with the apples.

TIM: Alar – that was going too far, taking them off the shelves. The way everyone got so worried all of a sudden.

HANK: What I meant was, we been eatin' apples like that all our lives [said with a funny accent]. If I stop now, what difference is it gonna make? I mean, I figure if you live to be 300 that stuff will get you at 200.

TIM: At least they don't use the really bad stuff they used to use – like DDT.

HANK: There's a whole mess of chemicals they banned, that were around twenty years ago.

MAUREEN [emphatically]: Then they just send them to other countries, so they use them there. [Turning toward the back seat, where Tim and I were sitting, and poking Hank gleefully, as if this is a really new and really funny thought] *Hey*! Isn't that funny?? They ban the chemicals *here* so the American companies keep selling them to other countries, and then they use them on food that they turn around and sell to us! So we get it anyway!

TIM: And we end up eating it!

MAUREEN [exaggeratedly deflated]: It's crazy.

HANK: They say they're regulating them more, but they're inventing new ones all the time. And they never know till way later what effect they have. And you don't know whether you're living near something, or whether it's toxic.

The problems about which they claimed never to think clamored around them constantly. Gathering information to transform into jokes was protection against being swayed by forces beyond their control. Displaying control in person was a way of making real control over these problems seem irrelevant. While the volunteers displayed control by silencing discussion of "big" problems, these Buffaloes tried to appear in control by being on top of information. And in the process of working to reassure themselves and each other, they talked about politics and joked much more than any other group I studied, exchanging enormous amounts of information.

Much recent social theory and newspaper editorial space condemns "the cynical society," saying cynicism makes earnest commitment impossible (Goldfarb 1991; Miller 1988, for example). The problem with that kind of analysis is that it cannot distinguish between the cynics and the activists, who, as I describe later, also often expressed opinions of political disgust, mistrust, and cynicism. The difference between the activists and the cynics was not just a difference in beliefs, but in implicit ideas of what interaction was for in the contexts where they met. For the activists, as we will see, joking about government and corporate misdeeds fueled activism. For the cynics, bitter joking allowed speakers to reassure each other that they were not alone in their political disgust. The purpose of the cynics' constant joking was to affirm to each other that they were together in a conspiracy against gullibility – their joking was a form of solidarity aimed at displaying immunity to politics. Thus, even though cynics' disgusted beliefs about the political system resembled those of the activists, their practice of connection and disconnection to the wider world differed.

The kernel of solidarity embedded in cynicism was especially important in relation to the other Buffaloes. They tried to make sure that no one thought of them as real "bubbas," as Maureen jokingly called Hank, her boyfriend ("bubba" is slang for "dumb country redneck"). For example, when the dance instructor announced at the Buffalo that we could all enter a contest for a free trip to Alaska, the majority of the recreation group participants sat quietly listening to all of her announcements, probably relieved that they did not have to try to talk, letting her announcements stand in for general sociability without their having to produce it themselves. But the strenuously disengaged cynics were full of giggles.

MAUREEN [elbowing Hank]: Hey, it's a really great time to go to Alaska, now. Right, Bubba?
HANK: You bet. Come take pictures of the oil slick.
MAUREEN: Be part of history – you can say to your grandkids, "I was there when Alaska was destroyed so that Exxon could make a profit."
HANK: Miles of black beach.
TINO: Take home a souvenir dead sea otter.
MAUREEN: Take home the last of its kind – the last living sea otter.
TIM: I read that the ship there is still leaking. They cleaned up one beach and then the wind shifted and blew all the oil right back onto it.

Whether they joked about local refinery fires, local industrial explosions, acid rain, extinct otters, toxic T-bone, or the national, media-oriented wars on crime and drugs, they were protecting themselves from being taken in, reassuring each other that they still had not become bubbas, that there still are people in the world who are not as gullible as they imagine others to be. When alone, they sometimes sounded less cynical, because they did not have to worry about reassuring the others.

Since the cynics did not also subscribe to the cozy overlay of nostalgic community given by country-western culture, they did not have to worry that they, as individuals, did not fit into the down-home community, but took the Dixie flag, the drawling lyrics, the lace and the ruffles, as obviously camp and ridiculous. There was no effort at paying homage to imagined traditions that "everyone is supposed to already know," such as Betsy's list of rules for when to throw the bouquet at a wedding, when to throw the rice, when to throw the garter, when to dance with the parents. Their refusal to take commercial culture's "recommended use" freed them to be cynical about everything, and not try so desperately to save out some sacrosanct bits of down-home wholeness. This cynical solidarity is the silver lining of cynicism – it is perhaps preferable sometimes to Pollyanna-ism in its solidarity against the forces that create bubbas, since it allows for some kind of publicly minded exchange.

But they tried to enforce this regime of irony and disengagement on every-one else, too, though – their approach was to laugh at society, not to try to change it. During one class, Tim mentioned that the previous Sunday was "real rowdy" because the band sang one song that was an imitation of rap music, "with grunts and u-u-ee-ee [monkey sounds] and words were some-thing about 'gotta get back, to makin' my crack, nine to five,' and all about 'your lovely big flat nose.' I noticed that the band looked around real careful before doing that number – and there were a few blacks there." I asked what they did. Tim said "I'm sure they took it as a joke. Like that black couple over there. They dance all the dances. I'm sure they don't take that stuff too seriously." He had never talked to them, though, so his guess was based on assumptions about what being at the Buffalo Club was for.

Mention of the "country rap" song led to a conversation about other songs that were not to be taken seriously – one about how much better a big Cadil-lac is than a Subaru. They all sang together, "Some say it's too old, some say it's too fast, some say it uses too much gas," and laughed. Then Maureen did an ironic rendition of the classic country song, "Stand By Your Man," with praying hands and yearning eyes gazing to the sky: "He'll have good times and you'll have bad/ But don't try to understand him – he's only a man." She knew all the words, to the whole song. Her point was that *she* was not like that, so Hank took up the joke, saying, "I think that's what you should do tomorrow morning." Maureen pretended to whack him, "Get outta here!" Tony added, "Like that Merle Haggard song, 'I'm Proud to be an Okie from Muskogee.' You wonder if they were serious about that one." Maureen said, "Especially the part about 'We don't smoke marijuana in Muskogee.' Who were they kidding?" This posture – lovingly committing to memory every single absurd word of a song while simultaneously pushing it all away – pervaded their approach to the wider world. They were fasci-nated and repelled, attentive and loving, and could not stop thinking and talking about it, as if documenting it would keep it safely at bay.

But they were ambivalently related to "bubbadom" and commercial country-western culture, since they saw no trustworthy alternative institutions on the horizon. Right after Maureen's joking rendition of "Stand By Your Man," Hank said happily, "Country-western is a place that women's lib hasn't gotten to yet," and he and Tino made nasty jokes about one newly divorced woman who, they said, tried to lead in dancing. While they scorned the institutions that served them, there was no available alternative in circu-lation. When Hank, Tino, Tim, and about twelve other men were initiated into the National Order of the Buffalo, Maureen, Sandra, and I sat together in the audience in the windowless Buffalo Hall, surrounded by paintings of praying children and Last Suppers and Buffalo flags. Before we sat down for

the ceremony we rushed over to the photo gallery of ''Women of the Buffalo,'' to laugh about the photos of 1950s-style women with giant beehives
and pink swathed monobosoms forming a shelf under their necks.

The ceremony struck them as funny. Hank said that the line about ''Suffer
the little children to come unto me'' did not make sense and sounded like
bad grammar. The speeches emphasized ''not just thinking in terms of mercy,
but acting mercifully; not just having loving thoughts, but acting with love;
peace, instead of war; charity, instead of meanspiritedness.'' Buffaloes should
draw a ''Circle of Care'' around themselves, and all Buffaloes should be
welcome into it.

Afterwards, Hank contrasted that ideal with the reality. He said, ''The
words are nice but it's a joke 'cuz half of those guys there are members
of the NRA,'' implying that membership in the National Rifle Association
contradicted the idea of acting with charity, peace, and love. He also made
several jokes that night about how he would go over to the owner of the
Silverado, who was a Buffalo, to say that he should draw the ''Circle of
Care'' that we were told Buffaloes feel for each other, and let us all have
free drinks – or at least free ice water, which normally cost $1.50 a glass. In
sum, they made a point of making fun of the organizations in which they
participated. They were not just feeling nervously distant or lacking firm
footing, as the mainstream country-westerners were. Instead, they were
strenuously declaring, ''I am not a member,'' constantly referring to Exxon,
to the NRA, the IRS, to a wide range of institutions that they were trying to
ignore.

Like that of the mainstream Buffaloes, cynics' ''civic etiquette'' was
organized to avoid commitment. The cynics' context let all participants demonstrate their intelligence and knowledge in order to reassure the others that
there still were people who could avoid getting swallowed up by whatever
institutions were surrounding them. The context justified and reproduced disconnection to the wider world. Power worked here by not allowing any air
space for forthright political engagement.

Vocabularies of strenuous disengagement

Cynics were incredibly knowledgeable about politics. Cynical solidarity
relied on first invoking the world's problems to show that I recognize the
problems and, along with you, am not a ''bubba.'' The second step was to
say why the problems do not affect me. Usually, the answer is that I have
rendered myself impervious, through laughter. So, the image of powerlessness peeps in, but the door quickly slams on it. Knowledge of one's own
powerlessness was a taken-for-granted prerequisite of conversation but when

it became an explicit topic, participants quickly showed that they were not so powerless after all: they were impervious and had somehow exempted themselves.

For example, after the group interview with Tim, Maureen and Hank, Tim told me, ''The big corporations made money off of Vietnam; they're making it now off Nicaragua – nothing's changed. Nothing I was gonna do was gonna make a difference so I just gave up with it. Now, I just don't participate . . . I realized nothing was gonna change, but *I don't participate*. That's what I do. I don't pay taxes.''

Tim has exempted himself from the problem by telling himself that he does not participate. It does not seem to affect him. They talked about the Army as another sick institution from which they learned to distance themselves. At the bar one night, Hank, Tim, and Tino entertained themselves by talking about a television documentary that they had all seen, on the Vietnam war. (This was, parenthetically, yet another instance of how different their idea of ''having fun'' was from the others'. They went into awful detail about the program, talking about how ''Americans would kill grandmothers and children and old men and stuff their bowels into their mouths to scare other Vietnamese from helping the Vietcong.'') The lesson these recreation group participants learned from their basic training twenty years before was one of ironic and disgusted disengagement. In basic training,

you have to go under barbed wire this high from the ground while they shoot right overhead, and as soon as you smell the gas you have to put your gas mask on, but not till you smell it, and you can't raise your head. There was a guy who was having trouble, you know, a little trouble putting his mask on, and he gets it on and I see his eyes bugging out behind the eye goggles – and then I look over again and he's got it on real snug and he's going [retching sound]. *I just laughed.*

Hank ''just laughed''; Tim ''did not participate'': there was a required conversational barrier at the end of anecdotes, that snugly protected speakers from the problems. The world is a problem, but they always ended by asserting that they were untouched, not implicated, in control after all, laughing. Their powerlessness formed the implicit backdrop for most of their jokes; they could not explicitly talk about their perceived powerlessness as a topic without reassuring themselves and each other that the sorry state of the world did not really affect them. The punchline of their complaints about institutions always had to be an ironic expression of anti-membership.

The problem affects other people, not us. It also originates in other people, not us. For example, we were talking about how stupid the news usually is. I asked why, and Tim said, ''The news is stupid because people are stupid. It's simple. If people were more interested, they could buy the *New York*

Times, which they don't. If they did, the price would go down because it would be a mass market.''

Like private people, they focused on facts when discussing politics. But unlike the private people, they were data hounds. Sniffing out grim facts was a form of self-protection for them. Of all the non-activist groups I encountered, only they had heard of the planned toxic incinerator down the road. The strenuously disengaged Buffaloes knew about all the nearby toxic plants, and referred to them freely. One day we were talking about our home towns, and they said that mine must have been charming if it was in New England. I said that, in fact, people used to plug their noses when they drove by it on the turnpike. Hank said, ''That's what people used to say about it here.''

MAUREEN: *Used* to? But I'll tell you what's really stinky though, is that Brighton plant up on Linda Vista Highway.
SANDRA: You mean Exxon?
MAUREEN: No, they got that, too. This is Brighton refinery.
TIM: Plastico?
MAUREEN: They got it all there: Plastico, Brighton, Exxon, Gasco, you name it.
HANK: Exxon's really in trouble now [referring to the Valdez oil spill].

Gathering facts as a form of self-protection did not work, though. Cynical Buffaloes were exposed nerves that turned any touch into pain. Maureen told us about a dream she had: ''There were explosions and fires in the chemical plants [that surrounded her home], and I was trying to run away, and there was a woman running away with me doing weird things. Then Lucille Ball, looking like a bag-lady, was smoking crack while we were trying to run away.'' There was no respite from social problems, not even in sleep.

Unlike the mainstream country-westerners, the cynics were confident enough in their own intellectual abilities to assume that their ignorance comes from factors like government secrecy and the power of moneyed interests, not from their own lack of intellectual abilities. As citizens, the cynics knew that they were supposed to have a say in politics and that political problems affect the ways people think and live. The cynical Buffaloes would never just flatly state that they have no say in the workings of our government, as the majority of the country-westerners did. The cynics, unlike the other Buffaloes, held an ideal of political life, but assumed that the ideal was unattainable in today's world.

The mainstream Buffaloes considered themselves too ignorant to talk about politics (as the next chapter will more clearly show), but this comparison case shows that knowledge alone is not enough to make displays of political engagement possible. More talkative, more familiar with each other, less willing to swallow commercial culture whole, better informed, more clever and confident: the cynics' style was quite different from that of the mainstream Buffaloes. But the grounds for membership ended up being remarkably similar in that, in both cases, the purpose of conversation was to assert nonmembership and disengagement, to appear irreverent and impious, not to take the group or the wider world too seriously. So, the seemingly perfect freedom of leisure time posed two contrasting obstacles to political conversation. For the first group, conversation was too difficult; for the second, too easy. Mainstream country-westerners were too closed to political ideas, doubts and worries; cynics were too open, giving such abundant expression to the horrors and degradations of the world, they were immobilized. Both discourses presume that participants can extricate themselves from the wider world.[2]

7

Activists carving out a place in the public sphere for discussion

Part 1: *"Is this a tangent?": activists in meetings*

> We're good at having discussions but bad at deciding anything. We'll have a meeting and someone'll ask us what we decided and we'll say, "We don't know but we had a *great* discussion!" That's why we're having a strategy meeting with a regional organizer.
>
> Neil, an activist in CESE (Communities for Environmental Safety Everywhere), sounding guilty but a little pleased

> I have a little sermon I wanted to give – it's short, but I just want to say a little something about what I was thinking after I met with Wilma Balinsky's campaign for governor. She asked to talk to us, and see the incinerator site, and she wanted to know that we're not just alone, that we're not just babes in the woods or flaky liberals. I think we really convinced her, but we'll see. But it really made me think: we're getting somewhere! What we're doing here matters!
>
> We're not in this for a big splash – we're in this to protect our future. If you care about the future, or even if you've ever had a child, or even if you haven't, you know that you're not in this just to make a scene or get attention. We're not doing this for ourselves, or because we want to make a fuss just for the purpose of making a fuss – we're in this to protect everyone's future. So, we've got to keep at it: this group is here only because all of us are working together, so it's important that we all volunteer. Anyway, that's my little *"sermonette"* [makes a funny mock bow and abruptly sits back down].
>
> Chris, another activist in CESE, giving a self-deprecating but a little proud pep talk a few months later

The riddle for these activists was: How can citizens' own open-ended political conversations become valuable? In their meetings, activists had to work against their own common-sense assumptions that political discussion is a waste of time, that activism is something for radicals and people who just want to make a big splash, that talk is not a source of power. They had to counteract the cultural current that considers citizens' public political discussion rude, or out of place, or irrelevant and tangential.

In meetings with officials, activists also had to struggle against the devaluation of citizens' discussion. Officials assumed that public meetings are for the purpose of distributing technical facts – one way, from officials to citizens – and not for reasoning together aloud. After about a year of diligently attending officially sponsored meetings and quietly absorbing seemingly neutral facts, the activists began to challenge that official civic etiquette that called upon citizens only to ''speak for themselves'' in the public sphere.

To value public-spirited conversation, the group had to strike out into a new cultural political territory – there was not an obvious and well-known cultural niche for thoughtful activism, such as there was for volunteer groups. One of the group's accomplishments over the course of its development was to carve out that niche for itself. That meant, above all, redefining the purpose of talk itself; over time, participants decided that becoming active citizens in a democracy was inseparable from valuing their own speech, in meetings and other public spaces. They had to convince themselves that *publicly minded talk* was not, as volunteers said, just a waste of time and energy; and not, as Buffalo Club members said, just something that ''flaky'' show-offs do to ''make a big splash,'' ''get attention or make a scene.'' They had to convince themselves that holding reflective, broad-minded political discussions was, itself, an important part of citizenship.

A strong force working against that valuation of talk itself came from officials and reporters, who pushed activists to sound like volunteers – like people who are involved only out of concern for their own families, who speak only for themselves in public, and who thus should be convinced when officials tell them the incinerator is safe. Activists often met this pressure half-way, by sounding much less publicly minded in public than they sounded in private, using that Mom discourse that I described in chapter 1. Thus, activists themselves played their part in the cycle of political evaporation: they relished publicly minded conversations in their informal gathering – backstage – but rarely found a ''place'' for it in public – frontstage. And when activists did manage to squeeze publicly minded ideas into the constricted public sphere, officials and reporters ignored them, anyway; the cycle of political evaporation continued.

The groups

The chapter focuses on Communities for Environmental Safety Everywhere, a group that was trying to prevent a toxic incinerator from being built in

Evergreen City. I worked with that group for over two years, going to its demonstrations, meetings, informal gatherings, press conferences, watching members interact with reporters, helping with petitioning, poster-making, and publicity. There were about two dozen sporadic members and twelve core members, including a local realtor; Chris and Maryellen, two homemakers (Maryellen later got a job in a pre-school); Neil, a corporate chemist; Al, a carpenter; Ginny, a schoolteacher; Eleanor, a retired schoolteacher; Henry, a social worker; Nikky, an owner of a used clothes store; Donald, a musician, and several office workers.

I spent less time with another group, Testament for Humanity, a coalition that was protesting arms shipments to the Third World from the local weapons depot. I collected their leaflets, watched them interact with the press, attended many of their demonstrations and three meetings of one of the groups involved in this coalition. I also attended an election night party of a fundamentalist Christian's city council campaign, and interviewed some members, including two leaders. I also closely followed the newpaper coverage of, and editorials written by, a group that was trying to prevent a homeless shelter from being installed in its neighborhood, and interviewed people who were trying to start a homeless shelter in a mall. But CESE was, by far, my main focus of attention.

The first part of this chapter shows how activists came to value political conversation itself within their own meetings. The second part portrays activists' efforts at challenging the officials' definition of the purpose of "public" meetings, and simultaneously but tenuously beginning to locate themselves on a map that included an alternative set of institutions: local unions, statewide grassroots groups, and national political groups like Greenpeace.

CESE's way of creating a sense of togetherness veered between three different styles, or genres of participation. Were CESE members "citizens of a democratic republic," who debated and did not shy away from talk about structure and conflict? Or was CESE a "radical" group, since it worked with eccentrically dressed hippie environmentalists from Pacific City who seemed flamboyantly to reject the American way of life altogether? Or was CESE a "volunteer" group, doing non-conflictual and wholesome activities to protect the children? Participants tentatively wanted the group to answer "yes" to the first question, but this category – "democratic citizen" – was one they felt they had to make up from scratch. Every now and then I heard tenuous allusions to "our American democratic heritage" that permits citizens to speak out and make a difference, but these tentative references to democratic ideals were usually vague enough to be easily mistaken for references to volunteer-style participation.

"Democratic citizens in a republic": a genre in the American tradition

Every meeting of CESE included an argument like Chris' "sermonette." Item no. 1 on the agenda one day was about another incinerator plan that had just been canceled in a nearby town, Airdale. Neil, the meeting chair, said the Airdale activists had fought long and hard since 1983. "It really counts!" he announced, as if he had to argue against the going assumption of futility. It was as if the members were saying, "Yes, of course we all know that in America, citizens are supposed to be able to make a difference, and of course we all assume that it's just a line they tell civics classes or that it's based on a defunct idea of American politics: but really, it really *is true!*" This constant implicit argument against expected disbelief was like Ripley's "Believe It or Not" or the *National Enquirer*, which also anticipate readers' disbelief.

Clearing away the disbelief and finding a positive role for citizens seems to take so much effort, it would take a long time for any grassroots group to reach the point of exploring what the positive contents of good citizenship would be – to find a comfortable etiquette for deciding what grassroots groups should want. Maybe this helps explain why so many grassroots groups in this country are organized simply to say "No," and so rarely develop a vision for positive change.

In its first year, CESE hardly met at all, mostly meeting only the way volunteer groups did – at people's houses, one-on-one, informally. After that, for another few months, they held informal meetings, but still did not regularly have publicly announced meetings. Public meetings followed the bureaucratic process, happening only when the state called a hearing or issued a report. During this period, Maryellen told me that Neil and Ginny thought meetings were a waste of time, but that she herself thought they were a way to get people involved. Since she, her husband Neil, and Amy, one of their two daughters, were all active in the group, their house was a center for organizing. Maryellen said, "People are always calling me up asking how they can get involved and there's nothing to tell them!"

A few months after Maryellen told me she thought meetings were a good way to foster involvement, she met with Neil and Donald, and, as Neil put it, "convinced us to try to figure out how to *allow* people to participate. We've been not *allowing* people to participate. Everyone is waiting for someone else to tell them what to do, but why can't the publicity committee be in charge of getting publicity even when there's not an *event* for them to publicize?"

In other words, at first, their approach echoed the volunteers'; as one volunteer put it, "there is little to do . . . What would I do? You could write the *letter*, but otherwise I wouldn't know what to do.'' Activists decided that there *is* little to do; that is, except talk, talk to each other and to neighbors in meetings and rallies and pickets, talk to people in other locales working on similar issues; and write leaflets, write the letter to the official, to the editor, to other people working on similar issues.

Later, after the group had changed course, and begun to value conversation more, I asked Diane in an interview, ''How much influence do you think a person like you can have over government decisions?'' She answered that survey question with a laugh: ''A *lot*, if I get committed to running my mouth!''

Social researchers Frances Fox Piven and Richard Cloward (1979) worry that activism easily gets lost in the halls of bureaucracy, where dead-end quasi-solutions rob people of the ability to organize themselves (see also Habermas 1979). The activists soon came to the same conclusion; dramatically reversing their earlier strategy, they began to hold monthly meetings. The group also organized itself into subcommittees – fundraising, phone tree and mailing, research, and others – that met at people's houses, in addition to the monthly mass meetings of about fifty people. Soon, the physical structure of the meetings changed, too. Earlier, Neil had chaired all the meetings, using a microphone, and the ''audience'' would sit in rows of chairs facing him or whoever was authorized to speak at the microphone. Later, the meetings changed shape: the microphone went away, and the rows became a circle (this shape was, of course, not an idea that they invented out of thin air. They got the idea for committees, a circle, and the importance of participation from a booklet put out by a national organization, the Citizens' Clearinghouse on Hazardous Waste, and adopted it as their own. As we will see, activists began to highlight groups like CCHW, and discovered a whole galaxy of alternative institutions on the horizon). Members said they were making a conscious effort to make more people feel more comfortable talking in meetings.

The group decided to value meetings, not only as a means of getting predetermined tasks done, but also as contexts for developing new thoughts. For example, in a discussion about making signs for a picket, one member suggested that people could just make their own, in their own time, if the group could find an easily accessible place to stow the magic markers and posterboard. But another member disagreed, saying that the group should set aside one particular time and place for all interested members to make posters together. Everyone agreed when she said, ''The poster committee might get together and think up stuff we'd have never thought of!'' The group also decided to start a newsletter, something members never would have done when the group was just tagging behind the bureaucratic process.

Backstage among activists

In these and other ways, activists made it clear that they valued free-flowing publicly minded discussion. Yet, they were still not sure how much of that rich discussion should enter public space – mostly, they kept it backstage. In informal get-togethers, members of CESE nimbly transformed seemingly private topics of conversation into public ones and back again. For example, when we met at Diane and Wilfred's house to make posters for an upcoming demonstration and eat Diane's homemade stew, we entertained ourselves for hours while designing posters, with conversations analyzing the incinerator plans and the politics of toxic waste production. Another time, over breakfast before the town parade (in which the group had a float), we had a long debate about unions, then speculated on the local newspaper owner's reasons for encouraging rapid suburban development and his relation to unions, and puzzled over the relationship between grassroots activism and citizens' advisory committees that are sponsored by corporations – Plastico wanted to form one, and had invited Neil to serve on it. At a lunch break during a special all-day meeting, members speculated about the connection between people's employment and ideals, noting that several members had recently obtained jobs in day-care and teaching, which allowed them to do something that fitted with their activism while making money; and then we talked about the profit-making capacities of incinerators. At another get-together, a conversation about home decor immediately led into a debate about the political pros and cons of buying Native American rugs on reservations – whether it was good to spend money on reservations and support them that way, or whether it ultimately harmed reservations to be so dependent on tourists; a conversation about buying a new car led to discussion of freon, ozone, and air conditioning, etc. There was no separating politics from the rest of life. Exchanging political analyses was a form of entertainment in these informal get-togethers. Such mental flexibility was less present in more frontstage settings.

No one was quite sure how much discussion was useful for meetings, and how much should be kept backstage. At one meeting, a new woman brought up the question of why taxpayers should pay for toxic clean-up, as she thought a new bill proposed. Was answering this going off on a tangent? Later in that meeting, the group began to discuss the relationship between the Evergreen County *Times* and the community. Was a discussion of the local paper's politics a tangent? In a discussion on fundraising, Henry, an awkward and dedicated schoolteacher, started off sounding very practical, talking about a topic that even volunteers would consider useful – fundraising – but ended up doing what the volunteers and Buffalo Club members would call soapboxing: "We should dig into our own pockets to pay for our stuff. That's a good form of fundraising itself, if each of us donated $25, that would come to $1400, and we're up against big money, with those Montgomery guys getting paid $500 a head to come to Local Hearing Commitee meetings." Was this a tangent? In many meetings, Victoria brought up the "for-profit" nature of Montgomery (in a discussion about how to recruit new members): "I find saying 'commercial' really gets people. It's not just that they're gonna burn toxic waste, but that they're going to make profits by importing toxic waste from all over. It's the profit-making that really convinces people." She said the company would have incentives to work quickly instead of carefully. Was this a tangent? None of these issues were on the agenda, and after a few minutes in each case, someone in the group would step in and say "We've gotten off track," and try to refocus the group. Yet, the group had devoted some time to addressing all of these questions.

I found Neil and Henry outdoors in the balmy evening air after one meeting, arguing over the recurrent question. Neil argued that it was too simplistic to say, as Henry had, that "we should just stop producing the stuff this minute." At another meeting, when the topic of "where should the waste go?" arose, Ginny tried to shut the debate down, snapping in a rapid and concise clip:

It's not up to us to come up with solutions. When people at a dinner or a party ask that, it's usually just a way of sidetracking you. Scientists have to solve that. If the companies put some of their millions of dollars of research efforts into studying that, they could solve it. But we can't. That's another meeting, another organization. It's not something we can figure out.

The problem was not just that members were unsure of the answer to the question (though Ginny sounded pretty sure of some good answers). They were unsure whether even to discuss it at all.

A frequent preface for a comment in the group was, "I don't want to make this into a rap session, but ... ", implying that just talking was not useful, but that on the other hand, it was, in this specific case, necessary. In another meeting, someone described a book that she said we all should read (*Killing Our Own* by Harvey Wasserman). Nikky and Al told the group that the US military was the nation's biggest toxic polluter, and that led into a small discussion of the irony involved in the government's being the watchdog over itself. But again, these were considered "tangents," though the group let them go on long enough for some discussion to get going before someone got the group "back on track." So, though the questions of where waste should go or what could be done to prevent its production were rarely on the agenda, they were discussed anyway, in every single meeting. And every time those ''tangents'' arose, new perspectives on them arose as well. In this way various analyses entered the meetings, but not at the center of discussion. And in fact, after meetings, backstage, most of the casual, one-on-one conversation was precisely about those intriguing ''tangents.''

Backstage was where activists voiced their important objections to the incinerator. One objection was that the government should be actively encouraging companies to stop producing toxic waste (''source reduction''); building incinerators, they said, encourages companies to keep producing toxic waste, because incinerators are so expensive to build and maintain, and can be profitable only if they are used to near-full capacity. Another was that the company had a bad track record and therefore could not be trusted, no matter how sound the design appeared to be. A third objection was that the local community would not itself see any of the profits. A fourth source of political objections was the idea, expressed ''tangentially'' in several meetings, that the military, which many members thought was a big waste in itself, was the nation's largest source of toxic waste – if the company could argue that toxic chemicals made everyday necessities possible, the activists would have said that they were mostly a by-product of useless weapons production. A fifth political objection was that there was no incentive for the company to operate its incinerator according to the rules: that a profit-making company would be loath to turn away trucks loaded up with chemicals that the incinerator was not designed to handle; and that government inspectors were too few and far between to do their jobs.

All this talking helped members clarify their positions. CESE held a series of meetings about an environmental initiative on the state ballot. The battle was confusing: like the Alcohol Tax Initiative faced by the volunteers that year, the environmental one inspired the targeted industries (logging interests and corporate pollutors, in the environmental initiative's case; alcohol producers in the alcohol tax's case) to mount a counter-initiative that looked pretty much the same to voters who did not ''read the fine print'' (and both the environmental and the alcohol tax proposals lost to giant corporate-funded campaigns). Yet, remember how the volunteers ''volunteered'' me in their meeting to collect signatures for the alcohol tax before I or any of the others had information about it? The volunteers had assumed that talking about it was not necessary. The activists, on the other hand, lavished time on discussion of their initiative. The first time it was discussed, Neil read a long list of organizations' endorsements; then someone described its basic programs; then Neil asked, with pretend pomposity, ''Being a democratic organization, does anybody want to endorse it, or object to it?'' From across the room, Diane hollered, ''Endorse it!'' Then, someone from the Stockport Greenpeace chapter, Ruth, with tangled curly hair and combat boots, said there was a "fake" one going around – a "counter-initiative" – and this led to more discussion of the differences between the two. CESE then held two evening meetings about the measure, partly in order to find out more about the industry-sponsored counter-measure, and the group hosted two public video screenings. A few months later, the group held a little demonstration supporting the initiative (that the local newspaper got wrong, saying the group opposed it!).

The relation between "getting things done" and "talking" was tense. The group considered its petition drive to be both an educational effort and an effort to prevent the waste from entering town. But what was the relation between the two types of effort? If signature-gatherers in front of Safeway engage in long debates with each individual, they miss streams of people entering the automatic doors – this was Henry's approach. The rest of the group thought that getting enough signatures to give the petition teeth would help the group publicize the incinerator, and that in turn would lead more citizens to talk and question the issue, later – less talk now would mean more talk later. But the process of signature-gathering sat uncomfortably next to activists' own desire to ignite discussion, now.

Many times, I observed members changing their opinions during or after discussions. For example, at first, members were excited about Earth Day, 1991; the national event seemed initially to be making environmentalism mainstream, not just a marginal activity of leftists and granola eaters. But later, after backstage conversations with Greenpeace members and others, they decided it was corporate window-dressing – "big pollutors like Hewlett Packard and McDonald's, for public relations – you know, plant a few trees in front of the refinery and everything'll be OK." Having the opportunity to change their minds through discussion was part of what they liked about activism. Unlike country-western dancer Betsy, who thought that all she could do was "snip her rings" on six-packs, the activists learned about environmental politics by talking. They had a less static idea of knowledge and power – that they grow through talk. The difference between the two groups was in their beliefs about interaction.

The danger for "democratic citizens"

In direct contrast to the volunteeeers' neatly organized, quick meetings, the activists' meetings often risked overwhelming members. Once the dam against political talk opened a little, everything came flooding through, threatening to drown the meetings altogether. At one meeting, for example, a member, Jimmy, said that the group should tell people to walk the mile to a planned demonstration at the proposed incinerator site. Maryellen said it was too dangerous to walk along that windy, narrow road, but that they could tell people to park nearby, at an asphalt company. She hesitated at that, thinking aloud, "That's polluting, asphalt."

Jimmy, a long-haired surveyor for suburban developers, who rode a bicycle everywhere instead of driving, said, "But you'll be driving on it instead. It'll look ridiculous. People will say, 'They say they're for clean air and they drive a bunch of vans.'"

In the same meeting was a long debate about using paper to write letters to officials. A newcomer said, "The most polluting industry is production of paper, particularly bleached paper. By the way, is all the literature on the table printed on recycled paper?"

Neil answered, guiltily, "As much as possible." Maryellen said she also felt funny about using so much paper. Since activists had decided to let seemingly unsurmountable problems into the realm of discussable reality, they were not sure where to stop. All aspects of everyday life were up for questioning, making someone wonder aloud if it was environmentally wasteful even to use paper for writing letters to politicians and leaflets! It was difficult to sift between issues of personal morality, like paper use and driving, and the ones that addressed issues in a more structural way.

In interviews, this danger of feeling overwhelmed became even more apparent. In interviews, I asked activists whether they would ever think of joining an anti-drugs group and when they said no, I explained that volunteers thought drugs was a good issue because it was urgent, "close to home," and "do-able." Maryellen said,

> I'm concerned about them, in a *way* [in a sing-song tone, as if she is not sure why she is being asked – see Labov (1972) on the meaning of this tone], because of the peer pressure, we try to teach them, and – but, so it is close to home, but not – I don't know, that is a good question. Is it close to home? It definitely is close to home. It's close to home to all of us . . .
>
> *All* of these issues are close to home because they're human and we're all human and it's all international like I said, and there are very few places in the world that are independent . . .

NINA: The anti-drugs group says that drugs is a good issue to work on because it's do-able. What do you think – Is the drugs issue a do-able one?

MARYELLEN [describes her daughter's fifth grade anti-drug program, saying it was not enough]: Maybe a real grassroots type of thing will snap the government into shape . . . But I don't think the government's gonna help them until they really push hard. I think it's gonna be a real struggle for them to straighten it out . . . But [after more on the pros and cons of her daughter's program] I don't know, I really feel as if the whole society, to me, is falling apart . . . It's gonna take a lot of strength and it's gonna take a lot of people to pull out.

Whether I asked environmental activists if they would join an anti-drugs group, or a schools group, or *any* group, *whatever* the group was, activists convinced themselves that every issue was really important and that they really should care deeply. And in contrast to volunteers and recreation group members, activists made every issue feel both personal and political at the same time:

NINA: Does the nuclear stuff seem close to home?

GINNY: Sure it does. It's more though, it is more of a personal kind of issue – you know, that Ground Zero kind of approach. As serious of an issue [as] it is, just other issues have taken precedence . . . I certainly believe it's absolutely *the* issue . . . But you know, it's the whole international military establishment that you've got to stop. It's our whole system that depends on the military for our economic well-being.

Addressing the same question, Eleanor declared, "Absolutely, that's as close to home as anything. Sure it hits close to home. My word! And I think we have to do something. I think we have to take action, we have to do something." Diane said, "It scares the hell out of me, it really does," but then concluded, "I'm not saying we should just lay down and get screwed, but what can a local group do?" All of the interviews with activists gave me the dizzy feeling of perching on the edge of despair.

It was not clear what "doing" was, when faced with such problems. Thus, in interviews, even the most active activists – Neil, Maryellen, Eleanor, and Diane – all claimed not to be very active, and claimed to be very "private" people. At the same time, they all mentioned, in passing, scores of "little" tasks they did for the group. In contrast, volunteers were more certain what "doing" meant for them, and could more easily feel secure that what they were doing did matter. They proudly listed all of the volunteer work they did, and were more convinced than activists that their work did make a difference.

One way that activists avoided feeling overwhelmed was to talk about institutional, and not just individual, solutions to social problems. Thus, activists' approach contrasted with the other two groups' – they talked about solutions that would not depend so completely on each individual's personal feelings of generosity and personal ability to donate money, space, and time, but on solutions that would be built into official institutions:

ELEANOR: We can pressure our county supervisors; we can pressure the state legislators; we can pressure the US government – after all, we *are* the government. And we can – again, we can make a difference with individual people. When you see kids who don't have a home address in your classroom, and you know damn well they're living in a car, that's hard. That's unbelievably hard. And there should be some kind of program, local program, for developing housing – some kind of low-income housing.

A problem could thus be both very personal and "close to home" and *also* "big" and political. For volunteers, calling something personal was a way of making it seem smaller and more "do-able"; for activists, in contrast, ferreting out a problem's institutional origins did not make it less personal, but *did* make it feel more "do-able." They expanded from personal feelings to structural solutions, instead of treating personal and political as opposite.

Democratic citizenship: "It's what America's all about, isn't it?"

Evergreen City had a big celebration in the park every Fourth of July, with booths, music, concession stands, and games. CESE made a booth, festooned in red, white, and blue, with a "Stuff the Stack" game, in which players who tossed the fuzzy ball into a model smokestack won a prize; all passers-by got a leaflet and an offer to sign a petition. Nikky joked about Diane's "patriotic" garb, a red shirt with white stars. Diane said wryly, "Well, what we're doing *is* patriotic. It's what America's all about, isn't it?" She added that she would have brought her American flag, but her back hurt and the flag was heavy.

Reference like this to the American tradition of active political participation was rare. The other explicit reference I heard to that tradition was in a speech Neil gave at a rally to support a state initiative on the ballot. Dumping tea into Swift River, he decried Montgomery, a foreign company, saying that two hundred years ago, Americans dumped tea in the harbor in Boston to assert local rule against British forces, and here he was, doing the same, with the same goal in mind. The activists were tentatively trying to redefine the meaning of "volunteers" – they wanted to be the kind of volunteers that held the Boston Tea Party: people willing to stand up for themselves, even if it meant disagreeing in public and confronting powerful institutions, rebelling, and speaking in terms of principles. While the group did know about this cultural category for political involvement, it was a very abstract and distant concept. The activists had to reinvent it, as a practice and not just a static belief.

A rejected genre of citizenship: cynical radicalism

Early in the group's life, members of CESE assumed that style and political conviction went together automatically. Like the disengaged people of the

Buffalo Club, the new activists assumed that criticizing people's political opinions was like criticizing the way they decorated their home or styled their hair: a matter of taste that is very personal and not open for debate. One woman called me to tell me when the next meeting was, and she felt compelled to add, "I can't believe I'm doing this – I was never one of those types who went out and protested and wore sandals in the '60s." This implication, that political commitment is a character trait, helped make engagement seem inaccessible to many of the people I met, who said they were not "political people" by nature.

After about a year of meeting regularly, though, members began asking what was the relation between personal style and political ideas. The group explicitly discussed the conflict between looking respectable and expressing feelings, and tentatively decided that it was more important to "play the game." At a publicity committee meeting, for example, seven of us sat in Diane and Wilfred's antique-filled, manicured living room, muzak on the radio; our task: to design a logo and name for the group. We considered acronym titles that the group decided sounded too negative or "radical," like "GASP" and "STINK," and ones that they said sounded too "mealy-mouthed," and "sappy," like "SHARE" and "CARE." CESE – Communities for Environmental Safety Everywhere – was positive – not "against" or "anti" – without sounding "sappy." As Chris said, it showed that the effort was both grassroots and statewide and made it clear that it was "groups of little people all over the place just working in neighborhood communities." In other words, it was not "radical" and not "volunteer" style, but sounded like something for responsible citizens. Finding a way of representing themselves was much more difficult for activists than it was for volunteers, and also more important, since there was not already a comfortable cultural niche for activists. Activists had to invent themselves.

Volunteers' political etiquette felt natural, part of their personalities, dovetailing nicely with the institutions surrounding the groups. But the activists' etiquette did not feel natural at all; it was thus much harder to enforce, sometimes leading to incongruous mixes of styles. Donald, the unemployed actor from Europe who prided himself on being cosmopolitan, fitted the "radical" mode. He came to one outdoor picket in a hot pink shirt and tie, fluorescent green sunglasses tied to his head with a day-glo pink safety strap; behind him was the towering gray Plastico plant; underfoot was yellowish gray grass coated with forty years of chemicals and grease. Almost everyone else in the group dressed up, trying hard to look respectable and responsible: they were not portraying themselves as self-interested plain folks in plaid flannel, but as informed, responsible, and powerful citizens. Diane picked through the scrubby grass in black pumps, trying not to snag her panty hose. Al, a hippie carpenter, wore a suit.

Despite activists' efforts at appearing responsible and not "radical," an angry journalist accused the group of not bothering to arrange a public meeting with Plastico before calling the picket. Afterwards, Chris worried that the journalist was right; yet, even at the picket, she had proclaimed that "with a history like theirs, Plastico should be coming to us with its tail between its legs to explain the blow-up. And," she had added, "the problem is not just Plastico, but the whole alley of industry all up and down the Swift River, from Carthage to Amargo." On the one hand, Chris wanted to cooperate and not look "radical," but on the other hand, she was pretty sure that the proper channels had already proven themselves useless – as the group's signs said, the plant had had "eight major explosions, spills or fires in the last eight years." She wanted to participate in political decision-making, but did not want to be rude or out of place. She had criticisms, but they were about policy, not just technology. Until activists carved out public space for their own talk, there was no *place* for a participant like that.

The importance of style became a matter of debate. For a few months, part of every meeting was devoted to questions of radical style. One debate was about whether Greenpeace members' purple pants were a problem or whether it was their political ideas or both. At another meeting, the group decided that the previous demonstration had been too short, but that long speeches "get boring fast," so they tacked a big sheet of paper on the wall and asked members to call out suggestions for a demonstration, in which the activists were to give Montgomery a "Bad Neighbor" award (this was part of a national campaign in which toxic pollutors around the country received such awards):

> A town crier on stilts
> Smokestack on wheels, with a fan to blow dry ice smoke upwards
>   (this they learned from activists in Airdale, a town nearby)
> Songs
> Black balloons
> Ugly flowers, weeds
> A coffin with Evergreen City written on it

Members were clearly having fun thinking up proposals, but at this last suggestion, Al said,

> People respond negatively to such negative images. The common man. The more common, straight, normal, we look, not a bunch of hippie types; the more totally normal and regular we look, the better.
>
> NIKKY: We all look regular, but we should wear street clothes. People don't want to be scared ... They look for a wide range of people, and not just radicals.

[Murmurs from the rest of the group:] Oh, why not! Go for it! [that is: Oh, why not shock the public?]

AL: Well, that's where I am [with the "radicals"] in my *heart*!

Later in this meeting, Victoria said, "We were a threat to Montgomery at the last event because we were orderly – there were no cat-calls." She compared this orderly event to another more rowdy one at the site of the proposed incinerator, on Montgomery Company property.

At that rowdy event, demonstrators audibly gasped when they first glimpsed the several acres of square, bright, crayon-yellow and green sludge. Montgomery said it had been in the process of cleaning up the psychedelic toxic ponds since buying the site, nearly thirty years earlier. While they did graciously offer a company spokesperson a turn at the microphone, demonstrators also jeered and cat-called and pointed at the surrealistic ponds when the spokeperson told them that the company was going to have "brand new state-of-the-art storage modules."

After the demonstration, some members chastised those who laughed at the company speaker. Chris offered the principle that "if we want them to treat us like good neighbors, we have to be good neighbors, too." Diane, thinking more of strategy than principles, said that in any case it did not look good. Another time, Maryellen told me that "if we treat the hearing process with respect, they'll treat us with respect." On the one hand, CESE found that the cost of acting "radical" was too high. On the other hand, conflating a "radical" style with public-spirited discussion was tempting, since the hearing process was set up in a way that made publicly minded debate rude and out of place.

Why was that style so tempting, then? It was difficult for Henry and others not to sound "radical" when talking to corporate spokespeople. Leaving the meeting one day, Henry encountered Mike, the plant manager. Henry, trying unsuccessfully to be friendly after having been told that he was too confrontational, said,

Put yourself in my shoes. How would you feel, knowing your property values will go down?

MIKE [in a comforting, reassuringly paternal voice]: Well, that remains to be seen. That's what the financial impact report is about.

HENRY: Just think about it. Of course it will. And what gives you the right to take something away from all the people of Evergreen City? I've lived here a long time – what gives one person the right to take away all our rights – never mind the health risks? What right do you have?

MIKE: It's gonna go somewhere. If you don't like the result, don't drive a car. Most of the waste in this country comes from that automobile – when you stop driving it, we might get somewhere. But most of us enjoy the freedom cars give us, and the hairdryers and convenience foods and the rest.

HENRY: How much waste is generated by cars? I'll own that much. What must it be? Half? fifty percent? It can't all be in cars!

The weight of everyday life was on Montgomery's side. Activists had to live as if everyday acts, such as driving, were not inevitable. They had to invent a language for something that does not yet exist, develop an etiquette for living in the subjunctive tense: "*If* our society *were* different in many ways, *then* we wouldn't have to drive and there would not be as much toxic waste." They constantly had to treat everyday acts as irrelevant.

The "radical style" was tempting, not just because it was so dominant an image of activism. It was tempting because the pressure to appear like volunteers in public – calmly and politely seeking facts – cost members, especially women, dearly. Many often felt on the verge of exploding at the company representatives. Maryellen defiantly told me:

I'm going to the LHC meeting Thursday and I'm gonna give them an earful. I'm gonna tell them how I feel – let those Montgomery people know how people in the community feel. "How would you like it if your kid was the one in a million [projected cancer deaths]?" And it's not just one in a million, because there's Plastico and Pantox and Chemfill and Gasco. I'm gonna let them have it!

NINA: That sounds fun but what about the people in the meeting saying all this about being respectable?

MARYELLEN: We've done that and there's a time for that but I want to tell them straight. I haven't told anyone I'm going to do that – not even Neil [her husband] – because I don't want anyone to convince me not to do it. Beside, it'll be before the meeting actually starts, so it won't upset anything. I just want them to know how the people here feel.

Independent-minded Diane felt the way Maryellen did. She said, annoyed, "If Neil and Wilfred weren't always telling me to hold it, I would just explode at those guys from Montgomery – no more of this kissy-face, huggybear!" And she never did explode at them.

The "cynical radical" genre, theater and farce

This "radical" style summoned some of the Americans' worst fears about activism: it came close to making the whole issue appear to be a show aimed at self-promotion and attention-getting, and to make activists appear to have no respect for the average American. At the group's beginning, the two aspiring stage performers tried to run the show. "Donald Ghetto" and "Tom Haystack" both had stage names, both loved to talk, and both enjoyed making fun of average Americans. At a small meeting when the group was new, Tom, a skinny actor with a fashionably jagged haircut, said he liked to do an audience IQ test, licked a finger and held it in the air (that is, most audiences' heads are wind-tunnels). Donald, a robust fellow with a big, booming musician's voice, proclaimed that posters publicizing the event should "bill it as a free concert and comedy" and put the "intelligent" stuff in small print at the bottom. "People will go, 'Duh, a free concert – let's go!' and then notice who put it on. 'A toxic incinerator – huh! What's that?' " Donald and Tom kept up a constant, amusing banter, quickly railroading the others into planning a concert with music, speeches, and comedy. The two joked that the group could appeal to musicians' vanity, declaring that musicians play for only three reasons: money, publicity, and to have a good time. Only later did Donald add a fourth reason: for a good cause. Neil and Maryellen asked several times, "What *else* can we do, other than just music?" but no one listened.

Tom ordered Maryellen to reserve the Oil, Chemical and Atomic Workers' Union hall for two hours. Henry asked, "Why not four? Why not be straight with them?"

Tom said, "Oh, right, I forgot. I been wheeling and dealing all day, I forgot."

This kind of radicalism assumed a great distance between "radicals" and "the public" – the assumption would be that if most people are just stupid, then there is no harm in manipulating them. The relation between spectacle and message, between cultural radicalism, political analysis, and winning their immediate battle was a topic of recurrent debate. Activists worried that the public forum was hopelessly poisoned by people with money and power, who could explain themselves by greasing palms and twisting arms. They worried that maybe the "radicals" were right in thinking that "the public" is unable to distinguish a good, solid argument from a bad, flashy one. On the other hand, they did not want to engage in publicly unmasking Montgomery's glib and oily efforts at deceiving the public.

After the city council voted to accept CESE's petition, Maryellen gave me her standard line to the press when I interviewed her on the phone for a radio story: "It's a major victory. There's a lot of work ahead of us, but it's a victory and it feels good to be marching forward together." But then, a minute later,

But *just between you and I*, Nina, the problem is, industry is so powerful, and with their money they can put out ads for a month solid, brainwash the people, and the next thing you know, the people say, "Oh, *well*, this for sure is safe because they told us so and they have beautiful colored ads in the paper: they've *got* to be honest!" So many people are bought out, just by ads, not consciously. And that's the part that would be scary, I think, but maybe people are becoming more intelligent. I don't know. I rather doubt it.

There was no way to express these doubts about the public without sounding "radical" like Tom and Donald, without insulting the public. Since most activists did not want to sound arrogantly scornful of the public, they could not voice these concerns.

A contrasting case: bandana radicals

Demonstrators at the Evergreen Island Naval Air Station vigil had fewer qualms about expressing the idea that the public is easily fooled. After demonstrator Augie Bradley lost his arm when a weapons truck ran over him during a sit-in there, about ten thousand people gathered to protest at the dusty, hot station and listened to speakers who had flown in from around the world. Before the speeches ended, about a hundred demonstrators broke away. Wielding pickaxes and crowbars, red bandanas tied over their noses and mouths, guerrilla-style, they began dismantling the concrete highway. Back at the main event, speaker after speaker begged them to stop, saying that the group should be trying to convince people through civil disobedience, not direct destruction of property, and bringing up the examples of Gandhi and Martin Luther King.

With these costumes, and with their habit of using Spanish pronunciation for Latin American country names ("Nee-cah-rah-gwaah," for example) and shouting Latin American slogans in Spanish, it was hard to imagine how the bandana radicals could have thought of themselves as communicating to disengaged, mall-shopping readers. However, one highway dismantler told me that physically ripping up the highway *was* a way to convince people to get involved. He said that most people feel too powerless to get involved, but if demonstrators can show them that the highway was built by humans and can be unbuilt by humans, then they will feel less powerless. The spectacle will break through their everyday assumptions about the inevitability of the political and material world. He quoted a poem by Bertolt Brecht.[1]

In activists' argument about how important spectacle is, the highway dismantlers could realistically claim that, if not for them, vigils would not make it into the news. Most participants in the Evergreen Island vigil opposed the highway dismantling – they were extraordinarily prolific leaflet writers, whose messages bore the stamp of the quiet, solemn religious groups that wrote them. But indeed, not a word from those leaflets ever made it into the news. In fact, nothing those religious groups had to say made it into the news.

A third genre: mandatory public Momism and the temptation of the volunteer discourse

A third style for citizenship was the ''volunteer.'' The image of ''the volunteer'' went with the ''melodramatic'' (that is, ''melodrama'' in the sense used by literary theorists, to mean intimate drama about domestic issues) Mom discourse portrayed in chapter 1. In this genre, activists sounded like volunteers, highlighting concern for their own health and their own children. Melodramatic Momism was activists' standard fare for their frontstage discourse, despite their wide variety of discourses in more backstage settings. And (aside from a single exception, in one local newspaper article) it was the only discourse of theirs that ever made it into the news.

At a demonstration on a chilly rainy day in February, over ten people spoke, from groups all over the western United States, and again, the reporters zeroed in on the Moms. First, Neil gave an information-oriented speech analyzing the three possible kinds of toxic emissions from a toxic incinerator: those occurring in the plant's normal operations, accidents, and leftover toxic ash. Of course, none of the reporters quoted him, except Andrea, who did not quote the informational speech, but focused on his emotional state, saying that Neil ''shed a tear'' for his community.

Other speakers advocated laws requiring corporations to reduce their use of toxic chemicals, or offered ideas for making local industries more trustworthy through active government regulation. One activist from a nearby town reported on major changes her group had just won, and discussed the interlocking powers of military pollutors and government regulators. Another drew parallels between his town and dozens of others.

Some speakers, though, used the Mom discourse. Ginny said,

I see lots of kids that I know and love, and they go to school right in the direction of the wind from the incinerator. And I think of how fragile their little lungs are ... Raise your hand if you live in Evergreen City [many raise their hands]. OK, so *you* have a vested interest in keeping these people healthy. You have a vested interest in making sure that we don't have a whole lot of funerals in one week.

The next speaker invited all the children in the audience to come up onto the stage with her, and surrounded by children, played a Mom, pleading, ''Will they notify schools when accidents happen?''

I was there this time as a participant observer of the press, covering the story for a small Newton radio station. Every story about this demonstration, including mine, began with a description of the chilly weather, implying that the demonstrators displayed personal fortitude to stay out in the drizzling rain. In the precious little space afforded to some journalists, that was what mattered. To reporters, activists' *personal* dedication and commitment, their individual actions of the moment, mattered more than the principles they were advocating. In stories written by reporters who sympathized with the activists, the main message was that the activists ''believe in standing up for what they believe,'' and we should respect them for standing up for their beliefs.[2] The context of a news story was, apparently, not the place to discuss citizens' political *analyses*.

In every event the group put on, at least one activist said something about trying to change policies regarding hazardous waste production, but it was not easy to get into the news as a ''democratic citizen.'' For example, at a press conference in the courtyard of city hall, Maryellen said:

We are very concerned that, rather than reducing and reycling, which EPA and DHS says they are proud to say that's their #1 way of taking care of our toxics, that rather, they are putting their money into incinerators, and we're concerned *about* the effects of the incinerators. We're real glad to have Greenpeace in town to help us in our fight, which the rally this Saturday at the riverfront park will help a lot. And we urge all residents *in* Amargo and Evergreen Counties *to* come *to* that rally.

She was trying to sound respectable, like the kind of citizen who should be taken seriously. But in their stories, no local reporters quoted what she said about reducing and recycling. The reporters all turned to the nervous Mom who spoke next, surrounded by her kids: ''We have Plastico and Pantox and ChemFill and various other industry in our city. We also have families and sick people and elderly people – people trying to survive and have a life in this city. We feel we are the dumping ground for all the cities in this county ... We're *scared* to have any more.''

Reporters were clearly more interested in her, taping, videotaping, quoting her and the frizzy-haired, ''radical''-looking Greenpeace organizer.

Whether or not activists used the Mom discourse as a conscious strategy to get air-time is an obvious question: at some point, do people really start to believe their own rhetoric, and feel fear for their own health more deeply than they feel indignant about a set of policies they deem unjust? Or can people continuously and indefinitely claim in public that they are simply ''afraid'' and still privately retain a sense of concern for the common good, a sense of justice, a wider vista than their own self-interest? A few times, Ginny, the long-time activist and veteran of the civil rights movement, con-sciously tried to get attention any way she could, and calculated that Momism would get her a foot in the door. But then she was dissatisfied, unsure how to go from this way of getting a foot in the door to airing her broader, more publicly minded activist agenda.

Much more typical than Ginny was Eleanor, who, as she mourned after the press conference described at the beginning of this book, experienced herself as having truly forgotten her more public-spirited motives when speaking in public. The question of whether claims of ''self-interest'' soak down into deep feelings might be interesting to ask, but whatever activists felt in their hearts, for all of these activists, *if opening up public discussion and debate was part of their goal, emphasizing their own self-interest and fear would not help.* Mandatory Momism just made the activists seem to have interests that were just as undebatable as the corporations'.

At one point, they thought of inviting children and teenagers to come to their events – working not just ''for the children'' but also *with* them. Chris had had the idea of inviting children from an article about the incinerator she had seen in a high school newsletter – clearly, some of ''the children'' themselves were worried. She said, ''It would be great to have them come to the Good Neighbor Rally, so it's not just a bunch of old people worried about their property values, but young people worried about – well basically, about their *lives*!'' It seemed, as with the volunteers, as if children and political conflict could not be thought of in the same breath; this suggestion seemed to make the group into a volunteer-style group. Neil humorously intoned, ''The Youth of Our Country,'' switching back to his ''radical'' persona, laughing at himself for being involved in a cause that could be called wholesome.

Now, the fact was, Neil's daughter Amy and several other teenagers and children already did come to meetings and demonstrations. In fact, the teenagers knew more than most adults about bureaucratic politics and local environmental issues. Maryellen was proud of the ''education'' that she was giving 13-year-old Amy by taking her to meetings and demonstrations; they even went to Airdale a few times to protest a radioactive incinerator there.

Yes, personal fear and personal health and personal self-interest were among some activists' reasons for objecting to the incinerator, but not all; and for many, the longer they were involved, the smaller that component became, eventually demoting personal fear to a ''besides,'' as in Maryellen's ''Where are you gonna move? It's everywhere – or it will be. Everyone can't just move away from it. Besides, we *like* Evergreen City.'' But the activists were involved for reasons that embraced people far beyond their own kin. The question of what could be done, as Maryellen put it, to prevent ''some other community . . . from being stuck with it'' plagued members and constantly forced open debate.

Second-guessing "other people's" motives: the attribution of selfishness

Like volunteers, activists often assumed that *other* people – the people in their imagined audience – are short-sighted and self-interested, even if they themselves had more publicly minded, long-term motivations. Diane's succinct stock phrases included: "They don't think it relates to them," and "People will do anything as long as it doesn't involve getting up off their fat butts." In other words, members often relied on volunteer-style explanations, despite the fact that most of the people who *did* live near the proposed incinerator site were not involved and many of those who were involved did *not* live very close to the proposed site, and could, in any case, have easily moved in less time than working on the issue consumed. Yet, when activists heard people say they would get involved if an issue were "close to home," they took them at their word. This would often be a mistake, as the chapters on the volunteers showed: some people use the language of self-interest to protect fragile feelings of empowerment within a small circle of concern.

Ginny and Victoria said that the group should find out what the incinerator would do to local property values. Eleanor mourned that when she told neighbors about the planned incinerator, their first response was, " 'Oh, what'll it do to my property values?' not 'What'll it do to my health?' " Ginny said instructively, "That's where you have to get Americans – in their pockets."

Eleanor let Ginny define the situation, resigning herself to the reality that she assumed that Ginny had portrayed. She said, "It's true, but sick." They, along with the rest of the group, assumed that even though they personally were not just in it for themselves, that *other* people must indeed operate according to the logic of the market. Strangely enough, though, neither Eleanor nor Ginny was herself involved for her own bank account or her own health. Both had earlier been involved in other causes that did not benefit them: Ginny had worked in the civil rights movement, going off to Oklahoma when, she proudly grinned, "not too many pregnant, blond ladies got involved in that kind of thing." Eleanor had attended disarmament demonstrations and farmworkers' rallies and more. Both were dedicated schoolteachers who worked many extra hours without pay. So, their equation of "practical" with "appealing to self-interest" was not based on autobiographical experience, though they tried, unconvincingly, to portray themselves as self-interested.

A favorite topic for casual discussion concerned the Montgomery plant managers. "What do they think? Their kids live here, too – how could they not care?" they would ask, sometimes leading to a discussion of the different "mind-sets" of the managers. Often, but not always, the explanation was that the managers are self-interested, that most people are self-interested, and that self-interested people run the world. Still, if activists had been totally convinced by this argument, they would not have had to spend so much time speculating on the question.

"Self-interest" developed a life of its own, even when it flew in the face of members' own motives. Members thought that not only did they have to appeal to others' self-interest, but that they themselves must really be self-interested. They were resigned to the fact; it was considered common sense, and they sometimes even scrounged for self-interested sounding explanations of their own involvement. Neil even claimed that he was involved just because he was self-interestedly looking for amusement for Saturday mornings! The discourse of self-interest pinched discussion, sometimes even backstage, far from reporters' ears.

Two contrasting cases: activists without publicly minded discourse

In contrast to CESE were two other local groups that could be called activist but actually operated, in face-to-face contexts, with a volunteer style. Neither made connections to national politics, either backstage or in leaflets and public writings. One group in town, a group that was trying to prevent a homeless shelter from being installed in its neighborhood, did not bring national policy into the picture at all, simply saying, "We don't want them here" (the parallel between the homeless and toxic waste is painfully obvious). Members said they feared that the homeless men were crazy and would harm their children, or, more altruistic-sounding, that this residential neighborhood was the wrong place for the shelter because it was not near anything else a homeless person might need. So they gave reasons why this particular neighborhood was a bad site for the shelter, but did not offer any suggestions for preventing homelessness in general.

A fundamentalist Christian organization in Honey Ridge, a nearby city, was working to repeal a gay rights, anti-discrimination ordinance in the city. Its campaign T-shirts bore the slogan, "Sometimes it's time to draw the *line*," but when I interviewed two heads of the organization separately, they both emphatically denied that they were interested in "drawing a line" to keep gays and other minorities out of town, saying that they simply did not want to give them privileges denied to other people. The leader hid his very active membership in the well-funded national Christian Broadcasting Network. The local organization thus did not seem "political," but simply "moral," since the leaders misrepresented their political involvement as simply means to ends that were not "political," not discussable, but God-given and natural, static, beyond human control. In fact, the organization was part of a national group with a clear political agenda that went far beyond the local, immediate issue (Diamond 1989). This is a very different kind of group from the grassroots CESE. It is "political" in the sense of trying to influence policies, but not "public" in the sense of involving citizens in open-ended discussion of issues. Since members of these groups assumed that their opinions were simply natural and God-given, they were not debatable. In contrast to the volunteer-style groups, the activists in CESE tentatively decided that working together as citizens meant redefining taken-for-granted ideas of power and talk.

Part 2: *Personal passion and dry facts in the public sphere: two sides of the same coin*

Local government and corporate authorities did not *appear* to discourage anti-toxics activism. They appeared to accept it: they spoke of citizen participation in vaguely positive terms, and they usually responded to citizens' requests for information. Yet, their thin model of citizen involvement corresponded to the volunteers': citizens should get involved in solving local problems, with hands-on work. Citizens can attend meetings about other sorts of issues, but officials should be in charge of calling the meetings. Citizens can request information, but cannot be sources of information themselves. Citizens have a right to be concerned about their own health and safety, but are unreasonable if they are motivated by political principles or analyses that go beyond "self-interest." Thus, officials invited citizens to speak for themselves, but only for themselves. Public-spirited questioning was considered rude.

In a country that calls itself democratic, powerful institutions have to appear to include the people's will. Local agencies like the ones that dealt with the activists bear much of the burden of making the government appear legitimate. Messages about how to treat citizen participation come from above, filtered through those often well-meaning local officials as loose rules of political etiquette that invite certain kinds of citizenship and exclude others. The contexts of public events, not inner beliefs, shaped how these lower officials could act in public, shaping what they could hear and what they could say. These contexts managed to make corporate pollution into an issue that resists volunteer-style action, and then officials were annoyed by activists who tried to treat the issue more politically, with open debate.

Officials defined citizens' power and citizens' talk the way the volunteers defined them, and this official image of how to be an involved citizen put immense pressure on the activists, to define their groups in accord with official definitions. Officials assumed that their job was to distribute technical facts to an overly emotional, befuddled, self-interested citizenry. And activists often – though by no means always – implicitly tried to comply with officials' definitions of participation, by sounding more like volunteers in official, public forums than they sounded in their own meetings and in casual contexts.

To offer cultural explanations of officals' treatment of activists is not to deny that some officials rapaciously calculate corporate interests. There are strong ties between many high government officials and toxics-producing corporations in fields like petroleum, lumber, and chemicals (Domhoff, e.g. 1989). For such high officials, perhaps their short-term need to make a profit blinds them to their long-term need to breathe and eat, so they think they have an interest in preventing strong environmental regulation of industries (and even so, one could certainly imagine officials discovering the profit-making possibilities in environmental protection). But whatever their interests are, even they must have strategies for presenting their interests to the citizenry, of convincing people, themselves included, that their own particular form of environmental destruction is in the interests of all.

While such single-minded profit-makers may dwell in the high ranks of the elite, most local and county health department officials down below in Evergreen City thought of themselves as being "on the community's side" against the corporations. Many local officials were more like grassroots citizens than like high government and corporate officials – for example, one city council member fumed to Henry and me that she had just wasted an entire day on the phone trying to find out what an upcoming "public" hearing was going to be about. Many local health officials also expressed backstage, off-the-record frustration to me about the companies' secrecy and federal officials' inaccessibility. One quit her job, joined an anti-toxics group herself, and went back to school. Another had been active in a socialist party for many years before signing up as a state environmental regulator. Many had been active in grassroots environmental groups before. As *individuals*, nearly all were very sympathetic to the activists' publicly minded concerns. *But they could not hear them in official contexts.* Officials played by the rules; that meant inviting citizens to ask questions only about their own personal safety, and excluding larger political debates.[3]

Technology and democracy

By treating all questions from grassroots activists as requests for technical information, officials kept open-ended discussion out of the public arena. Why *should* the corporations and the state assume that average citizens have the technical – legal or scientific – knowledge to participate in making decisions? What if citizens make uninformed, panic-based decisions? Certainly, it is true that citizens sometimes object to something because they *are* ignorant, like people who do not want people with AIDS to swim in public pools because they think the virus is transmitted through water.

But citizens produce knowledge in a variety of ways. Sometimes citizens oppose something on moral principle, no matter how scientifically safe or unsafe it is, like pro-choice or anti-abortion activists, who will never be convinced by scientific arguments about "when life really begins" or when a fetus – or egg or sperm or cell – could be cultivated to become a viable human. Sometimes citizens object to something because they are bigoted, like whites who do not want blacks swimming in public pools. Sometimes citizens object because they have access to a body of knowledge that differs from officially accepted information, like people who said cigarettes caused cancer even when tobacco corporations claimed otherwise. Sometimes citizens have publicly minded objections, because of the political context, and will not be convinced by facts produced outside of that context, like CESE members who objected to the for-profit nature of the incinerator, the lack of accountability, and the lack of government and corporate investment in preventing hazardous waste production, no matter how safe incineration seemed in laboratory experiments; or like political conservatives who value free enterprise so much, they object to public funding for health care, even if experts show that people in societies with public health care spend less and live longer. Not all questions of citizenship can be addressed with information alone (Steven Epstein [1991] explores these questions in interesting ways).

In principle, activists have no reason to object to technical and bureaucratic language. In principle, scientific language discovers physical, chemical truths; in principle, bureaucratic language discovers rules for democratic accountability, by tracing decisions through the agencies that control decisions. But activists did come to object to officials' approach, because officials used bureaucratic and scientific languages to crowd other ways of talking and reasoning out of the conversation. Publicly minded reasoning and moral reasoning were "out of place" in public.

If all we needed was an expert to make decisions for us, we would not need democracy – we could just have a scientist, a lawyer, and an economist make our decisions for us. The officials treated knowledge as an object which they had stored up and could deposit into the spongy brains of the citizenry – the "banking theory of knowledge" (Freire 1970). Activists, in contrast, wanted to help produce knowledge, through discussion. As a result of these clashing ideas of what citizen involvement is, and specifically, of what its relation to technical knowledge is and of what kinds of knowledge count as valid, the officials and activists not only disagreed with each other, but also thought that their opponents were unreasonable and rude.

The clash over civic etiquette in official settings developed slowly. When the incinerator was first proposed, the state and Montgomery Chemicals set up the Local Review Committee (LRC), a committee of residents who volunteered to survey the information neutrally on behalf of the community, and conduct bi-weekly public meetings. At every meeting of CESE, especially at the group's beginning, activists strongly urged newcomers to go to LRC meetings; for the first year, this was the most often repeated concrete piece of advice given to newcomers. As CESE began regularly holding its own meetings, members grew a bit more equivocal about the LRC. Most guiltily stopped going to LRC meetings after about a year. As Diane put it more than a few times, "I find those meetings thoroughly discouraging. I'm just not that into the bureaucratic aspect. Everyone at the meeting was so blah."

These bureaucratic agencies had a place, but they could absorb citizens' energy so that there was none left over for political debate.[4] The state produced a steady, rushing stream of these sorts of agencies and regulations. I told Diane about a meeting I attended in Evergreen City, of regional anti-toxics groups. I said, "there were people there who really seemed to know an incredible amount, who work at a full-time job and still have time to learn this amazing amount about the EIRs and the EISs and the RCRA process and CEQA and who knows what else. Like Laura, from Airdale ACES. Or Neil." Diane grinned, "Thank goodness there are people like that," in an unsanctimonious tone, as if to say that she would not really want to be one of those people.

Why were members not unequivocally pleased that the LRC had been created to respond to their demands? As we heard, in activists' casual conversations there was no separating politics from the rest of life. Yet that was precisely what the LRC meetings attempted to do: focus solely on health questions and leave politics out. But, as backstage conversation made clear, most of the activists' objections to the incinerator were, in fact, political. So, even if, theoretically, the company could have proven that incineration could be safe, the activists would have said that this technology would be unsafe (and possibly unnecessary) *in this political context*.[5]

To activists, this relentless avoidance of political debate made meetings boring; with no openings for political and moral discussion, there is not much for citizens to do in the public forum. For example, when CESE was still religiously attending LRC meetings, Neil was excited to discover something that he said would "make a splash" at the next meeting. In his after-hours independent research, he found out how the legal limits for exposure to toxic chemicals had been set: many human limits for toxic exposure had been set by a committee of four scientists, two of whom were defending the chemicals their own corporations produced! He also found that the committee would not divulge its research methods for public review. Disclosing this information did not make a splash at all. It was a short item on the agenda, quickly passed over.

A few times, CESE members explicitly vented indignation about the civic etiquette required in official public meetings. For example, I missed a meeting that Maryellen said was "really good."

The Risk Assessment Report came out and the people who prepared it were there, and they were really deceitful. They went on and on for the whole meeting about how it was really no danger to anyone, with these .03 percentages of this and that [demonstrating that the cancer risk of the incinerator's emissions would be less than one in a million, the standard figure for demonstrating lack of serious risk], and then at the very end of the meeting, I asked, "What about *fish*? Is there a danger to fish?"

Then she figured out that all that time, the scientist was referring only to the emissions coming out of the smokestack, not the chemicals that would be going into the water, and not the ash that would be left over in the incinerator, after incineration. "The part about the water goes into the Environmental Impact Report, not the Risk Assessment, which is supposed to be about health, not the environment. But people eat the fish!" Not a soul in CESE ate fish from the mucky, polluted Swift River; only very poor recent immigrants dared eat from that river. "And the other thing that pissed me off was the way these guys talked about the wind patterns. 'Oh, the way the wind goes, it just takes the stuff high up and scatters it.' So great, it'll be all over *everyone* instead of just here. What do those guys think – all we care about is Evergreen City?" There was no public opening in which Maryellen and others could voice disgust at being treated as people who cared only about themselves and not the poor people who ate the fish, or the faraway people who would be sprinkled with the leftover ashes from the incinerator. Evergreen City activists were outraged at the danger of having an incinerator in town, but only because they were convinced that something could be done to eliminate toxic waste for everyone.

Bureaucratic meetings were not the only public places in which activists – like Victorian children – were considered best when seen and not heard. Being polite at local celebrations meant acting like volunteers – upbeat, inspiring to all, cheerful, concerned without engaging in debate about the wider word. So, CESE had to fashion itself after a volunteer group in order to participate in local celebrations and parades. The translation was sometimes a transformation. For example, CESE built a float for their local Pioneer Days Parade; it was a black-sheathed pick-up truck, carrying children and adults, a big lump of ugly-colored cotton sticking out of a cardboard smokestack, and the "Wizard of Ooze," slimy and smiling in a gown, waving like a prom queen, holding a grayish-black artichoke on a stick to look like a malignant Statue of Liberty's torch. Behind it strode Donald in a Grim Reaper outfit. Every few minutes, we all broke out in a scary yell.

But the city forbade the group to pass out leaflets at the parade. Marching behind the glittering and handspringing Central Riverton High School Marching Band, Diane told me that when she had called to get the marching permit, she had had to "twist the arm of the guy who was in charge of signing people up for the parade even to let us in it *at all*. He was hesitant because, he said, 'This is a family event, not a political event.' " He echoed the common distinction between "family" and "political." Diane had to argue, "What's political about a toxic incinerator? It's not political!" The official said that people do not all agree about it, but Diane countered with, "Everyone in town agrees! The only people who don't agree are the ones who would make money off it, and they don't even live here, most of them." The official said he would have to ask the parade committee when it met on Monday.

Wily Diane said to me, "So I said to him [and here she put on a wheedling, mock feminine voice, octaves above her real one], 'Geeee, we'd *really* like to work on the float this weekend.' So he said, 'Oh, heck, go ahead and work on it – what the hell.' "

As long as they got into the parade, I had the impression that Diane had convinced herself that indeed, the float was not "political," so she had honestly convinced herself that the group was squarely within the volunteer genre. But Henry was not content with mere theatricality, and leafleted under separate cover. Diane commented wryly, "If it's against the rules, you can be sure Henry will be out there doing it." In this incarnation of the ongoing debate over which genre of citizenship to embody, Henry was being too "radical," but without the leaflets, the float just looked like an early entry for Halloween.

So that is how CESE got its spot in the parade. Members were forbidden from handing out flyers *explaining* the issue, because that would be "political" and politics was as out of place in a family parade as it was in a public hearing.

"Just the facts": what counts as knowledge?

Officials tried hard to keep their role as sole purveyors of information, even when activists tested the limits of that approach. Holding a panel discussion following a Plastico explosion, CESE had wanted to look respectful and responsible. They asked the League of Women Voters to supply a moderator, and arranged to write down all their questions ahead of time, on tiny scraps of paper. The moderator was charged with reading the audience's questions to a panel of officials – firefighters, police, and Navy emergency squad spokespersons (all in full uniform), along with Plastico representatives and air quality control personnel – instead of letting the audience shout out questions.

Fielding the questions from the audience, the experts answered them as if they were requests for information, not combative challenges or invitations to debate. For example, one audience member asked, "Why should we trust Plastico to monitor itself, when it blows up or has a spill every year?" Another asked why Plastico lobbied so hard against regulation of pesticides when the only real solution to the blow-ups and spills was to cut back on toxic production. The very short answer to that was that "we all use pesticides now, and they are beneficial for many purposes." As Diane put it, smiling her ironically fed-up, lopsided half-humorous half-grin, officials' response to the initial question, about what could have prevented the explosion, was that "they just read us their job descriptions and then said that they did their jobs."

By treating the questions as requests for information, the authorities avoided debate. Had the questioning citizens been *volunteers*, not activists, officials would have been right to interpret their questions as simple requests for information. When the social service workers, police, and probation officers at the anti-drugs public meeting did the same thing, volunteers left happy. Officials would have deposited, and volunteers received, the desired information. But the debate-oriented *activists*, in contrast, wanted more variety. Were the officials consciously trying to avoid debate? Perhaps, but if the audience had been full of volunteers, the treatment given the questions would have been just right. When officials offered activists the same treatment, the activists were not satisfied at all. Activists were trying to make political analyses count as knowledge; officials were trying to keep the focus on what they considered to be "the facts." The argument was not just about Plastico's blow-up; it was also about what counts as legitimate, real knowledge in the first place.

The moderator from the League of Women Voters did not help matters when she used her volunteer-style cultural repertoire to edit all the questions. In an intermission, Diane muttered that the moderator was garbling the questions. In the very front, wearing a flaming pink dress, CESE member Victoria stood up toward the end of the hearing, angrily stating that the moderator was "editing the sense out of the questions." After that, the moderator started stumbling though the embarrassing scraps of handwritten questions. Afterwards, Diane, Donald, and Victoria all fumed, saying that the volunteer-style moderator rewrote the questions to make them not sound "confrontational," but that in the process, she made them impossible to understand. She had transformed them from argumentative challenges into requests for information.

State documents did not include statements from oppositional organizations like Greenpeace or local environmental research groups. One devoted a little section to reprinting residents' questions; the officials' answers were very cool and technical, written in full sentences, while the questions were taken verbatim from residents' handwritten notes and oral questions at a meeting. Aside from the question-and-answer section, the document of over five hundred pages relied heavily on the company's own data, and did not mention citizens' complaints in the other towns across the country that housed Montgomery plants. Most crucially, the report solely addressed local residents' safety. There was only a brief, one-paragraph introduction, outside of the main text, about the politics of toxic waste production. This paragraph baldly stated that toxic waste was an inevitable, unfortunate fact of contemporary life; the only question was how to dispose of it. The document never addressed activists' demands to limit toxic waste production, and never asked why more capacity for toxics processing was needed when the government was loudly proclaiming that corporations should produce ever-dwindling amounts of toxic waste.

Another industry and government co-production was an informational pamphlet telling citizens what to do in an emergency. This pamphlet was intended to "clear up . . . misconceptions" about petrochemical production, that it said were "primarily due to a lack of information . . . The CAER Program is an effort to open communications between industry and surrounding communities . . . There is no hidden agenda, no pressure for industry to participate, and no cause for alarm." The brochure, or CAER "tool," as it called itself, focused on how citizens could get the information they needed from authorities (for example, it contained a full paragraph explaining the use of 911 – the nationwide emergency phone number that all children know – for those who found 911 a difficult concept). Its message was that if citizens just had information, they would agree with the chemical industries.

Similarly, public relations personnel at Montgomery's East Coast headquarters repeatedly informed me, when I interviewed them on the phone in my radio reporter persona, that the activists were "confused": the plant would not be a "toxic waste incinerator," but a "waste minimization and recycling facility!" The company sent me, by overnight express mail, a glossy 9×12 booklet with that title on the cover, with answers to possible objections to the incinerator. The company sent a similar set of expensive, elaborate brochures to most local households.

The presentations at the bi-weekly LRC meetings were numbingly, exclusively technical. There was no time in this forum for citizens to debate public issues. Instead, almost every time, someone from the company gave a slide show or verbal presentation on a specific aspect of the proposed plant's technology, without ever directly answering questions from the audience. One meeting, for example, contained a presentation that lasted over an hour describing the plant's one-way valves, showing that the chemicals could flow only in the directions in which operators intended them to flow and at the rates intended. The presentation included six slides of the valves, and the company representative described each part of each valve, one by one, in excruciating detail. Thus, little by little, the whole official public sphere was filled to the brim with exchanges of unanalyzed facts.

"All the media people want is a Mom and an Expert." – Ginny

If something was not a neutral, dead fact, officials considered it an emotion. Montgomery and Plastico spokespersons charged, in article after article, that activists' emotions conflicted with reason. One article, for example, cites the company's toxic incinerator plan in Arizona which was vetoed. " 'The atmosphere had become so emotionalized, there was no chance for dialogue,' [the company spokeperson] said. She blamed Greenpeace for creating a 'confrontational atmosphere.' " (And naturally, the charge rang true to the newspaper readers I interviewed; since activists' public-spirited ideas did not appear in the paper, the only people who could have heard their publicly minded reasoning would be those who had actually attended the rallies.) Officials' implicit division was between passion and rationality. Pete, the anti-drugs volunteer, expressed the "common-sense" view when he said that it is better not to be too "passionate" about political issues; he believed that passion clouds rationality.

According to this line of thinking, passionate protesters are, by definition, not rational. At the same time, passion is considered more "real," more involved. Officials and reporters assumed that readers will assume that "raw" emotions are more authentic; that feelings are more real than thoughts. And reporters, as I will discuss later, thought this way themselves, as well as assuming that their readers did. Working within this common-sense framework, it is hard to imagine how passion sometimes *enhances* rationality, as Neil's impassioned after-hours hunt for the scientific basis of legal exposure to toxic chemicals did. Though there are no doubt many irrational activists in the world, news stories amplify all activists' irrationality, and muffle their reasoning, when portraying the activists to the world. In this lopsided model of citizenship, the only thing citizens can do is "speak for themselves," from personal experience. The irony is that this passionate speech is, at the same time, just the thing that most Americans do not value, do not consider rational.

Indeed, some activists decided that the *only* way they could effectively participate in public debate was by becoming technical experts themselves. Connie, the city council member who supported the activists, said at a party that she wished she could follow the technical discussion more easily. Cathy said,

> You could go to the university in Newton and take a chemistry course – I know someone who did that, and said it was really fun.
>
> CONNIE: I wouldn't do that. I would be too lazy to do that, and if I were to take a course, it would be at Evergreen County Community College anyway, but I haven't done that either.

Chris actually went back to school to get a BA, not in political science or sociology or journalism, but in environmental science, convinced that the most important knowledge she lacked was not political, but technical. Some activists were indeed homegrown experts, having devoted years of study to local environmental problems and the convoluted bureaucracies that oversee them; and, of course, most activists spent time poring over the state's scientific documents, doing independent library research, and trying to master the scientific reasoning behind the company's technical assurances. This is part of the route to good citizenship, but as CESE itself showed, not the whole route.

The Expert man

Sometimes, activist men who spoke in public tried to sound like experts, even if they were not. While Mom is a passionate and self-interested warm body, the Expert is rational, disinterested, and lifeless. The Mom is a woman, the dark side of the moon; the Expert is a man, the moon's relentlessly bright face – but not a caring, personally involved "Dad." For example, at a press conference in front of City Hall, Martin tried to display expertise, saying,

what we're seeking to do through the initiative *process* is to prevent the incineration of hazardous and toxic waste from ever being a permitted, erh, conditionally permitted use in the heavily industrial zoning district of Evergreen City. It's not even there now. They're, they've submitted an application – in this particular case, we have to refer to Montgomery Chemicals, because they're the only ones that are currently proposing anything. Their original application was for a use permit, and that is a land-use decision. And that's how it became the purvey [*sic*] of the – of the city council – of the planning commission to deal with it. And we, through the initiative process, are seeking to give them enough teeth in their ordinance to deal with it summarily.

After Martin went on for a very long time like that, the reporter turned the camera off altogether. But then the reporter heard a few sentences that made his ears perk up again, and switched the camera back on, trying to get Martin to repeat them. The off-mike lines the reporter had liked were "passionate":

MARTIN: I think it's ludicrous that a corporation such as Plastico [the reporter had asked why CESE did not feel futile, considering that no authorities seemed able to do anything about Plastico and other local pollutors] can fall under the order to clean up and just thumb their nose and walk away. Ultimately, I guess that's what they make shotguns for [chuckles]. But . . .

Here, he realized that he sounded much more "passionate" than he had planned to sound; the rest of the sentence remained unspoken. But when the reporter tried to elicit this violent, dramatic statement again, Martin could not (or did not want to) reproduce those lines on camera, or anything like them, and went back to his usual distant, stiff tone. At this point, another CESE member chipped in, rescuing him by changing the tone.

What made most of Martin's speech "Expert" was a starchy vocabulary, arranged in starchy constructions, with quibbling qualifications. Nobody says, at a picnic, "What I am seeking to do is to locate a spoon," for example. Martin was not unusual in that regard. But in front of the press, he was full of words like "currently" and "summarily," and painfully precise legalisms and malapropisms. He thought that the reporters wanted that kind of speech because it showed that he really knew what he was doing. I heard four people in the group say that that kind of precise, technical speech is the *only* kind that counts in official hearings. Maryellen, for example, said, "You have to respond to very specific points."

"Page 7, paragraph 4, line 2," added Neil.

"Otherwise it doesn't count," said Maryellen, completing the thought. The enforced precision for responses to technical and bureaucratic questions shaded easily into the painful legalisms of the sort Martin offered.

Martin was trying to imitate what researcher Dana Kaminstein aptly calls "toxic talk" (1988): official, technical speech that is delivered not for the purpose of helping or increasing public knowledge, but that does an excellent job of stopping the conversation. For example, Evergreen County safety planners brought giant blow-up pictures of big station wagons to meetings about Plastico's proposed waste plan, declaring them "safety equipment." They were shiny and new, but nothing unusual. Nobody in the audience was fooled by these displays, but they were good conversation-stoppers. Officials had vocabularies full of double negatives – "We do not think Fair Share cannot work''; passive voice verbs – ''consequently, a process was developed whereby . . . ''; and qualifications –

STATE OFFICIAL [in LRC meeting]: It is my understanding of the historical record of the legislation, and this is only my understanding of the record because I wasn't there and can only report the historic record as I see it . . .

I was not alone in having difficulty following officials' answers to questions in LRC meetings. One LRC member, a chemistry professor at a major university, was one of the only people in town who was not afraid to confront officials. He did not have to worry about being considered a person who ineffectually ''spouted'' with no knowledge base or power base; and he was usually able to follow the meeting's proceedings. Still, most of his objections to the incinerator were political or logical; one did not need any special education to understand his frequent, ten-page critiques of state documents. In fact, his critiques *offered* an education, in making presuppositions clear, in logic and scientific method, in connecting politics and technology.

For example, one state document ignored the results of five out of ten experimental ''trial burns'' of toxic chemicals, saying that in those discounted trials, the incoming chemicals had impurities, or that mistakes had occurred in the burning process. All the other trial burns came out nearly perfect, with few toxic residues from the burning process. The professor pointed out that in real life, chemicals are impure and mistakes are made, too, especially when a company is hurrying to make money by processing waste quickly. He requested that the state divulge those discarded results and include them as part of the experiment's results.

Another time, the professor boldly asked a regional Air Quality Board member an obvious question that none of the documents had addressed: ''What incentives are there to minimize waste production?'' The answer (I had taped this meeting):

Methodologies of systematizing incentives will differ from county to county, to determine hypothetical facilities needed. The ''Fair Share Process'' [the latest state law which called for each county to take in toxic waste in proportion to the amount of waste the county generated] was used to determine sitings. We're waste minimizing to the economically feasible maximum . . . The state is not for or against Fair Share – we should use Fair Share as an implementation facilitation process. The process we have been indicating to the county that we believe are the appropriate ones is what we call the ''overlay process.'' [Note that even the speaker himself could not keep track of the nouns and verbs in this paragraph, switching randomly from singular to plural.]

THE UNIVERSITY PROFESSOR: So, they'll pick some state sacrifice areas that can't be saved and let 'em go to hell? It'll be called "Incinerator Alley" instead of "Swift River."

The professor's style was much more confident, and less polite, than the others'. All the other citizen-members of the LRC were much more apologetic in their style, often prefacing their questions with, "I might be misunderstanding . . . ," or, "Let me make sure I'm getting this right . . . ," or, "I'm sorry to make you repeat this again . . . ," or, "Now, let me just get a bit of information here that I must have missed . . ." When inconvenient facts emerged, officials sometimes managed simply to bury them in the flood of toxic talk (for example, the Environmental Impact Report on Montgomery cited several studies of the human health effects of Swift River industries. The studies contradicted each other, but the report paid attention only to the one that said that the cause for high cancer rates in the area was smoking, not industrial pollution).

Despite their efforts at sounding like experts, no reporters ever quoted the activists when they tried to replicate experts' "toxic talk." Only officials were allowed to be experts. Thus, mandatory Momism made participation from "dads" and other non-"Moms" difficult. And indeed, throughout the US, women are much more heavily involved in local environmental movements than are men. Women are more often the leaders of grassroots environmental groups. The standard explanation is that women *care* more about their children and communities, and experience the effects of environmental degradation more directly – when their children get sick, for example. But I offer a different explanation for women's predominance: women have easier access to the Mom discourse, a more legitimate-sounding language for citizen involvement than the Expert discourse. It is more difficult for a man to cry "Save Us!" (as Ginny had earlier named the group, before members decided the name was too pathetic and possibly evangelical-sounding).

The problem was, when women tried to sound like Moms, they were called emotional and unreasonable; and when men tried to sound like Experts, no one listened. Only experts were authorized to use the neutral-seeming, rational languages of bureaucracy and science (Bourdieu 1982). Citizens were relegated to overly narrow, "passionate," devalued professions of self-interest. And even if the male activists had managed to get themselves quoted, they might never have gained full access to necessary information. Officials refused to disclose the information that would make informed citizen participation possible. For example, Plastico issued a report describing its toxics production at one hearing, but blacked out over half of it, claiming that these sections divulged "trade secrets" that would let competitors copy

Plastico's chemical formulas.[6] Not convinced by the authorities' scientific claims, activists would have liked to come up with a set of alternative facts, but did not have the resources. Diane said that my arduous and unsuccessful trip to the library, to hunt down a fact about Montgomery Chemicals, was typical for the group: "We're just starting, we don't have the money, the set-up, the know-how all in place. And we never will have the money, compared to what they have." Even so, activists had so many other moral and political objections to the incinerator, they did not really need access to the company's secret chemical formulas or a fully funded set of researchers.

Clumsy ways of silencing activists

Of course, officials also used some more overt, clumsier, coercive and intentional ways of silencing activists' publicly minded statements and avoiding debate with activists, but these were not as deeply cultural and were thus easier to notice. These included:

1 Holding secret public meetings

Officials can simply to refuse to meet activists; or not publicize meetings; or not tell activists what is on the agenda of upcoming meetings; or hold meetings during working hours. This overt strategy for ignoring activists required a "radical" response from activists, one that turned the official floor into a farce – picketing, or, in one story from a state organizer, environmentalists wangling tickets to a semi-private benefit dinner with the governer after he had refused to meet with them, and shaking his hand up and down and up and down and up and down – "He just *had* to stay and chat!"

2 Muzzling citizen watchdogs

Privately, the mayor met with Maryellen and Neil, asking them for information about the incinerator and claiming he supported them. But publicly, he was totally silent on the matter. Privately, many city council members said they supported the group, but publicly, they too were silent. Why? The answer was always, as Neil put it, "The city council wholeheartedly endorsed the petition drive and the group and said it's great you're active on it, but can't make any out and out commitments. They have to appear impartial, or else, when the time comes for them to actually vote on the issue, they will be disqualified, because they would already have a known opinion." (Some members of CESE agreed with Neil, but others insisted that "government officials have the right of free speech" and *must* take stands on issues that affect their constituents.) Similarly, the volunteer LRC panel members were not allowed to make public statements for or against the incinerator, since that would make them appear to be partisan, not neutral observers. Joining the committee forced some of the most concerned citizens out of the public sphere. Neil declined an invitation to join it, saying that he would rather be able to say what he thought in public about the incinerator and other environmental issues, and not be silenced for however many years it took to make a decision. A couple of years later, Plastico tried to set up a similar committee, and invited CESE to send members. At first, some were pleased and honored, saying, "Isn't this just what we've wanted?" But after discussing it for quite a while, CESE members all declined the invitation to join the corporate-sponsored committee, saying, "It'll be another LRC; it would take people out of grassroots."

3 Erasing activism

This clever approach for making active citizenship invisible involves making sure that officials appear always to be the ones to call meetings, and that no one finds out that citizens' pressure made a difference. CESE held a march to the smelly industrial site of Montgomery's proposed incinerator, to tell the company to "be a good neighbor and drop your plans to burn hazardous waste." The activists had put great effort into organizing this event. They wondered whether any Montgomery representatives at all would show up at the Saturday protest; and whether the demonstration would be turned away by guards at the gates, before even entering the site.

Not only did Montgomery representatives show up to greet the soggy demonstrators after their march through the cold, greasy rain, but the Montgomery public relations expert passed out a press release that made it impossible to tell who called the demonstration. The press release made it sound as if perhaps the company had cordially invited the public to visit its muddy, slippery property on that rainy Saturday (for brunch, perhaps?). It began:

In keeping with the company's policy of openness and cooperation, representatives of Montgomery Chemicals met today with county residents to discuss plans to process hazardous waste at the company's facility here.

"We recognize that any proposal to process hazardous materials will arouse local concerns. It has been our policy from the beginning to address those concerns head on," said Mike Santoro, Montgomery's plant manager. "This meeting today is a continuation of that process."

... There has been some confusion as to what is being proposed. We are not building a hazardous waste incinerator ... The facility has been safely recycling [a chemical] from the local chemical company for decades. What we are proposing to do now is process additional waste classified as hazardous in the existing facility.

The press release managed to make the activists seem like misinformed, curious, "confused," passive members of the public, whom Montgomery had graciously invited over to educate. Remarkably, this was not an isolated incident.

Even when activists did win disputes, there was no public acknowledgment that they had won. Scientists and lawyers from both sides spoke at one hearing regarding Plastico's permit to build new facilities to process the toxins produced at the plant; activists spoke also. The company actually lost the battle, but nobody – not the state, not the company, not even the activists themselves – ever said why. After the hearing, the activists were erased from the struggle, as if they had made no mark, even though they had technically won. This vanishing is not unique: studies of the US anti-war movement of the 1960s (Wells 1994), and the Western European and US disarmament movements of the 1980s (Breyman 1989) show activism not getting credit for making a difference. This remarkable lack of credit keeps citizens unsure of their ability to judge and speak and question effectively, even while corporations and governments actually end up doing exactly what the activists want.

But again, much more often than these clumsy, direct strategies for making active citizenship impossible or invisible, I heard officials keeping their monopoly of legitimate-sounding knowledge more subtly and often unintentionally, by simply assuming that public debate would not generate interesting or useful ideas. However, there were some institutions that helped activists challenge that assumption.

The alternative institutions: "outside agitators" as ears

The power field surrounding groups includes not just corporate and government institutions, but politically oppositional institutions and activists, and the broader public. The groups looked not just up, at the officials in institutions, but also down and around, to figure out what grassroots groups were capable of accomplishing. In this way, the activists reassessed their power and their relations to the public over the course of the group's development.

Having other groups and alternative national institutions as an audience provided a welcome counterbalance to the ears of the state and company officials. The study of speech usually does not include the study of listening – of speakers' anticipation of listeners' reception – but I propose that these elements are inseparable. In mass communications textbooks, a commonplace holds that the world's most expensive commodity is Americans' ears; advertisers and politicians pay millions for the opportunity to occupy them for just a few seconds. In public life, too, ears are precious, but for another reason. Here, a diversity of ears was valuable because they made it possible for activists to say, and to think, different ideas in public contexts than they could if all ears were equally closed to public-spirited discourse. Getting beyond the language of self-interest required explicit discussion of the relation between national policy and local activism, and to carry on that kind of discussion, the group had to discover that someone might be willing to listen to it.

At first, the group played only to the audience of local authorities, trying only to convince them of the irrationality of building a toxic incinerator. Later, CESE added on the local public as an intended audience; that was when the group began having regular, open, publicized meetings. Still later, the group added on another layer of audience – other local, national, and international environmental groups. Members realized that the group's endeavors were affecting groups all over the region, as the group became part of a regional network. Members found out that other groups were intently scrutinizing CESE's victories, just as CESE could learn from others. They figured out the inseparable ties between local and national issues. And they discovered, through new readings, new acquaintances, newsletters, and computer networks, that groups around the world were working on a web of political, ecological problems inseparable from their own. All of this meant valuing citizens' publicly minded deliberation as a centerpiece of democratic participation.

So, CESE joined a network with other anti-toxics groups in the region. Eventually, reports from network meetings regularly peppered CESE meetings, with greetings and encouragement from other groups. Donald, for example, came back glowing from a network meeting, saying that people all over the state were talking about a recent CESE victory; he exclaimed,

We didn't realize we'd be a model. Everyone wanted to know, "How did you do it?" [get a city law passed outlawing the importation of hazardous waste into Evergreen City]. It shows how much we've networked. Word has gotten around! They held us in high esteem. We didn't know how valued we were, how people looked up to us: we're a hot little team! Somebody noticed us!

He then described some other groups' achievements and projects, explaining how CESE could learn from them, as these groups had learnt from CESE. Having an encouraging audience made a difference in the group's speech; this meeting was the first that had time specifically set aside for a long political discussion that would not be labeled "a tangent."

When Greenpeace organizers and members of other anti-toxics groups attended CESE meetings and events, their ears also offered an alternative to the officials'. CESE members learned to talk to people who did not just want to locate the hazardous waste "elsewhere," but wanted broad changes in government regulation of industrial production. At the first meeting of the statewide network of anti-toxics groups, Neil and Cathy both spoke comfortably of "grassroots democracy," and "empowerment," and the problem of profit-making incineration. I had heard them talk about all of these things "backstage," but at this meeting, they easily talked about them frontstage. Learning this new language allowed the activists to vocalize these other, more analytical sides of themselves.

They did not, could not have invented this new valuation of talk from scratch, or simply from a disembodied American tradition that they had learned in books. National environmental organizations and other organizations had to be there, to help them value their own talk, and their own political participation. Without these alternative institutions' encouragement and listenership, inventing democratic citizenship would have been even more arduous than it already was.

Discovering power in the spaces between people

Groups like CESE might seem to lack "resources," but creating "resources" is, in part, a work of interpretation, interaction, discussion, magically creating power from the warmth of human togetherness and discussion (Morris 1984). The respect that members accorded discussion and education made the difference between a "nimby" issue and a movement that might change national policy through publicly minded discussion. After one hearing, Chris said, "I'm glad those scientists and lawyers came. We need them. Without them, we just sound like we're whining 'not in my backyard, nimby, nimby.' " Chris wanted to be right, not just to win.

Making connections to other little grassroots groups around the state was another way of creating a "resource." After the group had existed for two years, members began proposing contacts with churches, doctors, realtors, hospitals, schools, the PTA, and regional city governments. Even if they conceived of these groups in volunteer-style terms, the fact that they even thought of contacting them showed that the group had discovered another "resource" that could make it at least equal to a volunteer group in legitimacy. A year earlier, the group had not even held regular meetings amongst its own members.

Marching in the parade and bringing the Stuff the Stack booth to the July 4 festival made use of an unnoticed local "resource." CESE's participation in these events seized on the ideas of "community" and "celebration" and redefined them in ways that included politics and active citizenship. Onlookers might have considered the activists spoilsports, to invade a "family event" with politics, as the parade organizer put it. But actually, it is only in the past forty or so years that American public festivities have been so empty of explicit politics (Hanson and Ryan 1991). The activists considered the possibility that their neighbors would think they were wet blankets on the happy consumer events, and emphatically decided that their group was part of "community," too. CESE's implicit challenge to the volunteer-style image of the non-conflictual, self-interested community opened up new contexts for public participation, and began to redefine "community" to include "attention to the wider world."

An obvious type of grassroots activism with which the group did not consider aligning itself was unionism. This puzzled me. When I was petitioning one day in the supermarket parking lot, many chemical plant workers and ex-workers told me stories. One woman said her husband had had a stroke at Plastico but could not prove that it was caused by working conditions because the other workers were too afraid of getting fired to testify on his behalf. Three greasy bikers, slouching toward Safeway, stopped to tell us about a fellow worker. "He fell into the wrong acid bath at ChemFill and never was heard from again. He just never showed up to work again. The company didn't say anything, but all that was left of him was his rubber boots and the buttons of his pants." As tall tales go, this one says a great deal about local workers' suspicions of ChemFill.

When a union organizer started coming to meetings, Neil welcomed him in a very polite, formal way, introducing him in the general meeting but not going out of his way to invite him to smaller meetings and not proposing any concrete activities for union members and CESE members to do together. At the meeting, the union activist said, "The companies bring in low-budget, outside workers who don't care, don't live here, aren't gonna want to take care. But we don't want to kick out the non-union workers or the companies, because they'll just go somewhere else, and it's the *world's* environment." Another time, a union scientist testified at a hearing about Plastico's on-site incinerator, saying basically the same thing the Amargo union organizer said: that non-union workers are not as careful or skilled, so the risk of accidents is greater; and that companies use toxic solvents to clean machinery because they do not want to pay workers to do the work. In other words, the unions were working on stopping toxic production at its source. At another meeting the unionist who often came to meetings offered to try to convince a billboard owner in Amargo to put up a sign on the highway about the incinerator. Nobody encouraged him one way or another.

CESE members did not think of helping unions or getting help from unions. Their frame of reference was volunteer groups, "radical" groups, and other environmental groups. Unions, like genuinely different political parties, are generally off the American political cultural map, and this group's map was no exception. This was not because members were anti-union in their inner beliefs: a conversation at a party revealed that Diane, Chris, who used to do layout at a newspaper, and her husband Jim, the retired school-teacher Eleanor, and others actually were, or had been, active in their own white-collar unions. Neil's union experience was less positive. In college, he had had to pay a union membership to a man "sitting behind a half acre of marble." Privately, Neil told me that he was surprised that unions, which he thought of as being filled with rednecks and "hardhats," would be interested in CESE. But when he was at a little party talking to Chris, Diane, and Jim about unions, he formulated a more nuanced opinion of them.

This lack of response was especially remarkable since, that year, a union had won a major environmental victory when local workers on oil tankers forced companies to equip the ships with vapor-recovery mechanisms, so that the petrochemical vapors would not poison the boatworkers – and the air in general – when fuel was loaded and unloaded. Yet, as will be described in the chapter on media coverage, this major victory barely appeared in the press, so most activists probably did not know about it.

The group had never sat down and talked about "talking with other types of groups" as a form of action. If it had, perhaps it would have discovered that unions were an important and obvious ally. The image of the passionate, engaged "union" was not a salient style for involvement, for citizenship, and for togetherness. This powerful, taken-for-granted cultural understanding of grassroots activism undermined activists' ability to gain a potentially powerful ally.

Conclusion: keeping activism out of place

CESE began as a group that did not have meetings and thought of discussion as a waste of time – agreeing with the volunteers that open discussion was "just rhetoric." The activist group gradually began to value its own talk, deciding that political ideas and political knowledge are not static, but grow when people talk about them. This allowed members to generate a magical kind of grassroots power. In teaching each other to value their own talk, they broadened their circle of concern, and challenged the dominant political etiquette that demanded that citizens "speak for themselves" and no one else, in public.

Local government officials assumed that their duty was to dispense information, and citizens' duty was passively to ingest it. Mandatory Momism allowed women to speak, but only for themselves. It shut men out, because they could not be Moms, and if they tried to sound like Experts, they were ignored; only officials were authorized to speak as Experts. Either way, citizens had no place speaking in public: Mom's passion was devalued and Dad's expertise ignored. Everyone's reasoned analyses were ignored.

Because of this prevalent etiquette for civic participation, even politically sympathetic local and county officials were stuck in the position of appearing to defend the incinerator. The context made this so, even when they agreed with the activists. There were no contexts for citizens to air public-spirited questions and grievances, or for officials and the rest of the public to hear them.

Officials' exclusive focus on technical information came from a general cultural assumption that citizens get involved only out of personal fear. To appear respectful, officials had to act as if honest, raw fear, not politics, was activists' motivation. So when CESE began to try forcing public-spirited discussion, the two parties started talking past each other; at least if CESE had stuck to the volunteer-style Mom discourse, they would have been operating within the same cultural universe as the officials. Both would have assumed that there is no room for debate, no common ground for political discussion, no room for questioning and analyzing moral and political issues, only the bickering voices of purely self-interested actors, minimally restrained by inert, indisputable facts and rules. Thus, the impersonal language of facts and the personal language of self-interest turn out to be two sides of a coin.[7]

But CESE ended up trying to redefine the relation between the two poles of impersonal facts and personal passion. They wanted to say that there were moral and political decisions hiding within the seemingly neutral expertise, and they were convinced that citizens did indeed have a place in the public arena, revealing and discussing those hidden moral issues that concern citizens even when the problems do not immediately affect them personally. Backstage, especially after LRC meetings, a constant line of questioning asked who was included in the various official "risk" reports: Did it include people who work in the plant? Did they include people who eat the fish from the river? What about people who will receive the ashes from the incinerator after the burning in Evergreen City? Other constant backstage questions were: How expensive would it be to convert all the factories that produced the toxic waste into non-toxin-producing plants? Who should pay? How would the profit-making mission of the incinerator affect the burning process?

All of these were questions of scientific method, as well as questions of politics. Interpenetrating lines wove between science, politics, and interest.

To say this is not to collapse science and politics, nor to say that science is simply a political tool of corporate interests; activists made it clear that these political insights into scientific assumptions could have helped *strengthen* the scientific inquiry. But instead, public conflict came in two packages, both lacking in public spirit. For technical languages, the goal is pre-set: to build the incinerator or whatever project most efficiently. For the ''close to home'' language of self-interest, the goal is also pre-set: to defend one's own interests without questioning them. If the goals are pre-set in both languages, the only question is how to reach them.

Breaking through these static ideas of knowledge and power was the challenge for the activists. Initially, activists complied with the official civic practice, letting the public spirit evaporate out of the public arena, sounding less public-spirited in frontstage than in backstage contexts. But later, activists began to challenge that etiquette, trying to show how regular citizens could contribute political ideas to the public forum. Official institutional power worked by making politics invisible and always ''out of place'' in public contexts. But activists carefully began germinating a different kind of power, through talk itself.

8

Newspapers in the cycle of political evaporation

Reading the local newspapers in Amargo and Evergreen City did not help citizens make connections between politics and everyday life, did not help them learn about the art of political debate, and inadvertently discouraged them from speaking out in a public-spirited way. Far from the sober gray world of national news, the world of local news is simultaneously lurid and down-home. The news in local Amargo and Evergreen papers was a rushing stream of unpredictable, curious, and scary events that happen to other people, usually elsewhere – lost children in other states, Siamese twins somewhere who ride a bicycle built for two, freak poisonings, the random, and the weird – and advice about cholesterol, dogs, yard care, consumer advice on brands of cough drops and local shopping. That is, the local papers were mainly tabloids with tamer headlines (Bird 1990) plus consumer gazettes.

Still, they did cover many local events, using serious local reporters, and they devoted two pages per issue to national and international news. And they were most people's source of news, aside from TV – everybody I met who read newspapers read either the *Amargo Herald* or the Evergreen County *Times*. Every now and then, a few activists and cynics read nearby city newspapers, but those papers rarely had news about suburbs. No one read national newspapers such as *The New York Times*, *Washington Post*, or *Los Angeles Times*. These local, suburban papers, then, were their sources of news; indeed, most Americans who pay attention to the news at all read or watch the *local* news where they live, in the suburbs (Kaniss 1992).

This chapter examines coverage of CESE, Testament for Humanity, the volunteers' Just Say No team, and other volunteer groups. Since there were few articles on these groups, I supplemented them with coverage of other local grassroots activism, and also read a systematic sample[1] of entire editions of the Evergreen County *Times*, the larger and more news-oriented of the two regional newspapers, to see how coverage of activism and volunteering fitted into the general flow of news (Williams 1975). I ask three questions about this news coverage:

1. Balance: Do articles show debate, giving voice to important actors' reasons for concern?
2. Human consequences: Do articles make the human effects of this decision-making clear?
3. Human responsibility: Do articles show how human decision-making is responsible?

In addition to doing this more systematic study, I regularly read the local papers, and put myself on several news "diets," reading nothing but these local papers for several weeks at a time, to find out first-hand what this nourishment would do to my political health.

Balance: usually unnecessary

The importance of "balance" in the news is not that it tells the entire, objective, "truth," since recording the infinitude of occurrences of a day – or a minute – would be impossible, but that it illustrates a *process* of decision-making: debate, in which each side musters its analysis, its evidence, and its form of public reasoning. Ideally, "balance" presents a model of political dialogue. It is typically presented in journalism textbooks as the rule, the ideal form for news stories. The problem is, journalists do not follow their own rules.

The most astonishing thing about "balance" in these local papers was just how very few stories required it. If metaphors for newswriting come from playgrounds, a dizzy, loud, unfocused merry-go-round ride is a better image than a creaky, slow, "balanced" see-saw. Most sections of the paper – sports, home and garden, science, real estate, entertainment, the funnies, and the obituaries, and of course, the pages and pages of ads – were exempt from the balance rule. Tales of demon babies, mysterious poisonings and freak accidents, zoo animals, nature, weather, health, consumer tips: none of these usually required balance. A long story entitled "Murder Charge Filed in Riverfront Freeway Shooting" (January 5, 1990) told that "a man driving home with his wife after celebrating their anniversary was shot to death [near Pacific City] by another motorist who allegedly wanted to speed up traffic so his passenger could use the bathroom." Most of these stories were about unusual individuals, whose behavior was presented as not having any social explanation at all; but even with the bathroom-seeking motorist, one could imagine a debate. For example, coverage of shootings never once asked about control of the sale of ammunition or guns, or if the US's high murder rate, compared to that of other nations, might be connected to gun ownership.

Stories about volunteering and charity were another genre that did not require balance. A story on an educational program sponsored by the local refinery, in which high schoolers were trained in semi- or unskilled work, came as an unequivocal tale of good things that happen in the community, with a picture of a youth wearing a clean uniform, standing in front of a machine. A long, page two article (September 1, 1988) about a local Mothers Against Drunk Driving campaign quoted the spokesperson offering the volunteer-style refrain, "Even if we keep one person from drinking and driving for one day, that's an improvement." Needless to say, there was no opposing perspective in this article – though public transportation and dense development probably could prevent some of the 50,000 highway deaths per year (Gusfield 1981), MADD does not raise the controversial idea that mass transit could preventing drunk driving (Reinarman 1988).

Balance was not considered necessary for understanding volunteer-style politics. An article about an anti-drugs parade in the *Amargo Herald* did not have to cite studies demonstrating that communities with many parades have less drug abuse than communities with few parades. Nobody had to be quoted saying that pupils should be in class learning to read and write instead of engaging in school-time anti-drugs festivities like the banner-making assembly – children's participation was to drizzle red paint on their little hands and then stamp them on a giant white sheet that had an anti-drugs slogan on it. Similarly, when police and volunteers said that the family problems were the root cause of children's problems, no "experts" were asked to debate whether disturbed families *are* the root problem or just another symptom. Or again, for stories about drugs, reporters never had to interview dealers, users, or even pro-legalization advocates.

Another exemption from the "balance" rule came for stories in which *nobody's* side of the story is told – stories which *did* describe conflict but did not make the conflict comprehensible. The Evergreen County *Times* often avoided the difficulty of explaining conflicts by simply stating that there *was* a conflict, enumerated deaths or injuries if any, described the heat of animosity, and ending at that. For example, a story about a strike quoted a union official saying, "We're going to the mat," and gave many more illustrations of both parties' anger, but did not offer either party's analysis of the dispute, except to say that the union wanted a contract and the companies did not want to recognize the union (April 8, 1989). A story about a protest in Pacific City described the arrests but neglected to say what the two parties had to say about the issue under protest (August 11, 1989).

When I went on my "news diet," reading only the local news, I felt very much in the dark about the causes of conflicts and upheavals, including some of the ones I had understood earlier that year. I found myself not remembering what conflicts were about and not remembering the various sides' arguments. That made concentrating on stories, especially foreign stories, quite a challenge.

Many brief stories, such as "Private Garbage Haulers May Now Store Radioactive Weapons Waste" (February 6, 1989) and "Nuclear Licensing Relaxed" (April 8, 1989) were so short, they did not mention opposition. In my sample, only an average of two stories per issue devoted more than two lines to explaining opposing perpectives. These were usually disputes between local officials. The other kind of story that sometimes had "balance" was about local activism. But this was a very strange, lopsided balance.

Balance in reporting on local activists: Experts and Moms

Public hearings were presented as efforts on the part of officials to convey neutral information to ignorant, frightened citizens, not as disagreements about what kinds of knowledge should count in the first place. Thus, stories "balanced" the sides by asking whether or not enough good information had been dispensed by authorities: officials say "yes" and opponents say "no," but the debate was portrayed as being over the quality and quantity of information dispensed by experts, not over opposed political policy positions.

Recall from chapter 7 the many examples of reporters ignoring activists when the activists tried to offer policy suggestions and speak as responsible citizens of a democracy. Instead of portraying activists as politically concerned citizens with possibly useful policy suggestions, reporters presented local activists as simply worried about their own health, children, and finances. One article quoted an activist saying, "I'm starting a family; I've got a 19-month-old daughter . . . and this could affect her future." After the Plastico chemical fire had filled the sky with bruise-colored clouds – purple, yellow, brown, and green, visible eight miles away – CESE picketed, with signs advocating recycling, better regulation of toxic production, non-toxic alternatives to toxic production, and specifically advocating two laws for the government to pass, to begin to reach these goals. Signs detailed the accident-prone plant's bad safety record, enumerating Plastico's major accidents of the previous eight years. But the reporters ignored them. Even reporters who were sympathetic to the group's cause – in fact, especially reporters who were sympathetic – tried to portray them as simple, emotional people who cared only about what was close to home.

All five reporters (myself included!) flocked to a bystander who was not even a member of the group. Sobbing, she described her panic: when she heard the boom at Plastico, she grabbed her children as fast as she could and tried to get away, but did not know where to go. She presented herself as a Mom, wildly frightened for her own children; whether she had any analysis of the problem or its solution, or if she was connected to any grassroots group was irrelevant for the news stories. Later, a story said CESE "wasn't satisfied with Plastico's assurance, and [said] that the company should have done more to explain itself and its record." The reporter was clearly trying to make the activists sound reasonable in this article; in doing so, she fitted them into the volunteer model of citizens waiting for knowledge from experts. She ignored the group's signs and leaflets calling for more strict government regulation and for other political solutions – demands that were not quite requests for more information. Similarly, another article paraphrased the group's leaflet, skipping the policy suggestions and quoting the part that said that the incinerator should not be in a populated area or near a crowded highway, and that trucks shipping the waste might get in accidents. In another story about the Plastico explosion, indignant citizens claimed that the soot from the fire ate away the paint on their cars. A Plastico official tried to undermine the image of righteously indignant citizens by placating them: "For goodness sakes, call and deal with us on a one-to-one basis. We don't want to panic anyone." (For decades, Plastico had dealt with these fires by reimbursing people whose cars had been corroded by soot rather than publicly arguing about whether the corrosion was indeed caused by Plastico's soot.) Similarly, in a story about a pornographic bookstore that neighbors wanted shut down, there was a pull quote in large type, from a man saying, "You're not talking about constitutional issues, but the emotional and physical safety of our children."

In all of these cases, frantic citizens were portrayed as doing just what they should: defending their children and caring about what was "close to home." As Francis, a reporter for the Evergreen County *Times*, told me later, the press likes it when the story is "the little guys are saying they've had enough." It is a formula that is so standardized, this reporter said, it is a standard newsroom joke to mimic exaggerated versions of it. In an interview with me, he laughed, giving an example of his most recent version of that formula: the owner of a trailer park was going to force a dying trailer dweller to get rid of his three cats. Francis said he felt bad about doing that story, it was "so one-sided and silly." But it is a formula for local news, which he said editors like and local news readers recognize.

Even when citizens did present information, it was not printed. CESE sent numerous letters to the editor of the Evergreen County *Times* about the incinerator, but the only letter opposing the incinerator that the paper published was sent by someone who was unknown to the group. This letter had no information in it, while the letters sent by group members were always full of information about Montgomery Chemicals in particular, and toxic inciner-ation in general. The editor told the group that those letters could not make it into the letters column because they would require too much fact-checking.

In contrast, members of the anti-drugs group were satisfied with coverage of their issue, and said that the local paper would print any letter they sent. At my very first meeting with them, I was asked to write a letter to the editor. Activist groups would never have asked a newcomer with so little knowledge of the issue to write a letter. And when I said to the anti-drugs group that I did not know enough about the issue, it sounded strange, because the drug problem is not seen as an issue that demands specialized information of a person who wants to have an opinion.

Three exceptional articles on CESE activists violated all the rules for coverage of citizenship; I will describe these in depth at the end of the news analysis. Aside from those three, only one article in my sample portrayed citizens' desire to participate in meaningful debate. It quoted Neil neatly stating, ''I'm disappointed. The EPA held a public hearing, but they ignored everybody.'' For the activists, the process of distributing information was as objectionable as the information itself: even if the company could convince residents that the soot that ate paint was safe to inhale, activists had other demands. They wanted a more regular system of accountability; they wanted more control over the corporations and government. This was not just a matter of disputing facts.

Balance and Testament for Humanity

Testament for Humanity was a coalition of religious and political groups participating in a vigil protesting arms shipments from the local weapons depot. The vigil produced piles upon piles of dense leaflets, explaining the participants' reasons for protesting. After the vigil had been going on for a year, one protester, Augie Bradley, was run over by a weapons truck during a sit-in on the highway into the weapons depot. Several articles on the vigil appeared each day for a week after that, and then about one a day for another month. I read them all.

Incredibly, out of the dozens of articles in the Evergreen County *Times*, only one presented Bradley's, or any other protesters', reasons for objecting to US arms shipments to Central America. It said, ''images of burned-out Vietnamese villages and homeless peasants led [Bradley] to oppose with increasing vehemence, what he perceived as another Vietnam in Central America . . . [On a trip to Central America] he saw poor people being brutal-ized. [He] talked with survivors and families of people who disappeared, who were tortured and killed.'' But even this exceptional article did not say what he found out. A typical reader might have wondered, "What is this war about? Is the US involved?" and then, after that, "Why does he think the US is on the wrong side?" Considering the depths of most Americans' political ignorance (Rosen 1987; Neuman 1986, for example), journalists should not assume that we do remember much of this information. The passive voice verbal constructions – "being brutalized" by whom? – made it difficult to see the connection between his lying on the highway here, and Central Americans brutalizing each other there.

Trying to be sympathetic to protesters, one article interviewed some who talked about their upbringing: one had parents who were activists in the civil rights movement, another's parents asked during World War II, "Why did the people of Germany let it happen?" Along the same lines, one other article tried perhaps to be sympathetic, saying that Bradley and his wife "met and fell in love on an anti-war visit to Nicaragua ... Their wedding invitation included a collage of photos of their anti-war activities." These efforts at exposing protesters' emotional worlds offered "balance" in one sense: they tried to make the protesters sound human, and they were hailed for "believing in standing up for what they believe in." But this kind of "balance" did not offer readers any opposing analyses of policy.

No other articles came this close to providing even this much balance, this much analysis, from any side. Instead of presenting the contending parties' competing analyses of the issue of arms shipments, articles focused on the logistics of the protest itself – enumerating arrests and timetables, describing the traffic jams caused by the protest, describing police strategies for dealing with the protest, tallying every day how many tax dollars the protest (but not the war) was costing the county. Numerous articles gave information about whether or not the drivers of the truck could have stopped on time, whether they knew that the protesters had vowed not to move, whether drivers were exceeding the speed limit when they ran Bradley over, and initially, daily reports about the condition of Bradley's arm and head.

For example, the local columnist, who usually confined her topics to "Baby-Killing Mom Hits Lecture Circuit" (January 5, 1989) and "How Should Parents Protect Their Children from Kidnapping?" (November 3, 1988), was typical in avoiding the issue of arms shipments to Central America and elsewhere. The day after the injury, she wrote an editorial entitled "Injured Protester Crossed the Fine Line," saying that he should have moved. In the middle of the article, she conceded, "I do not wish to argue here with Bradley's political philosophy. In fact, much of it I share. The Vietnam veteran's conviction is commendable. He is prepared to stand up and speak out for those things in which he believes and that's what this country is all about." This is the "he believes in standing up for his beliefs" formula; we eagerly await a description of his beliefs, his reasons for believing in this particular issue.

Instead, the columnist then spent the next six paragraphs on detailing the difficulties of stopping a heavily loaded eighteen-wheel truck, including a physics lesson about the relationship between weight and velocity, and a quote from a truck driver. And for all these lines about "standing up" for beliefs, it was interesting that at least two big photos *showed* protesters lying down, placidly napping in the sun! Similarly, the paper's editor conducted a poll, not asking whether Bradley was right in his analysis of US policy, but asking "who was to blame for the truck accident at the weapons station protest" (and when some readers answered the survey, deeming Bradley responsible, the editor wrote that "the public" was against Bradley, and that the local congressperson was out of touch with his constituents, since he voted against aid to Central America). Carefully attentive to public opinion about the *injury*, the local news neglected opinion about the issue itself.

The disarmament protesters did try to publicize their analyses, though. Their political analyses just never made it into the news. In speeches and leaflets, they offered detailed analyses of the relations between US involvement and corporate profit-making in Third World countries, usually focusing on the exploitation of cheap labor and an unprotected environment. For example, in a speech at Evergreen Island Weapons Station, following Bradley's accident, then presidential candidate Jesse Jackson spoke about how factories close up shop in the US and open up in the Third World where labor is cheap and pollution unregulated. He said that when people in those countries try to raise their wages, then our government, using our taxes, sends arms to keep the low-paid workers down, and that in turn keeps workers' pay here low. But local papers did not report this portion of Jackson's speech, and never once quoted other protesters' similar arguments.

Balance in other local protests

Activists were not portrayed as particularly knowledgeable. They worried and asked questions, but were not shown as having "done their background," as Cathy of the country-western club put it. Typical was "Toxics May Always Be With Us" (April 27, 1989) an article about a protest in Pacific City. It devoted five paragraphs to experts' saying that the total elimination of toxic waste is impossible; one paragraph went to a Greenpeace spokesperson who said that the government was encouraging toxic incineration by permitting new incinerators to be built. But the article did not explain the Greenpeace member's statement, so it sounded nonsensical, unless one already knew Greenpeace's analysis of how more incinerators could create more waste. An accompanying photo showed a demonstrator holding a big picture of a Cupid's arrow and heart, with "POLLUTERS -N- EPA" written inside, and another saying "WHO'S IN BED WITH WHOM?"

The big photograph went to the colorful demonstrators, but there was no space for them to offer *reasons* for the colorfully flamboyant show. Like officials, reporters characterized activists as "emotional" and experts as rational. "Hazardous waste issues are so emotional it's hard to come to a rational, technical solution," an official claimed in one article ("Swift River Vote Bars Waste of ChemWaste Corp. from Plant"). The "balance" was portrayed as being between reason and feeling, not between two competing analyses.

In another local conflict, over two hundred citizens had flooded hearings twice in one year, mustering a range of publicly minded arguments against a proposal to build mammoth new reservoirs in Evergreen County. They argued that having more water would make more county development possible; they wanted more dense development in the nearby cities, which they said was more ecologically sound than the car-centered sprawl in mall-filled suburbs like Evergreen County and Amargo. And they said that new water supplies would justify continuing profligate water use – green lawns, flowerbeds – and destroy the soil of this fragile, dry, desert-like ecosystem. And they said that the water to fill the reservoirs would come at the expense of small farmers' water supply, whose farms would suffer. And they said that poor quality water for small farmers would harm the state's economy. And they said that these new reservoirs would very likely become the first steps in a proposed massive statewide water system which they said would be expensive, unecological and unnecessary. One article described a former senator voicing part of this last criticism, clearly assuming that readers were already familiar with the history of this water system proposal.

Aside from the former senator's cryptic objection, the only argument opposing reservoir construction that made it into the Evergreen County *Times* was that flooding canyons to create the reservoirs might endanger an obscure species of snake (in two articles, both on June 10, 1989). On local TV, I also heard the argument that these particular canyons were pretty places to stroll. The arguments in favor of construction – cleaner, safer water, more water to put out fires and for other emergencies – far outstripped concerns for the snake. A similar debate, about damming a river, pitted "people who like to go river-rafting and fishing" against the "1.1 million water users" of the region (February 6, 1989). In fact, the opponents of the dam argued that there were more long-term solutions to the problem of local water quality and that damming the river would ultimately harm water quality throughout the region.

Whether or not the opponents' arguments were good is not my point. My point is that they were not reported in the news at all. The only way one could know about them was to attend hearings; but then again, most of those hearings were as technical and strict about avoiding political arguments as the LRC meetings described in the previous chapter. Really, the only way a citizen could learn of these objections was to happen to meet an activist – that was how I learned of them. Specifically, I met this activist when interviewing him for the Newton radio station. Doing this story myself drove home to me that reporters' lack of time was not the reason for their lack of analysis. I wrote a story (and edited the tape on very archaic equipment – a time-consuming process that a print journalist would not have) in half a day, the same amount of time that print reporters have to write theirs – this is not to brag: I was very slow, by the radio station's standards.

To present analyses, reporters would not have needed to produce the rival interpretations themselves; they would have simply had to call up the non-governmental organizations, the research institutes, politicians, academics, or activist groups that would gladly have offered their analyses. But for most reporters, like most citizens, the public sphere was empty of such institutions (Hallin and Mancini 1985). The lack of analysis sometimes made stories impossible to follow, and certainly made the art of debate, of mustering evidence and reasoning, seem irrelevant to politics.

Human consequences

Does political decision-making affect everyday life? Stories that described how real human beings were affected by something followed the human interest model: not showing how citizens could influence the problem (and not requiring "balance"), but showing dramatic, graphic effects on common people. A suburban high schooler inhaled butane for a high and died; investigators now thought they knew why a boy in faraway New Jersey had died the year before from tainted yogurt (a brand not even sold in the Pacific City region). Disaster happened to civilians in foreign countries – "Lebanese Pack Bomb Shelters," or "Bus Crash in Mexico Kills 12." "It's a shame," is what a Buffalo member would say about these stories.

Aside from descriptions of effects on those particular individuals, portrayals of consequences were often very abstract. A short (twelve-line) article beginning with a passive voice phrase, "Higher amounts of two suspected carcinogens will be tolerated by the state [in drinking water] ..." sounds much more distant than "The state's drinking water may soon contain two

more suspected carcinogens,'' for example. Nearly all articles about hazardous waste simply said a chemical was "potentially hazardous," without
saying what the potential hazards might be. Most graphic descriptions were
reserved for effects on lower animals: "When scientists tried to grow plants
or breed earthworms in the soil [at the Evergreen Island Naval Air Station],
the effect was immediate. 'It killed them,' said Barton Clay, a soil scientist
with the US Army Corps of Engineers," said one article ("20 Toxic-Waste
Sites May Need Cleaning at Evergreen Air Base" [April 20, 1990]).

The only time human consequences seemed necessary to report was when
local plants blew up and killed or dismembered people or when they sent
clouds billowing visibly into the sky. In these cases, the paper reported the
effects on those specific workers who died, were disfigured, or dismembered.
The clearest effects described were the "fear" and "panic" that the
explosions and fires, smoke and soot, leaks and smells, inspired.

The "human consequences" of union activism were reported as being
wholly negative; readers were not addressed as potentially benefitting from
any union activities. This complete blackout on the possible positive effects
of union activism was especially remarkable in this region, where unions
were in the forefront of environmental activism; could this help explain
CESE's lack of attention to making alliances with unions? An article blandly
reported that the state had a new rule regarding the handling of gasoline on
freighters: "The new rule will eliminate 30 tons per year of benzene, a gasoline ingredient that has been declared cancer-causing by the state Air
Resources Board" (January 5, 1989). The article reported that "environmentalists" won this victory, naming some lobbying groups based in Pacific City.
Eliminate from what? Emissions from where? How much will they still be
allowed to emit? And why the elaborately passive verb construction when
scientists have long agreed that benzene exposure can cause cancer (as well
as other deadly problems)? Compare this to a dockworker's description of
benzene's effects: "cirrhosis . . . high blood pressure . . . chronic insomnia,
heart disease, lead poisoning, benzene leukemia, and the consequent tearing
at family life . . . cancer of the pancreas, throat and kidney . . . dizziness . . .
irreversible chronic effects, [including] memory loss . . . workers would go
home without remembering that they had ever left the job." The union said
that all of these effects added up to "death rates [that] surpass those in any
other occupation in the state."

But aside from problems caused by long-winded and legalistic writing,
articles about this ecological coup left out the key actor: the union of dockworkers who unloaded the gasoline products. The union had been on strike,
and "began publicly to count their dead," according to the union's local
newsletter. The union worked for years to change laws about benzene vapors,

claiming that the airborne chemical affected not just workers' health, but everyone in the whole region. This was an issue that had aroused activism and concern among union members' children and spouses, and non-union members as well. Yet the paper did not refer to it as a "community issue" or a "family issue." On the contrary, the stories implied that if consumers were dissatisfied, union workers were to blame (Goldman and Rajagopal [1991] found a similar pattern in coverage of mine strikes). Readers were not addressed as potential fellow workers or even possibly fellow air-breathers, but as potentially dissatisfied consumers of the services the union workers produced: prices might go up, or implausibly in this major international port, tankers might just go elsewhere.

Human consequences of Testament for Humanity's vigil

After Augie Bradley was run over by the weapons truck, a flurry of articles addressed the effects of the protest on local traffic (bad), local police (long hours, paid for with residents' taxes), and on the protesters themselves (they are having fun, or suffering from the dry weather, or "at long last . . . in the international spotlight . . . The protest of US arms shipments to Central America, had, at long last, a symbol [in Bradley]"). Aside from the one article described above, that quoted Bradley on burned-out villages, none of the dozens of articles mentioned any possible effects of the war or the protest on people in Central America.

Human consequences of volunteerism

Citizen responsibilty was presented in a way that was harmonious with the volunteers' own sense of it. A front-page story in the *Amargo Herald*, for example, showed the annual Just Say No team event in which a thousand Amargans encircled a park with a giant red ribbon. The year before, they had spelled out the words, "I Don't Do Drugs," so that they would be visible from the sky. In these events, the content was taken to be the form: that is, the celebration was not supposed to be "about" some other thing, any more than a Little League game is. Every quote and paraphrase in the long, 150-line article had the same message: "It shows that someone cares," said one parent. "It signifies we're committed to the war on drugs like everyone else," said the police chief. People came to the event "to symbolize unity in the war against drugs . . . The red ribbon serves as a reminder to children not to use drugs and alcohol," wrote the reporter. The consequences were so clear, they did not even require analysis from opposing perspectives.

Human action and responsibility

In my sample of whole newspaper editions, only four stories, none local, described American citizens' efforts at trying to influence national politics: two small anti-abortion meetings, a huge pro-choice demonstration in Washington, DC, and one of the three exceptional stories about CESE (the other two exceptional stories were published on a day that was not in my sample). There was, however, a steady stream of articles inviting people to volunteer in solitary charity efforts – donating clothes to homeless people, doing carpentry in a home for abused children, recycling, doing other important tasks quietly and alone, without having to talk about it, volunteer-style.

Citizens' action sometimes disappeared altogether. A person reading the Evergreen County *Times* might learn that the mayor of a nearby town argued with the giant corporations that owned her town's chemical plant, but no one could tell from news articles that *citizens* worked with her in these two disputes. Another example was that article about the new law controlling air pollution from tankers, that did not mention the dockworkers' union.

Citizens did not appear in stories offering positive solutions to environmental problems. " 'Do Something' Pesticide Plant Area Residents Tell Health Officials" (April 14, 1989) was the title of one story, which pitted the beleaguered, seemingly helpless black neighbors of the plant against the state's and company's experts. Another article about the same neighborhood, headlined "Odors Permeate Life in Hillview," cited many residents' vague, helpless, or humorous complaints: " 'It's like a big underarm,' says one lifetime resident of the smelly, toxics-laden area." Remarkably, these articles never mentioned the very un-helpless black activist group in Hillview that was fighting the smelly plant. Instead, Hillviewers' plight fitted into the "It's a shame" frame preferred by Buffalo Club members.

Articles about local activism did not report on national activism or policy and vice versa, even though local groups linked up to various national networks. And there were no stories comparing US domestic policies to other countries' policies, to ask how policies affect life. It was therefore difficult to see the effect of local activism on national politics, or the effect of national policy on local residents.

Instead of analyses of how policy-making affects people, or how people affect policy-making, readers got technical information; at least one long or mid-sized article per issue named the brand and make of weapon used by a drug dealer, gave the weights, lengths, widths, and names of the missiles carried on a sunken submarine; or otherwise gave technical details that would not add to a reader's understanding of the politics of a story.[2]

The three exceptional articles

An extraordinary reporter at the Evergreen County *Times* managed to break through these frames, or at least twist them, in three articles. One article was a decade summary piece, printed on a New Year's Eve Sunday (December 31, 1989), on local environmentalism and its ties to national movements. Another was an individual profile of an interesting local person, a standard feature of the Thursday paper, except that this was about a local activist. A third was about an event.

Two of these articles were "balanced," describing differing interpretations, giving space to both sides' reasoning. The year-end summary piece did not just make activists sound like volunteers. It quoted activist Neil's saying, "This is a democracy. If people are loud enough and persistent enough, they can be heard, but it's not going to work on its own. Not doing anything guarantees that the will of the moneyed few will win out."

This piece and one other made a link between local and national, thus making the local activism sound potentially politically effective: the two articles said that the local group was part of a national network. And the year-end wrap-up piece gave credit to local environmental activism for changes already in place: curbside recycling, and the closing of the toxic dump in Swift River a few years before. None of the articles gave the activists credit for educating themselves about the scientific and legal issues surrounding toxics and their regulation. But still, the articles certainly broke rank on the other grounds.

"How did these extraordinary articles happen?" I asked the reporter in an interview, "and why was this sort of article so rare?" His answer is part of the mystery unraveled in the second half of this chapter, on relations between citizen groups and the press.

News-gathering routines and the market definition of local

To find out why the media coverage of activists was so thin, I spent time at some activist events standing and talking with reporters, and working as a reporter myself, for an out-of-town volunteer-run community radio station. I also worked side by side with reporters covering other local issues. In addition, I interviewed the two reporters who were most sympathetic to the CESE activists, to find out how it could be that reporters' political beliefs made so little difference. Again, I will stick to the three questions of this chapter: Do stories show balanced debate and analysis? Do they show citizen responsibility? Do they show how policy decisions have consequences for regular people?

Balancing the obvious

Most reporters were friendly and practical people who just assumed that most everyday stories were straightforward, not full of options and choices for framing, not really in need of analysis. For example, the Navy held a press conference, in which it shuttled all the reporters on a little barge out onto the Romano-cheese-smelling river, to show off a new device for cleaning chemical spills. This skimmer could clean any of the many anonymous, undocumented toxic and oil spills; these anonymous spills and leaks were the major source of river pollution, the Navy claimed. The device looked just like the red and white striped buoyed ropes that keep children out of a pool's deep end.

I asked one reporter how he planned on doing his story. He laughed, ''Well, I'm just gonna report what the Navy said and show some pictures. What else?'' as if it were obvious. And that was just what he did, in a quite long television news story, showing beautiful, long, slow, wordless pictures of Navy skimmers on the glassy river.

Considering that several activist organizations claimed that the Navy itself was by far the river's largest polluter, just taking the Navy's word and showing pictures was not the only obvious approach. This pattern, of simply playing a story as if it had no need of balance, was repeated in other stories as well – though of course, when the source was a group like CESE, the reporters always consulted the corporate or government officials against whom they argued. But again, to obtain ''balance'' in the oil skimmer story, reporters could easily have called up one of the dozen regional activist organizations that researched river pollution; reporters do not need to provide rival interpretations, themselves, but simply to call people who can provide it.[3] Some reporters said that space limitations caused their lack of analysis, but in the same amount of time and space, reporters could have offered some analysis if they had had a good file of phone numbers.

For commercial radio news reporters, in contrast, time and space did indeed limit content. One balmy evening, I was standing outside with a reporter waiting for a particularly boring section of a CESE-organized panel discussion to end. Janet, a radio reporter, sauntered over, snorting with annoyance,

> Now I have to go figure out how to boil this whole thing down. I don't even know how much time I'll get. Sometimes it's just forty seconds for the whole story.

NINA: Forty seconds? You're kidding! How can you say anything?

JANET: Oh, hey, that's not so bad – sometimes my cuts are only one or two *words*!

Citizen responsibility

Even if Janet, the radio reporter, had had more time and space, her story probably would not have had much counterpoint, since she, like many reporters, professed active disinterest in politics. Making conversation at one event, I asked if she knew which reporter covered the recent Plastico explosion for National Public Radio. She sneered, "Pfah! I never listen to the news on my day off. I listen to the country music station! And when I'm working, I only can listen to [the commercial station at which she worked]." She was typical in her jaded, annoyed approach to the news. It was not cool for reporters to display anything but supercilious cynicism regarding activists – even if the reporter him or herself was privately rooting for them.

As Francis, the self-reflective reporter who wrote one of the exceptional articles on grassroots environmentalism, said, in a taped interview with me,

Many reporters think it's unethical to be involved, because they think it compromises journalistic objectivity. So they keep themselves willfully ignorant of movements both right and left. You always hear about the famous "liberal bias of the press." Most reporters are liberal: they scorn bigotry, they're for equality of the sexes, and they recycle. But they're not politically active, and are suspicious of people who are.

At events, reporters are at the scene in a different capacity from regular participants. So, even though most of the reporters I met were congenial and jolly, this difference fostered a cynical solidarity amongst reporters that amplified their suspicion and distance from activists. For example, one evening, while the activists sat on hard little orange folding chairs in a hot, fluorescent-lit city hall chamber, the three reporters were free to move about, wander outdoors in the cool shade, sit in a special little room above the city council chamber, with one-way windows and sound that was piped in but did not go out. So, while the regular folks are stuffed into uncomfortable rows below, the reporters can gather up top to laugh and put their feet up on the table and make fun of the whole thing. We ordered a pizza. Andrea kept grimacing and saying that the event was planned wrong, that one of the activists was a flake for not understanding the laws, another was a pest for calling her up on Sunday, a third was a pain for pushing her to get CESE's event announced in the "Community" section of the paper, which "everyone knows is reserved for lost dogs and keys." Neil and Maryellen were "adorable hippies, but too pure for politics." Reporters have the scoop on everyone. As usual, we did not talk to each other about the politics of their news stories.

At another event in nearby Hillview, black anti-toxics activists got in an argument with regulators and started shouting at them. Everyone had to take a side, either shouting at the regulators or telling the shouters to quiet down – everyone except the reporters, that is. While everyone else was getting hot and excited, the reporters were a cool pack of James Bonds, aloof, observing, taking notes, shooting the most dramatic speakers from behind a camera. Almost all reporters left events after only ten or fifteen minutes, long before the rest of the crowd.

Most local suburban news reporters took an especially ironic attitude toward the local news. They thought that they were not Edward Murrows reporting on world-shaking events, but were just little local newswriters reporting for little newspapers on little events in Evergreen and Amargo Counties that were not central to anything. Most lived in cities, and wished they were city reporters, who get more time and money and job stability to report on more important-seeming issues. They made jokes about the triviality of the stories they covered, or laughed at how often overly earnest activists called them up, even at home, with urgent announcements.

Human consequences of political decision-making: "local" according to the local news

The local news made it seem that politics happens elsewhere. The emphasis on and definition of "local" combined with time constraints to make the news, and coverage of activists in particular, trivial. While all reporters complained about getting "stuck" with local stories, they rarely made their stories bigger, by drawing out their national or global implications or causes. This would take research, which was considered impossible in such little time. They thought that they could not cite activists' leaflets without checking the facts independently, and no one had time for this. Now, they *could* have simply cited the activists and said that the "fact" in question was the speech act – the fact that the activists said what they said, and that the officials rebutted (just as one would report on racial strife by reporting the racial slur A shouted to B, without the reporter him or herself having to verify that in fact, B did embody the characteristics described by the slur).

For example, I told Andrea about a story I had read that said that Montgomery Chemicals had illegally experimented on humans to test its new line of cosmetics and, through a series of corporate buy-outs, was owned by the same company that had had a notorious chemical accident that killed thousands. I said it would fun to do a story on that for the local news. She agreed, but said she could not because, "How could I demonstrate that the connections really matter? I could be sued for libel, or run the risk of the newspaper getting sued, and ruin my credibility in any case." But why couldn't she simply call up the sources that were consulted in the story I had read, and call up Montgomery spokespeople for their rebuttal? Similarly, Francis would have loved to describe the effects of the state's property tax cuts in the stories he did about cities. But he said, "it would be difficult to get time from the editor to do a statewide story asking, 'What did the tax-cutting initiative of 1982 do to the state?' not because editors think the tax cut is the greatest thing since sliced bread but because they'd say, 'It's not local.' " He said that a story like that would require research, which takes time, while all editors really care about is that reporters get the right number of lines done in the right amount of time.

Politics happens elsewhere

FRANCES: You have to do local, local, local, local! The Evergreen County *Times* is *never* gonna do an in-depth story about El Salvador. [It is] not perceived as local. *If* the protesters were from Evergreen County and Evergreen were getting refugees from El Salvador, then a reporter *could try* to give it a local angle and get by editors that way. On the other hand, the people who *work* at Evergreen Island Air Station *are* local, do live in Evergreen, a lot of them, so they get better coverage. Editors never say, "That's too liberal a story," but "What does that have to do with our readers?"

Local news had a very specific definition of "local": our circulation area. The Amargo paper, which was supposed to cover events in Amargo and Swift River, did not touch Evergreen City, which was a short swim from both. The Evergreen County *Times* sometimes covered events in Amargo and Swift River, since the paper was sold in those towns (coverage came after the market expansion). So, the news' definition of local helped create the public's definition. And the news' definition of local was based not on political or social boundaries, or ecological or geographical ones, but market boundaries.

The sense of localness is created first by the market, and second, by the ease of explanation without research. If there is no time to explain *causes* that go beyond the "local," then all stories that are local seem apolitical, and all political stories seem not local. Readers and reporters assumed that an issue is not political if it is local. They assumed that local stories do not require knowledge or analysis, but national and international stories do. Newsroom customs (of not consulting opposing actors, not being authorized to report actors' own views without fact-checking) fostered this assumption, by making it difficult for reporters themselves to explore analyses of local problems' political roots – political causes and solutions that would not immediately boil down to a local individual's visible actions (handing the blanket to the homeless person, feeding the hungry person, for example).

This second meaning of local helps solve a puzzle: even while "local" was confined to a very strict geographical boundary, other towns' "local" news often made it into the Evergreen County news – more often, in fact, than national policy debates. One could read all about unusual, "local" events in small towns a thousand miles away if the events seemed otherwise to fit this second definition of "local"; and thus were a network of "local" towns connected through their unusual, quaint occurrences – their teenagers who die while ice-fishing ("Fumes Kill 4 Ice-Fishing Teens") in distant Wisconsin (February 6, 1989) (had any readers in Evergreen City ever even witnessed ice-fishing?), tainted yogurts in far-off New Jersey, eccentric neighbors, weird criminals.

The problem is, first, that reporters did not make connections between local and global; doing so ideally would necessitate presenting *debates* about *how* to think about that connection.[4] To get beyond "local, local, local," newspapers would have to illustrate a practice – debate – rather than just explain facts. This lack of debate resonated with citizens' political etiquette.

Conclusion: political evaporation in the news

The local news did not follow reporters' own rules. It almost never showed balance and debate, and rarely showed how the news would matter to everyday citizens, except as defenders of their own very specific and narrowly defined interests, or as well-meaning volunteers. Reporters wanted to draw readers in by focusing on feelings, as if feelings exist apart from thoughts. Stories focused on the "local," but as fewer and fewer important issues are purely local any more (if they ever were), this narrow focus unnecessarily constricted reporters. In avoiding analysis and debate, and focusing on citizens' feelings, and neglecting to locate interesting news sources who could argue over how to interpret local news in light of wider policies, reporters made their own work nearly superfluous (Rosen 1994).

The famous "liberal bias of the press" deserves a rebuttal here. Rightwing media critics (Lichter, Rothman, and Lichter 1986, for example) make the erroneous assumption that reporters' vaguely "centrist" or even "liberal" political preferences and anti-authoritarian personalities influence their reporting. On the other hand, others (influenced by Edward Epstein's *News from Nowhere* [1973]) say that while most reporters are "liberal," they are not politically active, and distrust people who are, so their liberal tendencies have little effect on coverage of grassroots issues. Reporters are not highly committed to their beliefs, Epstein says, but take a kind of distant, ironic stance toward *all* political involvement. And above all, reporters are committed to their own careers, and will do almost whatever they think it will take to further those careers.

While the "liberal bias of the media" thesis clearly misses reporters' deep lack of political commitment, this second explanation – that calls journalists' scornful aversion to activism politically neutral – is also lacking. It *is* part of reporters' jobs to unmask hypocrisy, dogmatism, and stupidity wherever they find it, so in a way, reporters' suspicion of activists makes sense.[5] But their suspicion and irony easily sounds like cynicism, and this cynicism systematically filters only certain kinds of ideas out of public circulation. Press cynicism leaves all but the most cynical, overtly self-interested activists sounding silly and naive – or at best, sounding like well-meaning volunteers who do not need to debate about their obviously good works – thus undermining public-spirited grassroots activism and debate.

9

The evaporation of politics in the US public sphere

Examining everyday political conversation reveals an often ignored dimension of public engagement and disengagement, rebellion and acquiescence, curiosity and complacency. This seemingly shallow dimension is the intangible realm of unspoken political etiquette, where citizens delicately but very firmly establish a sense of *what the public sphere itself is* – of what can be questioned and discussed, where and how. In the contemporary American public sphere, paradoxically, what marks a context as clearly "public" is often precisely the fact that the talk there is so narrow, not at all public-minded.[1] Civic etiquette made imaginative, open-minded, thoughtful conversation rare in public, frontstage settings. The more hidden the context, the more public-spirited conversation was possible. Politics evaporated from public circulation.

The people I met wanted to create a sense of community, but did not want to talk politics. Though they did gather together, they missed a chance to ignite that magical kind of power that can sparkle between people when they self-reflectively organize themselves. Such reflection does not necessarily entail ignoring local, individual suffering or abandoning local hands-on projects. In the process of alleviating real people's suffering, citizens *could* wonder aloud about the political forces that may have helped create that suffering. While building the playgrounds and selling tickets to the local Halloween fair, parents *could* casually talk about whatever came to mind, including politics. People *could* learn to use their collective imaginations to improve what they can improve – to lend a hand, but also an imagination.

Common sense and much social research directs our attention to two common ways of understanding apathy and engagement: one focuses on structural power, the other on beliefs. Examinations of structural forces typically focus on the seemingly "outer," seemingly impersonal, objective, and automatic systems of money and power. Examinations of beliefs focus on the seemingly "inner," seemingly personal, subjective, and active realm of feelings, meanings, and experience. Neither the "inner" nor the "outer" approach pays enough attention to the "in-between" – to the ways people talk to each other about the political world and their place in it.

Beliefs and the missing public sphere

On the first side of the seemingly common-sense dichotomy between "inner" and "outer" is the idea that if people appear not to care, they just must not have the right values, attitudes, beliefs, the right inner selves, or maybe they are not smart enough to be good citizens, or maybe they have bought a dominant ideology and think the world is fine as it is. But none of the people I met just thought everything was fine as it was. There were just too few contexts in which they could openly air their political discontent and their curiosity about the wider world.

A longstanding argument in political research declares that most people are just too dumb or narrow-minded to be good citizens. These studies are both right and wrong: on the one hand (as discussed earlier), there is overwhelming evidence that most people simply do not know the most basic facts about politics. On the other hand, many fascinating studies show that *being interviewed* can make interviewees *into* thoughtful citizens; the interviews opened up free, unjudgmental space, maybe for the very first time in the interviewees' lives, for talking through vague political ideas, playing with their ideas in the light of day; interviewees then could notice inconsistencies and begin to reconcile them.[2] For example, several studies (J. Hochschild 1981; Hart 1992; Halle 1984) beautifully demonstrate that people arrive at different opinions, using different logics, depending on whether they assume they are speaking as consumer, church-goer, worker, parent, citizen, or wearing some other "hat," as Steven Hart puts it.[3] But the potential is usually hidden, because usually interviewees have different contexts in mind when voicing contradictory beliefs; when the beliefs remain nicely packed away in separate closets, the interviewees can avoid noticing the contradictions.

This insight is one key to understanding how contextual political opinions are, and these studies dramatically show that people are fully capable of *becoming* good citizens, if a social researcher who prods them with good questions should happen along. But these studies do not set out to ask how different real-life contexts called for different "hats," or why so few contexts ask citizens to wear their "democratic citizenship" hat. Thanks to these studies, we know that the hats are in the closet; the next question is how people decide which ones to wear to which occasions.

Power and the missing public sphere

On the second side, the "outer" side, of the seemingly common-sense division between inner and outer, is the idea that rigid structural inequality prevents average citizens from having an effective voice in politics. Non-elites have good reasons for believing that what they say about politics does not matter: it usually does not. Political battles are usually pitched in favor of the people who already have money and power. But this simple "outer" explanation would not tell us why the people I met censored their *own* speech, even when they were far from oppressive institutions. The people I met assumed that powerful institutions would not pay attention to common citizens' public-spirited talk; authorities' long shadows deeply colored the kinds of conversations that groups had, even in seemingly unpressured, voluntary situations, seemingly far removed from official settings. Lisa and Carolyn, for example, held such authorities in their peripheral vision when they pronounced "big" and "political" problems to be "not close to home," beyond the range of serious concern. They steered their attention toward problems and solutions that they felt they could address without challenging those authorities' definitions of citizens' proper role; they did so without the powerful institutions' having to exert any direct influence at all.

Luckily, while those in power can monopolize wealth and material production, nobody can control all the tongues in the world. As culture scholar Steven Tipton tidily puts it, "[s]ocial and economic circumstances influence our thinking, but they do not do it for us" (1982: 281). Whether actively challenging, actively embracing, passively embodying, or selectively transforming the seemingly rigid forces that surround them, citizens somehow have to enact a life within these institutions, and have to make sense of their world. In the process of doing that, they create the organizations of civic life. And these organizations become a force in their own right.

Some of the more useful ways of thinking about power take inspiration from Antonio Gramsci's concept of "hegemony" (1957),[4] that highlights the *meanings* that dominated people give to their circumstances. This focus on meaning-making offers a way of understanding how oppressed groups have accepted or transformed their political powerlessness. According to this line of thought, practical, everyday knowledge and intuitions actively but implicitly connect people's ideas to the powerful institutions around them; the way people make sense of everyday experience usually discourages them from thinking thoughts that might challenge the status quo (Gramsci 1957; Williams 1977, 1980; Hall 1977). A society's political imagination is, according to this explanation, patched together in a way that makes domination seem natural and inevitable, odorless and invisible, "to such a depth that the pressures and limits of what can ultimately be seen as a specific economic, political and cultural system seem to most of us the pressures and limits of simple experience and common sense'' (Williams 1977: 110). This ''hegemony'' is the ongoing cultural process that gerrymanders the boundaries of perception.

A more nuanced rendition of hegemony shows that subordinates' social vision is *not* so hopelessly small at all. What Gramsci calls ''contradictory consciousness'' allows people both to notice *and not* to notice these ''pressures and limits of simple experience.'' Experience turns out not to be so simple at all; people constantly have to rely on their relentless, active interpretations of experience, to stitch together mismatched pieces of contradictory reality and draw the contours of their shared, discussable reality. An example of a good study that starts to reveal this process is John Gaventa's investigation of an impoverished and polluted Appalachian mining town, *Power and Powerlessness* (1980). Gaventa says that the government and mining company crushed dissent over decades of struggle, and the newspaper ignored or condemned dissent, so that by the late 1970s, all that was left was silence; and poisonous water, and acid-filled mountain streams, and mudslides. After years of political domination, he says, valley dwellers created a culture of political silence, too hopeless even to voice feelings of outrage, too powerless even to formulate their own interests even to themselves. This silence may have sounded just like political acquiescence, but Gaventa says it was not. Valley residents told themselves that they did not care about their ruined home, but their resentment still could be heard in very subtle ways – and the culture of silence collapsed as soon as a plausible opportunity to challenge or avoid the mining company arose.

Following Steven Lukes (1974), Gaventa names this silence the ''third dimension of power'': the first is coercion – A's ability to make B do something against B's will. The second dimension is A's power to set the public agenda, to exclude some organizations from arguing for their interests at the public negotiating table. A ''three-dimensional'' study of power would understand that conflicts may be so deep and institutionalized, subordinate people might not even be conscious of them:

is it not the supreme and most insidious exercise of power to prevent people, to whatever degree, from having grievances by shaping their perceptions, cognitions and preferences in such a way that they accept their role in the existing order of things, either because they can see or imagine no alternative to it, or because they see it as natural and unchangeable . . . ?   (Lukes 1974: 24)

To take an example from Amargo, when anti-drugs group member Lisa said the nuclear battleships were ''not close to home,'' while detailing her painstakingly microscopic insider knowledge of the spills, and dwelling on workers' unsafe habits, she *was revealing* a social conflict, but one that she herself did not overtly recognize. Producing apathy and powerlessness was not so invisible after all, but revealed itself in her convoluted speech. "Contradictory consciousness" was audible.

Still, a study like Gaventa does not go far enough in showing how citizens actively create "hegemony." His valley dwellers' silence seems simply to have happened as an automatic, natural, invisible response to the relentless cruelty of their situation. In Gaventa's story, when a man whose water supply has been poisoned by strip mines declares "Black is beautiful," referring to coal, he is explicitly declaring himself well served by the companies. If he says nothing else to reveal his understanding of the situation, the only way we outside observers could feel sure that he was experiencing anything other than simple complacency would be to assert a connection between his attitude and our understanding of the valley's history. That is, we would have to bypass the meanings the man himself gave to the situation.

But probably, if Gaventa had listened to more interactions between valley-dwellers, he could have told us how they actively created this culture of silence. Gaventa assumes a stable community, with a long history of heavy, shared oppression, and he does not show how people communicate and re-create this cultural knowledge in everyday conversations. But even in a new community like Amargo, with little shared local past, groups manage to create a civic etiquette that outlaws political conversation; the heavy hand of history alone does not force citizens to speak or hold their tongues.

These hegemony theories still focus too much on rigid outer conditions, on the one hand, and on what people can *think*, on the other, and do not focus enough on what people can *say in public*; in other words, they are both "outer" and "inner" at the same time, but the in-between is still missing.[5] In the mining valley, "hegemony" seems to float everywhere and nowhere, seems simply to work the same way for a dominated person, in all situations, front- and backstage, public and private. Gaventa is talking about the boundaries of consciousness; now I want to know about the boundaries of interaction – the boundaries of the public sphere – that keep people even from considering bringing some ideas into public debate *even if they can think those same ideas in some other contexts*. How, and in what contexts, do people manage to convince themselves to care, or not to care, about politics? How do people build the contours of "the public" together?

Beginning to retheorize beliefs and power together: love of one's fate

Citizens have to talk themselves into their political ideas together, and that means having everyday places for casual political conversation. Talking ourselves into our feelings and opinions may seem like simple dishonesty or lack of self-awareness – you may be wondering, why can't we just say what we *really* feel and think? Because thought itself is dialogue; a conversation that we imagine ourselves to be holding with someone, with ourselves, in which we talk ourselves through our thoughts and feelings.[6]

Pierre Bourdieu deftly reveals everyday methods of convincing oneself to love one's limitations (lack of money and education, for example) – he ties these methods to a person's lifetime experience as a member of a class. This "love of one's fate" is "embodied history, internalized as a second nature and so forgotten as history . . . a kind of immediate submission to order that inclines agents to make a virtue of necessity" (1990: 56; 1983: *passim*). In *The Managed Heart*, Arlie Hochschild elegantly traces a similar alchemy, showing how flight attendants manage their emotions, forcing themselves to have kindly feelings toward rude customers. Flight attendants no longer even realized how much effort it took to ignore their anger. Not only did they regulate their desires, they also had to forget that they had ever done the regulating. "Feeling rules" tell them what to feel, what to want to feel, and how to go about trying to have the right feelings. Consider the examples of an unhappy bride trying to feel joy, a happy funeral attendee trying to suppress his glee, and a blasé star halfback trying to "psych himself up at a game." For these souls, Hochschild argues, there is "emotion work," that bridges the "discrepancy, between what one does feel and what one wants to feel (which is, in turn, affected by what one thinks one ought to feel in such a situation). In response, the individual may try to eliminate the pinch by working on feeling" (Hochschild 1979: 562). For the unempowered volunteer trying to feel confident that democracy is working according to its promise, there is also "emotion work."[7]

Bourdieu and Hochschild get at the energetic, culturally regulated process of matching feelings to social structure, of embodying a culture's possibilities and limitations, transmuting limitations to desires. Both scholars describe the ways individuals digest imperatives from the social structure – the ways individuals seemingly voluntarily, seemingly easily, seemingly painlessly, stay within the strict confines of their social positions. Both reveal the coercion behind the voluntarism, the struggle behind the easy performance, the pain behind the painless appearance.[8] Both reveal a double insult: not only are dominated people powerless, they lack the power to name their own powerlessness; this lack is itself a kind of powerlessness.[9] Both address *how* people enact the third face of power – how people learn to make the heavy burden of powerlessness feel natural and freely borne. Both sensitize us not only to people's different interests, but also people's different methods of producing interests.

Even this approach would not pay enough attention to interaction for my purposes. Both Bourdieu and Hochschild focus too much on the individual biography, on the one hand, and the strict structural limitations that confine it, on the other. That is, on the one hand, they highlight feelings and tastes, instead of tact and manners. On the other hand, both scholars assume a rigid structural context – a workplace, in Hochschild's example, that members assume they have no power to change.

Instead, asking primarily how *individuals* adjust to *predetermined* contexts, I focus more on *groups'* processes of *producing* contexts; less on individuals' efforts at saving face and more on the group's efforts at getting along and making sense together. Here, in civic life, citizens themselves believe themselves to have at least some control in creating the contexts. Here in the public sphere, fragile, voluntary togetherness depends on the manners of members.

Civic etiquette is not just a passive, obvious response to powerlessness. Amargo volunteers, for example, desperately wanted to show the rest of the community how effective regular citizens can be; this *very active desire* prevented them from directly and publicly discussing anything that might expose their sense of powerlessness. Even in stable communities, and even in seemingly routine, rule-bound settings, like schools, hospitals, labs, or courts, participants inadvertently, constantly, relentlessly make inferences about the nature of those settings, improvising rules that participants do not recognize as improvised, to patch together an unruly reality that participants do not recognize as unruly (Garfinkel 1967; Schegloff 1987: 221).[10] In Amargo's civic life, there is an extra layer of uncertainty: in contrast to these rule-bound or traditional settings, in which participants think that they know what is going on and how to act, participants in post-suburban civic life *themselves* say that they are unsure about how to act. They *know* that they have to figure out the rules as they go.

Making the path by walking it

The power to create the organizations of the public sphere is missing from "inner" and "outer" descriptions of beliefs and power.[11] How do people create "the public," and give meaning to the act of participating in public life? We make the road by walking it; we create "the public" in practice. Our civic etiquette takes our perceptions of our own power into account, but is not simply *caused* by an "objective" wider world. Participants constantly "contextualize" any interaction, trying to make sense of it and the wider world, simultaneously. Through this process, civic practices inevitably empower or challenge institutions that the group implicitly holds on its social horizons (Gumperz 1989; Cicourel et al. 1974: 70, 1981: 65).

This focus on conversation overcomes the dichotomy between inner and outer, subjective and objective, personal and structural. Instead of focusing on individuals and the inner dispositions they carry with them from one context to another, as studies of beliefs do, I listened in on the spaces *between* people – on the ways political ideas circulate, coursing through spaces that are neither "subjective" nor "objective," but "intersubjective" (Habermas 1985). And instead of examining broad institutional hierarchies, as many studies of "hegemony" do, I tried to understand how people *made* those power relations relevant for everyday conversations and reality, by systematically sifting certain ideas and ways of talking out of some contexts and into others. If we listen carefully, we can hear just what it is about the wider world that members are taking for granted, instead of assuming that members somehow simply intuit everything about the institutions that an outside observer might notice or might learn through research. And, even more to the point, we can hear just how citizens create their own institutions – the seemingly free institutions of public life.

Political beliefs and political power are embodied in this elusive but very firm sense of what is appropriate to do or say in the contexts of the public sphere. How and why do some contexts evoke political conversation, and others discourage it? Citizens in Amargo and Evergreen City spoke, and interacted, and perhaps even thought very differently in different contexts. Understanding what speakers say in public is an important step in understanding what people assume talk itself is for in those contexts, and ultimately, what they assume public life itself is for and what democratic participation is. We answer the question, "What is democracy?" in practice; scrutinizing our practice might reveal to us that our implicit definition of democracy is not satisfying.

Backstage public where rules are not preordained

"When the great lord passes, the wise peasant bows deeply and silently farts." James Scott's wonderful study of quiet rebelliousness[12] begins with this Ethiopian proverb; the point is that if we listen carefully, we will hear subordinates' "hidden transcripts": fierce, subversive, often funny protests whispered backstage, behind their public bowing and scraping to elites. Peasants, working-class high school students, slaves, dissidents, and other subordinate groups creatively make room for themselves in the crawlspaces of the dominant culture; much more room than their powerless positions would seem to offer: big spaces, all the more glorious for being right under the noses of, and invisible to, the oppressors. In these situations, oppressed people know they are dominated, and do not like it.[13] But they cannot realistically protest in public, so they make jokes behind the rulers' backs while publicly staging a big, lavish display of obedience and respect.

Many such studies of "cultural resistance" show striking differences between front- and backstage political conversation, in societies with stable, longstanding, clear domination. Scott explicitly says that citizens in Western democracies do not develop "hidden transcripts." People like the Americans portrayed here, he says, have "the luxury of relatively safe, open political opposition"; we can openly declare our political resistance (p. 199), and can potentially move up, to become the oppressors ourselves, one by one (and, I add, any person might be on the top of some hierarchies and on the bottom of others). So, why did I still find enormous differences in public and private talk? The people I encountered could not openly express their political sentiments frontstage, but the reason for their self-censorship is much more complex than straightforward fear and oppression.

The people I met believed that they *were* free to speak their minds in public. Here, this shift between private and public speech must work differently. Here, openly bowing and scraping, genuflecting toward public power is not considered legitimate. Citizens' public poses can, in principle, display opposition, anger, earnestness, calm independence, bemused observation, mild questioning, distance from politics and power; almost anything but grateful, unquestioning dependence, adoration, and subservience that the serf or slave must display toward grand public figures. In a democracy, people create the public by talking; implicit definitions of citizens' public conversation define the public sphere, in practice. While Scott asks how people create the "public transcript," I am asking how they create "the public." In a democracy, this power – to make the public itself – is a supreme power. It tells us how to conduct ourselves as citizens, what being a citizen and a member of society means.

Practical beliefs: the "invitation to talk"

What does this emphasis on how people make the public itself add to our understanding of politics? First, it shows a new way of thinking about beliefs. Beliefs about the purpose and place of open-ended conversation itself are at the core of political participation. A comparison of the uses of four "beliefs" in the different types of groups will help make this point: first, the belief in the importance of citizens' participation; second, the belief that the government and corporations are dishonest and do not have citizens' interests at heart; third, the belief that the best way to start improving society is to "think globally, act locally"; and fourth, beliefs and ideas about the role of local efforts in solving homelessness.

1 The ideal of the democratic citizen

In different ways, all the groups shared a belief in the responsible, informed, concerned citizen, active in his or her community – de Tocqueville's good citizen of a democratic republic.[14] In surveys and interviews, all explicitly stated a belief in the importance of self-reliance, self-determination, and "community." But in practice, this idea called for different styles of interaction in the different types of groups:

> *Mainstream country-westerners*: The ideal of the democratic citizen called for no interaction. In fact, the most responsible thing Buffaloes thought they could do to be good citizens was not to talk about issues which they felt unqualified to discuss.
>
> *Cynics*: These frustrated populists talked politics incessantly, in order to show that they themselves knew that living up to the democratic ideal was impossible within the current political and economic structure.
>
> *Volunteers* wanted to embody the republican ideal, but were loath to face the difficulty of living it out in communities that are more inextricably enlaced in national and global politics than in de Tocqueville's day. The result was that they encouraged one another not to talk about issues that could not be solved simply by local citizens' banding together and looking out for one other. The belief called for political avoidance.
>
> *Activists*: Eventually, the democratic ideal came to mean talking with other activists in the state and nationwide, talking to other citizens, and talking with each other to try to learn more about the vast complex organizations that they assumed caused many local problems, and it meant engaging in often discordant verbal clashes with institutions. The core of the the belief was a call for public conversation.

2 Faith in corporate and state institutions

Two people I met tried to convince me that they were basically content with corporate and state power, but both speakers – despite their best intentions – unveiled glaring images that exposed their lack of faith in the powerful institutions that were supposed to protect them. One of these speakers was Gladys, a volunteer who revealed her awareness of troubling connections when she casually remarked, several times, that the skin cancer on her nose was probably due to the thinning of the ozone, about which, she said, she could do very little. The other was Ron, also a volunteer, who gave himself away when he tried to convince me in an interview that he never, ever worried about the nuclear battleships docked a mile away from his house, but then turned to his wife and son four times to tell them that the ships could melt down any minute, and officials would never tell nearby residents. But both ended up revealing their doubts in ways that they did not make explicit, not even to themselves. A third volunteer, Pete, also tried hard to maintain a sense that the world is in balance, repeating the phrase "no issue is black and white" like a mantra, as if to say that nothing is really seriously, irreparably wrong; but then he ended up saying the opposite when he brought up the case of environmental destruction, saying that "if it dies there is no getting it back," then chuckled to himself, adding, "so I guess that one *is* a black and white issue." All the other people I met openly expressed, at some point, a clear lack of faith and anxiety about the wider world:

> *Mainstream country-westerners* assumed that the best way to avoid the institutions' polluting influence was to stay away from them, and avoid talking about any institutional anchors (religion, place of employment, residency). They wanted to avoid taking any of it seriously; the goal was just to "be yourself," and try not to make references to "outside" positions in society. The only accepted references to the outside world were made for the purpose of deriding outsiders and violating taboos, to show just how very distant one was from rules – racist, homophobic, and sexist jokes, for example.
>
> *Cynics* were overflowing with information about, and disgust at, government and corporate dishonesty. They tried to distance themselves from greedy and despicable institutions, by displaying vast knowledge about them, feeling proud that they were no longer disgusted, but were just amused.
>
> *Volunteers* thought that it would undermine their present work if they allowed themselves to think and talk about how it was connected to broad social problems. While it became completely clear backstage and in interviews that volunteers lacked faith in the government or corporations to solve problems, they did not want to talk in meetings about how these institutions might be connected to poverty, disintegrating school buildings, lack of child care or whatever other problems arose in the course of volunteer work.
>
> *Activists*: At times, many activists sounded like cynics, brimming with horror stories of corporate and government greed. The difference between activists and the strenuously disengaged cynics was

that activists *spoke publicly as if* they had faith in the public's reasonableness, so their seemingly cynical criticism had a seed of hope. They were not just trying to display distance from institutions; their civic practice assumed that talk could lead to change. Unlike cynics, activists were not *just* amused.

In fact, they were more like Cora, a volunteer group member, sheepish about their "cynicism"; and like the volunteers, members of CESE were unsure at first whether criticizing was the same as complaining. When the group began to treat its talk seriously, members could acknowledge broad social problems without experiencing the acknowledgment as an admission of powerlessness, a threat to their group's own work, as the volunteers would have. By the same token, because of the perceived limitlessness of the issues, it was hard to manage meetings like the activists'; nothing was *a priori* off-limits for conversation.

Members of all these types of groups assumed corporations and government were dishonest; but unlike the activists, members of the other groups did not imagine that talking publicly about these untrustworthy institutions would accomplish anything good. The belief's meaning depended on members' unspoken assumptions about how their own talk mattered in the wider world – their beliefs about the connection between talk and citizenship.

The beliefs were similar; what they could *say*, and where they could say it, was different. Out-loud additions to survey responses (volunteer Carolyn's "I'd like to *think* that [the government can be trusted]," for example) showed that volunteers and activists, for example, shared skepticism about the government, but habitually expressed it and displayed it differently. It was not their "inner" beliefs that differed so much as their "outer" ability to voice some ideas and feelings and not others, in some contexts and not others. And this ability to *express* political concern opened or closed down the ability to acknowledge *feeling* concern. Beliefs, ideas, and feelings cannot be stuffed and labeled and put in a museum, but have to be observed in their natural habitats, slinking quietly among the trees, or howling loudly from the mountaintops.

3 *"Think globally, act locally"*

Like the first two examples, this concept accompanied different kinds of interaction in the different groups, depending on the different institutions members implicitly held in their peripheral vision.

Mainstream country-westerners: When Betsy used the phrase, it meant, as she said, "I snip my rings [the plastic rings holding six-packs together] and recycle so there's not much else I can do." The concept did not call for interaction at all.

Volunteers: Julie, Pete, and Danielle also used the phrase in interviews. For them, it meant recycling and more; it also meant being the kind of person who made the local community better, so that if everyone voluntarily brought hot meals to the elderly and watched the 5-year-olds on the pre-dawn winter playground, there would be no more local problems. In this understanding of the phrase, "thinking globally" meant that "if everyone thought like me, a good-hearted volunteer, the world would be a better place." It did not mean questioning why more people were not like them, or changing the institutions that perhaps prevented more people from being like them. Rather, it meant showing other people through deeds, not words, that such community membership was possible. For volunteers, the concept "think globally, act locally" called for suppressing interactions that did not help make this encouraging point.

Activists: Neil, Maryellen, and other activists also used the phrase. For them, it meant tying local problems to national and global political choices, interacting with people who were working on a wider scale and with people working in other localities, expanding the definition of local to include the global. All this meant drawing out the connections, through discussion.

4 Solving homelessness

Unlike the other examples, this one seems to reveal a simple difference in beliefs, but again, the difference is actually more complex than that.

Mainstream country-westerners: When I asked about homelessness in the interviews, one Buffalo asked herself to help solve homelessness by letting a homeless person sleep on her couch in her little apartment (but decided that it might be dangerous); others pondered the benefits of giving homeless people spare change. They offered individual solutions.

Volunteers: All volunteers talked about donating time to a homeless shelter or soup kitchen – volunteering with a group. Whether the problem was illiteracy, pollution, homelessness, poverty, lack of child care, disability, or poor schools, their solution was to think

about taking time out of their busy days, to donate an hour or two
a day. They offered hands-on, local, community solutions.

Activists felt overwhelmed by that approach. They imagined all of
the social problems to which they would have to donate one hour
a day – one hour teaching children to read, another hour volunteering in a soup kitchen, another hour volunteering at the school,
and still there would never be enough volunteers to right all the
wrongs, and still the problems would not be addressed at their
roots. They spoke of political solutions to homelessness, like
funding low-cost housing and developing programs for homeless
mental patients.

Someone might argue that this last example explains all the political differences between the groups; maybe Buffaloes were just individualistic; volunteers just pro-community and anti-government; and activists just "pro-
government." If this difference explained everything, then someone could
say that the different groups' civic manners were *caused by* different beliefs
about how social problems are solved. But the arrows of causality go in both
directions at once; the beliefs were inseparable from cultural assumptions
about the power and place of talk itself: volunteers wanted to believe that
they could solve all problems with hands-on work partly because they
assumed that talking politics was "just rhetoric," as one volunteer put it, and
would undermine their efforts at building community. Buffaloes created no
group contexts in which to talk seriously about anything, let alone politics,
and they imagined themselves to be alone in the face of social problems –
but since they did not have to uphold a sense of efficacy, they allowed themselves to sound more forthrightly bleak and critical than volunteers in interviews. Activists had created contexts for public debate and for monitoring
the government, and wanted to welcome a challenge and even risk feeling
overwhelmed. Pedaling in tandem with the different groups' abstract political
ideas, beliefs, and calculations of efficacy were desires about what to
believe – "I wish I believed that" – and beliefs about what talking will
accomplish. Taken together, these elements shape the quality of public discussion.

The groups' different ways of understanding the concepts of democratic
citzenship, corporate and government irresponsibility, thinking globally, and
solving homelessness, accompanied different group connections to institutions. The groups' different understandings of these concepts were inseparable from the groups' different *valuations of talk* itself. In other words, *the
central difference in practicing a belief is in what members assume the belief
means for talk itself.* Does the belief in responsible citizenship mean citizens

should talk to each other? Does it mean *we* should talk to each other? How? Why?

This "invitation to talk" should be at the core of a definition of political belief. That is what distinguished between various groups. No one in the groups I studied ever verbalized this nuanced difference in interpretation of the democratic ideal or any other abstract belief. The differences are not ones that members abstractly formulated to themselves or could ever put into words in an interview; no one ever explicitly told me what their group's civic etiquette was. But members enacted the differences, in practice, in the potential contexts of the public sphere. This is one reason that paying attention to political etiquette, rather than trying to pin down individuals' static beliefs, is so important; nobody hears other people's inner beliefs directly. The only ideas that circulate are the ones that people can express; what really matters is what people can say to each other. Beliefs are, above all, beliefs about what it is right to say in real places.

Practical power: creating public contexts for talk

What does the concept of civic practices add to our understanding of power? Important institutions surrounding the groups I studied propagated an image of community that helped vaporize debate. Social service workers, commercial culture, corporations, and politicians favored an image of "community" that excluded disagreement, discussion of justice and power, social analysis, a sociological imagination. Volunteers and recreation group members wanted "community," and used the language of community; what they had in mind was strifeless harmony and mutual aid, acceptance and comfort. The problem was, the ideal of "community" offered a kind of togetherness that did not require publicly minded discussion – it was assumed that citizens all already shared more than they did, and thus did not need to talk about it.

This cloying, unconflictual simulacrum of community offered the groups a culturally powerful image of togetherness, seducing groups with the one potent, officially approved way of linking face-to-face interaction with the wider world. The image was hard to resist, since creating a sense of togetherness in a centerless suburb can be so difficult.[15] Nostalgic language was so enthralling, even activists spoke it in frontstage settings, even though backstage they imagined a new kind of global, communicative community about to be born. Power worked through political etiquette, as citizens cooperated with dominant institutions by defining community gatherings in ways that rarely opened up public space for questioning and debate.

The assumption here was that real, honest people do not need to say anything in public, but need only act – bringing the blankets to the needy, helping out on the dark playground, *doing* something without needing to talk about it. The people I met carefully avoided public grandstanding. They wanted to be unpretentious and accepting of all, and assumed that if publicly expressing ideas is just dishonest or useless, then political conversation would uselessly scare regular people off.

Yet with all this humble silence, the public sphere was still not just silent. Somebody's voices filled it – just not always the most well-meaning citizens' voices. These Amargans were like unpretentious Cordelias, put in a position of speaking only after their falsehearted sisters filled the speech context with their "glib and oily art/ To speak and purpose not." When King Lear assembles his three grown daughters, so that he can divide up his kingdom among them, he demands, "Tell me . . . which of you shall we say doth love us most, that we our largest bounty may extend . . ." In this flattery contest, he invites the two elder daughters to speak first, saving Cordelia, his most beloved – and most loving – daughter for last. While the two elder sisters falseheartedly pour out extravagant praises, Cordelia mutters to herself, "Then poor Cordelia!/ And yet not so, since I'm sure my love's/ More ponderous than my tongue." But aloud to her father, all she can say is, "Nothing." Her unwillingness or inability to speak in this flawed context costs her a kingdom and a life; it also destroys her father.

A spirit of unpretentious deflation of puffery has a long history in American political speech. At the nation's beginning, Americans tried hard to use "plain speech" in an effort to distinguish themselves and their speech from the stuffy, ornate, inaccessible political rhetoric of European aristocrats (Cmiel 1990). Later, disgusted at high-toned, secretly greedy Victorian politicians, Americans reinvented plain speech again, certain that emphasizing self-interest was better than bloated palaver that masks self-interest (Rodgers 1987). Indeed, piercing such blather *is* essential for straightforward political debate. The problem comes when people *always* emphasize selfish motives and *always* muffle analysis; when the effort to be unpretentious and inclusive actually *hides* citizens' public-spiritedness instead of letting it circulate. Not airing public-spiritedness leaves little room for people to gain practice in thinking public-spiritedly (besides, total protection from deception is impossible – the really manipulative liars will be clever enough to sound high-minded even in a rhetorical climate that is poisoned with excessive expressions of self-interest, so why not risk expressing trust and concern?). But for citizens of Amargo, the public speech context itself seemed so flawed that it was hard to speak public-spiritedly. The cycle of political evaporation begins here, when citizens assume that talking politics in a publicly minded way is wrong and "out of place" in so many frontstage places, and, like Cordelia, can only mutter their publicly spirited sentiments under their breath.

CESE activists wanted to go beyond the "close to home/for the children" approach, but were not sure how, without ineffectually "going off on tangents" or violating the standard political etiquette that asked citizens to speak in public only when they could "speak for themselves," and not to worry their heads about political policies, or other people's problems, or anything that could not be solved with healthy volunteer-style, hands-on, can-do spirit. Volunteer-style involvement was much more consonant with newspapers' and government institutions' approaches to citizen involvement, so it would have been easier to float along with the current.

Partly because CESE could not neatly slot itself into a predesigned cultural category, the pressures that made a volunteer approach impossible also forced new openings for the activists. The group could have continued sounding like volunteers, but then it would not have been able to advocate, or even conceive, national, publicly minded solutions to local problems. The government and corporations had already defined involvement in environmental affairs as conflictual and beyond ordinary citizens' grasp, unlike involvement in schools and drug abuse prevention. Schools and drugs are potentially very debatable, public, political issues, but powerful institutions presented school and drug problems to the public as requiring solutions that "begin with the family" and as obvious to anyone with common sense.

"For the children," mandatory public Momism, and the nostalgic community

What does it do to an issue, to say it is "for the children"? It is evidently part of what it means for an issue to become mainstream: it is not "political," it's "for the children." It is persuasive – who could be against children? The problem is that in this volunteer-style approach to children and politics, the "for the children" aspect colonizes the "political" aspect, rather than "politics" coming to be seen as a thing that is "for the children." A nostalgic image of family hooked into that nostalgia for the "down-home," caring community – in this dream of family and community, there are no seriously opposing positions, no deep disagreements, no opposing interests; this nostalgic dream prevented productive dialogue about family (Skolnick 1991; Coontz 1992) and about community. That is, rather than questions about the future and children becoming political, politics becomes invisible, smothered in the sanctimoniousness with which we Americans surround children. Our concerns suddenly seem no longer to be about power, justice, and democracy, but only about survival. "For the children," volunteer-style, assumes that children do not themselves want to discuss issues, debate, and learn. It assumes that children are *not* uncannily adept at intuiting social realities, but are just natural and static beings.

Activists' initial public use of the "for the children" language implied that debates and arguments among non-experts would be useless wastes of time, since accepting or rejecting the incinerator appears to be simply a question of technical knowledge – a question of "does it or does it not adversely affect my children?" If it were the case that debate did not produce knowledge, then there would be no use arguing, and the public sphere would exist just for distribution of technical information, top-down.

However, though activists were alarmed about their own children's physical health, they still did not consider their families' "self-interest" to be an undiscussable absolute. For them, concern for their children's future *included* concern for the social, as well as physical, environment in which the children would live. That meant creating a world in which their children were not living at the expense of "someone else's children, in some community that's less organized." For activists, protecting their own children meant creating a just wider world in which their children's lives would make sense.

Concern for oneself and one's family *seems* to be an absolute that requires no discussion. How could we possibly go wrong if we made policies "for the children"? It turns out that people can justify just about any social policy or war as being for the children, probably because people have different ideas about what is good for children, about which children matter, about what children need and about what children *are*. One argument says that "maternal thinking" (Ruddick 1991) helps people arrive at good political positions. Mothers' horror over sending their sons to war, for example, has often been a source of peace activism and political thought, that has led people to conceive non-violent alternatives to war. On the other hand, sometimes people seem to consider the sacrifice worth it, saying that even if they hate sending their children to war, or hate denying good health care to poor children, the alternative is much worse for the common good. In either case – whether their judgments lead to war or peace, funding for poor children or cutting of funds for poor children – people are not just simply "speaking for themselves," but also have their conflicted, ambivalent, tortured understandings of the good in mind.

Maybe all participants knew that the Mom discourse is unpretentious shorthand for concern about future generations in general, concern about our hampered "generativity" (Erikson 1963). But real mothers have brains, and know that meeting some demands for their children or themselves would be unfair, impossible, or unjust to other mothers and children – and would create a world that was more divided, more full of envy, less comfortable all around, even for their own children. Of course, mothers want their children to be physically healthy, but most also want them to inherit a good, socially healthy world.

In the Mom discourse, Mom's intellect never appears. Yet, in the activist *meetings, all* of these questions were negotiable; members did not want to protect their own children at the expense of someone else's children. Discussion in meetings and informal gatherings did not revolve solely around members' own raw, unanalyzed self-interest. The Mom discourse makes mothers sound like apolitical, natural animals protecting their young, but not at all like thoughtful human beings who live in a broad, wide world with a meaningful history and an uncertain future. We can be both.

Interpreting the language of self-interest

There are many possible interpretations of this strange cycle of political evaporation, that, if correct, would explain away the importance of political etiquette. None are completely satisfying.

One obvious explanation for this language of self-interest and mandatory public Momism is that people naturally fear disagreement, and "Mom" is uncontroversial. Is fear of disagreement universal? A comparison with some other society's political etiquette will surprise those Americans who think that it is obvious that "you don't talk politics and religion with your friends, because you might disagree," as the maxim goes. For example, Israelis, talking among casual acquaintances, "use political talk the way Americans use talk about sports: to create common ground, with political disagreements only adding to the entertainment value" (Wyatt and Liebes 1995: 21; see also Simmel 1971).

How could anyone enjoy disagreement? In a fascinating study of a Jewish senior center in Los Angeles, Barbara Myerhoff describes a community whose members love to argue about politics:

Among center people, all talk was an intrinsic good ... courtesy, parsimony, clarity, and relevance were not appropriate criteria for a good debate in their view. Rather it was the ability to ferret out a hidden angle of a question, unearthing a new perspective that others had overlooked – *that* was prized ... [quoting an interviewee]: "This is the Jew's idea of Paradise. Do we have angels peacefully riding on clouds with their harps playing, like the Gentiles? No, we have a big debate with God."

(Myerhoff 1979: 125–126)

Though Myerhoff implies that seniors enjoyed argument for the purely esthetic adventure of a good debate, in fact, they intuitively connected their debates to political activism.[16] They constantly referred to a highly organized political world; nearly every argument Myerhoff reports was about politics.

As one character protests, in response to another's accusing someone of being a leftist, "Everybody here was a Socialist, a Communist, an anarchist twenty years ago" (1979: 34). Most were still members of political and ethnic organizations, on all ends of the political spectrum, from a California migrant farmworkers' union to Zionist organizations to Democratic clubs.

The energetically arguing seniors held a set of political institutions in their peripheral vision. This vision cannot be separated from any traditional, transcendent "cultural style"; the two go together.[17] If American institutions were different, perhaps Americans would learn to relish debate; and conversely, if many Americans relished debate, American politics would be very different. In nations that have truly contrasting political parties and histories of organized opposition, public arguing is *not* a sign that oppositional parties have dropped off of the political map, as it is here (Merelman 1991; Hallin and Mancini 1985). For most Americans, disagreement feels more dangerous and less like a game, partly because we do not have such clearly defined teams.

Thus, another explanation might say that fear of disagreement is one case that illustrates a general principle: styles of political debate are simple responses to institutional power configurations. A fascinating, striking study by Michelle Rosaldo, for example, shows that the "crooked," indirect, metaphoric, traditional rhetoric of the Ilongots in the Philippines presumed an egalitarian society in which "none can enforce compliance" and all must acknowledge "the real differences among individuals and the elusiveness of human truth." In contrast, modern, Christian Ilongots adopted a "straight-talking," instrumental speech brought in from the West, that presumed a world "immensely more hierarchical and more powerful than anything they are familiar with . . . [a] social order which recognizes an ultimate and knowable authority – be it god, science, or the army" (1973: 222). This new world did not require a style that gracefully, indirectly acknowledged the value of the opponent's truth; the "straight" new style could draw on powerful authorities, overriding delicate differences with direct appeals to the presumed-universal truth.

This second explanation might conclude that American political institutions simply, unequivocally extinguish broad, deep discussion of issues that matter – not that "fear of disagreement" is universal, but that it is an inevitable result of American institutions. Some observers have tried to make that point; Hervé Varenne (1977) says Americans fear disagreement because there is very little holding us together; all public, unpaid association is voluntary and our definition of community is so voluntary, fragile, and amorphous, dropping out is easy. If dropping out is really easy, hot debate that raises big, challenging questions can make people nervous. Similarly, Baumgartner

(1988) says suburban America lacks energetic public debate because residents do not want to get entangled in each other's lives. She calls this unintrusive, individualistic ethic "moral minimalism," saying that it creates a kind of peace and order, not of mutual support, charity, and abiding community, but of privacy, tolerance, and resistance to interference in others' affairs.

But even this is not the whole story. On the one hand, Americans want this cool moral minimalism. On the other hand, almost everyone I met harbored intense nostalgia for the warm, totally enveloping community. They all ambivalently recognized that without anything thicker than moral minimalism holding anyone together, life could be lonely and dangerous. So, while moral minimalists may exist in the US, these ambivalently community-minded people were different. They just could not voice their broader desires in public.

A third explanation of the public language of self-interest might say that it expresses a real need; people just naturally want to savor the privateness of private life. Trying to carve out a private space in life for contemplation, intimacy, esthetic pleasure, relaxation, can be a rebellious political act in a society that overly politicizes every corner of everyday life, or in a society that applies religious dogma to every thought and action, or a society that denies private pleasures to some oppressed category of people. Paradoxically, this "valorization of everyday life" (Taylor 1989) can lead to activism and political debate, in societies in which the state represses this effort to keep some aspects of life out of the glare of political scrutiny – the 1989 student rebellion in China, for example (Calhoun 1994). In the US, in contrast, as scholars like Bellah and Etzioni rightly assert, private life is rarely attached *enough* to questions of the common good, morality and politics. The people I met were not defiantly asserting their right to be left alone; they were chased into a small, cloistered private world by an inhospitable public world.

Another explanation of political evaporation would apply to activists, saying that they knew that the Mom discourse would get them an audience, and they rationally chose to "frame" their causes in ways that they thought would grab reporters' ears and charm the public (Snow et al. 1986; McAdam, McCarthy, and Zald 1996). This approach assumes that the purpose of activism is to win battles, not to inspire general public debate and political participation. But the activists in CESE and Testament for Humanity (and, I would suggest, many other social movements) also had other, broader goals. They did not just want to win; they wanted to inspire broad discussion about society. Mandatory public Momism and the language of self-interest do not do that. Activists themselves were unsatisfied with that language because they wanted to instigate discussion, while mandatory public Momism preempts debate.

A similar approach would say that citizens rationally sized up their possibilities, and decided that political action would not be worth the investment. This approach imagines the individual as a "rational actor" who constantly conducts cost/benefit analyses in order to maximize his[18] ability to reach a fixed set of preferences.[19] But the rational actor approach misses what was most interesting about the groups portrayed here. First, all the people I studied were more concerned with making the world appear to make sense, and with appearing to be normal themselves, than with any other "benefit." In that sense, "moral action," in the sense of meaning-making, rather than "rational," in the sense of self-interested, action is a more suitable label.[20]

Second, people like the Buffaloes could not have conducted a cost/benefit analysis of political concern, since they did not have a mental category for politics.[21] They worried about problems that someone else would have called political, so their lack of involvement was not a simple result of lack of concern. They were engaged whether they wanted to be or not. Political life has no "exit" (Hirschman 1970); citizenship is not a market or a firm, which one can leave if the political system is destroying the planet or making it impossible for people to walk down the street safely.

Third, *how* groups take their power into account eludes those theorists. Citizens' groups do take powerlessness into account, but in everyday life, the *process* by which they take this into account is never a pure rational calculation. Most people I encountered assumed that political talk was irrelevant at best, dishonest at worst. How, then, did they discover their interests? Why did the anti-drugs Just Say No committee I studied meet? It was so obvious to them, they had never discussed it, but relied on powerful institutions to define their interests for them.[22] Working without reflecting on their work, groups are more likely to swallow powerful institutions' definitions of social problems whole – more apt, for example, to have to choose between jobs and a future planet, if that is how the nuclear industry poses the problem. In this way, many people "had" interests that were already in harmony with the possibilities they imagined to be open to them. People did not first "fix" their preferences and then enter into institutional relations, but molded their desires from the start partly around implicit assessments of the options. And then they forgot they they had made these assessments. Indeed, the effort of convincing oneself to make a virtue of limitations works *only* if the memory of the effort is obliterated (Bourdieu 1990: 49–51, 56). This molding process, and the effort to forget it, was part of who they were, not something they "chose," as if they first got a character and then entered into society with it. Could we imagine that volunteers run the costs and benefits of possible action plans through a psychic adding machine to decide on a plan that will most maximize their "investment" of emotional energy, thought, and time?

While rational actor models talk about how people act or avoid acting, these models do not talk about how people think or avoid thinking itself. If we were to extend the rational model of humanity to thought, we would have to assume that thinking and feeling have a cost, and avoiding thinking and feeling is free. But when there is no exit, avoiding thinking and feeling is not free. (And anyway, why would anyone imagine that thinking is something that humans want to avoid?) The people portrayed here tried hard to limit their thinking, not just their action. They all worked hard to create a feeling that the world makes sense. The ways they tried to reconcile the hopes and the possibilities came, in part, from interactions in the public sphere.

Yet another way of depicting political evaporation might say that people just simply are unaware and unconcerned about the wider world. Perhaps some people simply go through life without even suspecting that their personal woes are connected to social problems. They drink contaminated water but do not guess the cause of their illness. If such people existed, then the "cycle of political evaporation" would not apply to them, since there would be no sense of connection there to evaporate. But I did not meet *any* such people. Everyone I met intuited, and said, that a wider world had an effect on their lives. Somehow their intuitions evaporated before becoming publicly expressable thoughts. Perhaps some people do not experience the problems in the first place – robust people who do not get sick from the contaminated water, or who have their own private water supply. Perhaps such people think everything is fine as it is, or have successfully made their exit from the political world.[23] Perhaps, but I did not find any such people.

Some happy observers writing in the 1950s and early 1960s (Lipset 1960, for example; see also Neuman 1986) said that placid contentment explained Americans' political silence, lack of political passion, and low voter turnout.[24] Such citizens would exit from political participation because they were genuinely happy with their place in the wider world. These comfortable theorists imply that such blanket contentment could happen if people were so well served they felt no need to talk about politics, and felt fine without knowing or caring how the rest of the world managed to take care of them so well. Less cheery social observers called these fictitious types monads (Horkheimer and Adorno 1944), or "one-dimensional" (Marcuse 1964), and emphasized the inner torments that such semi-humans would have to endure, to anesthetize themselves against their basically curious, gregarious, open-eyed, trouble-making, active human nature (Habermas 1979; Arendt 1958, for example). In violating human nature, this passivity would breed a neurotic personality that sought too much deep gratification in toasters and electric can-openers, and could easily be swayed by any efficient dictator who captured its fancy.

In such a society, citizens would never fully become adults, but would rely on the state and the corporations to administer their lives as if they were helpless infants or pets who cannot grasp the global social webs that fill their food bowls.

As in Gaventa's story, without specifically examining interaction, the only way we could be sure that the toaster-and-percolator-loving semi-adults discovered in the 1950s were contented consumers or neurotic monads would be to bypass the current meanings that they gave to the situation, and go back to their neuroses' origins: in Gaventa's case, that means doing our own research to understand their history; in Adorno's case, it means psychoanalyzing them. While I agree that intelligent adults must perform psychological contortions if they can tolerate hiding at home while the moral and physical world around them disintegrates, there is no room in these theories, of either the happy consumer or the neurotic consumer, to think about the social, and not purely psychological, processes that could produce such apathy. If these theories had looked beyond the level of individual psychology, they would have noticed that citizens have to interact somehow, to validate such seemingly blank, effortless, non-citizenship. Apathy takes social effort to produce.

A final explanation of political evaporation in American politics would point to longstanding traditions of individualism in our political cultures (Wuthnow 1990; Merelman 1991; Etzioni 1988; Bellah et al. 1985; Ignatieff 1986, describe the same upside-down bragging in Britain). Robert Bellah and co-authors found that the Americans they interviewed tended to call themselves "self-interested" even when self-interest was clearly not an adequate explanation of their motives. The ideas that "it's best to look out for number one," and that people are all selfish and care only about issues that are "close to home," are standard, stock phrases that Americans have long used to justify and make sense of the world. C. Wright Mills called these "vocabularies of motive . . . justificatory conversations" which we silently hold with an imagined questioner, to convince ourselves that we are behaving reasonably: " 'If I did this, what could I say? What would they say?' " (1963 [1940]: 443). Bellah and the others trace the language of self-interested individualism to a long tradition in American public life; when Americans reach for an explanation of their habits, the closest on the shelf is this handy "vocabulary of motive."

Their approach steers attention to the social, and not just psychological openings for political concern, convincingly showing that language is not just a neutral conveyor of information about inner desires. The shared, traditional language activates and gives shape to feelings, wishes, and worries that are otherwise formless and uncommunicable. The language might even help convince speakers that they really are self-interested, and should act self-interestedly, and even should create institutions that reward competition and punish nurturance.[25]

These writers argue that what is missing from US public dialogue is more often discussion of the common good than discussion of privacy and private self-interest (Etzioni 1988). For example, pro-choice activists justify abortion as a private choice, instead of justifying it by claiming that only the woman herself is deeply enough *connected* to her family and social milieu to know what is right for them all (Kilroy 1992; Glendon 1991). But privately, the connection is just what women do talk about: one study shows (Condit 1990) that, when asked about their own particular cases, women who had considered abortion recounted self-searching decision-making processes that revolved around the good of their children, parents, husbands, relatives, schools, workplaces, and the other people who depended on them and on whom they depended. In other words, abortion was not just a personal decision about individual well-being. But when asked about abortion in general, they used the publicly available rhetoric of "personal, private choice." In the imagined public context, publicly minded explanations of the moral reasons *for* abortion evaporated.

Scholars like Bellah or Wuthnow say that the "language of self-interest" often crowds the "language of citizenship" out of American public discourse. But here, in Amargo, professions of self-interest worked to *protect* the volunteers' belief in the democratic ideal. The two languages were not opposed but worked symbiotically, the professions of self-interest working to protect the belief in the democratic ideal. This protective emotion work may often be behind the profusion of expressions of self-interest in American society in general. Tracing this protective process shows how the one language often comes to crowd the other out. These languages work hard; they are not always just stock clichés, easy to grab from the "cultural toolbox" (Swidler 1986). Unspoken concern for the wider world often helped *prevent* citizens from talking in a publicly minded way. When Lisa and Carolyn, for example, called the battleships and chemical plants "not close to home," they did so with the implicit knowledge that powerful institutions would make it difficult for citizens to stop the leaks, explosions, fires, and spills (Mills [1963 (1940): 440] makes a similar point). Such speech helped volunteers preserve their feeling that the world made sense. Their effortfully upbeat concern only for things that were "close to home" helped make them appear – and feel – effective and empowered. These vocabularies of motive help us explain ourselves to ourselves; they are part of the "presentation of self" which we display to ourselves to convince ourselves that we are behaving reasonably (Goffman 1959).

Furthermore, it matters that some languages are *usable* only in certain real-life settings. When activists could openly explore public questions in intimate contexts but not in public contexts, they drew on implicit knowledge of what the public context is *for* – knowledge about what citizenship is. A focus on very broad traditions would miss this startling context-shift from frontstage to backstage; the context-shift tells us something important about what speakers assume the very act of speaking in public means. The context-shift shows us how citizens define "the public" itself.[26]

The cycle of political evaporation

The beauty of the ideal public sphere is that it would allow the widest, most challenging and provocative ideas to circulate throughout the public. I found that ideas circulated in exactly the opposite way from what theorists would hope: the further backstage the context, the more public-spirited conversation was possible. Public spirit evaporated in different places for each group; but the same shift kept recurring: the farther the voice from a whisper and the larger the audience, the less eager were speakers to ponder issues of justice and the common good, to present historical or institutional analyses, to criticize institutions, to invite debate; to speak in a publicly minded way. Common sense considered the public sphere to be a place for dramatically airing self-interest and translating self-interest into short-sighted public policies; this folk definition of the public sphere kept most interesting debate out of public circulation.

Certainly, political conversation does not always, in all times and places, circulate in the way described here. But the fact that it did here, even if only in this one locale, illustrates my point about political engagement and power. Of course, this is not to say that all politically silent groups are actively avoiding politics. For example, members could gather not for the purpose of meeting people or establishing a sense of community, as the groups I studied were, but to accomplish a very specific task that required total concentration or silence or was very noisy or left no time for chatting. If participants did have some free time to converse, though, and yet no explicit references to the wider world *ever* arose, I would begin listening for some active exit-taking, to hear how and why the group managed to talk so much without bringing out the political aspects of the many topics of conversation.

Simple apathy never explained the political silence I heard. Inside of "apathy" was a whole underwater world of denials, omissions, evasions, things forgotten, skirted, avoided, and suppressed – a world as varied and colorful as a tropical undersea bed. Most of this book has taken us on an underwater adventure exploring the variety of ways that groups prevent themselves from letting their cares surface. There is no bottom layer to the cycle of political evaporation; citizens vaguely and ambivalently perceive or experience political issues but do not put them all into words: this is infinite, raw experience, that may in fact never be made recognizable, speakable, cultural. This bottom layer is made of the inevitable, unacknowledged connections we have with each other: dependence on unknown others for water and food, shelter and clothing, language and meaning. The way a person absorbs this level of experience is not observable to the fieldworker or to even the person experiencing it. It is like a dream; it happens, but we cannot grasp it in its entirety except in a theoretical, retrospective reconstruction, motivated by a theory of how the world works, and we all have such theories. One has to *learn*, for example, to connect or separate even something as basic as contaminated drinking water inward, to one's own sick body, and outward, to a particular source of pollution. And this urge to connect the dots is powerful; a wonderful study of children's understanding of politics (Connell 1971) shows just how potent is that human urge to connect the dots, to make connections even where there are none![27] Everyone I met was aware, in some way, that they were connected to a wider world. Beyond these first "exits" from political life, taken by mythically contented or disconnected or privately neurotic citizens, citizens have to be more active, creating a relationship to the facts, as they ambivalently experience them.

So, the cycle of political evaporation begins on a bed of ambivalence and curiosity; people are not born apolitical. Beyond this fictional apolitical layer, obstacles lie in the path of any group that tries to express publicly minded sentiments in public contexts: groups can amplify the sentiments of anti-connection of the most bigoted, sexist, and homophobic members, as mainstream Buffaloes did, and silence any members' expressions of connection to the world, thus making the group seem more mean-spirited than the sum of the individuals and evaporating any public expressions of tolerance and openness. Or groups can avoid talking politics in meetings, as volunteers did, trying hard not to notice problems that can be addressed only through group discussion, leaving individuals secretly whispering vague worries and questions backstage. Individuals can silence themselves in group meetings, as Luke did in the volunteer groups, but still be able to voice coherent political critiques in backstage contexts or in other groups' meetings. Groups can ignore members who insist on talking politics in meetings, as volunteers did with Charles. Groups can silence their public-spirited speech in frontstage context, as the activists did.

Finally, any public-spirited idea that struggles through all of these obstacles still has to make its way past official and journalists' roadblocks before emerging to the sea surface.[28] In this manner, most political debate never makes it to

Lukes' "second dimension of power" – the power to set an agenda, to put one's explicit demands on the table, to formulate an explicit belief to oneself. Even less debate makes it to the "first dimension of power" – the power to win or lose in an overt power struggle in the public arena. Challenges to the official definitions of citizens' political participation have dissolved long before that.

While conversation did not make it to the surface, action did. Anyone in town could hear about the extraordinarily good volunteers exhausting themselves for the community (and privately wonder if this was the only possible solution to the problems volunteers addresssed). Volunteer-style citizenship is the most temptingly easy, hegemonic format for involvement; it works by defining the floor for citizen participation in particular settings; by setting the boundaries for what citizens can say and how they can say it in the settings of the potential public sphere. People also knew about Buffaloes' bigoted joking, because, according to Buffaloes themselves, it sometimes translated directly into violence or name-calling – the first dimension of power. The aura of exclusion kept blacks and others out of one of the few "community" gathering places in town; just a few violent acts and a subtle atmosphere of exclusion bleed a frightening racist tinge throughout the society without even ever having to reach public discourse.

The cycle of political evaporation was also a cycle of misconstructions, in which volunteers and recreation group members represented themselves as self-interested and unconcerned, and activists then took them at their word and made dramatic efforts at rousing them from their supposed stupor. "Putting heads together to come up with solutions" was not the image that came to mind when volunteers and Buffaloes thought about activism. Disengaged people thought of publicly minded talk as "soapboxing" – standing up in a crowd and mindlessly yelling, to capture attention. Volunteers thought that criticism was bad unless people could do something about it. If all social problems are inevitable, then criticism is just theater.

News reporting about activism fitted well with these bystanders' understanding of activists, as people who are, at best, putting themselves on public display because they have a special kind of personality and "believe in standing up for their beliefs," or because they are self-interested, or because they want attention; and in none of the three cases offering any thoughtful, informed explanations for their concerns. The irony was, nobody really liked or admired self-interested speech and everyone detested theatricality. At an informal party after a small demonstration, Diane remarked drily that one of CESE's events never even made it into the local news at all. To another event,

the media came out because it was theatrical. They *asked* me whether it would be or not: "Is it gonna be dramatic? Theatrical?" They actually said they wouldn't come if it wasn't!

[Later at the same party] They're not interested in anything but good pictures. Last time we had an event, they had a big picture of Pacific Beach on the front page. And if they can get a picture of a black man accused of robbery? They'll *always* put *that* on the front page.

So, even though they disliked theatricality, activists thought that they had to stage dramatic events. Reporters did not like purely theatrical events, but thought the public would be entranced by enjoyable spectacles. The disengaged public read about activists' stunts with disgust, if at all. In this tragic cycle of political evaporation, public speech was dishonored. The cycle reconfirmed Americans' belief that public speech is nothing more than glittery self-aggrandizement.

On the other hand, the activist men who tried so hard to sound like neutral experts would have appealed to people like the Buffaloes; they would have appreciated their civic etiquette for its stuffy clauses and stiff vocabulary, for being difficult to understand; Buffaloes would have heard it and thought that politics is boring and that they themselves were not smart enough to understand politics, instead of thinking that the activists are stupid. Those citizen-experts seemed to display knowledge of official processes, and demonstrate that the activists are at least "screaming and yelling at the right people," as Buffalo member Ken stipulated. Volunteers would have thought that the stiff technical speech sounded authoritative but "distant" and "remote," not something that could "affect them personally." This kind of language thus would have reinforced all of these readers' understandings of politics, as requiring very technical solutions – but, speculating on how volunteers and Buffaloes would have responded to this kind of language is beside the point, since reporters never quoted activists using it. This technical speech and the emotional speech of the Moms formed two sides of the same coin, both leaving out debate and dialogue – the only kind of speech that could have opened up the public forum.

Nothing is lost in the "water cycle" that we learn about in elementary school; water circulates as rain, goes into the soil and into rivers, lakes, and oceans, and then back again as moisture that becomes clouds, then rain again. But in the cycle of political evaporation, something is lost, as if some water had somehow vanished at each turn of the cycle, the way it does in a logged rainforest.[29]

Reversing the cycle of political evaporation: honoring citizens' public speech

Commentators, politicians, and theorists on all ends of the US political spectrum applaud civic participation. Nobody ever comes out against it. After offering devastating critiques of the undemocratic nature of many institutions, many books and commentaries end with a general call for civic participation: participation in associations is hailed as the cure for many ills, from slow economic development (Putnam 1993) to a declining sense of community, rise of loneliness and excessive competitiveness (Kemmis 1990; Etzioni 1988), to inequality and excess corporate power (Stauber and Rampton 1996), to ethnic and religious dogmatism (Barber 1995) – or as a partial cure for most or all of these at once (de Tocqueville 1969; Walzer 1992).

I agree with de Tocqueville and Walzer: vibrant civic life can infuse *all* of the rest of life with a fresh spirit, giving people ground on which to stand when presenting arguments against the excesses and narrowness imposed by any of these other spheres of life (Walzer 1992: 100). But just advocating "participation" is not enough. The quality of public dialogue within these civic groups matters, too.

What can help reverse this cycle of political evaporation, bring life to the deserted public sphere, and help Americans learn how to care about politics? Institutions do not all necessarily inspire a cycle of political evaporation: they can inspire the opposite. The national environmentalist organizations that helped the Evergreen City anti-toxics group, and the black Baptist church that hosted one town-wide volunteer meeting, for example, implicitly told local citizens that publicly minded messages would not be ignored. By lending their ears, an irreplaceable resource, these national groups helped activists, and even some volunteers, to learn to speak in a new way in public contexts.

Without such counter-forces to the institutions that discourage public debate, there were no public places for groups to speak with a publicly minded voice. Little local groups all over the country could try to develop such spaces from scratch, but a group that has access to the ears of a national or international organization that honors publicly minded talk – a religious body, an activist organization, a governmental body, an unusual media outlet – has an easier time, building upon the spaces that are already there, expanding the small breathing spaces into spacious openings. Local groups could make it part of their goal to keep those "ears" healthy, helping foster those broader organizations. The more that groups are able to speak in public, the more citizens will expect publicly minded debate in public contexts, and perhaps accept it as a cultural pattern.

Encouraging political debate is not identical to encouraging citizens to lend a hand. Presidents regularly stage ceremonies to honor volunteers; honoring volunteer work is a start – national service like Vista, that would pay volunteers a subsistence wage, for example, or the Thousand Points of Light Foundation, could help make volunteer work seem as important as it truly is.

However, a problem could easily arise if these volunteers became like the volunteers of Amargo: eager to help people one at a time, but at the cost of blocking out awareness of the possibly overwhelming, systemic aspects of the problems.

Some political theorists and politicians suggest repairing Americans' bitter aversion to politics with call-in talk shows, or with call-in referenda (Barber 1984). These are not good solutions. Citizens have to *learn* how to connect their personal lives to political issues. A one-shot call to a radio talk show would likely reaffirm listeners' belief that political debate is bewildering and disembodied, that ideas come from nowhere, and the people who care about politics just want to hear themselves talk at weird hours of the day and night. Such disembodied citizen participation neglects the *process* of learning to talk about politics. The theory behind this suggestion is that people are ready-made good citizens, naturally equipped to discuss, debate, understand how their concerns are connected to a wider world. But as the interviews with Buffalo Club members showed, some citizens have had no practice in connecting their lives to politics; call-in talk shows and easy televised voting would open up a forum to unformed opinions that have not benefited from any reflection. And as the conversations between volunteers showed, many citizens already have trimmed their aspirations before voicing them publicly – like impoverished people who, when asked what they would do with a million dollars, can imagine only as far as buying a warm winter coat. In radio call-in shows, callers are usually supposed to present themselves as representatives of "the little people": powerless, simple, devoted to action and not talk. These shows often address politics with a spirit that is not open to debate; they dehumanize the other side instead of trying to engage in dialogue. These shows' civic etiquette does not invite callers to debate, but only to become what one talk show host's fans proudly call themselves: "dittoheads."

Confessional TV talk shows, on the other hand, seem on the face of it to open up public speech to all, letting new identities and new topics burst into the public realm in a way that is more liberating and introspective than the polemical call-in shows. Some scholars say that talk TV grasps just how the smallest, seemingly quirky issues can really matter to real people, making the unspeakable speakable (Nicholson 1996; Gamson 1995; Livingstone and Lunt 1994; Carpignano et al. 1993). But these shows open up the public sphere in a way that actually aids the cycle of political evaporation: in these self-confessional shows, citizens bare only the most private, intimate experiences for broadcast. They are like Cathy of the Buffalo Club, who described to me, in great detail, her ex-husband's drug problem and his failed efforts at quitting, and her unhappy childhood, and more, but said that disclosing how she voted for president or disclosing her party affiliation was too private.

This kind of talk show fits well into the cycle of political evaporation – Oprah and the others enforce only one style of speech: if talk show guests voice concern about the wider world, audiences chastise them for not really being truly authentic. Like the public sphere in Amargo, the confessional talk-TV show enforces a relentlessly small circle of concern and outlaws reflection on the common good in public. Volunteers are called upon to lend a hand, therapeutic talk show participants to bare their hearts; still missing from both styles is a thinking, moral soul that is loyally connected to the wider world.

Direct questioning of politicians in so-called "town meetings" on TV could raise the level of political debate among *politicians*, as the one 1992 presidential debate that included citizens' direct questions showed, and if debate amongst politicians were less silly, and if there were some way of preventing politicians from planting fake citizens in the audience to ask only questions the politicians are prepared to answer (as Bush was widely reported to have done), then citizens might be less disgusted, more inclined to talk reasonably with each other. But one-time events will not create ongoing public discussion. Volunteers had good, moral reasons for avoiding political discussion, and it took a long time for the activists to unravel their culture of political avoidance to learn to value publicly minded debate.

"Deliberative polling" is another intriguing suggestion aimed at rebuilding democracy: James Fishkin (1991) advocates gathering about 600 citizens from all over the country and all walks of life, to meet for several days to discuss the issues of the day. The group would represent a perfect cross-section of Americans, showing how we *would* think if we had had the opportunity to deliberate. The results of their deliberations would, he hopes, be widely reported in the media, possibly replacing the media's excessive reporting of the "top of the head" (Zaller 1991) responses that people usually give to standard poll questions. The deliberative poll and stories about it might raise the level of media discussion, and could certainly help avoid the often destructively mindless use of political surveys in the media, and could perhaps do a little bit to germinate a new political culture.

Unlike most groups in the US, the Christian right is better able than others to bring questions of the common good into public circulation, because religious language is not bereft of public-minded rhetoric – *political* language is. When Americans want to talk about the common good it is easier to use religious language. The problem is that the way fundamentalists understand "religion" does not include interpretation, debate, evidence – God already gave all the answers – and dehumanizes those who disagree – "humanists," gays, Jews, Muslims. Another language that purports to have all the answers without requiring public debate is the language of the free market. According to that approach, money talks, so people do not need to.

The irony in the United States is that while the "humanists" avoid talking about the common good, fundamentalists and free-market advocates join hands, using the language of the collective good to advocate private schooling, private health care, private charity instead of welfare, individual punishment instead of social compassion. The point for a modern public is to develop a way of talking about the common good of diverse citizens that remains open to debate (Lerner 1991). But when public spirit evaporates from everyone else's public discourse, the only "moral" voice left in public is the voice that calls for citizens to abandon the public good.

What if newspapers opened up spaces for grassroots groups to write columns explaining their positions, called public meetings, reported more actively on grassroots efforts, and did other "civic journalism" projects (Rosen 1991, 1994)? What if social service workers avoided the temptation to enlist volunteers one at a time to treat each problem one at a time?[30] What if political organizers learned how to listen to their constituents more acutely? Organizers who are interested in making the link between local and global politics often grow discouraged when so many citizens claim only to care about their own self-interest, only about issues "close to home." Organizers could listen to members talk in more than one context, and could pay attention to how different contexts amplify or muffle publicly minded analyses and concerns. Organizers could recognize that their ears are at least as important as their mouths, that just offering themselves as a public audience is perhaps the most constructive thing they can do, listening to the local groups offer political analyses in public, reassuring the local groups that it is permissible, and good, to discuss politics in public spaces.[31]

Strengthening the fragile public sphere

Most importantly, citizens themselves can cultivate a sense of respect for the power of talk itself. Of course, hands-on relief of suffering is important, but talking about the human causes of suffering is important, too, and the two could go together. Busy volunteer groups might feel that they do not have time to devote to such discussion, but often, talking about it in public-spirited terms would not take any more time at all, and in the long run, that kind of discussion could inspire people, and lead to more thoughtful and effective ways of addressing the problems. Rather than focusing on changing only the private beliefs and "inner" values or the "outer" powers that make participation so difficult, we could devote more care to opening up everyday contexts for publicly minded talk, and valuing those public places.

While the parking-lot-filled, toxin-laden suburban landscape surrounding the groups may seem unusually desolate, it clearly shows how hard it can be to develop a sense of togetherness in the suburban places where most Americans live. And while the polluted physical environment surrounding the groups may seem extraordinary, it clearly shows that citizens' lack of attention is not simply due to lack of danger or lack of perceived danger. How different are the rest of us from these neighbors of toxic industries, ringed around by military bases exporting weapons to the world, witnessing fires and explosions and watching the nuclear battleships float by? Perhaps we live a few more miles away, but how far? If the chemical plants moved to some country with lower environmental standards, would that be far enough? Perhaps we feel safe. If we do not, we, too, manage our feelings somehow, perhaps by telling each other that the problems are not close to home, as the volunteers did. In trying to get along, and make the world seem to make sense, we sometimes develop an etiquette for talking about political problems that makes it harder for us to solve them.

The act of carving out public space for open-ended, broad-minded political conversation could, potentially, implicitly call into question many unjust forms of power. When citizens assume that speaking in public is a source of power, public speech magically can *become* a source of power. But when we assume that public speech is untrustworthy, useless, and dangerous, then we lose a precious, magical gift: the ability to decide what goes on in public – to represent ourselves to ourselves – and to make sense of the world together. Tracing this process of political evaporation shows how some Americans create the local institutions of the public sphere, tells us what they think the public sphere is, tells us what they assume community and democracy are.

Recreation group members gathered because members wanted friendship and community, a home-base. Volunteers and activists gathered to try to make the world better. Yet, all the groups' sense of political etiquette prevented them from fully following up on their humanitarian impulses for gathering together, preventing their desires – for togetherness, for community improvement, for world improvement – from reaching full bloom. For most of the Americans portrayed here, and probably for most Americans, the public sphere is a dry and dismal place, from which intelligence, curiosity, and generosity have evaporated. Yet, the people I met also ambivalently knew that they were deeply connected to a wider world. Ambivalently, most wanted a wider circle of concern than they let themselves voice in public.

Appendix 1: Class in the public sphere

One typical kind of sociological argument examines a causal link between individual members' class background and political engagement. It would show how hidden structural forces inexorably work on people, steering them toward this kind of group, away from that. Such research would look at members' class, look at their political participation, see how they correlate, perhaps correlate these figures with some other "objective" measures, and call it a day (Verba and Nie's 1972 classic, for example). If I had focused on class, I would have shown how or if groups take on class-linked character-istics, and then how members interpret their class positions, as another "relation to authorities and institutions." This would have been one good way of doing this study.

I had empirical and theoretical reasons for not doing that. First, empiri-cally, it is impossible to control for class in real civic groups in the US; I had originally planned on doing so, and then decided it was impossible, and then, in a way, inadvertently succeeded in doing so, anyway. Class differ-ences between the different types of groups were minimal, especially between the activists and volunteers. Volunteers in the schools and anti-drugs groups included: three schoolteachers, one corporate scientist, one local realtor, two full-time homemakers (both with two years of college), some pink-collar workers. Activists in the anti-toxics group included, among others: two schoolteachers, one corporate scientist, one local realtor, two full-time home-makers (neither with college backgrounds, though one started going to com-munity college to learn about environmental issues after a year in the group – being in the group helped change her class ethos), some pink-collar workers; in other words, if we lined up activists and volunteers, we could couple off a Noah's Ark of paired occupations. Of course, there were inevitable differ-ences between the two types of group, but the overlap far outweighed the differences. Contrasting the demographic characteristics of the volunteers and activists empirically would not suffice. Recreation group members generally had less education than members of the other types of groups, but here too, most members had class equivalents in the other groups: people with two- or four-year college educations, working at white- or pink-collar jobs. All three types of groups contained few college graduates who worked at jobs which made use of their mental faculties, some manual laborers, and many low-paid white-collar employees and service workers. Members of the recreational, volunteer, and activist groups *interpreted* their class positions differently. In the country-western bars, there *were* some college graduates, who acted just like the other members. And in the activist groups, there *were* many manual workers and high-school-educated service workers, who acted just like the other members.

What is even more interesting is that some members' political choices determined their occupations at least as much as the other way around. Cynical country-westerner Maureen, for example, had a teaching credential, but after a year of teaching, she decided that she did not want to be in a position of "having to control kids," and chose instead a high-level secretarial job in the advertising wing of a pesticide plant. Volunteers Geoffrey and Pete, and activist Neil all had similar degrees and training in chemistry. Unlike the volunteers, Neil carefully picked a corporation that did not do military work, and was (or at least convincingly claimed to be) environmentally benign. Then, he did not have to be in the position of defending his work to himself. So, showing how class determined political participation would not have been very interesting.

Second, theoretically, I wanted to find out how people in groups interpret institutional, structural conditions other than class divisions. I tried to wrench the focus dramatically away from the usual sociological explanations that focus on individuals' biographies, and toward a more contextual, institutional, cultural one. Something happens when people enter a group context: simultaneously drawing on, and creating, a shared culture, they collectively create a sense of their group's place in relation to the institutions around it. What interested me here is how members present themselves in context – not their disembodied ideologies, but thoughts about the context itself. In addition to causal analyses that rely on external factors or individuals' internal characteristics, we need to understand how people create the *contexts* for the display and production of political engagement.

Working-class dispositions or publicly shared, institutional embodied practices?

If working-class people were psychologically incapable of developing political perspective, and had no opportunities for developing their imaginations outside of work, then they would never be able to change unless a leader came from above and told them how to think. Luckily, sociable public life can help counteract the effects of class on political participation: casual conversation can generate knowledge, and the sociable public sphere is more accessible than formal groups to lower-class people. A history of British coffeehouses, for example, quotes a broadside verse written in in 1677: "So great a Universitie/ I think there ne'er was any/ In which you may a scholar be/ For spending of a Penny [to buy a coffee]" (cited in Oldenberg 1989: 185; Verba and Nie 1972; Verba, Schlozman, and Brady 1995; Cayrol 1985).

The moral is that organized civic life can counteract the corrosive effects of class, so the next set of questions is: how can these organizations develop, and what goes on in them, and how do various forms of political powerlessness infuse what goes on in them? Drastic class inequality won't go away by itself; people in groups will have to do something to make it go away. Instead of talking about a static "social structure," perhaps we can inspect the "discursive structure" itself as a "practice which constitutes and organizes social relations" (Laclau and Mouffe 1985: 96). They say that social categories like class and ethnicity exist only through a web of culture; that is, they are "constituted in discourse." This is a good idea in theory – the trick is not to treat discursive practices as disembodied networks of meaning. Discursive agents appear only in social contexts, that make some practices easy and others difficult – this is rarely made clear in discourse studies.

Even if class and political involvement correlated, which they did not in the cases I studied, we would still need to know how to leap from the psychological predisposition to the enduring forms of group life, or from "agency" to "structure," as Anthony Giddens puts it (1984).[1] The enduring institutions of group life – like recreational groups, volunteer groups, and other institutions of the public sphere – in turn make various forms of political engagement possible. Focusing on the production of apathy on the group level requires rethinking typical sociological formulations of class and power.

Cultural capital and political habitus

Americans do not usually base their political participation on class membership – not explicitly, anyway. Instead of looking for explicitly class-based groups that perhaps should exist but rarely do, I took what was there already: groups that draw on some aspect of identity, consumer tastes, or tradition (parenthood, neighborhood, musical tastes). These kinds of groups are usually loosely connected to class, if at all. In fact, the groups I studied had a range of members from different classes.

But just let us say that it *were* possible to divide up the public sphere by class. Surely, if I had looked harder, I could have compared unions, or very small school districts or neighborhood associations, whose members all worked in very similar occupations. What might I have expected to find? The way many social researchers have examined the relation between class and political engagement has been to loop through a social-psychological perspective, focusing on childraising patterns and inner thought patterns – thus jumping from "micro" to "macro," "inner" to "outer," reproducing the pernicious dichotomy discussed in the conclusion, skipping the everyday, shared practices and meanings, embodied in institutions, through which people together make sense of their relation to the wider world.

For example, Seymour Martin Lipset's famous formulation calls political obliviousness a symptom of "working-class authoritarianism"; a narrow-mindedness that he says is the inevitable result of supposed working-class tendencies: too-strict childraising, a narrow range of associations, an inability to defer gratification (1959/60: 114). These psychological characteristics cause in workers a tendency to "view politics and personal relationships in black-and-white terms, a desire for immediate action, an impatience with talk and discussion, a lack of interest in organizations which have a long-range perspective, and a readiness to follow leaders who offer a demonological interpretation of the evil forces (either religious or political) which are conspiring against him" (115).[2]

In a more sympathetic vein, Basil Bernstein (1970) compared middle-class and working-class childraising patterns. He says that working-class people tend to presume the existence of "a backdrop of common assumptions, common history, common interests" against which they can interpret the intentions of speakers; middle-class people speak as if they share little common context, and thus, they assume that they need to make their background assumptions more explicit. In an experiment, for example, a working-class child, asked to describe a set of pictures illustrating a story about a boy who throws a football through a window, will assume that the listener can see the pictures. The child relies on pointing and referring to the characters in the story as "he," as if the listener already knows who "he" is. A middle-class child will assume that the listener does not necessarily have access to the pictures and is unfamiliar with the story's characters. "He" becomes "the boy who threw the football."

Bernstein's research poses an interesting possibility. A researcher could take Bernstein's work and use it to investigate how, or if, working-class people create spaces for discussion in the potential contexts of the public sphere. One could use his ideas to investigate whether lacking a common context made political conversation more difficult for working-class people than middle-class people. His research implies that it would be more difficult for working-class people to *invent* a common context where one does not already exist.

Perhaps this double jeopardy of working-class life in a decentered suburb helps, in part, explain the extra dose of nostalgia among the country-westerners. The lack of common, taken-for-granted history can make communication more difficult for them than it would for deracinated middle-class people, who can always find some general, context-free way of making themselves understood. Bernstein says word-oriented, middle-class parents train their children to have more portable personalities, able to strike up instant intimacy without long-term bonds, able to put words to feelings, able to make assumptions explicit.

The ''working class'' that most scholars have studied has been a more traditional one, living in stable, enduring neighborhoods, unlike the country-westerners. Unlike them, working-class people in stable neighborhoods can presume that they share a concrete history together. So the country-westerners constitute a new kind of working-class group, not previously studied; the research on class predispositions may not even apply to suburban people like these country-westerners.

Appendix 2: Method

Distinctions

Anthropologists and sociologists rarely study people whose identities are constructed *in distinction from, in opposition to*, to their own: country-westerners dance to a song that proclaims, "I ain't no doctor, don't got no Ph.D., but when you talk about lüüüüv, come to me!"; I, in turn, was jealous that they could so easily and straightforwardly lay claim to being "typical red-blooded Americans," while no one would ever call me a real down-home, plain-folks American. I worried that I was the wrong person to study regular Americans. Even if the Buffalo Club was not "really" cowboy culture, it was all foreign to me, an urban, bi-coastal, bespectacled, Jewish, Ph.D. candidate from a long line of communists, atheists, liberals, book-readers, ideologues, and arguers. I could not trade on my unwholesome background if I were running for political office. Some of my earliest fond memories are of my communist grandpa telling me about the joy of unalienated labor as we carefully made beds and cleaned dishes, or railing about the Vietnam War, or sitting at his little desk writing letter after letter to his local newspaper.

Theoretically, I know there is no such thing as a "mainstream American" – mainstream by ethnicity, class, race, region, religion, and everything else – and if there were, the mainstream would either have to be broad enough to include someone like me, or else it would represent only a small minority of Americans. Nevertheless, whatever the statistical reality, the people portrayed here laid a more firm claim on normalness than I.

All the jokes my friends and colleagues made about the people I studied had a twinge of jealousy: two separate people asked, "Did they make you eat bologna sandwiches on white bread?" (One added, "and lots of mayonnaise?") Of course, when we were children, we used to be horribly embarrassed not to have bologna and white bread. Face it, the volunteers and country-westerners were "tacky" by my usual associates' measures, and we were jealous.

Doing this project forced me to take up their challenge to use fieldwork to "understand ourselves by way of the other" (as Rabinow 1977, citing Paul Ricoeur, puts it). Normally, people comfortably take their own tastes for granted. But driving to the Buffalo week after week, I lost my ability to pick a radio station, having really grasped that somebody I knew really did enjoy the Jimmy Buffett station (or, as I exlaimed when I came home one day, "Somebody really does listen to Neil Diamond!''); buying clothes, I knew somebody in Amargo who would like the pastel-colored garments I would normally skip on the rack. Unlike an anthropologist traveling to a faraway place, I studied my neighbors; we exist in opposition to each other; we are who we are *because* we are not the other, and have probably been that way since junior high school. People "like me" distinguish themselves from people "like them" through tastes and styles of interacting, and vice versa; we do not do it on purpose, but avoid each other's styles as automatically as we avoid clothes we deem ugly on the department store rack. The fact is, somebody usually buys those clothes.

Sure, anyone can buy white bread and blinking Christmas lights, but I and my Newton colleagues could never attain that fresh, happy, and yes, unquestioning acceptance of normalcy, the assumption that common sense works and that there is not always some alternative, better universe that could exist "if-only ... " The volunteers, especially, had such a healthy, hearty life. I was driving past Amargo High on my way to the Buffalo one brisk fall evening – there was a football game with happy-looking families on the bleachers, everyone looking rosy-cheeked in the fresh evening air. A couple of parents were carrying a sleepy little boy, wearing a favorite helmet, home to bed. I know that fun football games are not enough to make a good society, but when I see them, I forget why. They make everyone happy.

And I admired, liked, and respected many volunteers: Julie was a pillar of the community; Danielle had two children and a full-time job and still managed to volunteer. They were really good, fun, and caring people. And more than that, I agreed with most of what they were trying to do. I hoped that my children would be encircled within something like a "caring adult network" of neighbors, extended family, and friends. I must be a fussy and precious crab, I thought, for wanting more – more for my children, the volunteers' children, them, and me, too.

As nearly all fieldworkers do, I "went native" while with the people I studied. To most readers, this probably will seem most implausible with the Buffaloes. After the relaxed evening listening to the peaceful crickets and frogs outside Sue's house, comfortably not having to "prove" anything to the other country-westerners, I was driving home on the dark highway and forgot why I thought it was important to live for a wider world. I came home asking, "Wouldn't it be great to just live for private life, and have time to be bored sometimes, and not always be worrying how your actions will affect the future?" What a relief that would be, in a way, not to worry that everything one did "meant" something. The personal tone allowed country-westerners to appreciate the croaking frogs and humming crickets at Sue's house, without having to speak. At parties in Newton, the university types I knew usually stood in a tight knot in the kitchen clutching beers, talking seriously. I would go home with a backache. I would leave the Buffalo pleasantly flushed from dancing (but wheezing from the dense cigarette smoke). My Newton friends rarely had time to talk on the phone for hours about personal life, but I relish it. In Newton, the worst taboo was to feel bored, especially in the company of others, or to be boring. Surrounded by constant, hyperactive exhausting chatter, I never felt bored in the cosmopolitan, globally conscious rush – overwhelmed perhaps, but never bored. At the country-western places, participants often allowed themselves to be relaxed enough to be bored, and say so, if there was no entertainment going on for a while. This time-expanding, peaceful boredom pleasantly reminded me of the long summer days I enjoyed before becoming one of those frenetic Newton types. I appreciated this quietude.

On the other hand, when I would get home to our shabby city apartment, I would have a wonderful feeling, as if I were taking off a hot itchy sweater, feeling at ease in the diverse street life with a splendid variety of olive, coffee, eggplant, and peach-colored people, all "typical Americans." I would shed the oppressive automobile that felt to me like a wheelchair encasing my body – a constant in the places where "real people" live – and use my trusty bicycle as transportation, until the next time I had to take the glaring highway trip to the suburbs.

> *Mutual* noblesse oblige*; mutual disdain, fear, envy;*
> *and mutual curiosity*

So, who is more culturally dominant here – they or I? I am, because I have more cultural capital, or control more means of mental production? Or they are, because they are the mainstream, and have more cultural girth for it – and we all know that? And they all have more money and stability than I. I gazed at the homes the "real" Americans owned, thinking I would not be allowed the luxury of such stability and comfort for a long time, if ever; they gazed at me thinking that I had the luxury of not having a full-time job.

Why would it matter who was more culturally dominant? Sociologists are supposed to maintain a lofty distance from the people they study and perhaps feel sorry for them. Hidden in this lofty distance is often a sense of pity. We are supposed to feel bad for the ''underdogs,'' and show how they are victims of circumstances. We are not supposed to honor our ''subjects'' enough to get angry with them or argue with them, not supposed to engage in personal relationships with them, and not supposed to vacillate between thinking, ''Well, after all, maybe it would be nice to be like that,'' and ''I thank my lucky stars I'm not like that.'' Sociologists, like anthropologists, usually study people who are sufficiently drastically different from themselves that automatic, active distinction-making between them and their subjects is not built into their relationship.

The ''lofty distance from underdogs'' stance can be insulting and inaccurate. The *very last thing* in the world the volunteers would have wanted anyone to think about them was that they were ''victims of circumstances'' or ''underdogs''! And they felt very sorry for me for not having children yet, not being married yet, living in a dirty city in a slummy apartment, not being able to afford a respectable-looking car or a four-wheel drive vehicle, not celebrating Christmas even. One told me she was afraid to let her son drive to Newton because it was so dangerous and parking places were so scarce. Another said she was afraid walking down the main street in Newton because it was so dirty and she had to keep her hand on her purse the whole time. A Buffalo Club member told me that the best thing about his huge recreational truck was that when he was behind one of those slow, little cars on the highway, if he got right on its tail, they would have to move because his truck was so much bigger – in an accident, he'd be fine; the little car wouldn't be. Of course, I drove just such a slow, little car. It is hard to maintain the requisite feeling of *noblesse oblige* when one is simultaneously pitied by the objects of one's graciousness.[1]

Hardly anyone from Newton ever ventured out into the rest of the Pacific City area, except to study the more fashionable subjects, suitably oppressed and preferably covertly rebellious peoples: people helping people with AIDS, undocumented workers, new immigrants, gay activists, African-American high schoolers, to take examples from a collection of student papers from a participant observation class (Burawoy et al. 1992). They avoided the ''normal'' types like the plague, making me wonder if a little direct engagement, even argument, between the two types would be a good thing. In fact, a deficiency in US political life is that US academics and social change activists rarely venture out of our enclaves and into direct interactions with the people about whom we fret and theorize. Academics move from one job to another so much, they tend not to ''live'' anywhere, or read the local press, or join local civic organizations; and progressive political activists often fear the "working people" on whose behalf they purport to work.

The people I studied were not a popular type for Newton students to study, especially not through participant observation. Yet, these are the Americans about whom Newton political activists and scholars like me pondered endlessly, sometimes even tried to "reach." Intellectuals and activists oscillate ambivalently, first extolling them as the oppressed "little people" who heroically and quietly resist the dominant culture and will one day rise up and save us all; and then reviling them as oppressive, gas-guzzling racists who consume more than their share of the world's resources.

It is easier to study "oppressed victims," and empathize with them. After meeting Fred, the racist in the Silverado roast beef line, I heard a panel discussion in which fieldworkers were discussing the benefits of doing research that helped the oppressed people one studied (see Fals-Borda, on "participatory action research," for example [1987]): examples given were working-class women, workers, blacks, even peasants. Are suburban white people who are racist but live next door to a toxic dump and have not organized themselves to fight it the "oppressed," or not? This participatory action research dovetails with feminist research, that purports to treat subjects as equals, humans, real people and not types, and to establish reciprocal, egalitarian relationships with subjects. The implication is that the researcher can bend down and become accessible to the researched. But when I tried being egalitarian, I found that my "bending down" to equalize the relationship made no sense. I wasn't in the position to equalize the relationship: I couldn't reach *up* high enough. It was obvious who was in control in the situations I studied. Perhaps because I was still a student, people assumed that I and my project were a bit quaint. Perhaps because I was purposely not interested in reporting on very intimate secrets, but was interested only in public displays, I felt less guilty than some researchers when I was told secrets. In fact, I did not take notes when people told me intimate secrets. I was less in control, since I was purposely studying whole group contexts and public speech.

Some fellow graduate students told me that it was immoral to study people like the Buffalo Clubbers without showing them that I disapproved of their racism, sexism, homophobia, and their other mean-spirited political opinions. In fact, some seemed to think even that it was immoral to study such people, period. Perhaps the disapproving fellow students thought that if I was holding my tongue and not actively distancing myself *in person* from Fred, the Buffalo who made the racist jokes, I must not really *be* distant from him. But I had never actually heard anyone say such racist things in person before, and was morbidly curious, wondering, "Is this what real Americans are like?"

and "How will I react?" And indeed, I discovered something important for my research, when trying to make a quick comeback that would make sense in that context: that it was actually easy to do just what the other silenced Buffaloes did when faced with racist and sexist and violent jokes. That is, in contrast to my usual habit, in my usual haunts, I found out why it was easy *here* to "not say nothin'." The point is, I could not have discovered this if I had automatically argued with them. Toward the end of my fieldwork stint, I started to force myself to express my own opinions once in a while, though this too was meant as an experiment, not as a means of self-expression. I did not argue with those particular racist individuals, whose narrow-mindedness would, in any case, pop up in other bodies with other names even if I won my arguments with them as individuals.

The fact was, in most groups, usually no one was interested in hearing anyone's opinions. I felt incredibly grateful to those members who did show interest in my project.

Country-westerners in the cosmopolitan eye

Just as academics and activists are scornful, afraid, and envious of the "normal people," so are media critics. The regional press of the area treated country-western music lovers, people they considered to be "normal red-blooded Americans," with disdain, fear, and envy. One review in the nearby Pacific City newspaper started out particularly favorably, describing the esthetics of superstar Clint Black as "unassumingly profound . . . strong and dignified," saying he "would be a major pop contender *if it weren't for his cowboy hat and Texas twang* [my emphasis]." Another musician at this same concert under review was "master . . . troubadour" Merle Haggard:

The crowd took Haggard's love-America-or-leave-it sentiments at face value, shouting as if at a pro-war rally, particularly at that "Okie (from Muskogee)" line about "the hippies in San Francisco." Stoked on these reactionary sentiments, some audience members seemed as willing to pick fights as the most belligerent rap or heavy metal follower. Whether Haggard was speaking from the heart or spoofing his conservative roots became irrelevant.

The Newton press was even tougher on the country acts. This review in a free weekly, of a Jimmy Buffett concert, for example, was only part tongue-in-cheek. After saying that she was almost raped at a Buffett concert in 1978, the critic goes on:

But why, I hear you cry, go see a meaningless pud like Buffett? Because he's the Antichrist and he's been ignored too long, I tell you. It's my job as critic to fend off evil wherever I find it . . .

The thing is, what Buffett and his laid-back good ol' boy woman-hating, responsibility-shirking, incredibly drunken-sailor act represents is the truly dark side of the American psyche, the side which goes home and gets fucked up after work every day and then beats the children for smoking pot. The side that thinks pink frothy drinks with a plastic parrot in them are the height of culinary sophistication and aesthetic pleasure . . . judging by the long line of ladies clad in pink and red Aloha shirts and white shorts who were doubled over garbage cans vomiting by mid-set, nausea – albeit alcohol-induced – is another all-American sentiment, just par for the course . . . The women bleach their hair and get real tan; the men are prematurely bald and have bright red faces and mustaches. I felt like I was contracting skin cancer just looking at them . . . I was seriously considering getting myself a shot of heroin for the ride home.

Jimmy Buffett was the most popular musician at the Buffalo; this critic's rendition of the physical scene is perhaps accurate. The problem is, she is just describing the world; the point, however, is to change it. Casting fellow citizens as enemies will not do the trick.

The antipathy between cosmopolitan critics and the country-western audiences was mutual, as the songs "Livin' on Tulsa Time" and the other, whose refrain went, "I ain't no doctor, don't got no Ph.D., but when you talk about love, come to me," attested. Country music lovers positioned themselves as anti-institutional, so they probably would have been pleased by the loathing judgments passed on them by critics, if they were aware of them. The mutual negative regard helped keep the big industry appearing to resist the dominant institutions. But calling this antipathy "resistance" or even subcultural would be inaccurate. As noted in chapter 4, country music got "discovered" in the early 1990s when computer scanners revealed it to be the most popular musical genre in the US; reporters and other intellectuals were now in the margin, with country music lovers taking up more and more territory on the cultural field. Again, it was unclear who was the underdog, who had to bend down to become equal with whom.

Recently, some anthropologists have found it important to recognize that there is in fact a relationship between the cultures they study and their own; to treat their subjects less like bugs on sticks and more like people with whom they can argue, from whom they can learn, whose ways of life are bound up through global ties to our own (see Rabinow 1977; Clifford and Marcus 1986, for example).

Given all this, it would have been odd to think about the people I studied *without* thinking of them in relation to and comparison to myself and my usual milieu; we all were members of the same society, voting in or staying home from the same elections, tuning into the same spectrum on the radio, represented by the same faces in the United Nations, usually avoiding each other's subcultures, all Americans.

Erotic sociology?

I had other, related worries about my relationship to the people I studied. Part of the reason we academics think we are "above" our subjects is that we value control of words and meanings so much more than most Americans. I worried that I was too verbal compared to them, and would miss too much because of it. Entering the Buffalo, I expected to find the headwaters from which the country-westerners' resistance to activists' political messages emerge. I slowly discovered that all of these descriptions of the country-westerners – "gas-guzzlers," "little people," whatever – are too ideological, too verbal; projecting intellectuals' and activists' ways of thinking through political positions onto people who do not strive for such seamless verbal coherence in their everyday lives.

I had assumed I was more verbal than most people, more portable, better at starting up a conversation with anybody and everybody. As Basil Bernstein proposes, someone like me, from my class, is supposed to be more verbal than a Buffalo, maintaining that possibly class-specific verbosity was impossible in this situation, especially for a woman. Verbalness is as much a function of context as of class predisposition. For me, being at the Buffalo was like being sent back to junior high school – I thought *I* had changed, but upon entering this scene, I saw that I had just succeeded in avoiding that kind of *context* for the past sixteen years. Still, I expected more talk, especially among the private people, even if I did not produce it.

This verbalness was not just my own personal characteristic. Sociology is a verbal enterprise. It inevitably means giving words to the unspoken. The enterprise of sociology should make this distinction, this *traducción/trahison* explicit, instead of assuming that all interaction *can* be translated into explicit words. The concept of practices is a way of bridging the gap between the implicitness of most life and the explicitness of sociology.

Sociology writing rightly aims at "clarity," but in novels and poetry, as in life, hazy, misty, flowery, dreamlike, haunting prose sometimes is more accurate. Describing people in "clear prose" enforces a coherence that is absent from life. Could you describe yourself in clear prose? Or your beloved? I would honor our mystery more than that. But the enterprise of sociology is not to celebrate the haphazard, the skewed, the chance. One of the great joys in life is walking down a city street, where everything seems arbitrary, serendipitous, customary, traditional, unusual, bumbling: an alley in the middle of a big city, where some restaurant is storing its cabbages and tomatoes, and little cloth shoes are for sale cheap. No doubt the sellers are refugees who at some point had to leave their countries of origin, to come to the US. Maybe they were forced to leave, as servants. In any case, it probably wasn't a joyous occasion.

Ornate Victorian houses next to warehouses, Vietnamese in Texas, Hmong in Milwaukee, Jews in San Diego, salsa music, Cuban-Chinese food: part of what makes American culture so fresh and weird and joyous is the combinations and misplacements. There are benefits to this erotic lack of control: the mixes and blends, salsa and blues. If you could understand everything and control everything, would you be happy? Once everything fits neatly and you know how, why bother living? Social science thinking is not erotic and joyous, though. It tries to preserve, replicate, abstract, find patterns, control, fit things together, verbalize. Erotic is unique, appreciative without wanting to explain, natural-feeling; going for the breezy stroll in Chinatown and noticing the tomatoes in the alleyways. It is making a life for oneself selling tomatoes and shoes. Social science is worrying why the restaurant owners had to flee their country, and possibly trying to control the problem that caused the exile.

Still, I have faith in sociology as one form of engagement with the world, among others. Sympathetic understanding requires both kinds of knowledge. Sociological clarity has its own breathtaking eros, when suddenly seemingly disparate social issues seem to click into place and make sense together; and this broad vision allows one to consider broad solutions to seemingly disparate problems. The trick is to try to instigate social change without letting everything in life become a means to that end. One of my worst difficulties in writing this book was in knowing that I was making explicit what could never be made explicit, making everything seem to "fit" in a way that life never does.

Definitions

Other researchers have made inquiries into the relation between political talk and action, but their findings do not readily translate into mine. For example, in a suggestive statistical study of American political participation, Sidney Verba and Norman Nie asked interviewees whether they "talked about politics" in the various civic groups in which they participated. Not surprisingly, the researchers found a correlation between "talking about politics" and "political participation." For inactive members who reported that they "talked inactive about politics" in their groups, however, there was no such correlation (1972: 188).

I suggest that what Verba and Nie really found was that the link between membership and political involvement held only for people who *defined* some of their group's conversation as "political." Verba and Nie asked interviewees whether they "have ever worked with others in this community to try to solve some community problem" and whether they had ever worked on "a local issue," begging the question of what members define as a "community" and "local" issue vs. a "national" or "global" issue. As Michael Schapiro points out (1981), *a priori* limiting the definition of the political realm (in Verba and Nie's case, the definition boils down to four activities: voting, contacting politicians, working on local issues, and working on electoral campaigns) cuts off the most interesting question of all, which is: what activities count as political? Is making racist jokes "discussing politics"? This is not something that is accounted for in the same way by all Americans. Deciding what *counts* as political involvement is in itself a powerful political move; the dispute over the boundaries of "political" vs. "non-political" discussion is part of my question. Researchers like Verba and Nie examine easy-to-measure forms of involvement like voting and contacting officials; their establishing these measures is like the drunk who lost his hat and searches under a streetlight two blocks away from where he lost it, because that's where the light is.

The clash of fieldworkers' and "natives'" definitions has been a hotly debated problem since social research began. On the one hand, ignoring the "natives'" perspective is wrong. Defining the categories "objectively," beforehand, renders much political activity invisible: making racist jokes, or blasting country-western music out of car speakers to drown out rap music in a nearby car, or talking at the dinner table about toxic waste or Navajo rugs or car air-conditioners. Verba and Nie also do not count protesting as "political," thus possibly ignoring members' own definitions. On the other hand, unquestioningly accepting members' definitions is wrong, too. If members do not consider the argument over whether men should ever cook for the potluck "political" and yet researchers do consider it political, there is an obvious problem – the researcher is missing a crucial element of those people's sense of political empathy and apathy. Verba and Nie's definition is both too subjective and too objective.

There is no way out of this dilemma. Researchers must accept that they cannot avoid having relationships to, and making moral judgments about, the people they study. Instead of ignoring that relationship, as scientists tend to do, the best approach is to acknowledge it and build it into one's research plan. My definitions of "political talk" and "publicly spirited talk" are aimed at illuminating a theoretical and activist agenda, focusing on the process by which citizens collectively create a sense of empathic connection or disconnection to the larger society. It is a dialogue between a very broad idea of what could potentially be considered "politics," and the everyday fact that most of the time, no one – not even the most politically attuned person in the world – can explicitly draw out the "politics" inherent in any situation.

Interview questions

In open-ended interviews, I asked roughly the same questions of all interviewees:

> Why are you a member of (the group in which you participate)?
>
> Why do people work on the following issue (here, I asked about
> three or four of the following issues: schools, drugs, nuclear wea-
> pons, homelessness, US relations to Central America, environ-
> mental issues)?
>
> If you had extra time, would you consider getting involved in a
> group working on any of those? Why or why not?

After having done the interviews with the volunteers, which I did first, I
added, about each of the issues: "Does that seem close to home? Does it
seem like something you could do something about? Does it affect you personally?"

I also gave interviewees a large-type, three-page survey, asking about
income, education, voting record, and political efficacy and alienation questions taken from other surveys. The purpose of the latter was mainly to hear
how interviewees negotiated their answers to the questions, not to tabulate
answers and compare from one group to another. So I tape recorded the
survey interview, or took notes immediately following it.

To enter the groups, I introduced myself as a student from Newton, studying community life and how people get involved. In subsequent conversations, I told members about the other groups I was studying. At the Buffalo,
I also told people right away that I had a boyfriend in Newton – he came
dancing sometimes.[2]

Taking fieldnotes takes practice. The way to remember conversation is to
remember the *flow* of conversation, not single, decontextual utterances. For
long conversations, like the one about the toxic cows buried under the soft
green hills off the highway, I came equipped with a little purse containing a
wallet, lipstick, pencil, and a scrap of paper. For that conversation and a few
others, I took shorthand notes in the bathroom while still at the Buffalo, and
then rendered them legible when I got home. In the volunteer and activist
group meetings, notetaking was easier, since there were usually other people
jotting down a few notes or doodles to themselves, and there was usually an
agenda passed out, on which I could comfortably take notes. Usually, I waited
till I got home to take notes. I took no notes on some conversations and
censored notes on others, sensing that the speaker was treating me as a confi-
dante, and most definitely not expecting the conversation to end up in "my
paper." This etiquette was fine for my project, since I was not studying
purely personal self-disclosure about intimate life in intimate contexts.

Notes

1 The mysterious shrinking circle of concern

1 I have changed names of people and places, and some distinctive features of the setting and people to protect subjects' anonymity.
2 See Lipset and Schneider (1983, 1978); Wright (1976), for some examples.
3 See, for example, Neuman (1988).
4 This project draws on a pilot study I conducted, trying to address the questions raised at the end of that article (1990).
5 These booming new suburbs have been variously dubbed "technoburbs" (Fishman 1987), "transformed suburbs" (Baldassare 1986), "multinucleated metropolitical regions" (Gottdeiner and Kephart 1991), "edge cities," or "post-suburban regions"; the definitions vary somewhat, but all describe a similar development.
6 Gottdiener and Kephart (1991) explicitly name the county that I am calling "Evergreen County" one such suburb; Amargo was the closest city to Evergreen County and also clearly fits the description.
7 Habermas (1984); Thompson (1984); Fraser (1987, 1992); Calhoun (1992), for example.
8 Barber (1985); Dewey (1927), for example.
9 Some excellent examples are in the collection edited by Craig Calhoun (1992); see also Eagleton (1985); Cmiel (1990).
10 Two splendid studies describe what I call civic practices, but in both, the theoretical agenda is quite different from mine. Jane Mansbridge's *Beyond Adversary Democracy* (1980) clearly and concretely documents the civic manners that reproduce class inequality. In the Vermont village she observed, everyone was supposed to participate as an "equal"; paradoxically, the egalitarian structure of participation cloaked the existence of real inequality, making the town's inequalities impossible to address directly. Citizens' practical intuition regarding "what is sayable" and "who can speak" systematically screened some ideas out of public life. I ask what *other* implicit etiquette – other than the kind that reproduces inequalities between members – filters ideas out of public circulation? In *The*

Search for Political Community (1996), Paul Lichterman shows that different environmental groups had different understandings of what "being a member" meant: members of a black anti-toxics group, for example, thought of their group as a mouthpiece for "The Community," while white environmentalists focused on making sure that each individual's voice mattered. His question is more about the boundaries of the self, and less about how groups create and enforce manners for political conversation.

11 The same set of organizations could also be called "civil society"; I use the term "public sphere" to emphasize the nature of conversation in these settings, and to avoid the confusion associated with various conflicting definitions of "civil society." For a good review of the two terms' histories, see Calhoun (1993).

12 This definition is borrowed from Terry Eagleton (1985).

13 In theorizing the kinds of citizen groups that could open up space for political conversation, theorists and historians have searched for public life in a wide range of places, all called "public." Jeffrey Weintraub (1990) outlines four different uses of the word: public in the sense of public administration; public in the sense of cafés and street culture; public in the sense of the polis; and finally, public in distinction from domestic.

14 See Oldenberg (1989) for a fun, if nostalgic, review of that sort of public life. Also see Goldfarb (1980) and Arato (1981) for more scholarly treatments of the relation between this sociable, esthetic public and the more official public sphere.

15 Habermas (1979, 1985, for example). Mary Ryan makes a similar criticism of Habermasian analyses in her study of the boisterous and sweaty, passionate public sphere in nineteenth-century party politics (1992). Kenneth Tucker (1992) makes the same point on a theoretical level. Habermas would agree with poet W. H. Auden, who quipped, "A man has his distinctive personal scent which his wife, his children, and his dog can recognize. A crowd has a generalized stink. The public is odorless" (1985). That image of the public sphere is to the sociable public sphere as e-mailing "I love you" is to waking up on a warm summer morning together after twenty years of a happy marriage: more in need of explicit verbalization, less grounded in the often non-verbal comfortableness of everyday life. The loud, happy public is not easily separable from the sober polis; in fact, Iris Young (1987) convincingly argues that striving to keep feelings out of the public sphere may have helped contribute to its downfall.

16 See Rosen (1987) and Neuman (1988) for some startling examples of widespread political ignorance.

17 Numerous feminist scholars have pointed out that, alas, Arendt really did just mean "men" here (for example, Benhabib 1990) – or, more precisely, I would say, she means "people who are not in charge of childcare." Arendt's division of the world into "instrumental," "housekeeping" efforts vs. lofty, non-instrumental public life would collapse if she thought about how children and children's education fitted into her division.

18 Drawing out this "public-spirited" face of politics is a theoretical move with a long lineage (Arendt 1958; Barber 1984; Etzioni 1988; Wolin 1960, for example).

But the way I define "public spirit" differs somewhat from their definitions, since I am, like Pitkin, not excluding expressions of self-interest, and am focusing on the form of expression as much as the content. On the other hand, many political scientists assume that "interest group politics" is the *definition* of politics; in contrast, my focus on openness to debate and reference to justice would exclude pure expressions of self-interest from the category "publicly minded discourse."

19 Chantal Mouffe brilliantly argues this point in recent work (1992, 1993); I want to show concretely what one would examine in such research – though the people I studied are clearly not very close to being the "radical democratic citizens" – feminists, gays and lesbians, environmentalists – she envisions.

20 Arendt famously separates the two kinds of power, imagining a sterile, innocent public sphere, untouched by any instrumental power. Habermas (1976) argues that her "communications concept of power" ignores how communicative power is impaired by, and props up, structural forces. While I would seriously amend the distinction he makes in this early article between "communicative" and "structural" power" (or, what he usually calls "system" and "lifeworld"), I share his goal of hunting for systematic distortions. As Calhoun suggests, "This break [between 'system' and 'lifeworld'] is not a break in reality, however, but in our approach to understanding it. A critical theorist needs continually to remind herself or himself that it is provisional; it must be unmasked recurrently to reveal the actual human activity creating the larger system" (1988: 223).

21 Boyte 1980; Delgado 1986, for some examples among many.

22 The question of how they intertwine is the subject of some of the most exciting recent debate (see Alexander and Giesen 1988; Calhoun 1988; Laclau and Mouffe 1985; Mouffe 1992, 1993; Sahlins 1976; Sewell 1992; Somers 1995).

23 Thus, the steady stream of articles in journals like *Public Opinion Quarterly* noting the "noise," as they call it, caused by such problems as interviewees' responding to interviewers' race or gender or status, even on questions that are not specifically about race, gender, or status. Of course, survey researchers recognize, and write about, all of these problems all the time. My point is that these stances are part of what "holding an opinion" means; they are not just obstacles to surmount before we researchers nab the real, context-free opinion. For other reviews of survey research, see Reinharz 1983; Eliasoph 1990.

24 The exemplar of this type of research is Almond and Verba's *The Civic Culture*, a classic cross-national survey published in 1963. This is true despite the authors' claim to be studying "culture," which they see as the link between psychology and social structure (p. 33). The way they study culture effectively reduces it to shared values and beliefs. This privatized understanding of "democracy" fits with their thin definition of democracy. Had Almond and Verba and followers paid more attention to the educational process of democracy, they would have been more tempted to focus more on the norms for political conversation that *make* democracy *educational*, and less on inner beliefs and values. For thorough critiques of this scrawny idea of democracy, see Carole Pateman (1973, 1980), Barber (1984), who both use the term "democracy" the way it I use it, emphasizing the educative process of political participation.

25 Lane writes that the idea to write a book based on open-ended interviews with common people came from his training in "the strategy and tactics of psychotherapy" that "launched [him] upon this study of the political mind and that shaped the character of [his] conversations with these fifteen men" (1962: 7).

26 Of course, the concept of practices has a venerable history; for relatively recent versions, see Wittgenstein (1953); Bourdieu (1977, 1990); Taylor (1989).

27 Goffman's works suffer from a frightening proliferation of overlapping metaphors, images, labels, and typologies. For example, in defining "footing," he says "a change in our footing is another way of talking about a change in our frame for events" (1979: 5). I adopt the term "footing," because the term "frame" is used, in recent studies of social movements, to mean something more cognitive and strategic, and less interaction-centered, than what I mean.

28 Early "community studies" could describe a *place* and find a set of relationships, long-term backyard interactions, neighbors who knew each other's names, chance grocery store encounters; an easy familiarity that came from homogeneity. They could examine local diners, local bars and pubs, local union halls and local political machines (Hoggart 1957; Young and Wilmott 1957; Kornblum 1974, for example). Familiarity is harder to come by in a diverse and scattered post-suburb. How do people voluntarily create a sense of togetherness out of such diversity, in such centerless, privatized places? Such tenuous togetherness clearly exposes the *process* of developing a feel for what is appropriate to say where (for a similar critique of most ethnography of communication, see my conclusion).

29 Bourdieu focuses mainly on how practices automatically take structural limitations into account. In contrast, the practices I examine reproduce ideas of what being a good person means – not just to reproduce the power relations that he emphasizes, but also relations of solidarity. In fact, the two intertwine and repel each other in surprising ways (see Lamont and Fournier 1992, for a similar point).

2 Volunteers trying to make the world make sense

1 Luke, the quiet, non-mainstream Parent League member, said to me in the individual interview, "I used to tell people I had three jobs: driving to work, work itself, and then driving home, you know, because it takes two hours to get to downtown Pacific City and it's *not* relaxing."

2 In some cities recycling is defined as an activist thing to do, and in others it is a city service, but in Amargo it fitted squarely into the ethos of voluntarism. I also studied a presidential electoral campaign in another city before deciding to focus on the area around the Swift River. Oddly enough, I would characterize this as a volunteer-style group – members never talked about why they were involved in this campaign; and there was a surprising degree of ignorance about the candidates' platforms on the part of the phone banking volunteers with whom I worked.

3 I went to all of the meetings in a series that the League of Women Voters held before an election, designed to help get out the vote and to get neighbors acquainted with one another. About six members and six non-members attended

each of these meetings. Members were all women, but the non-members who attended were evenly divided by gender.

4 Verba and Nie's term "communalists" comes closest to the category I call "volunteers."

5 Spending time in Amargo, I too developed a fear of "saying the wrong thing" about race. The benefit of taking field notes, rather than simply being a member of a group, was that I could assemble all the reasons *why* I felt that race may have been an important issue in town, and not just queasily wonder whether or not I was imagining things (Reinharz 1983). After all, I had not originally intended to focus on race, but it hit me as silently salient.

6 Suburban Americans have for a long time assumed that categorizing people is rude (Whyte 1956). Many conversations in their meetings were devoted to asserting the existence of equality. When the principal brought in school test scores, happily reporting that Amargo High's "socioeconomically relative" score was higher than Swift River's, his note of encouragement was not taken in the spirit he had intended. He said:

> These scores are based on the assumption that kids of parents with advanced degrees do better than kids whose parents didn't go to college or just didn't finish high school.
>
> SHERRY [who had not gone to college]: Hyuh. *That*'s their assumption, is it.
>
> Looking a bit miffed, she pursed her lips, her opinion of the principal as a snob reconfirmed.

7 If productive and reflective were mutually exclusive, in their minds, then my line of work was especially bewildering or pathetic, to them. Before an anti-drugs event, I ran into Ron, the big, bossy Republican from the Parent League. He teased me about whether I was "doing anything useful in life yet" or if I was still in college. That was the theme for his jokes all evening – though he himself had an advanced academic degree. Finally, I realized that he wanted me to tease back, to defend myself, so I said, in the same joking tone he used, "Well, I'm helping kids live a better life. You know, we get all those 18-year-olds and help them learn to think. You know, 'an unexamined life is not worth living,' and all that?" He joked back, "*They* should be out doing something productive, too!"

8 I also heard this at the country-western club, and indeed, few ballot measures passed. The moral is: if you want your measure to pass, word it so that a "no" means "yes" and you will win.

9 With this odd, jarring way of phrasing it, was the mayor alluding to the Biblical injunction to "see that your children understand these teachings, speak about them when you are settled at home, when at work in the world, when you lie down, and when you rise up, [etc.] . . . "? If so, the fact that the mayor's list is so curtailed amplifies my point, that he really did not imagine public discussion of important issues.

10 Sounds almost as painful as being "targeted," which is state agencies' current favored relation to black men, as in "this program targets black males."

11 In this and other oddly punctuated materials from interviews, I borrow some of

the useful notation originally developed by conversation analysts Sacks, Scheg-loff, and Jefferson (1974). The "=" sign refers to continuous utterances that latch onto one another without missing a beat but without interrupting, either.

12 This is an extreme illustration of Michael Mann's (1970) point about the effect of the US's lack of political parties on the country's political life. In a political world where every issue has to be considered separately and by separate individuals, it is impossible for everyday citizens to know where they stand.

13 This is not to say that there was no inequality in the 1800s in the US, since whole categories of humanity were not full citizens – slaves, women, Native Americans! In fact, maybe Americans' egalitarian speaking style was always tinged with an anxious, unspoken knowledge of inequality.

14 Of course, this is a more interaction-focused replay of the argument Habermas makes about the transformations of the public sphere (1974, 1989); see also Fish-kin (1991).

15 Versions of this critique have been made by numerous critics, from Jürgen Hab-ermas to Michel Foucault to Christopher Lasch. For an interesting, post-cutbacks discussion of this literature, see Davies and Schragge (1990).

16 Skolnick (1991) cites the statistic that "only" 30 percent of families now have no contact with kin or see kin less than once a month, to make the point that the American family is not in as bad a shape as critics think (p. 222). Whether 30 percent is high or not depends, I think, upon whether or not there are other stable, nearby adults firmly planted in children's lives for years and years at a time.

17 More Americans volunteered regularly at the beginning of the 1980s than toward the end (Brudney 1990), and the trend continues (Putnam 1996; Verba, Brady and Schlozman, 1995).

18 Arlene Kaplan Daniels (1988) studied upper-class women volunteers, and found them similarly devaluing their own work. She attributes their self-doubt and self-dismissal to internalized gender oppression. I would like to add a loop to her gender-based explanation: in American culture, unpaid work is considered "femi-nine" and soft, not tough and bottom-line, so that even when men volunteer, it is devalued, partly *because* it is unpaid, and it is unpaid for reasons much like the reasons childraising is unpaid.

19 I wondered whether this thought came to her because of a conversation she and I had had the night before, in which I asked where the groups talk about their purpose, their larger mission. It did not matter; the group culture was sturdy and firmly rejected the suggestion.

20 Theorists have delineated and questioned the boundaries between public and pri-vate (for example, Arendt 1958; Rieff 1966) and criticized these boundaries from a feminist perspective (for example, Fraser 1987; Elshtain 1981; Gamarnikov et al. 1983; Pateman 1988; Held 1989). But where people themselves draw the boundary, in practice, is an exciting question rarely explored (but see Hansen forthcoming; Sennett 1977).

21 Incidentally, the connection between expressing political concern and doing well in school were not just two connected symptoms of class differences; they varied quite apart from class.

22 Someone should write a history of the vocabulary used to described poor children. In the 1960s, they were "deprived" or "underprivileged," as if there was a wonderful world out there, if only the children could have access to it. In the 1980s, they were "at risk," as if there was a menacing world out there waiting for all children, but preying first on the most vulnerable. Along with that goes "prevention" (which teens should be prevented?) and "substance-free" (can we prevent all substances?).

3 "Close to home" and "for the children"

1 While none of us can make conscious the totality of our raw experience, we may inadvertently reveal bodily knowledge of some of it through slips, jokes, giggles, the speed and rhythm of our speech, even if we cannot make the knowledge verbal. For example, the naked ear rarely registers this kind of strenuous denial of a problem; it is usually observable only with a tape recorder. I sometimes did not feel I had a grasp on interviews until I transcribed them; then, I was startled by the poetry and music of everyday speech, the rhythms, evocative cadences, repetitions, even rhymes. It was as understandable as music as it was as speech. With this kind of speech, a gap briefly opens between what the speaker wants to believe and the vague perception of the world. The speaker does not overtly, explicitly close the door on the problem, but does, implicitly. Of course, conversation analysts and ethnomethodologists make this point, too. For more on the questions raised by ethnomethodology and conversation analysis, see chapter 9.

2 Her focus on it helped me decide to limit my study to that neck of the Sound – even though it meant ignoring a month's worth of my fieldwork notes from another area.

3 The volunteers were more likely than members of other groups to pick up certain vocabularies invented and disseminated by government officials, when the vocabularies fitted with their own approach. In this case, the language of "self-esteem," made popular by government officials and popular advice books and columns, made it easy to talk in terms that emphasized individual psychology over structure, and that fitted nicely with the volunteer ethos.

4 I did not interview him, since I was studying adults, and since there are special human subject protocols regarding children. But was it right of me even to have allowed him to stay in the room? Did he have nightmares?

5 Another related approach to citizen involvement says that Americans just want to be left alone, to sit in their backyards, play with their kids, and mind their own business. Richard Flacks (1988) and Herbert Gans (1988) both make this argument. It is compelling, but does not emphasize enough that people themselves know, on some level, that private life is constantly impinged on by social forces – and that this knowledge is a source of both anxiety and empathy.

6 Many others have noted that "preferences" are indeed not "fixed" or rated on one single standard; Amartya Sen (1977), for example, argues that each person has different, incommensurate modalities for ranking preferences.

7 Harry Frankfurt (1971) makes a similar point, when he says that the essence of human desire is that it is not just raw appetite, but culturally, morally determined "desires about desires" (as Albert Hirschman [1982] summarizes his article). What I am adding here is to show how people collectively shape those "desires about desires" in specific contexts; part of what forms those desires about desires is a group's moral efforts, that are different from individual moral efforts.

8 I borrow this phrase from Michael Schudson's (1984) description of the relationship between advertising and capitalism – advertising, he says, is capitalism's way of saying "I love you" to itself. Volunteering is to the common good as advertising is to capitalist profit-making.

4 Humor, nostalgia, and commercial culture

1 Arato (1981), for that reason, values this kind of public life even more than the more formal, instrumental kind.

2 In *Genealogy of Morals*, Nietzsche writes that the sovereign individual, "liberated again from morality of custom, autonomous and supramoral," is the final goal of moral history; editor Walter Kaufman notes that "when it was written, it must have struck most readers as paradoxical, but in the twentieth century it is apt to seem less paradoxical." The older view assumed that to be moral, one must be located in custom, mores, and good manners (1967 [1887]: 59).

3 For other versions of this "numbing" theory of humor, see Bergson (1914), Coser (1959) and in a way, Burawoy (1979).

4 This phrase no longer shocks the way it did even in 1981, when I first heard it. It jars people who are accustomed to thinking of "culture" as something whose production could not possibly be "industrial," but is basically sociable, interactive, traditional, human; part of what Habermas calls the "lifeworld," as opposed to the "system" of monetary exchange.

5 I observed several different subgroups of friends before settling into three. I will focus on only one of these – the one in which I participated most. The comparison case, the "cynics," were the third subgroup. Members of each subgroup sat near each other, greeted each other when they entered; the channels were open for talk, even if the lines were not full. Goffman calls this "being in a state of talk" (1981).

6 The dance classes, unlike the Buffalo Club as a whole, were open to both sexes; to become a Lady Buffalo, a woman needed a Buffalo husband.

7 "Why should I subject myself to making a fool of myself like that? Didn't I already survive eighth grade Physical Education class?" queried one Newton dweller when I invited him to come dance at the Silverado. Another, a professor, said I was brave to "go to a place like that," where there must be barroom brawls, and told me to "take care."

8 Edward T. Hall (1959) says that for all people to be able to take charge of their own governance, they need to learn to verbalize the way Basil Bernstein's middle-class people did (1970). But perhaps some societies are settled and rooted enough to be able to leave more unsaid than that.

9 Some feminist scholars say that this puzzling is the peculiar province of women, who are often in a role similar to that of a fieldworker: appreciative, quiet and understanding, adept at deciphering minimal signals, good followers, listeners (Reinharz 1983). An ideal study of this setting would have been conducted by a woman and a man team that could hear both genders' single-sex conversations.

10 This gathering forcefully demonstrated to me the attraction of the "strong silent type." Men like Doug remained silent, possibly aloof, during this teasing session, and thus the others could suspect that the silent men were deeper than the loud ones. And there would have been no way for the silent men to engage in the conversation without appearing argumentative or foolish.

11 Some scholars ascribe almost no force to the private intentions of whites, saying that what really matters is how their actions objectively reproduce racial oppression, as they buy the house in one neighborhood and not another, pick one school and not another, locate a business in one part of town and not another. David Wellman (1977), for example, trashes one of his interviewees for being a well-meaning do-gooder. Despite her own self-understanding as a person who works on projects that she thinks will help end racial antagonism, Wellman says that she really is racist, because she unwittingly maintains her own structural position on top of blacks in the economic hierarchy.

12 This chapter complements statistical studies of the "gender gap," by showing what one could call "the gender gap in practice." Usually, I could observe only women's backstage conversations. Someone might wonder if the difference between the backstage and frontstage conversations I could witness was simply a difference between women and men, or an all-women's group and a mixed group. It is true that cross-sex conversation was especially difficult in the country-western clubs. Men and women often have little to discuss, since their lives are so differ-ent, as researchers from Mirra Komarovsky (1962) to Lillian Rubin (1976) note. But gender does not explain all the differences I noticed; at the Buffalo, single-sex groups also often sat in silence, too. Parents also often sat in silence with children.

Men and women in the volunteer and activist groups I studied did not have the same lack of common ground. The difference was that in the country-western clubs, unlike in the other groups, members shared no common project that could help make their conversations seem less a reflection on the speakers' particular basic self; participating in volunteer and activist groups took the focus off the speakers and put it more on the project, the group, the common concerns. At the Buffalo, in contrast, the topics that members themselves considered most import-ant were not discussable. What was intimate was what really mattered to members, but that was too private to discuss in a group; and there was little public or shared grist for conversation that participants considered interesting.

Still, probably men were more racist and "rebellious" in their backstage settings than women were in theirs. In mixed company, the fierce joking and its complemen-tary silence fell somewhat along gender lines: most (but not all) men were eager to appear casual and unconstrained, while most (but not all) women were much less eager to appear totally relaxed and boisterous, and more eager to rely on that unspoken "community feeling" – for example, Jody did all the work of making her wedding publicly meaningful, and Betsy was the one who kept the wheels of sociability going in group activities. But women's participation was not as valued as men's; the men's mandatory casualness held more sway than the women's hugging intimacy. Men usually controlled the nature of the "stage"; for example, men could use racist joking to silence women, but I never heard it work the other way around. Thus, men had more say in determining how both men and women could contribute to the group context. The context devalued their already ambivalent desires for community, warmth, stability, decorum, respectfulness. The vast and contradictory literature on gender and language similarly shows that even when women talk more than men, men can still control the conversation by controlling what is taken to be an appropriate style of participation (Eliasoph 1987; Tannen 1990: chapter 8).

In his chapter on backstage and frontstage, Goffman quotes at length from a study called *Wartime Shipyard*, by Katherine Archibald (1945), done, coincidentally, in a city next door to Amargo, in the 1940s:

> In their ordinary relationships with women workers most of the men were courteous and even gallant. As the women infiltrated the hulls and the remoter shacks of the yard, the men amiably removed their galleries of nudes and pornography from the walls and retired them to the gloom of the tool box. In deference to the presence of "ladies," manners were improved, faces were shaved more often, and language was toned down . . . I have often seen men who wanted to use strong language, and with good excuse for it, flush with sudden embarrassment and drop their voices to a mutter on becoming conscious of a feminine audience. In the lunchtime companionship of men and women workers and in the casual chat at any leisure moment, in all that pertained to familiar social contacts, even amid the unfamiliar surroundings of the shipyard, the men preserved almost intact the pattern of behavior which they practiced at home: the respect for the decent wife and the good mother, the circumspect friendliness with the sister, and even the protective affection for the inexperienced daughter of the family.   (16–17, quoted in Goffman 1959: 131)

The difference between what she heard and what I heard could not be starker. Now, nobody's treated like a lady. Archibald notes that the men who corrected their foul language in the presence of the ladies seethed at the thought that they had to work side by side with them. Maybe the purposive crudeness of the men at the Buffalo was a bit more egalitarian and possibly even respectful of the women, since it did not hide anything from them. But, men clearly have retaken control of the frontstage. The lack of gallantry at the Buffalo was a male initiative (Barbara Ehrenreich [1983] argues that in the past thirty years, it has dawned on many American men that they could discard the restraints of family and marriage, and just be free-floating "rebels" who did not have to help care for children and women. Some might blame feminism for this, saying that women no longer wanted "their doors held and their cigarettes lighted" – the refrain Ehrenreich heard in reference to feminism – but in fact, women country-westerners would have enjoyed those favors. And since they made so much less money than the men, it could have seemed fair for the men to pay for drinks). What the lack of gallantry revealed was not very nice, and maybe this lack of common courtesy made its way into national political discourse; perhaps the change in manners has helped make *public life* less charitable and gallant, and more mean-spirited and violent now than in the past.

13 Other studies of the informal working-class public sphere (Halle 1984; LeMasters 1975) show a premium placed on jokes, one-liners and unequivocal speech (though the authors of these field studies do not themselves draw out this aspect of members' speech).

14 This contrasts to the "spiral of silence" of the sort Noelle-Neuman (1984) discusses, in which people who believe themselves to be in the minority are silent about their opinions for fear of antagonizing the majority.

15 There was a clear formula for treating the rare moments when a topic that could be taken as "serious" arose. It went: a person said something that could be taken as serious. The next thing said had to be a joke: rarely a joke on the topic, but most often, a joke on the speaker herself or himself. The next thing said had to be an even bigger joke that topped off the previous joke. So the pattern was: serious comment, joke on the speaker, bigger joke. If anyone was ever serious in the group context, the two jokes in a row would vanquish that illusion.

16 By extending themselves into the community, and taking the cultivation of a whole working-class culture as their mission, the Knights were able to unify disparate workers, skilled and unskilled, immigrant and anglo, that other unions left divided (Voss, 1988).

17 See Robert Wuthnow's analysis of grab-bags (1991), based on Bronislaw Malinowski's earlier analysis of gift-exchanges in the South Pacific.

18 Halle says that American collective representations tend to be "apolitical" and "trivial" because there is so little consensus about what being an American means. This would be a good argument but his evidence shows Americans who did not know whether they agreed or disagreed – citizenship seemed mostly irrelevant to the workers he studied. The emptiness of the rituals is not just an effect of the lack of consensus, as he says, but also a cause.

19 The institutions are not always traditional religious ones. After the French Revolution, weddings were held in halls dedicated to the ideal of Reason. In the early Soviet Union, weddings were held in communist wedding halls that celebrated the proletarian revolution, decorated with hammers and sickles. Later, as ebullience faded, hearts and flowers replaced hammers and sickles. Thanks to Mark Saroyan for this point.

20 A question that would have hit closer to home would have been whether I would be "making" honor or status from it, but that was not in his mind, since honor requires a community and a set of common standards to bestow it.

21 In other words, country-western clubs were what Bellah et al. (1985) call lifestyle enclaves; but most members ambivalently wanted more from them than just shared taste.

22 Bourdieu (1984) talks about "misrecognition"; that is, that people do not recognize the social origins of their own tastes and preferences. "Misrepresentation" analyzes the same process on the level of group practices, rather than of individual consciousness.

23 The fact that the "country-western" identity was born in urban, commercial music studios does not, in itself, make this culture less "real." For hundreds of years, all around the world, "imagined" communities (Anderson 1991) and "invented traditions" (Hobsbawm and Ranger 1983) have provided the basis of "real" identities; the cultural symbols that seem the most authentic and homespun turn out to have been invented – the "traditional" Scotch plaid kilt, for example, was invented by a British industrialist (Trevor-Roper 1983), and yet inspired great nationalist loyalty. Country-western culture itself was invented in Los Angeles, by dustbowl immigrants from the South; the music helped them form a shared identity (Gregory 1989). By the 1970s, listening to country music was a way of marking white working-class identity (Peterson and DiMaggio 1975). In large-scale communities, such symbolism has been a constant. The problem is, after we use these goods and symbols to establish commonality, we have to go on, because these images do not, in themselves, tell us how to act, how to make a joke, how to know when we are being tactful or rude.

24 Taylor (1989) and MacIntyre (1981), for example, argue for the importance of "moral narratives." This is a rather different proposition from the bloodless project of rational discourse set out by a modernist like Habermas. It relies less on abstract, disembodied reasoning and more on the sense of rootedness and common culture that the sociable public could offer. Bellah et al. (1991) weigh in on this debate, arbitrating in interesting ways between these two approaches.

25 For an excellent review of social research on humor, see Michael Mulkay's *On Humor* (1988) on which I am leaning in my own account; see also Morreall (1983); for the classic account of the "anesthetizing" side of humor, Bergson (1914).

26 Part of the contemporary distaste for critical theorists comes from a misinterpretation of their insights. Many essays cast critical theorists in the same mold as American critics of "lowbrow" culture (such as Dwight MacDonald, and others in, e.g., Rosenberg and White 1957), saying that Adorno and Horkheimer simply said that mass culture was stupefying and pacifying. In fact, the critical theorists presumed a more active listener than the American mass culture critics did. Unlike the scorned "lowbrow" Babbits of "mass culture" derided by MacDonald, critical theorists' monads actively created political and cultural passivity; their monads *do* have an inner life, but it is twisted.

27 Katz (1988) makes the same point, focusing on the socially integrated people, not the isolated ones; John B. Thompson (1990) makes a similar point on a theoretical level.

28 Similarly, for theorists – Baudrillard (1981, 1983, 1988), for example – "silence" and laughter offer the only true resistance against the flood of meanings thrown at us; even coherent subversion of domination plays along with the game offered

by dead, rule-bound, commodified culture: "But what does this 'subversive' reading actually amount to? Is it still a reading, that is a deciphering, a disengaging of a univocal meaning? And what is this code that opposes? . . . is it yet another controlling schema of interpretation, rising from the ashes of the previous one?" (1981: 183). Ultimate liberation is to "smash the code" (1981) and float in a sea of ambiguity, ironic detachment, meaninglessness: in a culture in which money measures everything, the only true liberation is that which refuses to be systematized or coherent, that rejects coherent meaning altogether (1988). Rather than trying to create shared meanings, we should not even try to find "community" in an incoherent world, these scholars say; the reality of contemporary society is that it does not all fit together into a coherent whole, and any attempt to tell ourselves that it does is self-deceptive and destructive: when people try too hard to be systematic, the result is Ceauşescu's Romania, or Nazi Germany. The problem with this line of theorizing is that resistance like the Buffaloes' relied on constant reference to an unspoken dominant set of meanings that Buffaloes imported from outside their own meaning-making contexts.

29 It is thus not surprising that country music appeals to exactly the same constituents that presidential candidates have wooed in all late-century elections: the white, suburban middle class (Feiler 1996). This genre's popularity became clear only in the early 1990s, when computer scanners of the sales of recordings replaced salespeople's estimates in measuring what sells. After all these years of store clerks' undercounting country music sales, computers revealed that country was the best-selling genre in America (*Newsweek* 1991). When the news came out about the computer scanners' discovery of country music's popularity, sudden "newsflashes" began beaming out on the regional country music station, announcing, "President Bush has a stereo built into his desk so he can listen to country-western music up close whenever he wants" (September 17, 1991), and affirming that country music was Bush's favorite. Presidential candidate Ross Perot played Patsy Cline in the 1992 election.

5 Creating ignorance and memorizing facts

1 The question comes from Verba, Nie, and Kim's (1985) study.

2 In a Neighborhood Watch group, police hold a meeting to introduce neighbors to each other; once the neighbors recognize each other's faces – which they might not otherwise do in many car-centered, pedestrian-less suburbs – they can tell when a stranger is entering the neighborhood and call the police.

3 Men usually focused on protesters' ignorance, while women usually focused on their own ignorance. In either case, the prime consideration was knowledge, but the women's focus silenced them more completely than the men's.

4 A book charmingly titled *A Just World: A Fundamental Delusion* (Lerner 1980) (and other experiments examining the "just world" phenomenon) shows that in experiment after experiment, Americans try very hard to find a reason to blame the victims for problems that befall them. This helps people preserve the illusion

that the world makes sense. This explanation makes more sense for the volunteers than the private people, who more often simply try to keep "the world" as far away as possible, not trying on a daily basis to tell themselves that it makes sense. And it makes sense more for Americans than for other people, with other political ideologies, because Americans like the volunteers want to preserve a set of empowering beliefs about their political system.

5 Bruce Williams (Press and Williams 1992) compared audiences' reception of news programs and sit-coms on political themes, and found that audiences were more willing to speak up after having seen, for example, a sit-com dealing with the question of apartheid than after having seen a news report on the topic.

6 Surveys confirm that political sophistication is not just an effect of class, but is also an effect of membership in civic life (Verba and Nie 1978; Neuman 1986; Verba, Schlozman and Brady 1995). What can happen inside that black box of group life, that can make members of citizens' groups more politically engaged? Ignorance is a scar, constantly rebroken or mended in everyday interactions. For more of my argument against the idea that being a member of the working class inevitably makes one "authoritarian" or politically unsophisticated, see the section in my appendix on class.

7 See Jay Rosen (1987), for some startling data on what Americans don't know; on what would happen if the "don't knows" were reported in polls; and on how vast Americans' ignorance about basic political issues is. A huge literature documents Americans' political ignorance – the classic study is by Philip Converse (1964).

8 He cites Anthony Downs, Samuel Popkin, and other rational choice theorists to affirm his point.

9 Some theorists call this "proxy voting," equating it with a wife's voting as her husband commands, treating it as a violation of the democratic ideal of personal independence. But selecting an *organization* in which to locate oneself is different from being bossed around by a husband in the voting booth. Being a member of a union, or of a real, issue-based party, or being a loyal subscriber to a party-based newspaper, can do more than give a voter a "crib sheet" to take to the polls, as theorists label proxy voting.

6 Strenuous disengagement and cynical chic solidarity

1 This conversation took place before these recreation group participants knew many details about my research. I had told them I was studying "community involvement, and what people do in their spare time," so they did not stage this conversation as a cooperative response to their image of my research agenda.

2 See Charles Taylor (1989) for a discussion of these paired problems associated with the illusion of total freedom.

7 Activists carving out a place in the public sphere for discussion

1 The idea that "the people" should be shown in deeds the rebellion that they are too afraid to say in words is also in the philosophy of Peru's violent guerrilla

group, Sendero Luminoso (Shining Path), taken in part from Regis Debray's *Revolution in the Revolution?* (1967). There is a tension, explicit in many groups that engage in such "direct action," about whether the main goal is *really* to shut down the objectionable institution, or to sway public opinion indirectly, through media exposure, or to get people directly involved in the democratic processes of the activist groups themselves, which are themselves conceived of as mini-utopian communities (Darnovsky 1990; Epstein 1991). At Evergreen Island, I heard all three reasons for demonstrating.

2 Richard Sennet (1977) noticed the same treatment, in coverage of speakers and demogogues in the nineteenth century, in which the public was entreated to admire a speaker simply for his "authenticity" – his insistence on standing up for what he believed in – and not pay much attention to his position. Sennet says this was an important step in what he calls "the fall of public man."

3 Alvin Gouldner (1973) warns social observers not to pit the underdogs – in this case, the activists and volunteers – against the "middle dogs" – local and county health, fire, police, and city officials and social workers. The real "overdogs" were far away, in Washington, Montgomery Corporation headquarters, and the state capital, making it clear which kinds of issues can be treated in a polite way and which ones should be condemned as conflictual and "big." My point is that even the overdogs and middle dogs have a culture.

4 Diane presents a more nuanced appreciation of the place of bureaucracy than scholars like Piven and Cloward (1979) who favor only "radical" participation. Clearly Piven and Cloward were only referring to the kind of participation they liked, not, for example, "radical" participation from people who want to keep blacks out of public schools, give a death sentence to drug dealers, or a gun to every citizen. For those "radicals," the authors would probably *like* some aspects of the rule of law. Furthermore, activists reasoned that "radical" style is sometimes unappealing to the audience. There is no single good genre of decision-making in a democracy, but a mix that depends on the time and place.

5 In not having a forum in which political discussion is the legitimate mode of talk, CESE shared the plight of other social movement groups that address technological issues. For example, the anti-nuclear-power movement of the 1970s and 1980s did not have to rely so heavily on the photos of the three-legged calves after the accident at Three Mile Island or the scary and ominous predictions of impossible evacuations. Many anti-nuclear activists objected to nuclear power on political grounds, arguing that nuclear power would not have been profitable in a political economy that forced companies to bear the real cost of free raw materials like water and air; to pay the costs of health care to cure the problems caused by nuclear power; and to pay for adequate processing of wastes. They argued that nuclear power was profitable only because the government paid for nuclear weapons production materials, which revolved in and out of power plants around the world. Without this unsavory political arrangement, they said, nuclear power would not have existed. Yet their public cases against it were usually couched in the language of fear. The language of fear, of personal self-interest, is not just

simpler, it is more legitimate than the language of public-spirited political analysis. But it is less educational.

6 Activists suspected that officials often simply hid inconvenient facts. In hearings on a government-sponsored nuclear power plant in Britain, Ray Kemp (1985) found similarly "systematically distorted communication" (Habermas 1979): there was no way for citizens who opposed the plant to match the government-sponsored research funding of proponents, and the government refused to divulge much information to citizens altogether, citing "security risks."

7 The discussion here parallels one in the realm of moral theory. Alasdair MacIntyre, for example, proposes that absolute relativism in moral theory goes hand in hand with the illusion of total objectivity (1981). As Bellah et al. put it in *Habits of the Heart* (1985), discussing the symbiotic relationship in workplaces between psychotherapeutic management techniques (where managers try to help employees feel good inside) and bureaucratic neutrality (where managers simply tell the employees to follow the rules): "both conclude that there is no moral common ground and therefore no public relevance of morality outside the sphere of minimal procedural rules and obligations not to injure" (1985: 141).

8 Newspapers in the cycle of political evaporation

1 I read every article in twelve days' worth of papers, varying the month, day of the week and year. Each of the twelve days was in a different month; each day of the week was represented in the sample, and one of the days was in a different year from the others. I also read two issues of the *Amargo Herald* on two of the days in the sample (in addition to the Evergreen County *Times*). I had planned on a larger sample, but the pattern was so overwhelming after just a few issues, I did not need a larger set.

2 The people portrayed here were certainly not alone in honoring technical, scientific knowledge over political and historical knowledge, as necessities for political understanding. For example, during the 1991 war against Iraq, Americans were ignorant about the most basic facts of Middle Eastern politics and US foreign relations. Seventy-four percent thought that the US had threatened Iraq with sanctions before it invaded Kuwait; only 13 percent correctly guessed that the US had told Iraq the month before the invasion that it would take no action. Fifteen percent knew what the intifada, the Palestinian protest again the Israeli occupation, was. Considering this frightening dearth of political knowledge, it is peculiar that 81 percent of Americans knew that the missile used to shoot down Israeli Scuds was called the Patriot. The researchers who conducted this survey concluded, "Even after controlling for all other variables, we discovered that the correlation between TV watching and knowledge was actually a negative one. Overall, the more TV people watched, the less they knew. The only fact that did not fit in with this pattern was the ability to identify the Patriot missile" (Lewis, Jhally, and Morgan 1991). Probably, reading local news is not very different from watching TV.

3 Putting the problem this way shows that the narrative forms that put more weight on opposing interpretations, and less weight on the journalist's own narrative, make for more analytically rich news, news that can invoke more varied voices (see Hallin and Mancini [1985] for a comparison of reporter-centered US news forms and political party-centered Italian news forms – in the Italian case, the parties, instead of the reporter, provide the analysis).

4 Hamilton (1988) contends that it would be very easy for local reporters to draw the connection between "Main Street and the Third World," as he puts it, between the local and the global. But I add that that *debate* is what is missing, more than neutral, *World Book Encyclopedia*-style "education."

5 Sociologists and reporters share this problem. Bennett Berger (1981) poignantly writes about the difficulty of finding a sympathetic but analytical "voice" when writing up a fieldwork study. One does not want to cheerlead, but social research's usual analytic tone is slightly snide, working to provide the "inside dope," to demystify and unmask the strange customs of "weird natives."

9 The evaporation of politics in the US public sphere

1 There is no universal definition for "formal" speech; different societies enact formality in different ways depending on the ways that contexts defined by participants as "formal" fit into a larger cultural system (Irvine, 1979).

2 Some of the best examples are Reinarman 1987; Croteau 1995; J. Hochschild 1981; Hart 1992; Lane 1962. Croteau's book cites a vivid and hilarious four-page (184–7) conversation between workers in the factory he studied. The rest of the book is not about interaction *per se*; the other interactions he describes are question-and-answer sessions, between him and workers.

3 Another study that takes seriously the idea that imagining different contexts inspires different kinds of talk enlists teenage girls to write their own "advice columns," and notes that *when writing their own advice columns*, the girls took on the same breezy, Pollyanna-ish tone as teen magazine advice columnists, despite the girls' own criticisms of that tone (Frazer 1989). See also Wuthnow's ingenious study (1991), in which he asked interviewees to retell the tale of the Good Samaritan, and then analyzed what institutional contexts interviewees took for granted in their retellings of the tale.

4 As noted earlier, the original definitions of "hegemony" were highly contextual, but now, many researchers (Morley 1980, for example) who think they are studying "hegemony" are actually studying either ideological domination or what Gramsci would have called "common sense." For a similar point to this one arguing that "hegemony" should "not be used interchangeably with 'ideological manipulation,' " see Geoff Eley's discussion of Raymond Williams' and Gramsci's uses of the term. He says, rightly, that Gramsci used the term to mean something much more "contingent," and less "totalitarian" than most researchers do (in other words, it is better thought of as an activity than a static object): "[Gramsci] expressly links hegemony to a domain of public life (which he calls 'civil

society,' but which might also be called the 'public sphere') [Eley's parenthesis] that is relatively independent of such controls and hence makes its achievement a far more contingent process'' (1992: 323).

5 Referring to *The Un-Politics of Air Pollution: A Study of Non-Decisionmaking in the Cities* (Crenson 1971) as an example of a good study of power, Steven Lukes declares that "other things being equal, people would rather not be poisoned" (1974: 45). But each time he says that, he slips a crucial distinction in parentheses behind it, saying, "(assuming, in particular, that pollution control does not necessarily mean unemployment)" (on page 45, and again, in almost identical words on the next page). The problem with this formulation is that "other things" are never "equal." Short of death, problems are not universally recognizable, but have to be defined socially, in interaction (and sometimes people define even death as the greatest good, as in heroic death in battle). Paradoxically, without a focus on talk, and without the insight that talk is itself patterned culturally, Lukes' faith that an ultimate, bottom-line interest should transparently reveal itself becomes yet another "inner" approach that he assumes magically resonates with a big "outer" world.

6 This idea has several different long histories: one comes from John Dewey (1927), George Herbert Mead (1964 [1934]) and other American pragmatists. Another comes from Lev Vygotsky (1962).

7 In the process of becoming feminist activists, for example, a group of women can transform feelings of personal inadequacy and insecurity to feelings of political indignation and anger (Wasielewski 1989) – they have to override the usual interpretation they gave to their feelings – their feeling rules. In contrast to this approach, that assumes that political engagement is hard to avoid, many researchers assume that engagement needs explaining and apathy comes naturally. This approach was especially popular in the 1950s and 1960s, when political activism was considered a form of deviance. See, for example, Kenneth Keniston (1960).

8 There are, of course, differences between the two concepts, too. Bourdieu's works more automatically than Hochschild's; his works less actively and more as a shared habit developed over decades; his is less an individual "strategy" and more a culture than hers. So, "habitus" is closer to what I am describing here. But his concept lacks attention to context. True, in *Ce que parler veut dire* he talks about contexts, but only to analyze who controls them. As Rosaldo argues (1982), the study of speech must examine meaning apart from individual intentions. For a study of public life that devotes itself to shared meanings, shared assumptions, and processes of active "intersubjectivity," focusing on subjective intention misses the point.

9 Thus, Bourdieu (1985) and Laurent Thevenot (1987) both show that working-class people are less likely to assume that they have the knowledge necessary for participation, even when they *do* have the knowledge, and even when their knowledge is superior to an elite person's knowledge.

10 In different ways, Garfinkel, Schegloff, and Cicourel all advise an extremely close focus on the procedures by which people give order to their conversations, such

as how they know when to take a turn at talking, how they know how to end a turn, how they know how to question an inaudible or incomprehensible phrase. This is an interesting level of contextual analysis, but I am taking a different approach to the question of what defines a context. Going around with a microphone and tape recorder would have so deeply changed members' assumptions about the meanings of the contexts themselves, I could not focus on microscopic questions, that can be captured only on tape. When I *did* want the taping itself to be part of the nature of the setting (in interviews), I brought an absolutely giant phallus of a microphone, with a twenty-foot coil of heavy-gauge cord. Just in case people forgot, I fiddled with the microphone a lot, too! That way, I could be fairly sure we all knew exactly what the context was: a taped interview.

11 This point follows through on suggestions offered by a range of sociological theories, nicely reviewed by William Sewell, Jr., that "see . . . agency not as opposed to, but as constituent of, structure" (1992: 20).

12 For more on Scott's work and other "resistance" theories, see Eliasoph (1996) and chapter 2.

13 This kind of "private–public" existed in the former East Germany (Wilpert 1994) and Czechoslovakia (Havel 1989) – circles of friends who passionately talk politics around the kitchen table but *could not* enter a public forum for fear of imprisonment, assassination, or demotion at work. In those cases, the vibrant "private–public" was bursting with secret, subterranean political vigor; but, in contrast with the groups described in this book, participants *felt* repressed, and were conscious of hiding their subversive ideas. Ironically, according to sociologist Wilpert, when the lid comes off, when these societies become less overtly repressive, and people do have the opportunity to regain public space, both public and private space might be taken over by the market – commercial media, consumerism, overtime work to pay for new commodities. Wilpert says that ctizens in the former East Germany no longer assume that the private sphere is the realm of freedom in which all ideas are ripe for discussion, and so, this "private–public" is withering. At the same time, no equally vibrant public sphere is developing to replace the once vibrant kitchen table talk.

14 As Bellah et al. say (1985), all Americans say, "Get involved!" but grow vague when it comes to the particulars of this "involvement."

15 Alisdair MacIntyre (1981) aptly illustrates the problems with this simulacrum community. Imagine, he says, a world in which a natural disaster has destroyed all scientific knowledge except for a few torn scraps from various scientific articles. Suppose that many years later, leaders tried to resurrect science – it would be impossible. MacIntyre says that is what has happened with our language for talking about morality; we still have scattered words, phrases, and concepts, but the whole way of life, the sinews, ligaments, and cartilage that held the words together and made them move are gone. To most people, the skeleton seems inapplicable to everyday life. Perhaps the same has happened to "community" (though not as completely as MacIntyre's post-holocaust image suggests). Everyone talked about "community," and "family," but few talked about how to fill

in the blanks that could invent a sense of togetherness that would make sense in the contemporary, global world.

16 Myerhoff completely depoliticizes their love of debate, describing it instead as simply a cultural style. Marc Kaminsky also criticizes her work for this (1992).

17 Studies in the ethnography of communication (Basso 1979; Heath 1983; Hymes 1972; Philipsen 1992, for some examples) usually focus on traditional, stable settings, in which styles of talk or politeness (Brown and Levinson 1978) have sedimented for many years, or seem to map one-to-one onto a seemingly ascribed status like race or gender. These studies often leave "social structure" underanalyzed, and assume that members take for granted a "speech community" of the sort that rarely exists any more – or perhaps, as ethnomethodologists would argue, never did. Much recent work focuses on the ways speakers negotiate clashes between two cultures' different, clearly distinct speech styles – an American one that emphasizes back-slapping familiarity and a Chinese one that emphasizes respectful distance, for example (Young 1985; or see the essays collected in Gonzalez, Houston, and Chen 1994). Deborah Tannen's popular books on gender differences are good examples of this genre. Similarly, in Rosaldo's study, two clearly distinct, geographically separate, longstanding communities clashed; speech patterns could easily be traced to radically different institutions that enter from outside of a traditional society – in contemporary American society, both the cultural differences and the institutional differences are more complex. I hope that I have shown that focusing on cultural traditions and focusing on political institutions are not mutually exclusive; speech patterns neither mindlessly reproduce past traditions, nor do they simply respond mechanically to political institutions (Lichterman 1996). Focusing on both simultaneously is necessary (thus blending Burawoy's "extended case method" with an "interpretive case method").

18 I say "his" because the model assumes a person who is not fundamentally, always, centrally attached to others – children, perhaps, or loved ones. The model does not *primarily* imagine an actor whose "preference" is, above all, safety and happiness for the other person. Imagine calling the theories "rational actress models" and we see how jarring it sounds – "actresses" are never rational, but always exist in a tightly woven net of relationships and expectations. So do most "actors."

19 These theorists have added on so many extra loops to their ideas, they can describe almost anything as a rational, self-interested choice. Medieval scholars tried to preserve the Ptolemaic image of the earth as the center of the universe by adding backwards cycles and loops onto planets' paths, to "explain" their anomalous astronomical observations in Ptolemy's earth-centered terms. Similarly, these scholars can preserve the central conceptual nugget of the self-interested actor only by adding extra cycles and rings onto their theory until the "exceptions" outweigh the "rule." Then, the only problem is that they have a non-social theory of the construction of the individual and of society, surrounded by a sea of exceptions and anomalies. As Bellah et al. remark (1991: 290, fn. 3), such utilitarian

ideas are so deeply rooted in American culture, they die hard, even among sociologists.

20 Of course, Coleman (1990) has a residual category for this, saying first that some action is "expressive," not "rational" and then later saying that for many people, feeling good about themselves (by doing good deeds) offers a self-interested "benefit"; but, see the note above.

21 Critics of rational choice theory like Amitai Etzioni (1988) have made the point that no one can possibly have all the information necessary to make a decision that takes all the possible options into account, since that would entail "shopping" all day to make every decision. My point goes a bit farther though, since I am saying that some people cannot imagine one "choice" – political involvement.

22 As Alberto Melucci says, the state structures much of our experience before we can even start to develop needs and desires (1989: 170). He advocates research along the lines conducted here, saying that "Democracy in complex societies requires conditions which . . . enhanc[e] the recognition and autonomy of individual and collective signifying processes" (this is the message of Durkheim's *Division of Labor* as well).

23 Albert O. Hirschman neatly names three metaphoric responses to discontent in his book *Exit, Voice, and Loyalty: Responses to Decline in Firms, Organizations, and States.* "Exit" was the option the recreation groups *tried*: all spoke of moving out to the country. Betsy, for example, talked about moving to Colorado if Amargo got too crowded. But simply striking out for the frontier and "leaving the rest of society to take care of itself," as de Tocqueville put it, is no longer possible, and never was, so recreation group members had to work hard at adjusting their desire for "exit" to the impossibility of exiting from contemporary society. "Exit" required great effort of a sort untheorized by Hirschman, and was ultimately impossible.

Volunteers were what Hirschman calls "loyalists," low-level insiders, who considered criticism disloyal, and tried to convince themselves that nothing was really so bad. Of the loyalist, Hirschman says "one must be happy . . . This is illustrated in a story about two immigrants from Germany meeting for the first time after many years in New York. One asks the other: 'Are you happy here?' Reply: 'I am happy, aber glücklich bin ich nicht [but happy I am not]'" (1970: 113). For this immigrant, like the volunteer, *discontent is unsayable* in the American idiom. The sayable, in turn, helps shape the thinkable.

Hirschman recognizes that being a political "loyalist" takes enormous amounts of emotion work, but misses that dimension for the other two stances. His concept of easy "exit," in fact, makes sense only for "firms" and "organizations," but not states. He also misses the contextual nature of these three modes of participation; the three modes make sense in real-life *contexts*, rarely as abstract, cross-contextual values or personality-types adhering to individuals.

24 Of course, just a few years after all these diagnoses pronounced all well in the early 1960s, political discontent erupted, showing that beneath the placidity lay some less mild doubts.

25 Theories like Mills' "vocabularies of motive," and Swidler's "culture as a tool-box" (1986), Quinn and Holland's "cultural models" (1987), Lakoff's "schemata" (1987), and Schutz' "typifications" (1967 [1932]) reverse the causality of the "values" approach. In other words, Mills, Swidler, etc., say that the vocabularies, tools, etc. cause the thoughts. I offer a third model, in which neither "values" nor "tools" come first. Rather, as John Gumperz (1989) puts it, "the processes through which cultural and other types of background knowledge are brought into the interpretive processes" work simultaneously as tools and values, processes and products.

26 Similarly, William Gamson tries to unearth culturally shared methods of talking politics by conducting focus groups. Explaining his use of focus groups as stand-ins for more typical settings, he says that all settings are artificial: focus groups, he says, do not occur without some researcher contriving to gather a group, but "work-based interactions do not occur either without some employer who contrives to bring people together to do a job" (1992: 19). While I agree that all settings are the work of human artifice, I would rather examine the "contrived" settings that occur every day, in the usual course of a person's life, than say that all interactions are equally "contrived." Focus group research cannot ask what citizens assume the real-life contexts of public life are for – what the very act of speaking itself means to them – because the researchers themselves create the context: a research interview. Focus group research cannot reveal any persistent, patterned shifts in discourse from one setting to another, because it examines only one setting: a research interview.

27 As Chantal Mouffe suggests (1992), the process of analyzing and questioning these definitions will never end and never should – ideally, that is what citizenship *is*.

28 A musical rendition of this pattern might be the Passover song, "Dayenu":

> If the Eternal One had brought us forth from Egypt, and had not inflicted judgment upon the Egyptians, it would have been enough.
> If the Eternal One had brought us forth from Egypt, and had inflicted judgment upon the Egyptians, and had not bestowed their wealth on us, it would have been enough.
> If the Eternal One had given us their wealth, and had brought us forth from Egypt, and had inflicted judgment upon the Egyptians, and had not divided the sea for us, it would have been enough [etc.].

(as written in Passover–Ramadan Liberation Seder,
no attribution, anonymous, no date)

Any step might have been "enough." Another rendition might be "There Was an Old Lady Who Swallowed a Fly" (" . . . she swallowed the cow to scare the cat, she swallowed the cat to catch the bird, she swallowed the bird to eat the spider, she swallowed the spider to eat the fly, I don't know why she swallowed a fly, perhaps she'll die . . ." The last verse goes, "There was an old lady, who swallowed a horse, she died, of course." The horse would be the first dimension of power, but any of the other animals would have made her pretty sick anyway.

29 These ways of talking then must filter back into consciousness; for example, when I was a member of a women's disarmament group in the early 1980s, we spoke as "Moms" so often, we began to forget our other reasons for political involvement. It became more and more difficult to formulate a sense of ourselves and our group as having a larger, publicly minded agenda; political evaporation in public affects conversation in private as well.

30 For example, "transformative" public interest legal theorists (Trubek 1993, for example) discuss the importance of organizing clients, politicizing public interest legal work, strategizing to take on cases that will set important precedents; in the US, social service workers' interest in the political aspect of their work appeared to have petered out after a brief burst of "radical social work" in the 1970s (see the pages of the social work journal *The Catalyst*, for example, or speeches from early 1970s social work conferences – though even there, the "politics" in social work was seen as working mainly through personal transformation, personal rebellion, and freedom).

31 By so often taking proclamations of self-interest at face value, many left-wing grassroots organizers have been delinquent in providing a language other than self-interest to local groups. In fact, some scholars and groups elevate "self-interest" to a populist moral principle of solidarity-building. This approach made sense only when speaking of the universal working class in Marxian theory, whose "interest" was supposed to be everybody's interest as more and more people became dispossessed of means of production – became workers. This leftover, unquestioned bit of theory valorizing self-interest carries over into Harry Boyte's laudatory conceptions of "backyard politics," for example, or into research that cheers for groups agitating for stop-signs on their blocks (see Delgado 1986).

Appendix 1 Class in the public sphere

1 James Coleman says that we need to understand how people form institutions (1989). This book is thoroughly in line with that suggestion, but Coleman starts his conceptualization with the image of the autonomous individual, not the society into which he or she is born, thus missing the fundamental insight of sociological thought. He does not seriously complete the micro–macro–micro loop, since he does not take seriously the idea that the group creates the individual, as well as the other way around.

2 Many researchers have since disconfirmed this image, showing, for example, that in Nazi Germany, workers were less extremist than the middle class, and had only followed the lead of the extremist middle classes.

Appendix 2 Method

1 Arlene Kaplan Daniels (1967) offers a similar discussion, in her essay on being a "low-caste stranger," studying high-ranking military officers, to whom she was

supposed to feel superior, but who simultaneously felt superior to her, on another scale.

2 Despite this effort at informing my "subjects," I think that almost no one portrayed in most fieldwork studies *really* understands what the researcher is doing. Any academic with non-academic friends, relatives, or acquaintances knows how difficult it is to explain to them what academics do all day, what a dissertation is, why we are still in school at such an advanced age, why we do not get grades, what happens to a dissertation after it's done ("If you're not writing it to try to make it a bestseller, then does it just collect dust in the library?"). "Your dissertation" quickly translates into "your paper," and then everyone wonders why it is taking over a year to write.

References

ABC/*Washington Post* Survey, August 3–5, 1987.

Aho, James 1991: *The Politics of Righteousness: Idaho Christian Patriotism*, University of Washington Press, Seattle.

Alexander, Jeffrey 1994: "The Return of Civil Society," *Contemporary Sociology*, 23, January: 797–803.

Alexander, Jeffrey and Giesen, Bernard 1988: "From Reduction to Linkage: The Long View of the Micro-Macro Debate," in *Action and Its Environments*, ed. Jeffrey Alexander, Columbia University Press, New York: 301–334.

Allende, Isabel 1984: *Of Love and Shadows*, Bantam, New York.

Almond, Gabriel and Verba, Sidney 1963: *The Civic Culture*, Princeton University Press, Princeton.

Anderson, Benedict 1991: *Imagined Communities: Reflections on the Origins and Spread of Nationalism*, Verso, London.

Arato, Andrew 1981: "Civil Society against the State: Poland, 1980–1," *Telos*, 47, Spring: 23–47.

Archibald, Katherine 1945: *Wartime Shipyard*, University of California Press, Berkeley.

Arendt, Hannah 1958: *The Human Condition*, University of Chicago Press, Chicago.

Auden, W. H. 1985 (1962): "The Poet and the City," in *Poetry and Politics*, ed. Richard Jones, Quill, New York.

Bagdikian, Ben 1990: *The Media Monopoly*, Beacon Press, Boston.

Bakhtin, M. M. 1981: *The Dialogic Imagination*, University of Texas Press, Austin.

Baldassare, Mark 1986: *Trouble in Paradise: The Suburban Transformation in America*, Columbia University Press, New York.

Barber, Benjamin 1984: *Strong Democracy: Participatory Politics for a New Age*, University of California Press, Berkeley.

1995: *Jihad vs. McWorld*, Random House, New York.

Basso, Keith 1979: *Portraits of "Whiteman"*, Cambridge University Press, Cambridge.

Baudrillard, Jean 1975: *The Mirror of Production*, Telos Press, St. Louis.

1981: *For a Critique of the Political Economy of the Sign*, Telos Press, St. Louis.

1983: *In the Shadow of the Silent Majorities*, Semiotext(e), New York.

1988: *Selected Writings*, ed. Mark Poster, Stanford University Press, Stanford.

Baumgartner, M. 1988: *The Moral Order of a Suburb*, Oxford University Press, New York.

Bellah, Robert 1967: "Civil Religion in America," in *Beyond Belief*, Harper and Row, New York: 168–192.

Bellah, Robert, Madsen, Richard, Sullivan, William, Swidler, Ann, and Tipton, Steven 1985: *Habits of the Heart*, University of California Press, Berkeley and Los Angeles.

1991, *The Good Society*, Knopf, New York.

Benhabib, Seyla 1987: "The Generalized and the Concrete Other," in *Feminism as Critique*, eds. Benhabib and Drucilla Cornell, University of Minnesota Press, Minneapolis: 77–95.

1990: "Public and Private," paper given at American Political Science Association meeting, San Francisco.

Berger, Bennett 1981: *The Survival of a Counterculture*, University of California Press, Berkeley.

Berger Gould, B., Moon, S., and Hoorn, J. Van eds. 1986: *Growing up Scared?*, Open Books, Berkeley.

Bergson, Henri 1914: *Laughter: An Essay on the Meaning of the Comic*, trans. Cloudesley Brereton and Fred Rothwell, Macmillan, New York.

Bernstein, Basil 1970: *Class, Codes and Control*, vol. I, Routledge and Kegan Paul, London.

Billig, Michael 1987: *Arguing and Thinking: A Rhetorical Approach to Social Psychology*, Cambridge University Press, Cambridge.

Billig, Michael, Condor, Susan, Edwards, Derek, Gane, Mike, Middleton, David, and Radley, Alan 1988: *Ideological Dilemmas: A Social Psychology of Everyday Thinking*, Sage, Newbury Park, CA.

Bird, S. Elizabeth 1990: "Storytelling on the Far Side: Journalism and the Weekly Tabloid," *Critical Studies in Mass Communication*, 7, 4: 377–389.

Blumer, H. 1986 [1954]: "What Is Wrong with Social Theory?" in *Symbolic Interactionism*, University of California Press, Berkeley: 140–152.

Bourdieu, Pierre 1975: "Le langage autorisé," *Actes de la recherche en sciences sociales*, 5–6: 183–190.

1977: *Outline of a Theory of Practice*, Cambridge University Press, New York.

1982: *Ce que parler veut dire*, Librairie Arthème Fayard, Paris.

1984: *Distinction*, Harvard University Press, Cambridge, MA.

1990: *The Logic of Practice*, MIT Press, Cambridge, MA.

Boyte, Harry 1980: *Backyard Revolution*, Temple University Press, Philadelphia.

Boyte, Harry and Evans, Sara 1986: *Free Spaces*, Harper and Row, New York.

Breyman, Stephen 1989: "From Spears to Pruning Hooks: A Political Sociology of the West German Peace Movement", unpublished dissertation, University of California, Santa Barbara, Department of Political Science.

Brown, Penelope and Levinson, Steven 1978: *Politeness*, Cambridge University Press, Cambridge.

Brudney, Jeffrey 1990: "The Availability of Volunteers: Implications for Local Governments," *Administration and Society*, 21, 4, February: 413–424.

Burawoy, Michael 1979: *Manufacturing Consent*, University of Chicago Press, Chicago.

Burawoy, Michael, Burton, Alice, Ferguson, Ann Arnett, Fox, Kathryn J., Gamson, Joshua, Gartrell, Nadine, Hurst, Leslie, Kurzman, Charles, Salzinger, Leslie, Schiffman, Josepha, and Ui, Shiori 1991: *Ethnography Unbound: Power and Resistance in the Modern Metropolis*, University of California Press, Berkeley.

Calhoun, Craig 1988: "Populist Politics, Communications Media and Large Scale Societal Integration," *Sociological Theory*, 6, 2, Fall: 219–241.

ed. 1992: *Habermas and the Public Sphere*, MIT Press, Cambridge, MA.

1993: "Civil Society and the Public Sphere," *Public Culture*, 5: 267–280.

1994: *Neither Gods Nor Emperors*, University of California Press, Berkeley.

Caplow, Theodore, Bahr, Howard, Chadwick, Bruce A., Hill, Reuben, and Williamson, Margaret Holmes 1982: *Middletown Families*, University of Minnesota/Bantam, Minneapolis.

Carpignano, Paolo, Andersen, Robin, Aronowitz, Stanley and DiFazio, William 1993: "Chatter in the Age of Electronic Reproduction: Talk Television and the 'Public Mind,' " in *The Phantom Public Sphere*, ed. Bruce Robbins, University of Minnesota Press, Minneapolis: 93–120.

Cayrol, Roland 1985: "Le 'sans réponse' aux questions politiques," *Pouvoirs*, 33: 41–56.

Chomsky, Noam 1988: *Manufacturing Consent*, Pantheon, New York.

Cicourel, Aaron 1964: *Cognitive Sociology: Language and Meaning in Social Interaction*, Free Press, New York.

1981: "Notes on the Integration of Micro- and Macro-Levels of Analysis," in *Advances in Social Theory and Methodology*, eds. Karin Knorr-Cetina and Aaron V. Cicourel, Routledge and Kegan Paul, Boston.

1987: "Semantics, Pragmatics, and Situated Meaning," paper delivered at the 1987 International Pragmatics conference, Antwerp, Belgium.

Cicourel, Aaron, Jennings, S., Jennings, K., Leiter, K., Mackay, R., Mehan, H., and Roth, D. 1974: *Language Use and School Performance*, Academic Press, New York.

Clifford, James and Marcus, George 1986: *Writing Culture: The Poetics and Politics of Ethnography*, University of California Press, Berkeley.

Cmiel, Kenneth 1990: *Democratic Eloquence: The Fight over Popular Speech in Nineteenth-Century America*, William Morrow, New York.

Cohen, Stan and Young, Jock 1972: *Folk Devils and Moral Panics*, Granada, London.

Coleman, James 1990: *Foundations of Social Theory*, University of Chicago Press, Chicago.

Condit, Celeste 1990: *Decoding Abortion Rhetoric: Communicating Social Change*, University of Illinois Press, Urbana, IL.

Connell, R. W. 1971: *The Child's Construction of Politics*, Melbourne University Press, Carlton, Victoria.

Converse, Philip 1964: "The Nature of Belief Systems in Mass Publics," in *Ideology and Discontent*, ed. Alan Apter, Free Press, New York.

Coontz, Stephanie 1992: *The Way We Never Were: American Families and the Nostalgia Trap*, Basic Books, New York.

Crenson, Matthew 1971: *The Un-Politics of Air Pollution*, Johns Hopkins University Press, Baltimore.

Croteau, David 1995: *Politics and the Class Divide*, Temple University Press, Philadelphia.

Crozier, Michel, Huntington, Samuel and Watanukyi, Joji 1975: *The Crisis of Democracy: Report on the Governability of Democracies to the Trilateral Commission*, New York University, New York.

Daniels, Arlene Kaplan 1967: "The Low-Caste Stranger in Social Research," in *Ethics, Politics, and Social Research*, ed. G. Sjoberg, Schenkman, Cambridge, MA.

1988: *Invisible Careers*, University of California Press, Berkeley.

Darnovsky, Marcy 1990: "Direct Action as Living Theater in the Movement against Nuclear Power," paper given at The Seventies conference, Stanford University, Palo Alto, CA.

1993: "I Never Promised You a Rose Garden: Will Democrats in the White House Make a Difference?" *Socialist Review*, 22, 3, July–Sept.: 9–44.

1996: "The Greens Go to Market: US Environmentalists in Media Culture and Consumer Society," dissertation, University of Santa Cruz, History of Consciousness Board, Santa Cruz.

Davies, Linda and Schragge, Eric 1990: *Bureaucracy and Community*, Black Rose, Montreal.

Debray, Regis 1967: *Revolution in the Revolution? Armed Struggle and Political Struggle in Latin America*, MR Press, New York.

Delgado, Gary 1986: *Organizing the Movement*, Temple University Press, Philadelphia.

Dewey, John 1927: *The Public and Its Problems*, Allan Swallow, Denver.

Diamond, Sara 1989: *Spiritual Warfare: The Politics of the Christian Right*, South End Press, Boston.

Diskin, Jonathan and Sandler, Blair, forthcoming: "Essentialism, the Economy and Labor-Power: A Critique of Post-Marxism," *Rethinking Marxism*.

Domhoff, G. William 1989: *Who Rules America Now?*, Prentice Hall, New York.

Donzelot, Jacques 1979: *Policing the Family*, Pantheon, New York.

Douglas, Mary 1975: "Jokes," in *Implicit Meanings*, Routledge and Kegan Paul, London.

Douglas, Mary and Isherwood, Baron 1979: *The World of Goods*, Norton, New York.

Durkheim, Emile 1965 (1915): *The Elementary Forms of the Religious Life*, Free Press, New York.

Eagleton, Terry 1985: *The Function of Criticism*, Verso, London.

Ehrenreich, Barbara 1983: *Hearts of Men*, Anchor Press/Doubleday, New York.

1989: *Fear of Falling*, Harper, New York.

Eley, Geoff 1992: "Nations, Publics, and Political Cultures: Placing Habermas in the Nineteenth Century," in *Habermas and the Public Sphere*, ed. Craig Calhoun, MIT Press, Cambridge, MA: 289–339.

Elias, Norbert 1978: *The History of Manners*, Pantheon, New York.

Eliasoph, Nina 1987: "Rethinking Research on Language and Gender: Politeness, Power, and Women's Language," *Berkeley Journal of Sociology*, 32: 79–104.

1990: "Political Culture and the Presentation of a Political Self," *Theory and Society*, 19: 465–494.

1992: "Gender and Joking in a Postmodern Community Center," paper given at International Communications Association, Washington, DC, May.

1996: "Making a Fragile Public: A Talk-Centered Study of Citizenship and Power," *Sociological Theory*, 14, 3: 262–289.

Elshtain, Jean Bethke 1981: *Public Man, Private Woman: Women in Social and Political Thought*, Princeton University Press, Princeton.

Elster, Jon 1979: *Ulysses and the Sirens*, Cambridge University Press, Cambridge.

Epstein, Barbara 1991: *Political Protest and Cultural Revolution*, University of California Press, Berkeley.

Epstein, Edward Jay 1973: *News from Nowhere*, Vintage, New York.

Epstein, Steven 1991: "Democratic Science? AIDS Activism and the Contested Construction of Knowledge," *Socialist Review*, 91, 2: 35–64.

Erikson, Eric 1963: *Childhood and Society*, Norton, New York.

Etzioni, Amitai 1988: *The Moral Dimension*, Free Press, New York.

Evans-Pritchard, E. E. 1976: *Witchcraft, Oracles and Magic among the Azande*, Oxford University Press, Oxford.

Fals-Borda, Orlando 1987: "The Application of Participatory Action Research in Latin America," *International Sociology*, 2, 4: 329–347.

Feiler, Bruce 1996: "Has Country Music Become a Soundtrack for White Flight?" *New York Times*, Sunday, October 20, "Arts and Leisure" section: 38.

Fillmore, Charles 1975: "An Alternative to Checklist Theories of Meaning," *Proceedings of the First Annual Meeting of the Berkeley Linguistics Society*, eds. C. Cogen, H. Thompson, G. Thurgood, K. Whistler, and J. Wright, University of California Press, Berkeley, 121–131.

Fishkin, James 1991: *Democracy and Deliberation: New Directions for Democratic Reform*, Yale University Press, New Haven.

Fiske, John 1987: *Television Culture*, Methuen, New York.

Flacks, Richard 1988: *Making History*, Columbia University Press, New York.

Fox, Kathryn 1992: "The Politics of Prevention," in *Ethnography Unbound*, eds. Michael Burawoy, Alice Burton, Ann Ferguson, Kathryn Fox, Joshua Gamson, Nadine Gartrell, Leslie Hurst, Charles Kurzman, Leslie Salzinger, Josepha Schiffman, Shiori Ui, University of California Press, Berkeley: 227–249.

Frank, Tom 1995: "Dark Age," *The Baffler*, 6: 5–192.

Frankfurt, Harry 1971: "Freedom of the Will and the Concept of a Person," *Journal of Philosophy*, 68, Jan. 14: 5–20.

Fraser, Nancy 1987: "What's Critical about Critical Theory? The Case of Habermas and Gender," in *Feminism as Critique*, eds. S. Benhabib and D. Cornell, University of Minnesota Press, Minneapolis: 31–55.

—— 1992: "Rethinking the Public Sphere: A Contribution to the Critique of Actually Existing Democracy," in *Habermas and the Public Sphere*, ed. Craig Calhoun, MIT Press, Cambridge, MA: 109–142.

Frazer, Elizabeth 1989: "Teenage Girls Reading *Jackie*," *Media, Culture and Society*, 9: 407–425.

Freeman, Jo 1973: "The Tyranny of Structurelessness," *Berkeley Journal of Sociology*, 7: 151–164.

Freire, Paolo 1970: *Pedagogy of the Oppressed*, Herder and Herder, New York.

Fry, William 1963: *Sweet Madness: A Study of Humor*, Pacific Books, Palo Alto.

Gallup Organization, 1981: *Americans Volunteer*, Gallup Organization, Princeton, NJ.

Gamarnikow, Eva, Morgan, David, Purvis, June, and Taylorson, Daphne eds. 1983: *The Public and the Private*, Heinemann, London.

Gamson, Josh 1995: "Do Ask, Do Tell: Freak Talk on TV," *The American Prospect*, 23, Fall, 44–51.

Gamson, William 1992: *Talking Politics*, Cambridge University Press, Cambridge.

Gans, Herbert 1962: *The Urban Villagers*, Free Press, Glencoe.

—— 1988: *Middle American Individualism*, Free Press, New York.

Garfinkel, Harold 1967: *Studies in Ethnomethodology*, Prentice-Hall, Englewood Cliffs, NJ.

Gaventa, John 1980: *Power and Powerlessness*, University of Illinois Press, Chicago.

Giddens, Anthony 1984: *The Constitution of Society*, Polity Press, Cambridge.

Giddens, Anthony and Turner, Jonathan, eds. 1978: *Social Theory Today*, Stanford University Press, Stanford, CA.

Gilligan, Carol 1982: *In a Different Voice*, Harvard University Press, Cambridge, MA.

Ginsberg, Faye 1989: *Contested Lives*, University of California Press, Berkeley.

Gitlin, Todd 1980: *The Whole World is Watching*, University of California Press, Berkeley.

Glendon, Mary Ann 1991: *Rights Talk: The Impoverishment of Political Discourse*, Free Press, New York.

Goffman, Erving 1959: *The Presentation of Self in Everyday Life*, Doubleday, Garden City, New York.

—— 1979: "Footing," *Semiotica*, 25, 1/2: 1–29.

—— 1981: *Forms of Talk*, University of Pennsylvania, Philadelphia.

Goldberg, S., LaCombe, S., Levenson, D., Parker, K., Ross, C., and Sommers, F. 1985: "Thinking about the Threat of Nuclear War: Relevance to Mental Health," *American Journal of Orthopsychiatry*, 55, 4: 503.

Goldfarb, Jeffrey 1980: *The Persistence of Freedom: The Sociological Implications of Polish Student Theater*, Westview Press, Boulder.

—— 1991: *The Cynical Society: The Culture of Politics and the Politics of Culture in American Life*, University of Chicago Press, Chicago.

Goldman, Robert and Rajagopal, Arvind 1991: *Mapping Hegemony: Television News Coverage of Industrial Conflict*, Ablex Publishing Co., Norwood, NJ.

Gonzalez, Alberto, Houston, Marsha, and Chen, Victoria 1994: *Our Voices: Essays in Culture, Ethnicity, and Communication*, Roxbury Publishing Co., Los Angeles.

Gottdiener, M. 1987: *The Decline of Urban Politics*, Sage, Beverly Hills.

Gottdiener, M. and Kephart, George 1991: "The Multinucleated Metropolitan Region: A Comparative Analysis," in *Postsuburban California: The Transformation of Orange County since World War II*, eds. Rob Kling, Spencer Olin, and Mark Poster, University of California Press, Berkeley: 31–54.

Gouldner, Alvin 1973: "The Sociologist as Partisan: Sociology and the Welfare State," in *For Sociology: Renewel and Critique in Sociology Today*, Basic Books, New York: 35–69.

Gramsci, Antonio 1957: *The Modern Prince and Other Writings*, International Publishers, New York.

1971: *The Prison Notebooks*, ed. Quintin Hoare, International Publishers, New York.

Greenwald, David and Zeitlin, Steven 1987: *No Reason to Talk about It: Families Confront the Nuclear Taboo*, Norton, New York.

Gregory, James 1989: *American Exodus: The Dust Bowl Migration and California's Okie Subculture*, Oxford University Press, New York.

Grossberg, Larry 1988: "Wandering Audiences, Nomadic Critics," *Cultural Studies*, 3: 377–391.

Gumperz, John 1968: "The Speech Community," in *International Encyclopedia of the Social Sciences*, Macmillan, London.

1982: *Discourse Strategies*, Cambridge University Press, New York.

1989: *Contextualization and Understanding*, Berkeley Cognitive Science Report, No. 59, Institute of Cognitive Studies, Berkeley.

Gumperz, John and Blom, Jan-Petter 1972: "Social Meaning in Linguistic Structures: Code-Switching in Norway," in *Directions in Sociolinguistics*, eds. Dell Hymes and John Gumperz, Basil Blackwell, Oxford and New York.

Gusfield, Joseph 1981: *The Culture of Public Problems*, University of Chicago Press, Chicago.

Habermas, Jürgen 1974: "The Public Sphere: An Encyclopedia Article," *New German Critique*, 3: 49–55.

1976: *The Rational Society*, Beacon Press, Boston.

1977: "Hannah Arendt's Communications Concept of Power," *Social Research*, 44, 1: 3–24.

1979: *Communication and the Evolution of Society*, Beacon Press, Boston.

1984 and 1985: *Theory of Communicative Action*, vols. I and II, Beacon Press, Boston.

1989: *The Structural Transformation of the Public Sphere: An Inquiry into a Category of Bourgeois Society*, MIT Press, Cambridge, MA.

Hall, Edward 1959: *The Silent Language*, Doubleday, New York.

Hall, Stuart 1977: "Culture, Media, and the 'Ideological Effect,'" in *Mass Communi-*

cation and Society, eds. J. Curran, M. Gurevitch, and J. Woolacott, Edward Arnold, London: 315–348.

1980: "Cultural Studies: Two Paradigms," *Media, Culture and Society*, 2: 57–72.

1985: "Signification, Representation, Ideology: Althusser and the Post-Structuralist Debates," *Critical Studies in Mass Communication*, 2: 91–114.

Halle, David 1984: *America's Working Man*, University of Chicago Press, Chicago.

Hallin, Daniel and Mancini, Paolo 1985: "Speaking of the President," *Theory and Society*, 13: 829–850.

Hamilton, John Maxwell 1988: *Main Street and the Third World*, Delta Chi Foundation/Seven Locks Press, Cabin John, MD.

Hansen, Debra Gold and Ryan, Mary P. 1991: "Public Ceremony in a Private Culture: Orange County Celebrates the Fourth of July," in *Postsuburban California: The Transformation of Orange County since World War II*, eds. Rob Kling, Spencer Olin, and Mark Poster, University of California Press, Berkeley: 165–189.

Hansen, Karen, forthcoming: "Rediscovering the Social: Visiting Practices in Antebellum New England and the Limits of Public/Private Dichotomy," in *Public and Private in Thought and Practice: Perspectives on a Grand Dichotomy*, eds. Jeffrey Weintraub and Krishnan Kumar, University of Chicago Press, Chicago.

Hartz, Louis 1955: *The Liberal Tradition in American Politics*, Harvest, New York.

Havel, Vaclav 1989: *Living in Truth*, Faber and Faber, Boston.

Heath, Shirley Brice 1983: *Ways with Words*, Cambridge University Press, New York.

Hebdige, Dick 1979: *Subculture: The Meaning of Style*, Methuen, London.

Held, Virginia 1993: *Feminist Morality: Transforming Culture, Society, and Politics*, University of Chicago Press, Chicago.

Heritage, John 1987: "Ethnomethodology," in *Social Theory Today*, eds. Anthony Giddens and Jonathan Turner, Stanford University Press, Stanford, CA.

Hirschman, Albert 1970: *Exit, Voice and Loyalty*, Harvard University Press, Cambridge, MA.

1982: *Shifting Involvements: Private Interest and Public Action*, Princeton University Press, Princeton, NJ.

Hobsbawm, Eric and Ranger, Terence eds. 1983: *The Invention of Tradition*, Cambridge University Press, Cambridge.

Hochschild, Arlie 1979: "Emotion Work, Feeling Rules, and Social Structure," *American Journal of Sociology*, 85, 3: 551–575.

1983: *The Managed Heart*, University of California Press, Berkeley.

1989: *The Second Shift*, Viking, New York.

Hochschild, Jennifer 1981: *What's Fair?* Harvard University Press, Cambridge, MA.

Hoggart, Richard 1961 (1957): *The Uses of Literacy*, Beacon Press, Boston.

Horkheimer, Max and Adorno, T. W. 1972 (1944): *Dialectic of Enlightenment*, Verso, London.

Howe, Louise 1977: *Pink Collar Workers*, Putnam, New York.

Huizinga, Johan 1955: *Homo Ludens*, Beacon Press, Boston.

Hymes, Dell 1972: "Models of the Interaction of Language and Social Life," in *Directions in Sociolinguistics*, eds. Dell Hymes and John Gumperz, Basil Blackwell, New York: 35–71.

Ignatieff, Michael 1986 (1984): *The Needs of Strangers*, Penguin, New York.

Irvine, Judith 1979: "Formality and Informality in Communicative Events," *American Anthropologist*, 81: 773–790.

Jensen, Klaus Bruhn 1990: "The Politics of Polysemy," *Media, Culture and Society*, 12, 1, January: 57–78.

Kaminsky, Marc 1992: "Myerhoff's 'Third Voice': Ideology and Genre in Ethnographic Narrative," *Social Text*, 33 (vol. 10, 4): 124–144.

Kaminstein, Dana 1988: "Toxic Talk," *Social Policy*, 19, 2, Fall: 5–10.

Kannis, Phyllis 1991: *Making Local News*, University of Chicago Press, Chicago.

Katz, Elihu 1988: "Publicity and Pluralistic Ignorance: Notes on 'The Spiral of Silence,' " in *Mass Communication Review Yearbook*, eds. David Whitney and Ellen Wartella, Sage, Beverly Hills: 89–99.

Katz, Elihu and Lazarsfeld, Paul 1956: *Personal Influence*, Free Press, Glencoe.

Katz, Elihu and Liebes, Tamar 1990: *The Export of Meaning: Cross Cultural Readings of Dallas*, Oxford University Press, New York.

Kemmis, Daniel 1990: *Community and the Politics of Place*, University of Oklahoma Press, Norman, OK.

Kemp, Ray 1985: "Planning, Public Hearings and the Politics of Discourse," in *Critical Theory and Public LIfe*, ed. John Forester, MIT Press, Cambridge, MA: 177–201.

Keniston, Kenneth 1960: *The Uncommitted*, Dell, New York.

Kilroy, Bridget 1992: "The Rhetoric of Individualism and Community in Discourse about Abortion," unpublished dissertation prospectus, University of Washington, Seattle, WA, Department of Speech Communication.

Klatch, Rebecca 1987: *Women of the Right*, Temple University Press, Philadelphia.

Knoke, David 1981: "Commitment and Detachment in Voluntary Associations," *American Sociological Review*, 46, April: 141–157.

Knorr-Cetina, Karin and Cicourel, Aaron V. eds. 1981: *Advances in Social Theory and Methodology*, Routledge and Kegan Paul, Boston.

Kochman, Thomas 1981: *Black and White Styles in Conflict*, University of Chicago Press, Chicago.

Komarovsky, Mirra 1962: *Blue-Collar Marriage*, Vintage, New York.

Kornblum, William 1974: *Blue Collar Community*, University of Chicago Press, Chicago.

Labov, William 1972: "The Logic of Non-Standard English," in *Language and Social Context*, ed. Pier Paolo Giglioli: 179–216.

Laclau, Ernesto and Mouffe, Chantal 1985: *Hegemony and Socialist Strategy*, Verso, London.

Lakoff, George 1987: *Women, Fire, and Dangerous Things*, University of Chicago Press, Chicago.

Lakoff, George and Johnson, Mark 1980: *Metaphors We Live By*, University of Chicago Press, Chicago.

Lamont, Michele and Fournier, Marcel, eds. 1992: *Cultivating Differences: Symbolic Boundaries and the Making of Inequality*, University of Chicago Press, Chicago.

Lane, Robert 1962: *Political Ideology*, Free Press, New York.

LeMasters, E. E. 1975: *Blue-Collar Aristocrats*, University of Wisconsin Press, Madison, WI.

Lerner, Melvin 1980: *The Belief in a Just World: A Fundamental Delusion*, Plenum Press, New York.

Lerner, Michael 1991: *Surplus Powerlessness*, Humanities Press International, Atlantic Highlands, NJ.

Levi, Margaret 1988: *Of Rule and Revenue*, University of California Press, Berkeley.

Levine, Lawrence 1977: *Black Culture and Black Consciousness: Afro-American Folk Thought from Slavery to Freedom*, Oxford University Press, Oxford.

Lewis, Justin, Jhally, Sut, and Morgan, Michael 1991: "The Gulf War: A Study of the Media, Public Opinion and Public Knowledge," The Center for the Study of Communication Research Archives, Document #P-8, Department of Communication, University of Massachusetts, Amherst.

Lichter, Robert, Rothman, Stanley, and Lichter, Linda 1986: *The Media Elite*, Adler and Adler, Bethesda, MD.

Lichterman, Paul 1989: "Making a Politics of Masculinity," in *Comparative Social Research*, ed. Craig Calhoun, vol. 11, JAI, Greenwich, CT: 185–208.

1992: "Self-Help Reading as a Thin Culture," *Media, Culture and Society*, 14: 421–447.

1996: *The Search for Political Community: American Activists Reinventing Commitment*. Cambridge University Press, New York.

Lifton, Robert Jay 1968: *Death in Life: Survivors of Hiroshima*, Basic Books, New York.

Lippman, Walter 1924: *Public Opinion*, Free Press, New York.

Lipset, Seymour Martin 1959/60: *Political Man*, Doubleday, Garden City, NY.

Lipset, Seymour Martin and Schneider, William 1983: *The Confidence Gap*, Free Press, NY.

1987: "The Confidence Gap during the Reagan Years, 1981–1987," *Political Science Quarterly*, 102, 1, Spring: 1–23.

Livingstone, Sonia and Lunt, Peter 1994: *Talk on Television: Critical Reception, Expertise, Public Debate and the Audience Discussion Programme*, Routledge, London.

Lukes, Steven 1974: *Power: A Radical View*, Macmillan, London.

1975: "Political Ritual and Social Integration," *Sociology*, 9, May: 289–308.

1986: *Power*, Basil Blackwell, Oxford.

Lynd, Robert and Lynd, Helen 1929: *Middletown: A Study in American Culture*, Harcourt and Brace, New York.

McAdam, Doug, McCarthy, John, and Zald, Meyer 1996: *Comparative Perspectives on Social Movements*, Cambridge University Press, Cambridge.

MacIntyre, Alisdair 1981: *After Virtue*, University of Notre Dame Press, South Bend, IN.

Mann, Michael 1970: *Consciousness and Action among the Western Working Class*, Macmillan, London.

Mansbridge, Jane 1980: *Beyond Adversary Democracy*, University of Chicago Press, Chicago.

——— 1991: "Feminism and Democracy," *The American Prospect*, 1, 1.

——— 1993: "Feminist Identity: The Voices of African-American and White Working Class Women," paper presented at Graduate Faculty of the New School for Social Research.

Marcuse, Herbert 1964: *One-Dimensional Man*, Beacon Press, Boston.

——— 1965: "Repressive Tolerance," in *A Critique of Pure Tolerance*, eds. Herbert Marcuse and Barrington Moore, Jr., Beacon Press, Boston.

Mead, George Herbert 1964 (1934): *Mind, Self and Society*, University of Chicago Press, Chicago.

Mehan, Hugh 1978: "Structuring School Structure," *Harvard Educational Review*, 45: 322–338.

Melucci, Alberto 1989: *Nomads of the Present*, Temple University Press, Philadelphia.

Merelman, Richard 1991: *Partial Visions*, University of Wisconsin Press, Madison.

Merton, Robert 1968 (1949): *Social Theory and Social Structure: Toward the Codification of Theory and Research*, Free Press, New York.

Miller, Mark Crispin 1988: *Boxed In: The Culture of TV*, Northwestern University Press, Evanston, IL.

Mills, C. Wright 1979 (1940): "Situated Action and Vocabularies of Motive," in *Power, Politics, and People*, ed. Irving Horowitz, Oxford University Press, New York: 439–452.

——— 1959: "The Promise," in *The Sociological Imagination*, Grove Press, New York: 3–24.

Morley, David 1980: *The "Nationwide" Audience*, Television Monograph 10, British Film Institute, London.

Morreall, John 1983: *Taking Laughter Seriously*, State University of New York Press, Albany.

Morris, Aldon 1984: *The Origins of the Civil Rights Movement*, Free Press, New York.

Mouffe, Chantal 1992: "Democratic Citizenship and Political Community," in *Dimensions of Radical Democracy*, ed. Chantal Mouffe, Verso, London: 74–89.

——— 1993: "Feminism, Citizenship, and Radical Democratic Politics," in *The Return of the Political*, Verso, London: 74–89.

Mulkay, Michael 1988: *On Humor*, Polity Press; Basil Blackwell, New York.

Myerhoff, Barbara 1979: *Number Our Days*, E. P. Dutton, New York.

Myrdal, Gunnar 1944: *An American Dilemma: The Negro Problem and Modern Democracy*, w/ Richard Sterner and Arnold Rose, Harper and Row, New York.

Neuman, W. Russell 1986: *The Paradox of Mass Politics*, Harvard University Press, Cambridge, MA.

Newsweek, 1989: "The New Volunteers: America's Unsung Heroes," "Doing Well by Doing Good: A Growing Corporate Concept," "A Talk with Barbara Bush," and "A Salute to Everyday Heroes from All Over America," July 10: 36–66.

1991: "New Kids on the Range," David Gates, Marc Peyser and Michael Mason, October 7: 62–63.

Nicholson, Linda 1996: "Emotions and the Public Sphere of Postmodernism," paper given at Political Theory colloquium, University of Wisconsin, Madison, WI, March, 1996.

Nietzsche, Friedrich 1967 [1887]: *On the Genealogy of Morals and Ecce Homo*, ed. Walter Kaufman, Vintage, New York.

Noelle-Neuman, Elisabeth 1984: *The Spiral of Silence*, University of Chicago Press, Chicago.

O'Connell, Brian 1989: "What Voluntary Activity Can and Cannot Do for America," *Public Administration Review*, 4, 5, Sept./Oct.: 486–491.

Oldenberg, Ray 1989: *The Great Good Place*, Paragon, New York.

Oliner, Samuel and Oliner, Pearl 1988: *The Altruistic Personality*, Free Press, Glencoe.

Olson, Mancur 1971 (1965): *The Logic of Collective Action*, Harvard University Press, Cambridge, MA.

Parenti, Michael 1993: *Inventing Reality*, St. Martin's Press, New York.

Pateman, Carole 1973: *Participation and Democratic Theory*, Cambridge University Press, Cambridge.

　　1980: "The Civic Culture: A Philosophic Critique," in *The Civic Culture Revisited*, eds. Gabriel Almond and Sidney Verba, Little, Brown, and Co., Boston: 57–102.

　　1988: *The Sexual Contract*, Polity Press, Cambridge.

Paul, Kathleen 1992: "The Politics of Citizenship" (review of *Encouraging Citizenship: Report of the Speaker's Commission on Citizenship* [HMSO, London, 1990] and Geoff Andrews, ed., *Citizenship* [Lawrence and Wishart, London, 1991]), *Socialist Review*, 21, 3 and 4, July–Dec.: 177–185.

Peterson, Richard and DiMaggio, Paul 1975: "From Region to Class, the Changing Locus of Country Music: A Test of the Massification Hypothesis," *Social Forces*, 53: 497–506.

Philipsen, Gerry 1992: *Speaking Culturally*, State University of New York Press, Albany.

Pitkin, Hanna 1972: *Wittgenstein and Justice: On the Significance of Ludwig Wittgenstein for Social and Political Thought*, University of California Press, Berkeley.

　　1981: "Justice: On Relating Public and Private," *Political Theory*, 9, 3, Aug.: 327–352.

Piven, Frances Fox and Cloward, Richard 1979: *Poor People's Movements: Why They Succeed, How They Fail*, Vintage, New York.

Porpora, Douglas 1990: *How Holocausts Happen: The United States in Central America*, Temple University Press, Philadelphia.

Press, Andrea and Williams, Bruce 1992: "Television and Social Problems Discourse: Focus on Environmentalism and Abortion Rights," paper given at Speech Communications Association annual meeting, Chicago, IL.

Putnam, Robert 1993: *Making Democracy Work*, Princeton University Press, Princeton.

1996: "The Strange Disappearance of Civic America," *American Prospect*, 24, Winter: 34–48.

Quinn, Naomi and Holland, Dorothy 1987: "Culture and Cognition," in *Cultural Models in Language and Thought*, eds. Dorothy Holland and Naomi Quinn, Cambridge University Press, New York: 3–42.

Rabinow, Paul 1977: *Reflections on Fieldwork in Morocco*, University of California Press, Berkeley.

Radway, Janice 1984: *Reading the Romance*, University of North Carolina Press, Chapel Hill.

Reinarman, Craig 1987: *American States of Mind: Political Beliefs and Behavior among Private and Public Workers*, Yale University Press, New Haven.

1988: "The Social Construction of an Alcohol Problem," *Theory and Society*, 17: 91–120.

Reinharz, Shulamith 1983: *Becoming a Social Researcher*, Transaction, New Brunswick, NJ.

Reisman, David 1950: *The Lonely Crowd*, Yale University Press, New Haven.

Rieff, Philip 1966: *The Triumph of the Therapeutic: The Uses of Faith after Freud*, Chatto and Windus, London.

Rodgers, Daniel 1987: *Contested Meanings*, Columbia University Press, New York.

Rosaldo, Michelle 1973: "I Have Nothing to Hide: The Language of Ilongot Oratory," *Language in Society* 2, 2: 193–224.

1982: "The Things We Do with Words," *Language in Society*, 11: 203–237.

Rosen, Jay, 1987: "Public Knowledge/Private Ignorance," *Deadline*, Bulletin from the Center for War, Peace, and the News Media, New York, 1, 6, Jan./Feb.

1991: "Making Journalism More Public," *Communication*, 12, 4: 267–284.

1994: "Civic Journalism," paper given at Annenberg School for Communication, conference on Public Space, Philadelphia, PA.

Rosenberg, Bernard and White, David 1957: *Mass Culture*, Free Press, Glencoe.

Rosenzweig, Roy 1983: *Eight Hours for What We Will*, Cambridge University Press, Cambridge.

Rousseau, Jean Jacques 1969 (1758): "Letter to d'Alembert on Spectacles," in *Politics and the Arts: Letter to d'Alembert on the Theatre*, ed. Allan Bloom, Free Press, Glencoe, IL.

Rubin, Lillian Breslow 1976: *Worlds of Pain*, Basic Books, New York.

Ruddick, Sara 1989: *Maternal Thinking: Towards a Politics of Peace*, Beacon Press, Boston.

Ryan, Mary 1985: *Cradle of the Middle Class*, University of California Press, Berkeley.

1992: "Gender and Public Access: Women's Politics in Nineteenth-Century America," in *Habermas and the Public Sphere*, ed. Craig Calhoun, MIT Press, Cambridge, MA: 259–288.

Rybczynski, Witold 1991: *Waiting for the Weekend*, Viking, New York.

Sacks, Harvey, Schegloff, Emmanuel, and Jefferson, Gail 1974: "A Simplest Systematics for the Organization of Turn-Taking in Conversation," *Language* 50: 696–735.

Sahlins, Marshall 1976: *Culture and Practical Reason*, University of Chicago Press, Chicago.

Sartre, Jean-Paul 1948: *Anti-Semite and Jew*, trans. by George Becker, Schocken, New York.

Schapiro, Michael 1981: *Language and Political Understanding: The Politics of Discursive Practices*, Yale University Press, New Haven.

Schegloff, Emanuel 1987: "Between Macro and Micro: Contexts and Other Connections," in *The Micro–Macro Link*, eds. Jeffrey Alexander, Bernhard Giesen, Richard Münche and Neil Smelser, University of California Press, Berkeley: 207–236.

Schor, Juliet 1991: *The Overworked American*, Basic Books, New York.

Schudson, Michael 1984: *Advertising: The Uneasy Persuasion*, Basic Books, New York.

Schutz, Alfred 1967 (1932): *The Phenomenology of the Social World*, Northwestern University Press, Evanston.

Schwichtenberg, Cathy, ed. 1993: *The Madonna Connection: Representational Politics, Subcultural Identities and Cultural Theory*, Westview Press, Boulder.

Scott, James 1985: *Weapons of the Weak: Everyday Forms of Peasant Resistance*, Yale University Press, New Haven.

   1990: *Domination and the Arts of Resistance*, Yale University Press, New Haven.

Sen, Amartya 1977: "Rational Fools: A Critique of the Behavioral Foundations of Economic Theory," *Philosophy and Public Affairs*, 6, 4, Summer: 317–344.

Sennett, Richard 1977: *The Fall of Public Man*, Knopf, New York.

Sewell, William, Jr. 1992: "A Theory of Structure: Duality, Agency, and Transformation," *American Journal of Sociology*, 98, 1, July: 1–29.

Shakespeare, William 1963: *King Lear*, ed. Russell Fraser, New American Library, New York.

Simmel, Georg 1971: *On Individuality and Social Forms*, ed. Donald Levine, University of Chicago Press, Chicago.

Skolnick, Arlene 1991: *Embattled Paradise*, Basic Books, New York.

Snow, David, Rochford, E. Burke, Jr., Worden, Steven, and Benford, Robert 1986: "Frame Alignment Processes, Micromobilization, and Movement Participation," *American Sociological Review*, 51, August: 464–481.

Somers, Margaret 1995: "What's Political or Cultural about Political Culture and the Public Sphere? Toward an Historical Sociology of Concept Formation," *Sociological Theory*, 13, 2, July: 113–144.

Speaker's Commission on Citizenship 1990: *Encouraging Citizenship: Report of the Speaker's Commission on Citizenship*, Her Majesty's Stationery Office, London.

Spillman, Lyn 1996: *Nation and Commemoration*, Cambridge University Press, New York.

Stacey, Judith 1987: "Can There Be a Feminist Ethnography?" paper presented at Women's Studies International Forum.

Stauber, John and Rampton, Sheldon 1996: *Toxic Sludge is Good for You*, Common Courage Press, Monroe, ME.

Swidler, Ann 1986: "Culture in Action," *American Sociological Review*, 51: 273–286.

Tannen, Deborah 1990: *You Just Don't Understand!*, Ballantine, New York.

Taylor, Charles 1989: *Sources of the Self*, Harvard University Press, Cambridge, MA.

Thevenot, Laurent 1987: "Coding Data and Classifying Actors: Expert and Everyday Attribution of Social Status," paper given at A. E. Havens Center for the Study of Social Structure and Social Change, Department of Sociology, University of Wisconsin, Madison, WI.

Thompson, John B. 1984: *Theories of Ideology*, University of California Press, Berkeley.

1990: *Ideology and Modern Culture*, Stanford University Press, Stanford, CA.

Tipton, Steven 1982: *Getting Saved from the Sixties*, University of California Press, Berkeley.

de Tocqueville, Alexis 1969 (1831): *Democracy in America*, ed. J. P. Mayer, Doubleday, Garden City, NY.

Trevor-Roper, Hugh 1983: "The Highland Tradition of Scotland," in *The Invention of Tradition*, eds. Eric Hobsbawm and Terence Ranger, Cambridge University Press, Cambridge: 15–42.

Trubek, Louise 1993: "Critical Lawyering," paper given at A. E. Havens Center for the Study of Social Structure and Social Change, Department of Sociology, University of Wisconsin, Madison, WI.

Tucker, Kenneth 1992: "Saving Culture after Postmodernism: The Modernism of Giddens and Habermas," paper presented at the American Sociological Association annual meeting, Pittsburgh, PA.

van Dijk, Teun 1987: *Communicating Racism: Ethnic Prejudice in Thought and Talk*, Sage Publications, Newbury Park, CA.

Varenne, Hervé 1977: *Americans Together: Structured Diversity in a Midwestern Town*, Teachers' College Press, New York.

Verba, Sidney and Nie, Norman 1972: *Participation in America*, University of Chicago Press, Chicago.

Verba, Sidney, Nie, Norman, and Kim, Jae-on 1985: *Participation and Equality*, University of Chicago Press, Chicago.

Verba, Sidney, Schlozman, Kay, and Brady, Harvey 1995: *Voice and Equality*, Harvard University Press, Cambridge, MA.

Voss, Kim 1988: "Labor Organization and Class Alliance: Industries, Communities, and the Knights of Labor," *Theory and Society*, 17: 329–364.

Vygotsky, Lev 1962: *Thought and Language*, MIT Press, Cambridge, MA.

Walzer, Michael 1992: "The Civil Society Argument," in *Dimensions of Radical Democracy: Pluralism, Citizenship, Community*, ed. Chantal Mouffe, Verso, New York: 89–107.

Wasielewski, Patricia 1989: "Emotion as a Resource," American Sociological Association meeting, San Francisco.

Wasserman, Harvey and Solomon, Norman 1982: *Killing Our Own: The Disaster of America's Experience with Atomic Radiation*, Delacorte Press, New York.

Weintraub, Jeffrey 1990: "The Theory and Politics of the Public/Private Distinction," paper presented at the American Political Science Association meeting, San Francisco.

Weintraub, Jeffrey and Kumar, Krishnan, forthcoming: *Public and Private in Thought and Practice: Perspectives on a Grand Dichotomy*, University of Chicago Press, Chicago.

Wellman, David 1977: *Portraits of White Racism*, Cambridge University Press, Cambridge.

Wells, Tom 1994: *The War Within: America's Battle over Vietnam*, University of California Press, Berkeley.

Whyte, William H. 1956: *The Organization Man*, Simon and Schuster, New York.

Wildavsky, Aaron and Douglas, Mary 1982: *Risk Culture*, University of California Press, Berkeley.

Williams, Raymond 1975 (1974): *Television: Technology and Cultural Form*, Schocken, New York.

    1977: *Marxism and Literature*, Oxford University Press, Oxford.

    1980: "Base and Superstructure in Marxist Cultural Theory," in *Problems in Materialism and Culture: Selected Essays*, Verso, London: 31–49.

    1989: "Communications and Community," in *Resources of Hope*, ed. Robin Gable, Verso, London.

Willis, Paul 1977: *Learning to Labor*, Columbia University Press, New York.

    1978: *Profane Culture*, Routledge and Kegan Paul, London.

Wilpert, Gary 1994: "Public and Private in the Former East Germany," paper presented at the American Sociological Association Meeting, Los Angeles, August.

Winch, Peter 1958: *The Idea of a Social Science and Its Relation to Philosophy*, Humanities Press, Atlantic Highlands, NJ.

Wittgenstein, Ludwig 1953: *Philosophical Investigations*, Blackwell, London.

Wolfe, Alan 1989: *Whose Keeper?*, University of California Press, Berkeley.

Wolin, Sheldon 1960: *Politics and Vision*, Little, Brown, Boston.

Wright, James 1976: *The Dissent of the Governed*, ed. Peter Rossi, Quantitative Studies in Social Relations series, Academic Press, New York.

Wuthnow, Robert 1991: *Acts of Compassion*, Princeton University Press, Princeton.

Wyatt, Robert and Liebes, Tamar 1995: "Inhibition: Factors that Inhibit Talk in Public and Private Spaces in Three Cultures," paper given at Annenberg School of Communication, Conference on Public Space, University of Pennsylvania, Philadelphia, PA.

Young, Iris 1987: "Impartiality and the Civic Public," in *Feminism as Critique*, eds. Seyla Benhabib and Drucilla Cornell, University of Minnesota Press, Minneapolis: 56–76.

Young, Linda Wai Ling 1985: "Inscrutability Revisited," in *Language and Social Identity*, ed. John Gumperz, Cambridge University Press, Cambridge: 72–84.

Young, Michael and Willmott, Peter 1957: *Family and Kinship in East London*, Routledge and Kegan Paul, London.

Zaller, John 1992: *The Nature and Origins of Mass Opinion*, Cambridge University Press, New York.

Index